SUSTAINABLE FUTURES FOR MUSIC CULTURES

Sustainable Futures for Music Cultures

AN ECOLOGICAL PERSPECTIVE

Edited by Huib Schippers

and Catherine Grant

OXFORD
UNIVERSITY PRESS

OXFORD
UNIVERSITY PRESS

Oxford University Press is a department of the University of Oxford. It furthers
the University's objective of excellence in research, scholarship, and education
by publishing worldwide. Oxford is a registered trade mark of Oxford University
Press in the UK and certain other countries.

Published in the United States of America by Oxford University Press
198 Madison Avenue, New York, NY 10016, United States of America.

Library of Congress Cataloging-in-Publication Data
Names: Schippers, Huib, 1959– editor. | Grant, Catherine, 1977– editor.
Title: Sustainable futures for music cultures : an ecological perspective /
[edited by] Huib Schippers and Catherine Grant.
Description: New York, NY : Oxford University Press, [2016] |
Includes bibliographical references and index.
Identifiers: LCCN 2016038852| ISBN 9780190259075 (hardcover) |
ISBN 9780190259082 (pbk.) | ISBN 9780190259105 (oxford scholarly online)
Subjects: LCSH: Applied ethnomusicology. | Music—Social aspects. |
Sustainability. | Ecomusicology.
Classification: LCC ML3799.2 .S87 2016 | DDC 781.6—dc23
LC record available at https://lccn.loc.gov/2016038852

9 8 7 6 5 4 3 2 1

Printed by WebCom, Inc., Canada

Cover image: Street painting of mariachi musicians and dancers portrayed in the spirit of El Día de los
Muertos (Day of the Dead) in Mexico. Photo: Cameron Quevedo. Used with permission.

Table of Contents

Foreword

Anthony Seeger

IT IS AN HONOR to have been invited to write the foreword to this pioneering volume. It makes important and sophisticated contributions to contemporary thinking about how certain traditions thrive and others disappear; it presents readers with an original comparative approach to examining musical traditions; and it provides a model for collaborative projects in ethnomusicology. I think these achievements are worth expanding upon because I hope many readers will venture into the body of the book to read the general chapters, study the nine cases presented, consider their strengths (and possible weaknesses), and possibly use the model to undertake their own study, or to find ways to improve the sustainability of traditions with which they are involved.

Probably the most innovative feature of this book was the structure of the original research project, *Sustainable Futures for Music Cultures: Towards an Ecology of Musical Diversity* (from now on referred to as *Sustainable Futures*), generously funded by the Australian Research Council, the project partners, and in-kind contributions. Huib Schippers, without a preexisting model for doing comparative work, designed a project to examine how musical traditions are sustained in various cultures. He decided to include some genres that are quite successful in the 21st century and some that may no longer be performed in the next decade. The project proposed to examine five domains of music in nine different musical traditions in more than nine countries (at least two are transnational forms). The domains were systems of learning, musicians and communities, contexts and constructs, infrastructure and regulations, and media and the music industry. For each there would be a list of topics that each investigator would try to learn about to prepare a report that would be as distinct as the different traditions and situations they studied, but comparable to a degree because the same issues would have been addressed in each investigation and summarized in each report. This kind of comparison is rare in ethnomusicology. Ethnomusicologist Bruno Nettl (2005, pp. 60–74) discusses comparison in some detail, but this approach does not appear.

The next innovative and rarely attempted step of this project was that it began with the institutional collaboration of three Australian universities, three overseas universities, and three nongovernment organizations, as well as coordination with experts in various fields at other institutions. The reason such extensive collaborations are so rarely attempted is that they are so time-consuming and expensive to accomplish. An international advisory board of ethnomusicologists was formed. Huib Schippers, Dan Bendrups, Catherine Grant, and Myfany Turpin met with their advisors and presented sessions about the *Sustainable Futures* project at the conferences of several professional organizations, among them the International Council for Traditional Music, the Society for Ethnomusicology, and the International Music Council, as well as in other forums to see the reactions of different groups and to enlist support for the project. They also invited a number of scholars to Queensland Conservatorium Griffith University in Brisbane, Australia, to give lectures and consult with them in more depth on details of the project. This mixture of advisory groups, broad preparatory work, and intensive consultation is very rare in ethnomusicology. Although not all advisors were consulted on every step of the process, the consultations certainly greatly strengthened the eventual outcomes.

A third innovation was in the selection of the researchers. Most comparative projects of which I am aware have been launched by professors and undertaken by their graduate students who simultaneously do their dissertation research. *Sustainable Futures* might have used this model, but it didn't. Instead, experienced researchers who already knew a lot about the genre they were to investigate were contracted for most of the nine cases: James Burns for Ewe dance-drumming, Keith Howard for samulnori, Linda Barwick for Australian Aboriginal *yawulyu*, Peter Dunbar-Hall for Balinese gamelan, John Drummond for Western opera, Philip Hayward for Amami *shima-uta*, Huib Schippers for North Indian classical music, Patricia Shehan Campbell for mariachi, and Håkan Lundström for Vietnamese *ca trù*.

When a researcher was not a specialist in a tradition, he or she was paired with another scholar from the tradition itself. This means that most of the researchers already spoke the required research languages, had contacts among musicians practicing the music genre with the music institutions, and had contacts with in-country scholars who had devoted their lives to studying the music culture.

These skills and contacts allowed them to collect much richer information in a shorter time than would have been possible with less experienced researchers. The investigation of each tradition was tightly focused on the guidelines and questions. Their methods of obtaining the data varied, of course. In some cases there were very few practitioners and local communities, and most of them could be consulted individually (Australian Aboriginal women's music, Vietnamese *ca trù*, music in the Amami Islands of Japan). In other cases a selective approach was needed (North Indian classical music, Balinese gamelan, Ewe drumming in Ghana, samulnori in Korea, and mariachi in Mexico and the United States). In at least one case questionnaires supplemented selected interviews to learn about a transnational musical form (Western opera). The prior familiarity of the researchers with the traditions they were investigating was probably one of the key reasons for another success of the project: *all nine researchers finished their research, wrote about their cases, and are publishing their results in this volume!* This is an extraordinary success rate—far beyond any university PhD program of which I am aware—and it speaks to the determination (and patience) of the organizers, as well as the qualifications and dedication of those they selected to do the research itself.

Central to the conceptualization and development of *Sustainable Futures* is an approach to music that is broadly based on an ecological model. This is discussed extensively by Schippers in Chapter 1. He suggests that the important thing to study to understand how musical cultures are sustained is not primarily the structures of their sounds but rather the way the traditions are part of a larger conceptual, physical, and mediated environment of actions and values, resources and regulations, individuals and communities, power and hegemony, and markets and media. Developed from a reading of Jeff Titon's work (Titon, 1992, 2009, 2008–2016), this approach builds on some of the ideas of ecological studies and of ethnomusicology. The past 10 years have seen a considerable increase in the consideration of ecological models for approaching music in its contexts (Allen, 2013), and I suspect we will be refining our approaches and considering their implications for some time.

As Catherine Grant describes in Chapter 2, many attempts have been made to improve the sustainability of different musical traditions over the past century, though rarely based on a coherent theoretical model. Grant's chapter organizes a large number of projects according to the five domains of the project, which is useful for considering the details of the nine case studies that follow (Chapters 3–11), as well as the usefulness of using the five domains as an approach to reviewing previous attempts to prevent the disappearance of diverse musical traditions.

The nine case studies are rich in descriptions and background and they reveal how musical traditions are very differently transmitted, performed, regulated, and inserted into global media markets. They reward individual study, and many are fascinating to read. But they are also instructive when the reader moves from one to another looking at one of the five domains. This is a book that may be read linearly from beginning to end, but it may also be read horizontally, domain by domain. Chapter 12 draws some of the observations together, but the real gems will come from what readers discover as they read through the cases and think about other performing arts they know or participate in.

The book you are holding or viewing is only one of the outcomes envisioned for the *Sustainable Futures* project. In addition to publications for scholars, including this book, a chapter in the *Oxford Handbook of Applied Ethnomusicology* (Schippers, 2015), and a themed issue of *The World of Music* (Bendrups & Schippers, 2015), *Sustainable Futures* envisions several more broadly accessible online publications. At the center of these is soundfutures.org, a site where musicians and communities can explore possible options for increasing the sustainability of a valued performing art tradition. This includes a digital archive of key interviews and other collected materials that might be of use to researchers, and certainly would be consulted by members of the musical communities themselves. A related Internet project, undertaken by coeditor Catherine Grant and based on her excellent book *Music Endangerment: How Language Maintenance Can Help* (2014), encourages the public to review traditions they know on a scale of music vitality (http://www.musicendangerment.com). Other uses may be developed by readers and activists, as well as critics and improvers, who hone the ideas and data in this book in future publications and practical applications.

The editors, the authors, their assistants, all of the insightful people they interviewed, and the dedicated carriers of the traditions they value are to be congratulated on the results of the *Sustainable Futures* project and the work and dedication they have put into it. The rest is up to you, the reader.

REFERENCES

Allen, A. (2013). Ecomusicology. In *The Grove dictionary of American music* (2nd ed.). New York, NY: Oxford University Press. Retrieved from http://www.ecomusicology.info.

Bendrups, D., & Schippers, H. (Eds.). (2015). Sound futures: Exploring contexts for music sustainability [Special edition]. *World of Music* 4(1). Göttingen, Germany: Department of Musicology, Georg August University.

Grant, C. (2014). *Music endangerment: How language maintenance can help.* New York, NY: Oxford University Press.

Nettl, B. (2005). *The study of ethnomusicology: Thirty-one issues and concepts*. Urbana and Chicago, IL: University of Illinois Press.

Schippers, H. (2015). Applied ethnomusicology and intangible cultural heritage: Understanding "ecosystem of music" as a tool for sustainability. In S. Pettan & J. T. Titon (Eds.), *Oxford handbook of applied ethnomusicology* (pp. 134–157). New York, NY: Oxford University Press.

Titon, J. T. (1992). Music, the public interest, and the practice of ethnomusicology. *Ethnomusicology*, 36(3), 315–322.

Titon, J. T. (2009). Music and sustainability: An ecological viewpoint. *World of Music*, 51(1), 119–138.

Titon, J. T. (2008–2016). Sustainable music: A research blog on the subject of sustainability and music. Retrieved from http://sustainablemusic.blogspot.com/search/label/ecomusicology.

Acknowledgments

THIS PUBLICATION IS an outcome of the research program *Sustainable futures for music cultures: Toward an ecology of musical diversity* (2009–2014). The project was realized with generous support from the Australian Research Council Linkage Program and partner organizations: the International Music Council (Paris), the Music Council of Australia (Sydney), and the World Music & Dance Centre (Rotterdam). Nine research teams carried out the research, led by scholars at the University of Washington (Professor Patricia Campbell, Mariachi music), the University of London (Professor Keith Howard, Samulnori), University of Lund (Professor Håkan Lundström, *ca trù*), University of Otago (Professor John Drummond, western opera), University of Sydney (Professor Linda Barwick and Dr Myfany Turpin, Yawulyu; and Honorary Associate Professor Peter Dunbar-Hall, Balinese gamelan), Southern Cross University (Professor Phil Hayward, Amami Shima uta) and Griffith University (Professor Huib Schippers, Hindustani music). Griffith University also led and coordinated the project through its Queensland Conservatorium Research Centre with three successive Research Fellows: Dr. Myfany Turpin, Dr. Dan Bendrups and Dr. Catherine Grant. An International Advisory Board comprising of 28 senior scholars, performers, educators and industry representatives monitored the project as it progressed, and several hundreds of music professionals collaborated with the research teams for the case studies. Without such knowledgeable and generous support this project could never have been completed. They are acknowledged at the end of each chapter and on the project website: www.soundfutures.org.

List of Contributors

ABOUT THE EDITORS

Huib Schippers

Huib Schippers was the founding Director of the innovative Queensland Conservatorium Research Centre at Griffith University (2003–2015). As a recognized leader of major action research projects focusing on cultural diversity, he has published and lectured extensively on research, education and sustainability. He is currently Director of Folkways Recordings at the Smithsonian Centre for Folklife and Cultural Heritage in Washington, DC.

Catherine Grant

Dr Catherine Grant (Griffith University) is recipient of Australia's Future Justice medal for her research and advocacy on music endangerment and sustainability, and is former Endeavour Australia Research Fellow. Her book *Music Endangerment: How Language Maintenance can Help* was published in 2014 by Oxford University Press.

ABOUT THE AUTHORS

Linda Barwick

Professor Linda Barwick (University of Sydney) is an expert on Indigenous Australian music and language, as well as Director of PARADISEC, dedicated to the preservation of endangered cultures of the Asia-Pacific. She has co-written the Australian Aboriginal traditional music case study chapter.

James Burns

Associate Professor James Burns (Binghamton University) has conducted extensive and ongoing fieldwork and ethnographic research in Ghana, Togo and Benin with the Ewe-Ron, Akan, and Dagbamba (Dagomba) ethnic groups. He has authored the Ghanian Ewe case study chapter.

Patricia Campbell

Professor Patricia Shehan Campbell (University of Washington) is one of the leading figures on the intersection of music education and ethnomusicology, with an extensive track record in projects, publications and lectures. She has co-written the Mexican mariachi music case study chapter.

John Drummond

Professor John Drummond (University of Otago), author of the monograph *Opera in Perspective* (University of Minnesota Press), has a long track record in opera, composition, music education, publication, and a deep involvement in cultural diversity. He is author of the Western classical opera case study chapter.

Peter Dunbar-Hall

Honorary Associate Professor Peter Dunbar-Hall (University of Sydney) is a leading scholar of music education, who has published extensively on Balinese gamelan, Indigenous popular music, and cultural diversity at large. He has written the Balinese gamelan case study chapter.

Leticia Isabel Soto Flores

Dr Leticia Soto Flores (University of California, Los Angeles) is an ethnomusicologist with a specialization in Mexican mariachi music, and director of the Mariachi School of Ollín Yoliztli in Garibaldi, Mexico City. She has co-written the Mexican mariachi music case study chapter.

Phil Hayward

Professor Phil Hayward (Southern Cross University; University of Technology Sydney) is one of the first Australian protagonists of applied musicology, with a focus on music of small island cultures, on which he has published extensively. He is co-author of the Amami islands music case study chapter.

Keith Howard

Professor Keith Howard (University of London) is a leading scholar on Korean music and culture, a well-respected author on ethnomusicology and music education, and contributor to the UNESCO Masterpieces of Intangible Cultural Heritage program. He has written the Korean *samulnori* case study chapter.

Sueo Kuwahara

Professor Sueo Kuwahara (Kagoshima University), professor of anthropology, is currently involved in research in the Amami and Tokara islands of southern Japan, and is on the Editorial Board of *Shima: The International Journal of Research into Island Cultures*. He is co-author of the Amami islands case study chapter.

Håkan Lundström

Dr Håkan Lundström (University of Lund) is Dean of the Malmö Academy of the Arts, past President of the International Society for Music Education, and a scholar of Asian music. He is involved with a major project in Vietnam funded by development organization SIDA, and has co-authored the *ca trù* case study chapter of this book.

Myfany Turpin

Dr Myfany Turpin (University of Sydney) is an Australian Research Council Future Fellow with expertise in Aboriginal languages and song. Her current research explores the relationship between language and music in Arandic song–poetry. She has co-written the Australian Aboriginal case study chapter.

Esbjörn Wettermark

Mr Esbjörn Wettermark (Royal Holloway, University of London) is a doctoral candidate whose research focuses on the positioning of traditional music genres in contemporary Vietnam. He is co-author of the *ca trù* case study chapter.

About the Companion Website

www.oup.com/us/sustainablefuturesformusiccultures

Oxford has created a password-protected website to accompany *Sustainable Futures for Music Cultures: An Ecological Perspective*. We encourage readers to visit the site to accesses supplementary materials that illustrate and elucidate the nine case study chapters, including audio and video tracks, photos, web links, reading lists, and other resources. Further information and resources relating to music sustainability are also available on the site.

You may access the website using the following:
Username: Music1
Password: Book5983

SUSTAINABLE FUTURES FOR MUSIC CULTURES

1

SOUND FUTURES

Exploring the Ecology of Music Sustainability

Huib Schippers[1]

MORE PEOPLE HAVE more access to more music now than ever before in the history of humankind. Music once constrained to a single locale is available across the planet. The past hundred years have illustrated music's extraordinary capacity to transform and thrive in the face of major technological, economic, demographic, generational, social, political, religious, and artistic change. At the beginning of the 21st century, music as a worldwide phenomenon seems quite robust: many traditions, genres, and styles are flourishing. Yet, at the same time, there are thousands of music practices that struggle with the magnitude and rate of change. Many of these are at risk of disappearing in the course of this century, at a rate well beyond the "evolutionary" processes that governed the world's musical diversity in earlier periods. These dynamics invite an in-depth exploration of the ecology of music cultures to gain a greater understanding of music sustainability and its mechanics. This in turn will provide a basis for making practical insights available to communities around the world, assisting them in forging sound futures on their own terms.

This volume will address these complex issues by first investigating the emergence of *ecology* as a word and concept in ethnomusicological discourse, tracing

---

[1] This chapter is largely based on my essay "Applied Ethnomusicology and Intangible Cultural Heritage: Understanding 'Ecosystems' of Music as a Tool for Sustainability" (Schippers, 2015).

its origins in biology and its translation into contemporary musical thought. Next, it will critically investigate the relationship between ecology and sustainability in music, identifying the major (clusters of) forces impacting on sustainability. Sustainability initiatives to date and the constructs that underpin them are another subject for close scrutiny. Most importantly, we present nine, in-depth case studies of specific and diverse music practices in their 21st-century environments. These constitute the core of this volume and lead to the development of a model to guide the practical applications of understanding the ecology of music cultures in relation to music sustainability.

Such work is positioned in a well-established context. The challenges to maintaining global musical diversity have been widely recognized with increasing urgency since the beginning of this century. This is borne out by numerous initiatives at local and national levels, but perhaps most notably by a suite of UNESCO conventions, declarations, and initiatives from the *Universal Declaration on Cultural Diversity* (UNESCO, 2001) to the *Convention for the Safeguarding of Intangible Cultural Heritage* (UNESCO, 2003), the *Convention on the Protection and Promotion of the Diversity of Cultural Expressions* (UNESCO, 2005), and the *Declaration on the Rights of Indigenous Peoples* (United Nations High Commission for Human Rights, 2007). These four documents have been instrumental in raising awareness of the reality that although many music cultures have adapted successfully to changing environments, others find themselves at crossroads, with only few culture bearers surviving. Anthony Seeger, a central figure in the UNESCO *Masterpieces of Intangible Cultural Heritage* project through his role in the International Council for Traditional Music (ICTM) at the time, expresses it succinctly and eloquently:

Sámi / Sápmi

The problem is it's not really an even playing field: it's not as though these are just disappearing, they're "being disappeared"; there's an active process in the disappearance of many traditions around the world. Some of them are being disappeared by majority groups that want to eliminate the differences of their minority groups within their nations, others are being disappeared by missionaries or religious groups of various kinds who find music offensive and want to eliminate it. Others are being disappeared by copyright legislation. (Queensland Conservatorium Research Centre, 2008)

Technological developments, infrastructural challenges, socioeconomic change, failing educational systems, and loss of prestige constitute additional reasons for the decline of certain music practices.

The effect of these shifts on music practices is widely recognized. Over the past decades, numerous initiatives (many initiated by communities themselves others sponsored by governments, nongovernmental organizations [NGOs], and development agencies) have provided support for specific music cultures over a defined period of time, ranging from a single event (like a festival) to projects running for a number of years. They often constitute a positive impulse for the cultures supported. Another way to counteract decline in musical diversity is by documenting traditions in danger of disappearing. Archives are being created at a considerable scale across cultures and continents, often by qualified and highly motivated ethnomusicologists, and increasingly by musicians or community members themselves. The results are stored in various formats and locations, from local centers to various online repositories to international institutions. Through these initiatives, the sound of many traditions is being preserved for posterity. This allows future generations to reconstruct to some extent musical styles and genres that have disappeared as living practices, should they wish.

Valuable as they are, these efforts do not always provide sufficient basis for the actual survival of music practices as part of an unbroken, living tradition, which many will argue is a key condition for maintaining the essence (explicit and tacit, tangible and intangible) of specific styles and genres. To contribute to sustainable futures for music cultures in this way, there is a need for music practices to be examined within their contemporary global context, in close collaboration with the communities themselves. This benefits not only their histories and "authentic" practices but also their dynamics and potential for recontextualization in contemporary settings, which includes considering new musical realities, changing values and attitudes, and political and market forces.

Taking the previous reflections as a starting point, this volume is a key outcome of a 5-year international research collaboration enabled by an Australian Research Council Linkage Grant to test an ecological approach to music sustainability, focusing on nine case studies: Mexican mariachi, Ghanaian Ewe dance-drumming, Amami *shima uta* from Japan, Korean samulnori, Hindustani music from north India, Vietnamese *ca trù*, Indigenous *yawulyu* songs from Central Australia, Balinese gamelan, and Western opera.

The project, *Sustainable Futures for Music Cultures: Toward an Ecology of Musical Diversity* (2009–2014), made a deliberate choice to focus not only on "endangered" music practices (as has largely been the practice in other efforts) but also, equally, on "successful" ones. The rationale for this was that while the former may provide profound insight into the main obstacles encountered by living music cultures in need of safeguarding, vibrant practices can reveal possible pathways to removing such obstacles. So while much Aboriginal music from Central Australia and

Vietnamese *ca trù* are "in urgent need of safeguarding" in UNESCO terms, Ghanaian Ewe dance-drumming, Amami *shima uta*, and Korean samulnori have much less dire challenges, and Hindustani music, Mexican mariachi music, Balinese gamelan, and Western opera are largely thriving according to most observers and stakeholders, specific challenges notwithstanding. Similarly, the project aimed to consider *all* forces as part of the cultural ecosystem, accepting that music practices at the beginning of the 21st century are not immune to being globalized, mediatized, commodified, and/or politicized. In doing so, this volume aims to contribute to mapping and understanding the complex forces acting in and on present-day music cultures and specific music practices, both philosophically and as a basis for planning interventions that are effective and reflect the wishes of the communities that own, create, develop, perform, transmit, disseminate, and value the music.

AN ECOLOGY OF MUSIC CULTURES

While the debate on what music *is* is unlikely to abate or be resolved any time soon, we have made significant advances over the past decade in understanding what music, or *musicking*—"tak[ing] part, in any capacity, in a musical performance, whether by performing, by listening, by rehearsing or practising, by providing material for performance (what is called composing), or by dancing" (Small, 1998, p. 9)—*does* for people in terms of expressing and processing emotion, building a sense of identity, and relating to community, partners, children, ancestors, country, enemies, and worlds beyond. In that sense, it functions not unlike a GPS (Global Positioning System), providing a sense of place in the worlds of emotions, relationships, spirituality, and space.

We have also come a long way in understanding how music *works* in its environment. While the idea of "art for art's sake"—that music is something in itself without reference to its environment—continues to have a romantic appeal, music genres and styles in fact all demonstrably heavily depend for their survival on interaction with individuals, communities, governments, policies, buildings, funding, education, press, goodwill, reputation, and many other factors. Each music practice has a number of animate and inanimate forces working on it, whether symphonic music for Western orchestras, country music, Sufi chants from Turkey, polyphonic singing from Croatia, Chopi xylophones, or Chinese opera. As this volume aims to demonstrate, these forces can be approached as a complex, integrated system from an ecological viewpoint.

In the same year that Merriam refocused the attention of ethnomusicology as a discipline toward "music in culture" with his *Anthropology of Music* (1964),

William Kay Archer published a five-page essay, "On the Ecology of Music," in *Ethnomusicology*, in which he argues:

Widespread – Distribution

> In a time when the total pattern of musical dissemination, consumption and response is undergoing extraordinary changes, it may be as fruitful to consider sources of raw materials for instruments, patterns of leisure, technological developments, musical "listening-spaces" and the like, as to consider the music itself. (1964, pp. 28–29)

Archer does not develop this idea in any great detail, primarily focusing on social and aesthetic considerations in the following pages. Nevertheless, his article does help trace back the "wellsprings" of ecological thinking on music to over half a century ago.

In the five decades since, several authors have invoked ecology as an approach or metaphor to think about music cultures. Most notable among these is Jeff Todd Titon, who developed this view over a period of 25 years through his writings, his lectures, and his blog (http://sustainablemusic.blogspot.com/; 2008–2016), and in a themed edition of the journal *The World of Music* (2009) that he guest-edited. In that volume, he argues for strong links between ecological understanding and issues of music sustainability. Outlining the contents of the volume, Titon (2009a) provides an extensive list of factors influencing the sustainability of music, including:

> Cultural and musical rights and ownership, the circulation and conservation of music, the internal vitality of music cultures and the social organization of their music-making, music education and transmission, the roles of community scholars and practitioners, intangible cultural heritage, tourism, and the creative economy, preservation versus revitalization, partnerships among cultural workers and community leaders, and good stewardship of musical resources. (p. 5)

Critiquing cultural heritage management initiatives that approach preservation statically, he argues that stewardship in relation to musical ecology "offers the most promising path toward sustainability in musical cultures today" (Titon, 2009a, p. 11) as "living heritage 'masterpieces' are best maintained by managing the cultural soil surrounding them" (Titon, 2009b, p. 124).

Meanwhile, various other approaches to "ecomusicology" have emerged. Some researchers working in this area, most notably Feld (2015), focus on the meaning and relationship between nature and sound ("acoustemology"). Others, led by scholars like Pedelty (2012) and Allen (2009), link music and culture with environmental studies, sustainability, and change, promoting an interdisciplinary and activist approach.

Several ethnomusicologists have explicitly or implicitly used the ecology metaphor to elucidate the network of forces that impact on the sustainability of specific music genres. Daniel Neuman (1980) was one of the first to do so, dedicating a full chapter of his book on Hindustani music to "The Ecology of Hindustani Music Culture," covering "the producers of music, the consumers of music, the contexts of music events, and the technology of music production and reproduction" (p. 203). Other researchers to explore this theme include Slobin (1996) for Eastern and Central European music, Ramnarine (2003) for Finnish folk music, and Sheehy (2006) for mariachi music, to name just a few.

Directly or indirectly, in writing on the ecology of music, many of these authors consciously or subconsciously invoke the 1870 definition of ecology by the biologist Ernst Haeckel, who speaks about ecology as "the body of knowledge concerning the economy of nature":

> The investigation of the total relations of the animal both to its inorganic and to its organic environment including above all, its friendly and inimical relations with those animals and plants with which it comes directly or indirectly into contact – in a word, ecology is the study of all those complex interrelations referred to by Darwin as the conditions of the struggle for existence. (cited in Stauffer, 1957, p. 140)

Such a definition provides fruitful ground for looking at music cultures. Arguably, ethnomusicology (and to some extent historical musicology) has already used this approach extensively. We can find it in a wealth of focused ethnographic studies in regard to localized genres from the 1960s onward, and in writings on diasporic and global contexts since the 1980s. Individual musicians, instrument makers, communities, educators, the music industry, opinion leaders, and public authorities are among the direct actors, while the physical environment, climate, war, discrimination, and disease are among the indirect forces in such ecosystems.

Not everybody is convinced by this "ecological" approach to music. Keogh (2013) places what he calls the "trope" of ecology for the study of music cultures in a context of wider cross-disciplinary use of the term, referring to publications on the ecologies of mind, organizations, landscape, human development, behavior, cognition, information, and written languages, among others (p. 3). He is critical of this approach for music, as he sees its appeal to natural imagery primarily as a means "to justify critiques of the detrimental impact of transnational industry practices on sub-dominant music cultures and styles" (Keogh, 2013, p. 11).

Undeniably, it is both easy and tempting to make naively simple links between music ecology and sustainability efforts and imbibe them with implied social critique and moral righteousness. This has some analogy with the way the word *authentic* is often used in the context of music performance. As Cook (1998, pp. 7–14) points out, "authentic" is implicitly good, while "inauthentic" is dubious (cf. Schippers, 2010, pp. 47–50; Taylor, 2007, pp. 126–136), so that "music must be authentic, otherwise it is hardly music at all" (Cook, 1998, p. 14).

The most obvious pitfall to an ecological approach to music sustainability is a historically and intellectually unsound tendency to impose a static, preservationist approach on music. While many archiving efforts, recording projects, festivals, and even the highly visible *Masterpieces of Intangible Cultural Heritage* initiatives of UNESCO still run the risk of approaching music practices as artifacts rather than as part of organic systems, there is increasing consensus in the discipline of ethnomusicology that a dynamic approach to processes of change and sustainability in music is imperative (Alivizatou, 2012).

That approach, in turn, invites a consideration of the terminology and rhetoric used in this sphere, which is important for understanding the relationship between ecology and sustainability and the constructs underlying such understandings. As I have argued in the essay that informed this chapter,

> related terms such as preservation, safeguarding, and salvaging . . . run the risk of coming across as defensive and patronising. At a next level, they suggest risks of stasis, ossification and even strangulation, as well as disempowerment and other risks of government interventions or institutionalization. Maintaining, the favoured term in the preservation of languages, is certainly more gentle, but also suggests stasis. Perhaps the term sustainability has the best chance at transcending "tradition under siege" and static associations: its very etymology ("holding from below" rather than the "holding in the hand" of maintaining) suggests a more gentle and open process, and leaves room for taking into account more than a single force working on a phenomenon. (Schippers, 2015, p. 137)

On this reasoning, this volume adopts sustainability as the preferred terminology to refer to the condition under which music genres can thrive, evolve, and survive.

That in turn raises three questions on *whether* (any or all) music needs to be sustained, *what* aspects of music are to be sustained, and *how* and *whether* it is possible to make or help sustainability occur. As for the first question, it is useful to realize that not everybody is up in arms about the decline and disappearance of music practices at every single occurrence. For instance, the rise and decline of crooning was a process that did not cause indignation or concern from a sustainability perspective. As mentioned before, over the course of history, thousands of music practices have disappeared due to "natural causes," while others have thrived without ever needing support, adapting successfully to changing circumstances, and often benefiting from them.

Considering all these ideas, the practical focus of music sustainability need not be the preservation of *all* forms of musical expression, but rather supporting a future for those that musicians, communities, and other stakeholders feel are worth maintaining and developing as they choose, and which are currently at risk due to a range of circumstances beyond their control. Some of these circumstances can be influenced to some extent (like funding, education, or music industry involvement). Others are mostly or completely outside of human control, such as diseases, wars, or the slow effect of rising sea levels (see R. M. Moyle's 2007 description of Takū Atoll), and necessitate more creative lines of action to keep music vibrant.

Next, the answer to *what* is to be sustained has profound implications: Is it musical sound; performance tradition; transmission processes; audience; commercial value; social, cultural, aesthetic, or spiritual context; or the musical practice at large? The balance between these factors differs from tradition to tradition and stakeholder to stakeholder, but there is little doubt that they are interrelated. While it is perfectly possible to "freeze" a specific musical expression (e.g., on a video or audio recording), it is hard to imagine a music practice being sustainable without being embedded in a supportive environment. Characteristics of such environments may include solid transmission processes, strong links in the community, prestige, settings and infrastructure conducive for practicing the music, supportive media, an engaged music industry, and laws and regulations that do not impede the genre.

For most music cultures, these do not form a neat and static set of characteristics, but a diverse and not necessarily coherent one. But that very diversity may create the resilience to deal with inevitable changes. Efforts aimed at preserving music genres as objects or artifacts risk creating a false sense of security: Well-preserved recordings, carefully crafted slick productions of music catering to broad audiences, and institutionalized education or performance practices can lead to ossification by not allowing change, or an artificial "new life," which may be supported politically and financially but can be devoid of links to community or to creative lifelines infusing new ideas and practices. "Hold still, let me preserve you" may be convenient from a logistical perspective, but it is an altogether inappropriate approach to sustaining a living tradition. Howard (2012), among many others, argues that "cultural conservation needs to be dynamic" (p. 5):

> It can be conceived . . . as a way to organize "the profusion of public and private efforts" that deal with "traditional community cultural life" (Loomis, 1983, p. iv) and which "we together with our constituents, share in the act of making." (Howard, 2012, p. 6)

Related to this dynamism are interpretations of concepts like tradition, authenticity, and context. As I have argued elsewhere (Schippers, 2010, pp. 41–60), static approaches to each of those concepts may have done more harm than good to the thinking on, education in, and practice of music outside of the Western classical canon: "The nature of tradition is not to preserve intact a heritage from the past, but to enrich it according to present circumstances and transmit the result to future generations" (Aubert, 2007, p. 10). Similarly, as mentioned before, authenticity is highly contentious and laden. Paradoxically, it had opposite meanings in the emergence of early music practice in the 1960s and 1970s ("Authentic is as close to the original as we can get") and in rock music of the same period ("Authentic is as far from copying existing models as possible"). Moreover, the reference for authenticity, the "moment of authenticness," may well be rather randomly or even self-servingly chosen by an appointed or self-proclaimed authority. In that sense, it is similar to the idea of "the right context," while virtually all music practices reinvent, redefine, and recontextualize themselves as a matter of course. Varying degrees of hybridization and transculturation are not exceptions, but the norm. Few realize as they enjoy a symphony, for example, that there would be little left on stage if one were to exclude all influences on orchestral instruments that are traceable to the world of Islam. Such considerations present a potent case for regarding the past, present, and future of musical practices as part of a complex and often delicate ecosystem.

The final issue in discussing *what* is to be preserved is defining the scope of ecosystems of music. The literature on ecosystems at large allows room for both very narrowly prescribed boundaries and working on a vast scale (e.g., Pickett & Cadenasso, 2002). In some cases, it makes sense to draw a narrow circle around a geographical locus—a valley in the Swiss Alps or a Pacific island, say—that harbors the community; is the birthplace of its music creators, teachers, and performers; has provided the raw materials for instruments; and is the site of transmission processes, performance, and all other aspects of music making.

In such a scenario, influences from beyond the circle could be seen as intruders into the ecosystem, like an oil spill threatening a coral reef. However, as myriad external influences increasingly form an integral part of virtually all music practices, it may be more accurate and fruitful to regard *all* forces that impact upon the music as part of the ecosystem, including technology, commercialization, legislature, globalization, and media. As Wong (in Queensland Conservatorium Research Centre, 2008) reminds us, we are inevitably working in "environments which are going to be commodified, and mediatized, and globalized." This allows for a much more comprehensive picture of the potential and challenges for sustainability.

It also assists in addressing one of the concerns voiced by Keogh (2013): that the applied ethnomusicologist who works toward preservation or sustainability interferes with the ecosystem. I would argue that this is not the case; rather, ethnomusicologists who strive to preserve certain approaches to, or aspects of, a particular genre become *part* of the ecosystem. As Pickett and Cadenasso (2002) point out, the concept of ecosystems "now supports studies that incorporate humans not only as externally located, negative drivers, but also as integral agents that affect and are reciprocally affected by the other components of ecosystems" (p. 7). The key in this approach lies in not excluding *any* factors from the ecosystem to work from a comprehensive picture of forces impacting on sustainability.

FIVE DOMAINS INFLUENCING SUSTAINABILITY IN MUSIC

The approaches described previously suggest there is scope for an angle complementary to existing, more narrowly focused preservation initiatives: that is, for recognizing an ecology of music that includes organizational, media, industry, and political forces and, by extension, for exploring the sustainability of music cultures in closer collaboration with communities and other stakeholders. This would be in line with the third of Dan Sheehy's (1992) four proposed strategies of applied ethnomusicology: "providing community members access to strategic models and conservation techniques" (p. 331). It also resonates with Titon's (2009b) idea of stewardship that "repositions culture workers collaboratively, both as students of community scholars and music practitioners, and simultaneously as teachers who share their skills and networking abilities to help the musical community maintain and improve the conditions under which their expressive culture may flourish" (p. 120).

As argued before, such an enterprise requires a framework to map not only structures, histories, and "authentic" practices but also the dynamics and potential for recontextualization of music genres in their contemporary environment. The ethnomusicological literature of the past 50 years already presents a wealth of information on the nature and present state of many specific music cultures primarily based on wide consultation with musicians and their communities. More recently, we find increasing attention on the issue of music sustainability from other stakeholders such as public authorities, educational institutions, and the music industry, complemented by documentaries, press, policies, and data gathered from government sources, NGOs, educational authorities, cultural organizations, media, and business.

With such a vast body of information, the key challenge is choosing ways of organizing and analyzing data to generate insights and their impact on music cultures. *Sustainable Futures* developed a framework of five domains that contain crucial elements of the ecology common to most music practices: systems of learning music, musicians and communities, contexts and constructs, regulations and infrastructure, and media and the music industry. Table 1.1 overleaf summarizes the key aspects of each of these domains.

These domains arguably cover most key aspects relevant to the sustainability of almost any musical practice, irrespective of specific musical forms or content, and as free as possible from Eurocentric bias. Most of them are well documented. Domain 1 (systems of learning music) has been explored by music education and ethnomusicology; Domains 2 and 3 (musicians and communities, and contexts and constructs) have been at the center of much ethnomusicological research for five decades. Domain 4 (infrastructure and regulations) has attracted sporadic attention in the discipline but has been the realm of governments and NGOs, as exemplified by the International Music Council report on musical diversity commissioned by UNESCO (Letts, 2006). Domain 5 (media and the music industry) has gained increased attention since the 1980s from ethnomusicologists, and long before that from business and media scholars, as well as through professional publications from the music industry itself.

To understand the influence of these domains on sustainability, it is important to regard not only each individual domain but also the whole as the ecosystem. Each of the domains overlaps and interrelates with the others. For example, change in a music culture can be driven by a combination of changing values and attitudes, technological developments, and/or audience behavior. The nature of music transmission is often strongly determined by its institutional environment, and media attention, markets, and audiences can often be linked to issues of public perception and prestige. Television and radio broadcasting policies protecting local music, through laws that require it is allocated a percentage of airplay, have influence on sustainability. Opinion leaders can generate prestige for a particular genre or music practice, which in turn can drive funding, media exposure, and the creation of infrastructure. There will be many instances of each of these in the following chapters.

TABLE 1.1

The Five-Domain Framework: An Ecological Approach to Sustainability

1. Systems of learning music	This domain assesses the transmission processes that are central to the sustainability of most music cultures. It investigates balances between informal and formal education and training, notation-based and aural learning, holistic and analytical approaches, and emphasis on tangible and less tangible aspects of "musicking." It explores contemporary developments in learning and teaching (from master–disciple relationships to systems that are technology/web based) and how nonmusical activities, philosophies, and approaches intersect with learning and teaching. These processes are examined from the level of community initiatives through music education to the level of institutionalized professional training.
2. Musicians and communities	This domain examines the positions, roles, and interactions of musicians within their communities, and the social basis of their traditions in that context. It scrutinizes everyday realities in the existence of creative musicians, including issues of remuneration through performances, teaching, portfolio careers, community support, tenured employment, freelancing, and nonmusical activities, and the role of technology, media, and travel in these. Cross-cultural influences and the role of the diaspora are also examined.
3. Contexts and constructs	This domain assesses the social and cultural contexts of musical traditions. It examines the underlying values and attitudes (constructs) steering musical directions. These include musical tastes, aesthetics, cosmologies, socially and individually constructed identities, gender issues, and (perceived) prestige, which is often underestimated as a key factor in musical survival. It also looks at the realities of and the attitudes to recontextualization, authenticity and context, and explicit and implicit approaches to cultural diversity resulting from travel, migration, or media, as well as obstacles such as prejudice, racism, stigma, restrictive religious attitudes, and issues of appropriation.

(continued)

TABLE 1.1

Continued

4. Regulations and infrastructure

This domain primarily relates to the "hardware" of music: places to perform, compose, practice, and learn, all of which are essential for music to survive, as well as virtual spaces for creation, collaboration, learning, and dissemination. Other aspects included in this domain are the availability and/or manufacturing of instruments and other tangible resources. It also examines the extent to which regulations are conducive or obstructive to a blossoming musical heritage, including grants, artists' rights, copyright laws, sound restrictions, laws limiting artistic expression, and adverse circumstances such as obstacles that can arise from totalitarian regimes, persecution, civil unrest, war, or the displacement of music or communities.

5. Media and the music industry

This domain addresses large-scale dissemination and commercial aspects of music. In one way or another, most musicians and musical styles depend for their survival on the music industry in its widest sense. Over the past 100 years, the distribution of music has increasingly involved recordings, radio, television, and more recently the Internet (e.g., downloads, podcasts, iTunes, YouTube, MySpace). At the same time, many acoustic and live forms of delivery have changed under the influence of internal and external factors, leading to a wealth of new performance formats. This domain examines the ever-changing modes of distributing, publicizing, and supporting music, considering the role of audiences (including consumers of recorded product), patrons, sponsors, funding bodies, and governments who "buy" or "buy into" artistic product.

Reproduced from Schippers, H. (2010). *Facing the music: Global perspectives on learning and teaching music.* New York, NY: Oxford University Press.

To structure the project across nine very diverse case studies, guidelines were developed featuring some 200 questions and subquestions across the five domains to facilitate later cross-case analysis. For example, the following questions structure the section on Domain 5 (media and the music industry):

5.1. How widely is your music culture accessed by people within your community?

How is it accessed? (live performances/CDs/Internet/radio/podcasts)

How has this changed in the past 5/20 years?

How do you imagine this might change in the next 5/20 years?

5.2 In a typical performance context, are audiences expected or required to pay?

Is the price high, medium, or low, within the market?

How has this changed in the last 5/20 years?

5.3. How widely is your music culture accessed by people outside your community?

By whom is it accessed, and where, and how?

How has this changed in the past 5/20 years?

How do you imagine this might change in the next 5/20 years?

5.4. Is your music culture regarded by governments as a significant source of export income?

Does it contribute to international image?

Are exports or international presentations of your music assisted by the governments?

If so, how?

How do the national and international markets for your music relate?

5.5. Which legal means of *distributing* (disseminating) your music exist? How significant is each of the following: live performance (including festivals), recordings, radio broadcasts, television, Internet (podcasts, YouTube, MySpace), other file sharing (peer-to-peer), piracy, Internet downloads, or others?

5.6. Which issues of legality exist with regard to *distributing* (disseminating) your music locally, nationally, and internationally?

What arrangements of ownership exist, and how do they relate?

5.7. Which of the following play a role in *publicizing* your music, and how would you describe that role: print media (magazines/community bulletins/newspapers), Internet (e-bulletins/lists/emails/websites/wikis/blogs/e-networks), radio, television, word of mouth, or others?

5.8. How has the representation of your music in the media influenced the public perception of it?

5.9. Which of the following play a role in *financially supporting* your music, and how would you describe that role: patrons, sponsors, government, funding bodies, commissions, or others?

5.10. What is the interaction between your music culture and the tourism industry?

> How do they mutually impact each other?
>
> Is your music culture a primary or secondary attraction for cultural tourism, for example, through festivals or performances?
>
> Does the music or musical event alter when presented for tourists? How?

(QCRC, 2010, pp. 17–18. For a full list of questions and subquestions, see the companion website or http://www.soundfutures.org.)

Case study research teams were asked to seek answers to *all* questions across the five domains and indicate those that were not applicable, as these might point to areas unexplored in the music genre due to oversight, historical reasons, or simply irrelevance. Each case study leader did so by applying insights from (mostly many decades of) engagement with the specific culture, targeted fieldwork, and an average of two dozen interviews per genre, targeting a wide range of stakeholders across domains where possible.

The results of the case studies are presented in Chapters 3 to 11, after Chapter 2 presents an overview of initiatives by musicians, communities, NGOs, public authorities, and international organizations to safeguard, protect, maintain, and stimulate musical diversity. A final chapter formulates some key insights from the data across music cultures and domains. It presents a possible model for understanding music sustainability by approaching music cultures as ecosystems, offers a mechanism for documenting change in the vitality of genres over time, and proposes an instrument to assist communities to forge musical futures on their own terms.

REFERENCES

Alivizatou, M. (2012). The paradoxes of intangible heritage. In M. Stefano, P. Davis, & G. Corsane (Eds.), *Safeguarding intangible cultural heritage* (pp. 9–22). Woodbridge, UK: Boydell Press.

Allen, A. (2009). Ecomusicology: Music, culture, environmental studies and change. *Journal of Environmental Studies and Sciences, 2*(2), 192–201.

Archer, W. K. (1964). On the ecology of music. *Ethnomusicology, 8*(1), 28–33.

Aubert, L. (2007). *The music of the other: New challenges for ethnomusicology in a global age.* Aldershot, UK: Ashgate.

Cook, N. (1998). *Music: A very short introduction.* New York, NY: Oxford University Press.

Feld, S. (2015). Acoustemology. In D. Novak & M. Sakakeeny (Eds.), *Keywords in sound* (pp. 12–21). Durham, NC: Duke University Press.

Howard, K. (2012). Introduction: East Asian music as intangible cultural heritage. In K. Howard (Ed.), *Music as intangible cultural heritage: Policy, ideology and practice in the preservation of East-Asian traditions* (pp. 1–21). Farnham, UK: Ashgate.

Keogh, B. (2013). On the limitations of music ecology. *International Journal for Music Research Online, 4*. Retrieved from http://www.jmro.org.au/index.php/mca2/article/view/83

Letts, R. (2006). *The protection and promotion of musical diversity*. Retrieved from http://www.unesco.org/imc/

Loomis, O.H. (1983). *Cultural conservation: The protection of heritage in the United States*. Washington, DC: Library of Congress.

Merriam, A. P. (1964). *The anthropology of music*. Bloomington, IN: Northwestern University Press.

Moyle, R. (2007). *Songs from the second float: A musical ethnography of Takū Atoll, Papua New Guinea*. Honolulu, HI: University of Hawai'i Press.

Neuman, D. (1980). *The life of music in North India: The organization of an artistic tradition*. Chicago, IL: University of Chicago Press.

Pedelty, M. (2012). *Ecomusicology*. Philadelphia, PA: Temple University Press.

Pickett, S. T. A., & Cadenasso, M. L. (2002). The ecosystem as a multidimensional concept: Meaning, model and metaphor. *Ecosystems, 5*, 1–10.

Queensland Conservatorium Research Centre. (2008). *Twelve voices on music sustainability* [unpublished video recording]. Brisbane: QCRC.

Ramnarine, T. K. (2003). *Ilmater's inspiration: Nationalism, globalization, and the changing soundscapes of Finnish folk music*. Chicago, IL: University of Chicago Press.

Schippers, H. (2010). *Facing the music: Global perspectives on learning and teaching music*. New York, NY: Oxford University Press.

Schippers, H. (2015). Applied ethnomusicology and intangible cultural heritage: Understanding "ecosystems" of music as a tool for sustainability. In S. Pettan & J. T. Titon (Eds.), *Oxford handbook of applied ethnomusicology* (pp. 134–157). New York, NY: Oxford University Press.

Sheehy, D. (1992). A few notions about philosophy and strategy in applied ethnomusicology. *Ethnomusicology, 36*(3), 3–7.

Sheehy, D. (2006). *Mariachi music in America: Experiencing music, expressing culture*. New York, NY: Oxford University Press.

Slobin, M. (Ed.). (1996). *Returning culture: Musical changes in Central and Eastern Europe*. Durham, NC: Duke University Press.

Small, C. (1998). *Musicking: The meanings of performing and listening*. Middletown, CT: Wesleyan University Press.

Stauffer, R. C. (1957). Haeckel, Darwin and ecology. *Quarterly Review of Biology, 32*(2), 138–144.

Taylor, T. D. (2007). *Beyond exoticism: Western music and the world*. Durham, NC: Duke University Press.

Titon, J. T. (2009a). Introduction. *World of Music, 51*(1), 7–13.

Titon, J. T. (2009b). Music and sustainability: An ecological viewpoint. *World of Music, 51*(1), 119–138.

UNESCO. (2001). *Declaration on the promotion of cultural diversity*. Retrieved from http://portal.unesco.org/en/ev.php-URL_ID=13179&URL_DO=DO_TOPIC&URL_SECTION=201.html

UNESCO. (2003). *Convention for the safeguarding of intangible cultural heritage.* Retrieved from http://portal.unesco.org/en/ev.php-URL_ID=17716&URL_DO=DO_TOPIC&URL_SECTION=201.html

UNESCO. (2005). *Convention on the protection and promotion of the diversity of cultural expressions.* Retrieved from http://portal.unesco.org/en/ev.php-URL_ID=31038&URL_DO=DO_TOPIC&URL_SECTION=201.html

United Nations High Commission for Human Rights. (2007). *Declaration on the rights of indigenous peoples.* Retrieved from http://www.un.org/esa/socdev/unpfii/documents/DRIPS_en.pdf

2

MUSIC SUSTAINABILITY

Strategies and Interventions

Catherine Grant[1]

OVER RECENT DECADES, communities, researchers, and other stakeholders have developed and implemented a wide range of strategies to support music sustainability, from small grassroots festivals to international policies and conventions. Drawing on many specific examples, this chapter critically surveys this range of approaches to supporting music sustainability. The five-domain framework presented in Chapter 1 forms a lens through which to view them; although some initiatives fall across more than one domain. Given their extensiveness and centrality to the discipline of ethnomusicology, documentation and archiving are dealt with in a separate section toward the end of the chapter.

SYSTEMS OF LEARNING MUSIC

Many initiatives that aim to foster the sustainability of a given music genre focus on improving its transmission to younger generations. Specific examples illustrate the close connection between learning music and issues of sustainability—like the *Revival of Afghan Music* project, a music education initiative led by the Afghanistan National Institute of Music (2014). By training young musicians, who (it is hoped)

---

[1] This chapter is adapted from part of Chapter 1 in Grant (2014).

will eventually go on to become teachers and music educators themselves, the project aims to help rebuild and revive Afghan musical traditions. In this way, it has dual goals in the areas of music education and sustainability.

One successful model of a learning-based approach to music sustainability is the *Cambodian Living Arts* program of activities, which supports master musicians, students, and assistant teachers to develop income-generating skills while also helping to revitalize and celebrate their cultural heritage (Cambodian Living Arts, 2015). This nongovernment organization provides master-musicians with a wage, instruments, teaching space, and basic healthcare. For students, it provides musical instruments, public school stipends, and a limited number of university-level scholarships. A few years ago it opened its first teaching and learning center in Phnom Penh. This transmission-based model holds parallels with certain music apprenticeship schemes in the United States, funded by arts agencies as a form of "intervention" in cultural sustainability, in which younger members of an arts community learn from respected elders (Titon, 2009a, p. 13). In some ways, programs like these replicate time-honored apprenticeship systems of music transmission between older and younger generations.

In many parts of the world, education is playing an important role in music sustainability. Wettermark and Lundström (Chapter 11) describe the 2-month externally funded program that enabled musicians from several northern provinces of Vietnam to learn *ca trù*. Following these classes, many participants began teaching the genre themselves, leading to the establishment of *ca trù* "clubs," which then acted as infrastructure for teaching, learning, and performing. Tan (2008) offers another example from Southeast Asia, where changing values and attitudes to tradition and modernity among young people are precipitating the disappearance of some traditional genres. She describes a project in Malaysia in which youths were given training in local music traditions, which they then performed. The project stimulated interest in traditional music both among the young participants and the wider community. With regard to the link to musical sustainability, Tan writes that such

> community-based music and heritage conservation programs ... have empowered young people and the community to transcend ethnic barriers and take courage to speak for themselves. Empowerment ensures that musical traditions will be conserved in their traditional socio-cultural contexts of performance, rather than in the archives. (p. 81)

On the other side of the world, the *Kantele Project* is another striking example of a music sustainability initiative centering on transmission processes. It was initiated in 1982 by the Folk Music Institute in Kaustinen, in response to the low prestige and profile of the Finnish national instrument. By introducing the *kantele* into the music syllabus of all comprehensive schools, the project success-fully raised the instrument's national public profile and set a precedent for the introduction in 1983 of folk music into higher education. Ramnarine (2003) attri-butes the project's success to the endeavors of certain individuals, as well as "to the provision of instruments, teaching materials, and training for teachers—made available because of the value that the state continues to accord to folk music" (p. 64). The key role of transmission in the sustainability of music genres around the world, and its centrality to many initiatives aiming to support sustainability, is evident from the chapters in this volume, from *yawulu* song in central Australia to Ghanian Ewe drumming.

Theory relating to the relationship between learning and teaching music and issues of music sustainability is sparse, and rarely couched in general terms. In general, practical approaches to sustaining music genres that focus on teaching or learning are represented in the literature by specific instances such as those afore-mentioned. In describing a scheme with transmission at its core, Graves (2005, pp. 137–139) is one of the few scholars to abstract the key elements in reviving the transmission of an at-risk genre. The music in question is traditional English Northumberland *ceilidh* dance tunes. Their revitalization began around 1990, when a well-known local traditional-music performer rightly recognized that the genre could be given a new lease by engaging local school students with it, and through them, the wider community. From those modest beginnings the orga-nization FolkWorks was established. Under its auspices, teaching resources were created and disseminated, master artists were brought into schools to work with student ensembles, and summer music camps were organized for teens and adults. Some of the young adults involved in these programs became interested in a career in folk performance and eventually toured nationally. FolkWorks implemented a series of training workshops for schoolteachers, and in due course every school in Northumberland had a trained teacher able to offer basic instruction in the tradi-tion. Graves generalizes the whole process in this way:

> The basic components form an elegant circle: exposure of students to tradi-tional artistry in the classroom results in community performance oppor-tunities; these inspire the most interested and talented students to pursue extracurricular training; the best of these are given professional performance opportunities and are brought back for teacher training institutes; the teach-ers bring their new knowledge into their classrooms; and the cycle begins anew. (2005, p. 139)

One noteworthy feature of this model is that, like the Kantele Project in Finland, it illustrates the value of committed individuals in efforts toward music sustainability.

While some of the learning- and teaching-related approaches to supporting music sustainability are spectacularly successful, like those by Graves and Ramnarine described earlier, others are considerably less so. In Taiwan, educational infrastructure in the form of state-funded *nanguan* training courses in elementary and junior high schools cultivated some grassroots appreciation and skills in the genre, but also created tension among nanguan musicians over who would be involved in the program, how much they would be paid, and appropriate teaching methods (Wang, 2003, pp. 123–124). A number of scholars have tabled various risks in introducing music genres into the institutional environment (e.g., Cohen, 2009; Schippers, 2009; and several authors in this volume). These include risks of standardization of repertoire, stasis or ossification, decontextualization, and the various changes in attitude, values, constructs, and practices that may arise from assessment processes and procedures.

From another angle, the field of cultural diversity in music education may also contribute theoretical insights into learning-based approaches to sustainability (cf. Schippers, 2010, pp. 124–127). With a focus on approach and pedagogy, this area explores best ways to disseminate knowledge and practice about the world's music cultures in a range of formal and nonformal educational settings. The very practice of cultural diversity in music education may aid the sustainability of at-risk music genres, which may find a new lease of life through transmission in different times and places. Children or youth learning in schools, for example, may "start playing with and exploring the possibilities, . . . and expanding or in some way varying the tradition, . . . and actually give credence to a more inventive nature of the genre" (P. Campbell, interview, March 4, 2010). Although the field of cultural diversity in music education deals predominantly with transmission that occurs outside of the community whose music is being taught—sometimes with vastly different aims and in vastly different circumstances from transmission within its culture of origin—it nevertheless still holds potential to inform the understanding (and practice) of the dynamics of music transmission across contexts and cultures.

MUSICIANS AND COMMUNITIES

As several chapters in this volume indicate, one critical factor in music sustainability efforts is the involvement of musicians and communities themselves, and their commitment to the future of the genre in question. Top-down sustainability initiatives (such as those described later in this chapter) are only likely to be effective to the extent to which they involve grassroots collaboration and consultation and foster a sense of local ownership of the project.

Of all approaches to strengthening music sustainability that directly involve musicians and communities, festivals serve as perhaps the most powerful example. Since the 1920s, festivals have played an important role in revival movements (Rosenberg, 1993, p. 6); examples of festivals strengthening the vitality of music genres are scattered throughout the revival literature (Bithell & Hill, 2014). By creating a new performance context for Indian *dhrupad* from the mid-1970s, for example, festivals were a central catalyst in the revitalization of that genre (Sanyal & Widdess, 2004). Livingston's (1999) description of why festivals (and competitions) are fundamental to revival movements may hold true for approaches toward music sustainability too:

> These events are crucial to the revivalist community because revivalists meet each other face-to-face to share repertoire and playing techniques, to discuss the strengths and weaknesses of artists within the tradition, to actively learn and experience the revivalist ethos and aesthetic code at work, and to socialize among other "insiders." These events are fundamental to a revival's success for they supplement what can be learned from recordings and books with lived experiences and direct human contact. (p. 73)

For indigenous peoples, festivals can represent strategic spaces to recognize, celebrate, and renew their cultural traditions; arguably, they are

> one of the few consistently positive spaces for Indigenous communities to forge and assert a more constructive view of themselves, both inter-generationally and as part of a drive for recognition and respect as distinct cultures in various local, national and international contexts. (Phipps, 2009, p. 30)

By inspiring a community to identify more strongly with its music practices, or by confirming the value of those practices in other ways (financially, for example), even nonsubstantive community festivals and events can benefit the sustainability of music genres and practices well beyond the duration of the event. Hayward and Kuwahara (Chapter 8) describe the Hana Hana festivals held in 2005–2007 on Amami's northwestern coast, commenting that despite the success of these events in "showcasing a traditional form in a well-facilitated and modern outdoor context, the high levels of sponsorship required and complex logistical issues contributed to the festivals' discontinuance after 2007." On the other hand, it is also possible for the effect of these one-off initiatives to last barely longer than the events themselves. This depends a great deal on the level of community engagement, commitment, and ownership.

In Chapter 5 in this volume on Australian Aboriginal *yawulyu*, authors Barwick and Turpin suggest that regular performance-based events, including those that occur as part of festivals organized external to the community, can signal to Aboriginal people that their music is culturally acceptable and of interest to "outsiders," as well as instilling pride in their culture. The interrelationship between community-based festivals and constructs (such as prestige that festivals can bring to music genres) is raised again later in this chapter. Other authors in this volume investigate, with reference to specific genres, the link between performance events and constructs like prestige (see, e.g., Howard on *samulnori* and Wettermark and Lundström on *ca trù*).

With the rise of mass media, festivals and other community-based initiatives that directly or indirectly support sustainability can be global in reach. As in the case of Cape Breton fiddling in Canada in the 1970s, local events may increase public interest in a music genre, and this in turn may pressure the media to allot it greater importance (Feintuch, 2006, p. 6). But the vitality and viability of a genre may also be adversely affected by festivals, competitions, and other community-based attempts at support. Essentially a facet of the global music industry, the phenomenon of the "festivalization of world music" (Bohlman, 2002, p. 137) has left a residual effect on many genres (and their communities' perceptions of them), including their homogenization or standardization. In the case of *dhrupad* mentioned earlier, "festivalization" has arguably encouraged the growth of the genre as a "parallel culture," rather than its integration into the mainstream: Audiences are mainly local, and the festivals (and their embedded competitions) receive minimal press or national media coverage (Sanyal & Widdess, 2004, p. 281). Ellis (1992, p. 278) voices further ethical concerns about the competitive nature of some festivals and their impact on communities; on the other hand, competitions have been a positive impulse for other genres. Overcoming the challenges of these kinds of approaches may be difficult, but as with most sustainability initiatives, odds of success grow with a high level of community involvement in the process and product from the beginning. Many of these issues relating to musicians and communities overlap with the "contexts and constructs" that surround a music genre.

CONTEXTS AND CONSTRUCTS

In terms of contexts for sustainability initiatives, the borders are sometimes vague between approaches to sustainability that recognize, support, and encourage music at a local level and those that also work at a wider provincial, national, or international sphere. The Australian Aboriginal Garma Festival is one example: vigorously upholding local ownership while expanding to an event of national scope, and therefore now representing "an intercultural gathering of national political, cultural and academic significance, and, simultaneously, a very local gathering of Yolngu clans on Yolngu land for Yolngu purposes" (Phipps, 2009, p. 38). Another instance is the revitalization of *ca trù*, where the establishment of various *ca trù* "clubs" from the 1990s played a role in stimulating the recognition and celebration of the genre at the national and eventually international levels; the genre's raised profile fed back to surge local interest and engagement in it (see Wettermark and Lundström, Chapter 11). Music contests and competitions are another kind of initiative that may operate simultaneously in a local and broader context. For many genres (including *mariachi, ca trù*, Western opera, and others represented in this volume), these events hold significant prestige, and success in them can aid the career of a competing musician. Moreover, the media coverage they attract can play an important role in helping communities and others recognize and celebrate the value of the genres represented.

One particularly salient example of an initiative aiming to promote positive constructs around music genres, and that operates simultaneously in a local and a higher context, is the *Living National Treasures* (sometimes *Living Human Treasures* or *Intangible National Treasures*) system that operates in several countries, originating in Japan in the 1950s. These schemes identify, support, and celebrate individuals who hold the highest skills in an aspect of the cultural heritage of a people. They aim to persuade artists to continue and expand their artistic practice and pass their skills on to the younger generations, and to encourage younger people to "devote their lives to learning the skills and techniques of the identified cultural manifestations by holding out to them the possibility of future recognition and support, and national or international fame, if they are able to achieve the necessary level of excellence" (UNESCO Section of Intangible Heritage/Korean National Commission for UNESCO, 2002, p. 20). In this way, they are closely connected to the domain of "Systems of Learning Music."

Like festivals, competitions, and media promotion, these high-profile methods of recognizing and celebrating music and musicians have attracted criticism for their equivocal impact on the community (and cultural form) in question (see Smith & Akagawa, 2009, in relation to issues of intangible heritage at large). Howard (Chapter 9) discusses some of the challenges with the intangible cultural heritage preservation system in Korea, where, he writes, "camps of detractors and supporters in roughly equal measure critique and celebrate the [Important Intangible Cultural] Propert[ies] system." In Taiwan, the Ministry of Education

Heritage Award for outstanding traditional musicians, implemented in 1985, "not only created a sense of competition among musicians and groups but also enhanced the reliance of musicians on scholars or other cultural bureaucrats as their mediators and patrons" (Wang, 2003, pp. 117–120); the award was discontinued in 1994. Titon (2009b, p. 129) argues that UNESCO's discontinued *Masterpieces of the Oral and Intangible Heritage of Humanity* scheme (discussed in more detail in the next section) suffered from a lack of satisfactory implementation mechanisms and a focus on the "masterpieces" themselves, over and above consideration of the persons who produce and sustain them, or their wider music–cultural ecosystems. Thus, while "top-down" initiatives have proven an ability to promote prestige, recognize musical skill and knowledge, and celebrate and support musicians and music practices, they run the risk of being undermined by a complex set of issues, including a lack of grassroots understanding, resources, control, and ownership that typically characterizes approaches developed and implemented at the community level. In this way, issues of contexts and constructs are closely interrelated and are important factors in the success of efforts toward music sustainability.

INFRASTRUCTURE AND REGULATIONS

Infrastructure for music sustainability—from buildings to archives to instruments—may be supported at a community, regional, national, or international level, by stakeholders ranging from individuals to supranational bodies. Regulations, too, may be decided upon and effected across the range of levels by a range of players; among the most dominant are those operating at the international level and spearheaded by high-profile bodies such as UNESCO.

As a well-established and respected international agency for promoting the diversity and vitality of cultures of the world, UNESCO is an important player in cultural sustainability interventions. Its core aims in regard to intangible heritage are advocating, acting as a clearinghouse for the dissemination and sharing of knowledge and information, setting standards and forging international agreements, and helping member states implement national safeguarding measures such as ongoing inventories of cultural heritage, appropriate policies, and competent legal, financial, and administrative measures.

One of the most significant UNESCO mechanisms relating to music sustainability is the 2003 *Convention for the Safeguarding of the Intangible Cultural Heritage*, the first UNESCO treaty specifically underscoring the importance of such heritage. Resources to facilitate the implementation of the convention among states parties continue to be developed. Various other declarations and conventions also form tools of reference through which nation-states can take steps to protect their cultural heritage in spite of—or along with—mechanisms that promote it within a global market economy. The high profile of instruments like the *Universal Declaration on Cultural Diversity* (UNESCO, 2001), the *Convention on the Protection and Promotion of the Diversity of Cultural Expressions* (UNESCO, 2005), and the *Declaration on the Rights of Indigenous Peoples* (United Nations High Commission for Human Rights, 2007) means that they hold considerable influence in supporting and promoting cultural heritage and diversity.

A multitude of international and transnational nongovernment organizations have been established to further UNESCO's goal to protect cultural heritage, founded on its principles or operating under its auspices. The *Asia-Pacific Cultural Centre for UNESCO* (ACCU) is one example, organizing training courses for safeguarding intangible cultural heritage, hosting conferences around issues relating to the 2003 convention, and running the *International Contest for Better Practices in Community Intangible Cultural Heritage Revitalization*. The ACCU is largely subsidized by the Japanese government, and at times its continued existence has been at risk of discontinuation due to budget cuts (van Zanten, 2009, p. 42).

From 2001, UNESCO's *Proclamation of Masterpieces of the Oral and Intangible Heritage of Humanity* paid homage to manifestations of cultural heritage to encourage local communities to protect them and to raise awareness among local structures, national governments, and the wider public about intangible cultural heritage. While not without its problems, the *Masterpieces* program was successful in promoting awareness of the issues, creating a favorable environment for the drafting and ratification of the 2003 convention on safeguarding, and instigating a "surge in scholarly reflection" on intangible heritage programs (Seeger, 2009, pp. 114–115). This program was superseded in 2008 by the *Representative List of the Intangible Cultural Heritage of Humanity*, which at the time of writing (September 2015) contained over 300 entries. Another UNESCO list identifies *Intangible Cultural Heritage in Need of Urgent Safeguarding*; inscription on it typically escalates the local, national, and international profiles of the heritage in question, in addition to committing the relevant state party to undertake certain safeguarding activities. Wettermark and Lundström (Chapter 11) explore some of the impacts of inscription on this list for Vietnamese *ca trù*.

Especially if the principles of UNESCO's declarations and conventions are incorporated into evolving international agreements (like those on free trade or intellectual property), they hold promise to form a conduit by which many music genres may be kept viable. Yet UNESCO's approaches to supporting sustainability have not escaped criticism. For one thing, its safeguarding strategies have sometimes brought unforeseen and unwanted consequences, as mentioned earlier in relation to the *Living National Treasures* and *Masterpieces* schemes. The proclamation in 2001 of Bolivia's Oruro Carnival as a UNESCO *Masterpiece of the Oral and Intangible Heritage of Humanity*, for example, exacerbated conflict about the origins, ownership, and appropriation by Peruvians of Bolivian music and dance expressions (Stobart, 2010, p. 45). China's successful nomination of *khöö-mei* (throat singing) to the *Representative List* caused contention among some artists and officials in Mongolia, who argued the tradition is Mongolian, not Chinese (Higgins, 2011). In Croatia, certain proclaimed intangible masterpieces (not only musical ones) subsequently became "like a national park" where "you're not supposed to change anything" (S. Pettan, interview, July 30, 2010). In the case of the Royal Ballet of Cambodia, the UNESCO proclamation "entered local politics and worked against innovation, originality and development of new repertoire within the Ballet company" (Titon, 2009b, p. 127). In addition, the action plans resulting from the inscriptions to the *Masterpieces* list were sometimes considerably misconceived, and there were often insufficient financial means to implement them in any case, resulting in local-level disillusionment about the scheme (A. Seeger, interview, March 22, 2011).

There continues to be extensive scholarly theorization, deconstruction, and critique of UNESCO's approach to cultural heritage and safeguarding (e.g., in the volumes edited by Smith & Akagawa, 2009, and Stefano, Davis, & Corsane, 2012); and in 2013, UNESCO itself, through its Internal Oversight Service (IOS), began the process of evaluating the goals, methods, and impact of the six UNESCO conventions relating to culture (UNESCO, 2013). Ways to avoid (or even just accurately predict) the unanticipated ill-effects of well-intended initiatives like the *Masterpieces* scheme have been the subject of some ethnomusicological investigation. Titon (2009b) attributes the failure of that scheme to its very "remoteness" and a lack of "sufficient ongoing, on-the-ground connections (partnerships)" with cultural heritage workers and the culture-bearing communities themselves (p. 124). Within the context of the UNESCO cultural heritage schemes, the pivotal role of the community in safeguarding its own heritage has been problematized at some length (e.g., Blake, 2009, and others in that volume). Concern has been expressed too that experts in the relevant field do not have greater agency in moving forward UNESCO's goals (e.g., van Zanten, 2009, p. 42).

Some of these concerns also arise in relation to national-level infrastructure, regulations, and policies that aim to support music sustainability. National legal measures and policy instruments, for example, may explicitly or implicitly act to protect or promote music genres and music makers; laws relating to media, education, and copyright (among other matters) can all affect music sustainability. These instruments and regulations are dependent on the ideologies of those in power, and therefore vacillate from country to country and era to governmental era. Like international initiatives such as UNESCO's safeguarding schemes, the effect of national and international policy initiatives on local musics can be equivocal. While years of state intervention from 1980 brought Taiwanese *nanguan* increased visibility, for example, it also arguably contributed to a compromise of the integrity of its musicians, as well as the "commodification, vulgarization, and theatricalization" of the music itself—and this quite aside from the overall failure of state intervention to solve problems of transmission (Wang, 2003, p. 152). Burns (Chapter 3) notes that the lack of government support for traditional music in Eweland has certain positive aspects, including that musicians are free to practice their art without the restrictions imposed by regulations, taxes, or other dues. On the other hand, in the case of Western opera, its very existence is predicated on a complex top-down support system of infrastructure and regulations (Drummond, Chapter 7).

The various national and international regulations, policies, and mechanisms supporting the sustainability of cultural heritage may be supported locally, regionally, nationally, or internationally by the efforts of nongovernmental bodies. One example is the United States–based organization Future of Music, whose mission, through education, research, and advocacy, is "to ensure a diverse musical culture where artists flourish, are compensated fairly for their work, and where fans can find the music they want" (Future of Music Coalition, 2015, para. 1). Other examples include Freemuse (2014), which campaigns against unreasonable censorship and for the freedom of musical expression in all countries, and the World Intellectual Property Organization (WIPO), which aims to establish an appropriate relation between intellectual property rights and protecting traditional musical expressions. Responding to a call for guidance from Indigenous organizations, archives, and cultural researchers, WIPO develops and maintains guidelines, codes of practice, protocols, and other resources for dealing with intellectual property issues that arise when archiving, documenting, recording, digitizing, and disseminating intangible cultural heritage. It also describes best practice and management of intellectual property in relation to festivals, which, as described earlier, hold some risk of adversely affecting local music genres (World Intellectual Property Organization, n.d.).

Some community-level infrastructure initiatives have been described earlier in this chapter, such as festivals and educational projects. At a provincial, regional, or national level, infrastructural strategies may be represented by the efforts of cultural institutions, like the *Sangeet Natak Akademi* in Delhi, the *Sangeet Research Academy* in Kolkota, and the National Centre for the Performing Arts in Mumbai described by Schippers (Chapter 4). Governments and other bodies may also provide infrastructure in the form of buildings or other tangible materials required for the performance, rehearsal, and creation of music. At the international level, aside from UNESCO, several infrastructure mechanisms serve as means for stakeholders to explore and exchange views and information on promoting cultural heritage and cultural diversity. One example is the *International Federation of Coalitions for Cultural Diversity* (IFCCD), which facilitates cooperation and the development of common positions and actions between nations. The IFCCD played a role in developing the 2007 UNESCO *Convention on the Protection and Promotion of the Diversity of Cultural Expressions* (International Federation of Coalitions for Cultural Diversity, 2013).

Few international projects and networks deal specifically with the coordination of music sustainability efforts. Peak international music bodies such as the *International Music Council* (IMC) and the *International Council for Traditional Music* (ICTM; both with official relations with UNESCO) do have some engagement with the cause of musical diversity and music sustainability through policy recommendations and involvement in UNESCO activities (like the ICTM's input into the *Masterpieces* scheme). While IMC-commissioned reports by Mundy (2001) and Letts (2006) offer useful suggestions for developing ways to support the diversity, vitality, and viability of music genres and music cultures, many of these are still to be realized.

Research partnerships relating to music sustainability (such as the IMC's with *Sustainable Futures*), formal statements highlighting the need to support endangered traditions (such as the ICTM Australia–New Zealand Regional Committee's statement about the urgent situation of Australian Indigenous music and dance; Bendrups, 2011), and international conferences and events where sustainability is a theme (such as the 2013 Fifth IMC World Forum on Music) all demonstrate the ideological support of these peak organizations for the issues, but the administrative structure and financial resources that would enable them to play a more active part in coordinating approaches to sustainability are lacking. Thus, most ways in which these peak bodies might help improve and standardize administrative, ethical, legal, financial, and practical matters relating to music sustainability—say, by establishing guidelines and protocols for best practice, developing advocacy pitches, lobbying governments and other relevant bodies, evaluating practical efforts, centralizing information about potential funding sources, and creating networks for exchange of ideas and information—remain largely unrealized. In particular, infrastructure in the form of hubs, gateways, and forums to pool and share resources about ways to support music sustainability remains deficient.

MEDIA AND THE MUSIC INDUSTRY

Romero (1992) considers the mass media (and music industry) "*the* realm, *par excellence*, in which well-intentioned cultural policies could produce a positive effect" on music genres under pressure (pp. 191–192). While this may be so, the correlation between sustainability and engagement in media and the music industry is not necessarily a direct one. This is evident from some of the music genres represented in this volume, which span the gamut from having high media and commercial engagement (opera and samulnori) to little or none (Aboriginal *yawulyu*). It is hard to make claims that those with a generally positive and prominent media and industry profile and those with a checkered or low one are consequently respectively better and worse off in the sustainability stakes; some correlation seems to exist, however, though not necessarily a causal one.

Media, industry, and enterprise initiatives that explicitly or implicitly serve to protect or promote music genres and music makers are many. Blaukopf (1990, 1992) gives a number of examples of possible media- and/or industry-related legal or contractual policy measures that may help protect "small" music genres, not least by raising funds for archiving, documentation, research, training professional musicians, or revitalization initiatives. Many of his examples have now been implemented in some form or another, and some are relatively common practice. They include taxing media consumption via television or radio (or Internet!) license fees; encouraging or requiring broadcasters to pay royalties upon use of traditional music for economically gainful purposes (Blaukopf recommends those in turn be earmarked for cultural preservation or promotion purposes); implementing broadcasting policies that allocate a percentage of airtime to local music, thereby encouraging and celebrating local musicians and music and providing a platform for its performance; and copyrighting folklore so that the copyright is vested in the community.

In some countries, measures like these have been at least partly effective in protecting local music, such as in India, where All India Radio has played a significant role in preserving and promoting the Indian classical tradition (see Schippers, Chapter 4). In other cases (including in a number of sub-Saharan African countries), policies do not exist, are inadequately reinforced, or are perversely implemented (see, e.g., Burns, Chapter 3, who refers to the lack of enforcement of copyright laws and the repercussions for traditional Ewe musicians). Stobart's (2010) case study of music production and piracy in Bolivia explores the multifaceted nature of the challenges.

Online media are increasingly being used to store documentation of music genres and to disseminate the outcomes of these and other sustainability-related initiatives to the community and other interested parties. The *Plateau Music Project*, a grassroots cultural preservation program based in Xining City, China, is representative of some possible modes of media-rich dissemination and repatriation of the outcomes of music documentation (Bridge Fund, 2012). It made available video clips on YouTube, prints and distributes written information in the local language to local communities, lodges recordings with international archives like PARADISEC, and established links with the larger project *Digital Himalaya*, which continues to develop digital collection, storage, and distribution strategies for music, songs, and other oral traditions from that region (Digital Himalaya, 2015).

The vast possibilities afforded by mass media and the music industry point to complex issues around the roles of enterprise in supporting music sustainability, and cultural sustainability more generally. Drummond (Chapter 7) refers to the interesting case of shifts in the consumption of opera, as high-quality productions are being recorded and released for a "near-live" experience at the cinema. Cultural entrepreneurship and businesses, cultural tourism, cultural export strategies, and cultural enterprises as a part of economic development initiatives are just a few of the many possible links between enterprise and music sustainability. Some types of enterprise seem to be an integral and fundamental characteristic of music revivals, pointing to their possible role in sustainability. According to Livingston (1999), one feature of many music revivals is

> the emergence of a revival industry, by which I mean non-profit and/or commercial enterprise catering to the revivalist market consisting of concert and festival promotions, sales of recordings, newsletters, pedagogical publications, and instruments and supplies. Although many revivalists are embarrassed to admit this aspect of their movement given their general distrust of the commercial market and its massifying tendencies, it is an ethnographic fact. Indeed I would argue that it would be difficult for any revival to exist for more than a few years without entering into this phase. (p. 79)

If Romero and Livingston are right, the role of enterprise may be an important consideration in furthering practical approaches to music sustainability.

Vigilance should be exercised, though. As Graves (2005, p. 88) warns, powerful links sometimes exist between the protection and the exploitation of cultural heritage. Among approaches aiming to support music sustainability, perhaps nowhere is the threat of exploitation more real than in those where profitable enterprise and industry play a central role, whether those enterprises relate directly to culture (like music recording companies) or not (like mining companies, which often have a vested interest in being seen to be sensitive to the cultural heritage of the peoples on whose land they operate). Dunbar-Hall (Chapter 6) writes of the situation in Bali whereby "there seems to be little or no systematic control of what is recorded, by whom, or of royalty payments or responsibilities," despite the plethora of commercial recordings. Strategies "intended to buffer cultural heritage often result in consequences that are ruled by the model of the marketplace rather than the ecosphere" (Graves, 2005, pp. 88–89). Moreover, in some ways, cultural homogenization is an advantage for multinational companies, for whom fewer consumer tastes mean easier product and market development.

Recognizing this danger, governments and nongovernment stakeholders may develop mechanisms to support communities in protecting and promoting their cultural heritage. One example is *Stepping Stones for Tourism* (Stepwise Heritage and Tourism, 2008), developed in collaboration with the Australian Government Department of Environment and Heritage, Aboriginal Tourism Australia, and Tourism NT (Northern Territory). The program guides Australian Indigenous communities in developing and managing tourism that is sustainable for both themselves and their cultural heritage. Often working in connection with industry or enterprise, these kinds of mechanisms may yield outcomes with strong social and economic, as well as cultural, benefits for the communities involved.

DOCUMENTATION AND ARCHIVING

Of all practical approaches supporting the sustainability of music genres, documentation and archiving are almost certainly the most extensive. Hundreds of organizations and projects are involved with documenting and archiving local genres, many with an explicit goal to keep these cultural expressions for posterity. While these initiatives are situated within the domain of infrastructure, their extensiveness and centrality to sustainability efforts warrant a separate section devoted to them.

Documentation is not just about preservation; it can play a leading role in the maintenance and revitalization of genres. Ramnarine gives the example of the Sámi joik:

> There are numerous examples of researchers in the early 20th century . . . who were recording, notating Sámi joik traditions, and at that time they thought that they were recording something which was disappearing. And almost 100 years later, their work is now being consulted not just by other researchers, but also by the musicians who are seeking to reconstruct things that maybe have been slightly lost, or to become more familiar with traditions that they feel they should be familiar with. (T. Ramnarine, interview, March 16, 2011)

Many similar situations can be found across a range of genres and contexts.

In music revivals, historical recordings are often used as the basis for formulating repertoire, stylistic features, and history of a tradition (Livingston, 1999, p. 71);

notated music may serve some of the same roles, as in the case of the Northumbrian piping revival. Karpeles (1973) described an instance from her fieldwork on folk songs in the southern Appalachians:

> The bearers of the tradition, who had put aside their songs because they felt them to be no longer in the fashion, have had their confidence restored by hearing them over the radio and on gramophone records, and by seeing them in print. This was exemplified by a singer in North Carolina who said: "When I forget Mother's songs, I know I have only to look at Cecil Sharp's book, and they will come back to me just exactly right." (p. 101)

Historical recordings may also nourish the revival process. Recordings made by Hemetek over 30 years ago in Stinatz, Austria, "really are becoming important now for the people in this village, because most of the singers have died in the meantime" (U. Hemetek, interview, July 22, 2010); musicians are turning to these recordings to find new ways of musical expression based on the tradition. Norton recommends that as part of the ongoing strategy to revitalize the endangered north Vietnamese genre *ca trù*, historical recordings be used to inform contemporary understanding, performance, and transmission of it (2009, p. 215; see Wettermark and Lundström, Chapter 11).

The direct link that can pertain between the documentation of a music genre and its continuity in living form suggests an important role for documentation in both revitalization and preservation. As one example, documentation can play a role in promoting both public and community knowledge and awareness of the significance of a music genre. Thus, although the vision of the *National Recording Project for Indigenous Performance in Australia* is "to systematically record and document the unique and endangered performance traditions of Indigenous Australia" (Corn, 2011, "Vision" section, para. 1), it ultimately "hopes to aid Indigenous communities in sustaining cultural survival by stimulating lifelong interest in performance traditions through its serial recording and documentation initiatives, and the collections that it will deposit in local repositories for perpetual community access" (Marett et al., 2005, p. 88).

Sound archives are integral to effective documentation, serving the functions of "collecting, storing, maintaining, cataloguing, documenting, publishing and making available recordings of music traditions as they are now for the benefit of musicians, scholars and other interested people in the future" (Stubington, 1987, p. 9). Umbrella networks have been created as hubs, such as the Ralph Rinzler Archives that hold the collection of Smithsonian Folkways (which also functions as a digital educational resource; Smithsonian Folkways, 2010); the pan-European meta-archive DISMARC (*Discovering Music*

Archives), encompassing over 30,000 audio recordings; and DELEMAN (*Digital Endangered Languages and Musics Archives Network*), which brings together over 20 prominent regional and international archives including the *Archive of Maori and Pacific Music* (AMPM) housed at the University of Auckland, the *Pacific and Regional Archive for Digital Sources in Endangered Cultures* (PARADISEC), and the *Endangered Languages Archive* (ELAR) of the Hans Rausing Endangered Languages Program in the United Kingdom. Nettl (2005, pp. 161–171) gives an overview of the role of archives like these in musical preservation throughout the history of ethnomusicology.

Ethnomusicologists continue working to counteract procedural weaknesses in documentation and archiving processes, recognizing that high-quality sustainable data and metadata are crucial for accessibility and dissemination. Most major projects in Western countries (like the *National Recording Project*) are now routinely accompanied by extensive guidelines for ensuring that processes of recording and collecting data and metadata meet international archival standards. Recent research has aided the move toward sustainable fieldwork data and their interface with archives and digital repositories (e.g., Barwick & Thieberger, 2006; Fargion, 2009; Seeger & Chaudhuri, 2015). Nevertheless, from region to region and archive to archive, the processes of collecting, cataloguing, classifying, indexing, storing, and preserving materials all remain variable in quality and nature, with national and international standards relating to access and use of recordings being particularly erratically implemented and monitored. In the past, this has understandably led to ethical concerns among some communities and scholars about misappropriation and misuse of materials (e.g., Ellis, 1992). Much has improved in this regard in the last couple of decades, with issues of ethics now typically a foremost consideration in the development of guidelines and standards.

Beyond the challenges of achieving "best practice" in documentation and archiving, the efficacy of efforts may be further jeopardized by factors outside the immediate control of researchers and communities. Technology changes at a rate so rapid as to make it difficult to keep pace. Recent computer software may be expensive, or high-quality recording gear may require training to operate. Equipment required for playback of recordings has generally become more affordable over the past decades, but quickly becomes obsolete, leading either to those recordings falling out of the public realm or to significant infrastructure requirements in terms of personnel, time, and funds to enable the transfer of copies to more recent formats. Storage discs, hard drives, reels, and tapes are subject to loss, damage, and deterioration, and like copying, the restoration of recordings is often a costly and time-consuming procedure (Seeger & Chaudhuri, 2015). These factors need to be taken into account in documentation-related sustainability projects—including even at the stage of applying for funding, when the costs not only of recording but also of subsequent processes such as archiving and migrating the data to newer and usable formats should be factored in, as far as possible.

Internationally, researchers and fieldworkers are increasingly recognizing the value and importance of ensuring that communities have access to any documentation of their music genres, for example, by depositing recordings in local or locally accessible archives. Aside from the ethical reasons for doing so, facilitating access in this way sometimes has the intended or incidental effects of renewing interest in a genre, strengthening pride in it, stimulating memories of it, or forming the basis for further cultural reclamation projects. These were all outcomes, for example, of *The Federal Cylinder Project*, which repatriated some early wax cylinder recordings of songs and narratives of American Indian communities (Gray, 1996).

An even more collaborative approach to documentation provides community members with training in the skills required to undertake the documentation of their own traditions. This approach builds capacity within the local community, minimizes outsider bias in documentation, and maximizes community ownership of the process and outcomes, among other benefits. Self-determination was one rationale behind the UNESCO project *Ethiopia: Traditional Music, Dance and Instruments*, which aimed "to train a generation of local ethnomusicologists to collect and archive Ethiopia's diverse musics," including by establishing ethnomusicology courses at the University of Addis Ababa in 2005 (UNESCO/Norwegian Ministry of Foreign Affairs, 2006). Benefits of this type of collaborative approach notwithstanding, at times it proves challenging, not least due to the sometimes strikingly dissimilar aims of researchers and communities in documenting (e.g., Berez & Holton, 2006).

Repatriation of old recordings raises issues relating to community ownership, protection of works, and protection of knowledge. When efforts to maintain or revitalize a music genre include wide dissemination of recordings, concerns about copyright, economic rights, protection of works, protection of knowledge, and performers' rights may become acute. There are sometimes compelling arguments to make recordings available beyond academic circles and the communities themselves. A desire to promote knowledge about situations of music endangerment to as wide a public as possible may be one such argument, which clearly needs to be balanced against other considerations (including the wishes of the community itself). Several professional associations and archives now have formal codes of ethics that help navigate these complex issues.

To be most useful for sustainability, documentation should go beyond "the musical artifact alone," since "there is much more to music than the piece" (Nettl, 2005, p. 171). With regard to music documentation in written form, Aubert (2007) cites the case of the once-banned Ottoman genre *fasıl*, which survived largely due to musicological transcriptions made in the late 19th and early 20th centuries. However, he correctly observes: "We can see that having the writing as an exclusive recourse is not sufficient to preserve all the flavour and fluidity of an aesthetics so intimately connected with principles of an oral tradition" (pp. 72–73). This is also true of audiovisual music recordings (though arguably to a lesser extent), hence the importance of a range of types of other documentation (in books, articles, interview transcriptions, and so on) that record other important aspects of a music genre, like translations of song texts, meanings, and interpretations, and details of related performance traditions or ceremonies. However, there is still no substitute for culture bearers who can embody a tradition in all its tangible and intangible aspects.

In short, while documentation alone is not sufficient for the continuation of a vibrant, living tradition, with the engagement of interested individuals and communities it can undoubtedly be one resource for sustaining music genres.

REFLECTIONS AND IMPLICATIONS

Evidently, practical efforts toward supporting music sustainability are diverse in nature, and so are their aims and intended and actual outcomes. Many efforts are grounded in theoretical understandings of processes of change and revival, globalization, and cultural (and specifically musical) diversity. Documentation and archiving initiatives are extensive. Most sustainability projects show a keen awareness of ethical issues inherent in sustaining at-risk music genres (particularly in relation to documenting and archiving), especially the importance of the principles of equality, collaboration, and reciprocity. There are specific instances where these efforts have successfully supported music sustainability at local, national, and international levels, such as certain festivals, transmission-based projects, and policy measures. Extensive non-music-specific infrastructure and regulatory mechanisms can also support sustainability efforts, such as those administered or driven by organizations like UNESCO or WIPO. Another strength of the area of music sustainability, which becomes apparent when viewing this chapter as a whole, is the ideological readiness of researchers, certain organizations, and other stakeholders to engage with applied efforts to support it.

Clearly, though, considerable challenges to supporting music sustainability also exist. Some of these lie outside the immediate control of researchers or communities, such as the often-limited availability of substantive funding and resources for practical initiatives, political or legislative forces that override efforts to sustain at-risk music genres, and the impact on music genres of mass media, enterprise, and commercial ventures. While an understanding of these situations and processes is crucial to developing appropriate theory and practice of music sustainability, they may be factors that sustainability efforts will need to take into consideration, rather than trying to overcome them. The case-study chapters in this volume provide varied accounts of how these factors may be approached, and to some extent managed, in the course of making efforts toward sustainability.

REFERENCES

Afghanistan National Institute of Music. (2014). Letter from Dr Sarmast. Retrieved from http://www.afghanistannationalinstituteofmusic.org/letter-from-dr-sarmast/

Aubert, L. (2007). *Music of the other: New challenges for ethnomusicology in a global age* (C. Ribiero, Trans.). Aldershot, UK: Ashgate.

Barwick, L., & Thieberger, N. (Eds.). (2006). *Sustainable data from digital fieldwork. Proceedings from the conference at the University of Sydney*. Sydney, Australia: Sydney University Press.

Bendrups, D. (2011, October). Reports from ICTM National and Regional Representatives: Australia and New Zealand. *Bulletin of the ICTM, 32.*

Berez, A., & Holton, G. (2006). Finding the locus of best practice: Technology training in an Alaskan language community. In L. Barwick & N. Thieberger (Eds.), *Sustainable data from digital fieldwork: Proceedings from the conference at the University of Sydney* (pp. 69–86). Sydney, Australia: Sydney University Press.

Bithell, C., & Hill, J. (Eds.). (2014). *The Oxford handbook of music revival*. New York, NY: Oxford University Press.

Blake, J. (2009). UNESCO's 2003 Convention on Intangible Cultural Heritage: The implications of community involvement in "safeguarding." In L. Smith & N. Akagawa (Eds.), *Intangible heritage* (pp. 45–73). London, UK: Routledge.

Blaukopf, K. (1990). Legal policies for the safeguarding of traditional music: Are they utopian? *World of Music, 32*(1), 125–133.

Blaukopf, K. (1992). Mediamorphisis and secondary orality: A challenge to cultural policy. In M. P. Bauman (Ed.), *World music, musics of the world: Aspects of documentation, mass media and acculturation* (pp. 19–36). Wilhelmshaven, Germany: Florian Noetzel Verlag.

Bohlman, P. V. (2002). *World music: A very short introduction*. Oxford, UK: Oxford University Press.

Bridge Fund. (2012). Plateau music project. Retrieved from http://bridgefund.org/the-plateau-music-project/

Cambodian Living Arts. (2015). Home page. Retrieved from http://www.cambodianlivingarts.org/

Cohen, J. M. (2009). Music institutions and the transmission of tradition. *Ethnomusicology, 53*(2), 308–325.

Corn, A. (2011). National Recording Project for Indigenous music in Australia. Retrieved from http://www.aboriginalartists.com.au/NRP.htm

Digital Himalaya. (2015). Home page. Retrieved from http://www.digitalhimalaya.com

Ellis, C. J. (1992). Documentation as disintegration: Aboriginal Australians in the modern world. In M. P. Bauman (Ed.), *World music, musics of the world: Aspects of documentation, mass media and acculturation* (pp. 259–280). Wilhemshaven, Germany: Florian Noetzel.

Fargion, J. T. (2009). "For my own research purposes"?: Examining ethnomusicology field methods for a sustainable music. *World of Music, 51*(1), 75–93.

Feintuch, B. (2006). Revivals on the edge: Northumberland and Cape Breton. *Yearbook for Traditional Music, 38*, 1–17.

Freemuse. (2014). Freemuse: Freedom of musical expression. Retrieved from http://www.free-muse.org/

Future of Music Coalition. (2015). About FMC. Retrieved from http://futureofmusic.org/about

Grant, C. (2014). *Music endangerment: How language maintenance can help.* New York, NY: Oxford University Press.

Graves, J. B. (2005). *Cultural democracy: The arts, community and the public purpose.* Urbana, IL: University of Illinois Press.

Gray, J. (1996). Returning music to the makers: The Library of Congress, American Indians, and the Federal Cylinder Project. *Cultural Survival Quarterly, 20*(4). Retrieved from http://www.culturalsurvival.org/ourpublications/csq/article/returning-music-makers-the-library-congress-american-indians-and-federal

Higgins, A. (2011, August 11). A showdown over traditional throat singing divides China and Mongolia. *Washington Post.* Retrieved from http://www.washingtonpost.com/world/asia-pacific/a-showdown-over-traditional-throat-singing-divides-china-and-mongolia/2011/06/24/gIQASaZS7I_story.html?hpid=z9

International Federation of Coalitions for Cultural Diversity. (2013). About us. Retrieved from http://www.ficdc.org/A-propos-de-nous?lang=en

Karpeles, M. (1973). *An introduction to English folk song.* Oxford, UK: Oxford University Press.

Letts, R. (2006). *The protection and promotion of musical diversity.* Study carried out for UNESCO by the International Music Council. Retrieved from http://www.mca.org.au/research/research-reports/research-reports/640-the-protection-and-promotion-of-musical-diversity

Livingston, T. E. (1999). Music revivals: Towards a general theory. *Ethnomusicology, 43*(1), 66–85.

Marett, A., Yunupingu, M., Langton, M., Gumbula, N., Barwick, L., & Corn, A. (2005, September). *The national recording project for Indigenous performance in Australia: Year one in review.* Paper presented at Backing Our Creativity: National Education and the Arts Symposium, Melbourne. Retrieved from http://hdl.handle.net/2123/1337

Mundy, S. (2001). *Music and globalisation: A guide to the issues.* Paris, France: International Music Council.

Nettl, B. (2005). *The study of ethnomusicology: Thirty-one issues and concepts.* Urbana, IL: University of Illinois Press.

Norton, B. (2009, June). *Examination report for the nomination for inscription on the Urgent Safeguarding List in 2009: Ca trù singing.* Retrieved from http://www.unesco.org/culture/ich/index.php?pg=00246

Phipps, P. (2009). Globalization, indigeneity and performing culture. *Local-Global: Identity, Security, Community, 6*, 28–48.

Ramnarine, T. K. (2003). *Ilmater's inspiration: Nationalism, globalization, and the changing sound-scapes of Finnish folk music.* Chicago, IL: University of Chicago Press.

Romero, R. R. (1992). Preservation, the mass media and dissemination of traditional musics: The case of the Peruvian Andes. In M. P. Bauman (Ed.), *World music, musics of the world: Aspects of documentation, mass media and acculturation* (pp. 191–208). Wilhemshaven, Germany: Florian Noetzel.

Rosenberg, N. V. (1993). Introduction. In N. V. Rosenberg (Ed.), *Transforming tradition: Folk music revivals examined* (pp. 1–25). Urbana, IL: University of Illinois Press.

Sanyal, R., & Widdess, R. (2004). *Dhrupad: Tradition and performance in Indian music*. Aldershot, UK: Ashgate.

Schippers, H. (2009). From *ca tru* to the world: Understanding and facilitating musical sustainability. In B.-L. Bartleet & C. Ellis (Eds.), *Music autoethnographies: Making autoethnography sing, making music personal* (pp. 197–207). Bowen Hills, Australia: Australian Academic Press.

Schippers, H. (2010). *Facing the music: Shaping music education from a global perspective*. New York, NY: Oxford University Press.

Seeger, A. (2009). Lessons learned from the ICTM (NGO) evaluation of nominations for the UNESCO Masterpieces of the Oral and Intangible Heritage of Humanity, 2001-5. In L. Smith & N. Akagawa (Eds.), *Intangible heritage* (pp. 112–128). London, UK: Routledge.

Seeger, A., & Chaudhuri, S. (2015). The contribution to sustainable traditions through reconfigured audiovisual archives. *World of Music, 4*(1), 21–34.

Smith, L., & Akagawa, N. (Eds.). (2009). *Intangible heritage*. London, UK: Routledge.

Smithsonian Folkways. (2016). Smithsonian Folkways. Retrieved from www.folkways.si.edu

Stefano, M. L., Davis, P., & Corsane, G. (Eds.). (2012). *Safeguarding intangible cultural heritage*. Suffolk, UK: Boydell & Brewer.

Stepwise Heritage and Tourism. (2008). Stepping stones for tourism. Retrieved from http://www.stepwise.net.au/planning/steppingstones_tourism.php

Stobart, H. (2010). Rampant reproduction and digital democracy: Shifting landscapes of music production and "piracy" in Bolivia. *Ethnomusicology Forum, 19*(1), 27–56.

Stubington, J. (1987). Preservation and conservation of Australian traditional musics: An environmental analogy. *Musicology Australia, 10*, 2–15.

Tan, S. B. (2008). Activism in Southeast Asian ethnomusicology: Empowering youths to revitalize traditions and bridge cultural barriers. *Musicological Annual, 44*(1), 69–83.

Titon, J. T. (2009a). Economy, ecology, and music: An introduction. *World of Music, 51*(1), 5–15.

Titon, J. T. (2009b). Music and sustainability: An ecological viewpoint. *World of Music, 51*(1), 119–137.

UNESCO. (2001). *Universal declaration on cultural diversity*. Retrieved from http://www.unesco.org/education/imld_2002/unversal_decla.shtml

UNESCO. (2003). *Convention for the safeguarding of intangible cultural heritage*. Retrieved from http://www.unesco.org/culture/ich/index.php?pg=00006

UNESCO. (2005). *Convention on the protection and promotion of the diversity of cultural expressions*. Retrieved from http://www.unesco.org/new/en/culture/themes/cultural-diversity/diversity-of-cultural-expressions/the-convention/convention-text/

UNESCO. (2013). Intangible cultural heritage. Retrieved from http://www.unesco.org/culture/ich/

UNESCO/Norwegian Ministry of Foreign Affairs. (2006). *Ethiopia: Traditional music, dance, and instruments*. Addis Abbaba, Ethiopia: UNESCO Cluster Office.

UNESCO Section of Intangible Heritage/Korean National Commission for UNESCO. (2002). *Guidelines for the establishment of national "Living Human Treasures" systems (Updated version)*. Retrieved from http://unesdoc.unesco.org/images/0012/001295/129520eo.pdf

United Nations High Commission for Human Rights. (2007). *Declaration on the rights of Indigenous peoples*. Retrieved from http://social.un.org/index/IndigenousPeoples/DeclarationontheRightsofIndigenousPeoples.aspx

Van Zanten, W. (2009). UNESCO News: 2003 Convention. *Bulletin of the International Council for Traditional Music, 114*, 40–42.

Wang, Y.-F. (2003). Amateur music clubs and state intervention: The case of nanguan music in postwar Taiwan. *Journal of Chinese Ritual, Theatre and Folklore, 141*, 95–167.

World Intellectual Property Organization. (n.d.). Creative heritage project: IP guidelines for digitizing intangible cultural heritage. Retrieved from http://www.wipo.int/export/sites/www/freepublications/en/tk/934/wipo_pub_l934tch.pdf

3

SOUTHERN EWE DANCE-DRUMMING

Challenges for Performers in Contemporary Ghanian Contexts

James Burns

THE DANCE-DRUMMING MUSIC of the southern Ewe people of Ghana is a vibrant tradition that continues to form an integral part of funerals, religious ceremonies (including church services), and seasonal festivals. Nevertheless, prevailing cultural norms view traditional music as a free service to the community, and today artists face significant challenges as they try to survive in a modern, cash-based society. This chapter will bring to light contemporary discourse regarding the current state of Ewe music making from 20 important *henɔgãwo* (Grand Singers) and *azagunɔgãwo* (Grand Drummers) residing in the towns of Dzodze, Denu, Anyako, Tengekope, Dzita, Dagbamate, Klikor, Aflao, Kopeyia, and Ashiaman. Their observations and experiences reveal a tradition that is thriving socially but not economically within the context of contemporary Ghana, with obvious implications for sustainability.

Southern Ewe dance-drumming has a rich history of ethnomusicological scholarship, including detailed analyses of various performance genres, particularly their complex, multilayered rhythms and their association with traditional life cycle events (Agawu, 2003; Avorgbedor, 1986, 1987, 2001; Burns, 2005b, 2009, 2012; Chernoff, 1979; Fiagbedzi, 1977, 2005, 2009; Jones, 1959; Ladzekpo, 1971; Locke, 1979, 2010; Locke & Agbeli, 1987, 1992; Pantaleoni, 1972a, 1972b, 1972c; Pantaleoni & Ladzekpo, 1970). Southern Ewe drumming now features in many general discussions of African music in ethnomusicology textbooks and in trans-disciplinary studies of rhythm, dance, and oral literature (Alves, 2012; Anyidoho, 1983; Burns, 2009, May & Hood, 1983; Nettl, 2011; Okpewho, 1992; Shelemay, 2006; Temperley, 2000; Titon, 2008; Wiggins, 1999). This study seeks to address a previously unexplored topic of research, namely, the social life of Ewe musicians, and how they view their craft within contemporary society. A large portion of the data collected for this project, including the full transcriptions of all 20 interviews, an extended bibliography and discography of southern Ewe music, a glossary of Ewe music terms, and photographs and audiovisual recordings of each group, is available on the companion website for this book.

BACKGROUND

The southern Ewe form a distinct subgroup within the larger Ewe-speaking region located between the Volta River in Ghana and the Mono River in Togo. The Ewe people never formed a unified empire; instead, they clustered into independent city-states (*dukɔ*, pl. *dukɔwo*) that spread northward from the coast into the fringes of the Guinea forest belt (see Figure 3.1) (Agbodeka, 2000; Amenumey, 1997; Manoukian, 1952; Nukunya, 1997). In Ghana, the effects of history have created two broad divisions of Ewe *dukɔwo*: the southern Ewe and the northern Ewe. The southern Ewe are composed of the Anlo *dukɔ* (actually a confederation of 36 towns and villages surrounding the Keta lagoon), as well as several autonomous *dukɔwo* in the areas to their immediate north and east (Akyeampong, 2001; Greene, 1996). The northern Ewe are composed of independent *dukɔwo* that were established to the north of the southern Ewe, in an area extending about 150 miles north of the coast, which also saw extensive settlement and influence from other ethnic groups. As a result, the northern Ewe show marked differences in language, culture, and music from the southern Ewe people examined in this study (Agawu, 1995; Agbodeka, 2000).

Within the southern Ewe region, each city-state went through periods of war, cooperation, and peace over more than 200 years before British colonization began in 1874 (Amenumey, 1986; Asiwaju & Law, 1985; Ellis, 1965; Laumann, 2005). The Anlo confederation was the most historically important; during the 18th and 19th centuries, it fought many battles against regional empires like Akwamu, Asante, Ada, Accra, and Gen, as well as European nations such as the Dutch and English (Akyeampong, 2001; Fynn, 1971; Greene, 1996; Mamattah, 1979). In comparison, the other southern Ewe *dukɔwo* did not have much recorded contact with the outside world until the 20th century, so little is known of their early histories. Some states, including Klikor, Afife, Dagbamate, and Nogokpo, formed around a powerful *trɔ* or *vodu* (a divine spirit or pantheon of spirits), which protected the state

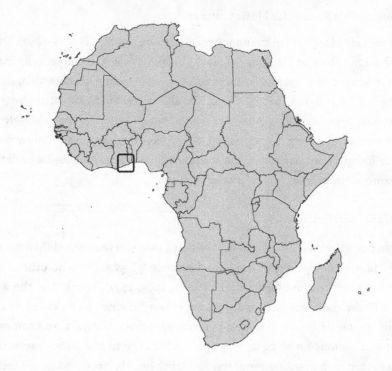

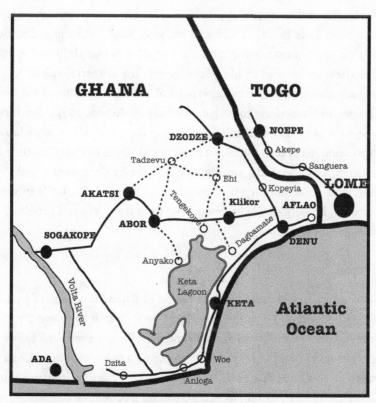

FIGURE 3.1. The southern Ewe region of Ghana.

Maps by the author. Top image adapted from http://bisteachers.cratercomets.com/sinks_jeremy/africa/
AfricaMapOutline.jpg (open source).

during periods of warfare (Amenumey, 1986; Greene, 1996; Nukunya, 1997). Other smaller *dukɔwo*, such as Dzodze, Tadzevu, Ehi, and Fenyi, grew organically from a main settlement that eventually incorporated surrounding satellite villages and farming hamlets (Burns, 2005a). There are also a few *dukɔwo* located along the border with Togo, including Aflao and Denu, which were formed relatively late by Ewe immigrants from Togo (Afokpa, 2005; Akyeampong, 2001). This arrangement of independent *dukɔwo* in the southern Ewe region produced a variety of local expressions of Ewe culture, including music.

Cultural and Social Positioning

The Ewe traditional belief system is based on a remote creator God (*Mawu*), who endows human beings with its spiritual essence (*gbɔgbɔ*) but who otherwise is not actively involved in human affairs (Gaba, 1965, 1997). To regulate the world and fulfill the daily needs of man, *Mawu* created divine spirits called *vodu* or *trɔ*, who act on its behalf. The Ewe perform sacrifices, festivals, and commemorations of various types to convey spiritual energy to the *vodu* in return for their assistance in granting requests, restoring health, or providing protection (Gaba, 1965; Rosenthal, 1998). The *vodu* are also believed to punish people who transgress their laws (*sewo*). *Mawu* and the *vodu* work with the god of destiny, *Se*, to bestow each human being with a set of talents and abilities (*aɖaŋu*) that will allow them to succeed in life (Gaba, 1997). The ancestral spirits (*tɔgbuiwo, mamawo*) are also a part of this supernatural realm, extending the network of divine power and sanctions to each individual (Nukunya, 1997). The Ewe refer to their system of traditional beliefs, including the music forms associated with their expression, as *dekɔnu* (culture or tradition). Over the past century *dekɔnu* has been competing with the worldviews brought by Christianity and Western education, and contemporary Ewe people are the product of the interplay of these diverse influences (Avorgbedor, 1986; Burns, 2009; Cornelius, 2000; Gbeho, 1954; Meyer, 1999).

Formal Features

Dance-drumming in the southern Ewe region of Ghana is organized by talented musical families within the various districts (*towo*) of each town and continues to be an integral part of the social and cultural life of every community. Ewe music making is generally called *vufofo* (drumming), and a music event is called a *vufofe* (drumming place/event; Fiagbedzi, 1977). Like many cultures in Africa, however, the Ewe use the term *vu* (drum) as a metonym for a community artistic event that incorporates several types of performance activities including drumming, dancing, singing, fashion, group interplay, solo displays, and occasionally theatrical plays (Anyidoho, 1983; Nzewi, 1997).

Most southern Ewe dance-drumming genres are performed using a common set of instruments. The foundation of every music form consists of a steady rhythmic background articulated by the *gankogui* (iron double bell), several *axatse* (gourd rattles), the *kagan* support drum, and spontaneous hand clapping by the audience and group members (Agawu, 2003; Burns, 2009). While community members with a modest amount of musical ability can play the *axatse* or clap along to the music, in Ewe towns like the ones we surveyed, there are only perhaps 10 to 20 individuals who are able to competently play *gankogui* or the *kagan* drum. These various supporting parts provide a steady rhythmic background for the lead singer and lead drummer to introduce musical dialogues between their corresponding chorus singers and response drummers.

In southern Ewe music, the lead drum part is played either on the *atsimevu*, a large drum tilted on a stand; the *sogo*, a medium-sized barrel drum; or the *gboba*, a large barrel-shaped drum (Burns, 2009; Fiagbedzi, 1977; Jones, 1959; Locke, 1979). The person who plays the lead drum is given the title *azagunɔ*, the "mother/nurturer" (*nɔ*) of the "Sacred Logo Drum Tree" (*azagu*; Burns, 2009; Fiagbedzi, 1977; Gbolonyo, 2012; Locke, 1979). In addition to playing the lead drum, the *azagunɔ* acts as the conductor of the entire ensemble, making sure that all of the parts are in alignment, and guiding the dancers and the lead singer through each episode of music. Virtually all of the lead drummers are male and, as we will see later, believe they have inherited the talent of drumming from *Mawu/Se*, as well as from one of their forefathers. Within the districts of the Ewe towns I have visited, there are only about 5 to 10 people with the ability to serve as the *azagunɔ* at a music event. Among a group of *azagunɔ*, a few will be given the title of *azagunɔgã*, Grand (*gã*) Drummer (*azagunɔ*). These elite musicians are able to compose their own drum-language variations (*vugbe*) and create their own musical forms. Below the *azagunɔgã* and *azagunɔ* in ability are perhaps 20 people in each district who can play the *kidi* drum, which responds to the dialogues of the lead drum (Burns, 2011; Jones, 1959; Locke & Agbeli, 1992; Pantaleoni, 1972c; Pressing, 1983). These drummers are often relatives of an *azagunɔ* and are known as *kidiƒolawo* (players of the *kidi* response drum).

Ewe singing is organized antiphonally between a lead singer and a group of chorus singers (Burns, 2009; Fiagbedzi, 2009; Locke & Agbeli, 1992). The person who leads the songs is given the title of *henɔ*, the "mother/nurturer" (*nɔ*) of the song (*ha*) (Burns, 2009; Fiagbedzi, 1977). The *henɔ* can be a man or a woman, but he or she must have a strong voice and impeccable timing. Most *henɔ* are illiterate, yet are able to memorize a corpus of perhaps 500 songs from different genres (Anyidoho, 1983; Awoonor, 1974). A *henɔ* who has composed his or her own songs and who is well known throughout a particular region is given the honorific title *henɔgã*, Grand Singer (Anyidoho, 1983; Awoonor, 1974; Ladzekpo, 1971; Seshie, 1991). Each *henɔ* has a group of 5 to 10 *hatsoviwo* (song elevators), who assist by singing along with the lead parts or by standing in when the *henɔ* needs to rest. Following the *henɔ* and *hatsoviwo* in ability are the *haxeviwo* (chorus singers), general community members who can sing the response parts for each song. The lyrics of Ewe songs touch on a variety of topics, including observations on life's difficulties, local gossip, insults and taunts, historical events, relations between men and women, and humorous stories (Fiagbedzi, 2009).

Dancing is the least specialized musical role in Eweland because every mature community member is expected to be able to dance common funeral dances like *Agbadza*, as well as the dances performed in their shrine or church (Fiagbedzi, 1977; Jones, 1959). Dancing usually occurs within a delineated space in the shape of a circle, square, or rectangle. Most music genres feature only a single dance sequence, which is easy to learn through observation. A *Habɔbɔ* (music club) performance will also feature dance soloists (*atsiawɔlawo*), who perform complex dance sequences (*atsia*) that would be beyond the abilities of a general community member (Burns, 2009; Locke, 1979; Pantaleoni, 1972a). Nevertheless, these solo dancers do not generally become well known like the *henɔ* or *azagunɔ*, and they are rarely given substantial leadership roles within their groups.

There are many ways to categorize Ewe music organizations, but the data collected for this project supports the model advocated in my other published work, which classifies ensembles into one of the following three types: District Funeral Ensembles, ad hoc groups of singers and drummers who gather to facilitate community music events at funerals within their district; Sacred Music Ensembles, groups that provide musical accompaniment at events held by their shrine or (Christian) church; and *Habɔbɔ*, voluntary musical organizations with recognized leaders, which perform at funerals and events to raise money for the group's mutual-aid society (Burns, 2005a, 2009).

SYSTEMS OF LEARNING MUSIC

In southern Eweland, learning music continues to follow an informal process that is completely aural/oral, without the use of notation, recordings, tablature, or learning aids of any kind. Instead of lessons, all of the artists interviewed followed

a long period of immersion into the music by attending countless funerals, ceremonies, and festivals during their childhood, where they accompanied the greatest
artists of their parents' and grandparents' generations.

Philosophies of Learning and Teaching

The Ewe musicians interviewed for this study believe that their musical ability derives from a special talent (*aɖaɲu*) bestowed on them by God/
Destiny (*Mawu/Se*) and from artistic gifts they inherited from their ancestors
(*amedzɔdzɔ*). Grand Drummer Jean Gamadi expresses this commonly held
sentiment in his own words: "In Africa, here, an *azaguno* is someone born into
it, with a spiritual talent given by *Se* (Destiny)" (interview, January 5, 2013).
Having an *aɖaɲu* (spiritual gift) that is recognized by the community is central
to becoming a respected musician. Grand Drummer Kwadzo Tagborlo elabo-
rates further on this concept: "If you are not born with the talent of drumming
you can never become a great drummer. Those that had to study drumming,
and those born with it, are of a different class" (interview, January 7, 2013).
A comment by Grand Drummer Richard Tuwornu connects divine talent with
ancestral talent:

> God sends us into the world with different abilities. If you are given singing,
> you will come down and be a singer; if you are given drumming, then you will
> come down and be a drummer. It all comes from the ancestral talents of one's
> clan. (interview, January 6, 2013)

The *henɔwo* and *azagunɔwo* interviewed in this study all acknowledged that
they had received the talents, abilities, and behaviors of a specific ancestor. Grand
Drummer Emmanuel Agbeli, for example, mentions his ancestor Adedi: "I inherited the spirit of music that was passed down from my grandfather [Adedi] to
my father [Godwin Agbeli] to me" (interview, January 4, 2013). Grand Drummer
Kwadzo Tagborlo informed me that he inherited the talents of Azakpo, an ancestor who was an *azagunɔgã* during the late 19th century (Burns, 2005a). When
asked about the source of his vocal talent, Grand Singer Freenight Awalekpor
replied, "The talent of singing incarnated with us from the spirits of our ancestors ... Kpenga Gbedzra Xokpeyisuxede and Kofi Aho Awalekpor" (personal
communication, January 10, 2013). This divine inheritance also gives the artist
special cognitive skills: "God gives them the mental ability to be able to process
and remember (the music) quickly; these are the people who become drummers"
(C. Agbenu, personal communication, January 8, 2013). Due to the prevailing

belief that God and the ancestors have chosen certain people for music, if an acolyte does not show an immediate aptitude for learning the basic parts, local artists will assume the person has not been blessed with musical ability and will move on to other prospects: "Like I said, it comes from the family heritage. Unfortunately, there are some families in this town who try and drum but it is not their talent" (A. Awalekpor, interview, January 10, 2013).

When asked about the specifics of the learning process, many respondents first proudly stated things like, "There has never been someone that came and taught us; we are born with it" (K. Tagborlo, interview, January 7, 2013). This stems from an important distinction in the Ewe language between the verbs *srɔ*, to imitate, and *fia*, to be taught/shown. Most Ewe musicians will tell you that nobody taught them (*fia*) how to play the drums or to lead the songs. Instead, they will emphasize that they learned their art through imitation (*srɔ*), a word that could also describe imitating someone's walk or manner of speech. Hence, the artists we interviewed described being exposed to the music at an early age by their parents and at some point being able to sing, drum, or dance by imitating the behavior of more competent people around them:

> My grandfathers played the drums, my maternal uncles played the drums, so we all got into it, and it caught us. That is how I started, they put me on the drum bench, then I was playing the drums as I was growing up. (P. Nudzor, interview, January 8, 2013)

Equipped with a divine inheritance that gives them the ability to quickly imitate what they observe, rather than formal instruction, drummers learn the music from participating in performances.

Learning and Teaching Practices and Approaches

"I can say that my singing, in the beginning, what happened was that when we were kids, our parents used to take us to music events, so we grew up around it" (F. Awalekpor, interview, January 10, 2013). Today most southern Ewe communities still have several music events every week, each lasting 4 or 5 hours: "Many times when you are an *azagunɔ* you will be called to some place to play and night will fall. You may even have to stay there for the night" (K. Tagborlo, interview, January 7, 2013).

Many drummers, including Grand Drummer Gbeti, report that in their toddler years their earliest attempts at drumming were playing on *ganugui*, a homemade drum constructed from a discarded metal can covered with a lid or plastic bag:

> I started with *ganugui*, and I was playing that as a kid for fun. Then my maternal uncles came and covered a drum for me, so if they were drumming I could copy them. (P. Nudzor, interview, January 8, 2013)

Youngsters carry the *ganugui* around the town, beating it with a pair of sticks cut from tree braches in imitation of what they have seen at local music events.

When a drummer progresses to adolescence, he will be given the opportunity to play the bell or one of the support drums: "My work with the drum . . . I started with *kidi* (response drum) and *kagan* (supporting drum)" (R. Tuwornu, interview, January 6, 2013). There is often a brief period at the start of each music event where a group of beginners and less talented musicians will be given a chance to play. This opening period of music serves as the main practice time for prospective drummers. When they are ready, support drummers will be given the chance to start learning the *kidi* response drum. In most ensembles there will be two or three *kidi* players, so a talented youngster can play on one drum while he observes the playing of the other musicians. If they do not immediately grasp a new drum language conversation (ʋugbe), one of the other response drummers will vocalize the part using mnemonic syllables. Young drummers who can quickly absorb the repertoire will be given more opportunities to play the *kidi* drum at music events.

"We started playing the gourd rattle, then the *kagan* drum, and then the other drums until we reached the level of the lead drum, and then we had mastered drumming" (K. Tagborlo, interview, January 7, 2013). By the time a drummer reaches 16 to 20 years of age, he will be given a chance to play one of the lead drums during the opening period of an event, and increasingly, during major parts of the main performance. Emmanuel Agbeli speaks about learning at his father's side until "it came to a point that I could play the master drum when he was not there" (interview, January 4, 2013). Speaking about his own evolution as a drummer, Donné Amegble says, "I started playing the *kidi* (response) drum in *Agbadza*, then my uncle (Kwadzo Tagborlo) showed me how they play the *sogo* (lead) drum in *Agbadza*. After that my study of the drum was complete" (interview, January 7, 2013).

"You cannot call yourself an *azaguno*—others will come to call you that" (E. Herman, interview, January 6, 2013). Over time, if community members are inspired by a drummer's talent and leadership, they will begin to call him an *azaguno*, lead drummer and conductor of the ensemble. A select few *azaguno* will become recognized as an *azagunogã* (Grand Drummer), based on a series of three qualities outlined by our informants: expertise in the local repertoire, moral rectitude, and having an original style. Nudzor's response aptly represents the first quality:

> From the effort I was putting into drumming and its related matters, people began to see that I knew all the dance-drumming genres in the Anlo state. Later, the townspeople realized that I could also play the drums from other ethnic groups in Ghana, so there they gave me the title of *azagunɔgã*, Grand Drummer. (interview, January 8, 2013)

Since an *azagunɔgã* has to be able to exercise his authority effectively, he must display a certain degree of moral and ethical awareness in his life and music making: "If your hand is playing well, and you are patient, they will call you an *azagunɔgã*, Grand Drummer" (K. Davo, interview, January 15, 2013). Emmanuel Agbeli believes that an *azagunɔgã* must be able to connect with the performers and audience: "To become an *azagunɔgã* you have to be able to move people with your music and to be able to use the drum to speak to people so that they understand" (interview, January 4, 2013). Ultimately, however, an *azagunɔgã* must have a unique style or "hand" (*asi*), as well as a certain performative quality that is both visually and sonically interesting:

> It's something in your hands, and thoughts. Drumming is all about one's mental ability—the kind of mental ability that lets you grasp the drumming quickly and to be able to transfer it to the hands so that people will say, "this person, they are really doing well, they are an *azagunɔgã*." (K. Tagborlo, interview, January 7, 2013)

The path to becoming a *henɔ* is similar to that of an *azaguno*. Singing usually begins in infancy, as a toddler is exposed to songs at music events. There is no emphasis placed on melodic instruction; singers learn by singing along with the chorus during performances. Like the young boys who practice drumming on tin can drums, young singers may get together spontaneously to sing and dance. Sometimes these impromptu groups will draw other kids who come to play small shakers or play on the *ganugui*. Those few who have been blessed with a divine talent for singing will eventually begin to lead the songs at local events, gradually assuming responsibilities from older singers in the district. At that point the community will recognize them as a *henɔ*, lead singer.

Among the *henɔwo* in a community, some will become known as a *henɔgã*, Grand Singer. When asked what qualities distinguish the average *henɔ* from a *henɔgã*, Grand Singer Christian Agbenu replied:

I can say that when we came out with a new type of music group, Novisi, and later the group Mikafui, I was composing songs for the group. Because of this, and my singing, the group members all started calling me *henɔgã*, Grand Singer. (interview, January 8, 2013)

As mentioned by Agbenu, becoming recognized as a *henɔgã* comes from composing original songs and having a group form around your music, points reiterated by Grand Singer Afaxoe Amenor: "When we brought out the Unity group, when I was singing and composing for this group, that is where I became known as a Grand Singer" (interview, January 15, 2013). These original songs have to be popular and make an impact: "If you know that you are a Grand Singer, you have to be able to bring out new songs for people to become interested" (F. Awalekpor, interview, January 10, 2013).

Nonmusical Influences on Learning and Teaching

"Singing . . . a song, it has an effect on people. Before you sing, something has to happen to you; if you are sleeping you will be thinking about the things worrying you, which you can take to compose a song" (P. Nudzor, interview, January 8, 2013). Some of the respondents report learning music in dreams, from ancestors or from other spiritual beings, a practice that has been noted in other studies of Ewe music (Anyidoho, 1983; Awoonor, 1974; Fiagbedzi, 2009). Adzo Ahiakpote, for example, describes inheriting a *hadzivodu* (divine spirit of song) from her father:

He had a *hadzivodu* called Azizaglu; when my dad died, it came to worry me, so it was I that came to look after the *vodu* and cook [ceremonial meals] for it. When the day comes for a music event, I give it alcohol. (interview, January 13, 2013)

A *hadzivodu* selects a person to serve it, usually a relative of the prior servant. In return for making occasional offerings of alcohol and food, a *hadzivodu* will protect its host, give him or her a brilliant singing voice, and teach him or her new compositions during dreams, such that he or she becomes recognized as a *henɔgã*.

"I learned to drum from the people in this house here," says Grand Drummer Kudzo Davo, using the Ewe word *afeme*, inside the house, as both a literal designation of his place of birth and as a metonym for the larger extended family, another important nonmusical influence to learning in Eweland (interview, January 15, 2013). Talking about his earliest musical experiences, Richard Tuwornu says, "In our family my grandfather, my mother, and other women played the drums, my mom played the drums. They used to take me with them to music events" (interview, January 6, 2013). All of the musicians interviewed in this study report growing up with their brothers, sisters, cousins, and assorted relatives, all of whom showed different degrees of musical talent: "I learned drumming in our house here, with my twin brother who is a singer. . . . In my case, I was around drumming during my youth; my elders were playing music in the house, and I was always around" (A. Awalekpor, interview, January 10, 2013).

Traditional music has been introduced into the Ghanaian educational system in the form of school cultural groups, which are formed by students, teachers, and local volunteers: "One experience I remember from my childhood was when our school group performed *Atsiagbekor* with me on the lead drum and people came out from all over the town to see us" (K. Tagborlo, interview, January 7, 2013). Grand Singer Freenight Awalekpor also reports a similarly formative experience in school: "My singing began when I was going to school, in the school and in the house; if there was a ceremony or festival, I was among the singers" (interview, January 10, 2013). His brother Augustine was also among the drummers at school: "When I started going to school I would drum for our assemblies and festivals. I was with my brother the singer, so in school I also began to be known" (interview, January 10, 2013). Nevertheless, school groups like these are only meant to provide a recreational activity for interested students, so the instruction is limited, and no attempt is made to prepare students to join one of the community music ensembles.

Implications for Sustainability

The belief in spiritual talent and divine selection in Ewe culture suggests that the ranks of musical leadership will continue to be filled in the foreseeable future. Moreover, music continues to be central to both funerals and religious occasions. Perhaps a greater challenge will be sustaining support for musicians and community participants, as there continues to be a lack of local institutions for learning traditional music. As will be discussed further later, there has been a gradual decline in community participation over the years, due to economic pressure and Westernization. Consequently, many groups are only able to maintain some of the popular dances of their parents' generation and do not have the level of community support needed to compose their own new music.

MUSICIANS AND COMMUNITIES

Ewe artists spend a great deal of their lives laboring at community events in return for simple gifts of drinks and food; therefore, they must maintain a separate career to earn an income. Most important community events require music, so musicians are given some degree of social prestige for what they do, but their lack of financial resources prevents them from attaining a decent standard of living. A very small minority of Ewe musicians have been given the opportunity to work in one of the national dance companies in Accra, or at an institution like the University of Ghana, where they earn regular salaries and can make a professional career out of music. Still fewer have been given the chance to work in Europe or the United States, allowing them to enjoy an even higher standard of living through their music.

The Musician–Community Relationship

All of the respondents indicated that music is still very important to their communities, stated best by Grand Drummer Emmanuel Agbeli: "Our drumming (and music) traditions are the cultural inheritance of the Ewe people." At the same time, they also acknowledge the challenge of maintaining the relevance of traditional arts in the modern world: "Musicians today are struggling to get people to recognize how rich our music traditions are" (E. Agbeli, interview, January 4, 2013). Some of the performers emphasize the former sentiment: "When we play we receive honor; they say we have done something great. It is important to the community" (R. Tuwornu, interview, January 6, 2013); some, the latter: "Music is very important, but the help that we would need to go forward in drumming and singing is not available" (D. Amegble, interview, January 7, 2013).

Musicians tend to come from certain lineages within each district, which may also be associated with the chieftaincy and with other forms of traditional leadership. This gives them a great deal of social prestige, and they are some of the most popular citizens in the town. At the same time, many drummers report being denigrated in the community due to their poverty:

Well, here, drummers get no respect from people. They will say you are pursuing a fruitless occupation. If something happens (like a funeral) people will come and praise you, or be asking you to play at their funeral, but outside, they will snub you and be insulting you. (K. Tagborlo, interview, January 7, 2013)

Grand Singer Afaxoe Amenor, who has devoted over 60 years of his life to singing, cynically observes, "You can say you are a Grand Singer or Grand Drummer, but there is no money in it" (interview, January 15, 2013). Many also feel that they lack the resources needed to preserve and develop their music, which impacts the sustainability of the tradition in the future. During funeral events, the audience may occasionally be moved to give a small tip. However, this practice is certainly not as common as in other parts of West Africa, where tips form a major part of a musician's income (e.g., Charry, 2000; Djedje, 2008; Tang, 2007; Waterman, 1990).

To survive, the male musicians we interviewed had to seek some form of self-employment such as farming (E. Agbeli, interview, January 4, 2013), driving cars (E. Herman, interview, January 6, 2013), doing manual labor (D. Amegble, interview, January 7, 2013), or weaving *kente* cloth (A. Awalekpor, interview, January 10, 2013). Female musicians can learn a trade such as tailoring or hairdressing, or can choose to sell goods at the market (Burns, 2009). As mentioned before, due to their lack of financial success, most of the artists interviewed report that despite the important role they fulfill within their cultural tradition, they are not given much respect in the community.

Being a Musician

Musicians spend a great deal of their lives at funerals and ceremonies: "If a funeral occurred in Denu, Adafianu, Tornu, or anywhere around there, I went and was learning (through immersion). Through this I became a drummer" (R. Tuwornu, interview, January 6, 2013). Drummer Ebenezer Herman talked about having to be ready to play at any given moment: "If something happens they will call you that there will be drumming at a certain funeral" (interview, January 6, 2013). Performing constantly at funerals and ceremonies entails certain hardships, including spending several days and nights at a time for each event, where the exertion of energy for continuous hours in the hot climate takes its toll on a musician's body. The strain of a weekend funeral or ceremony can cause an *azagunɔ* to feel run down and sick for several days, similar to an athlete in a contact sport.

There is a lot of competition between musicians and groups in each local community. Most of this competition occurs because of interdistrict rivalries between *Habɔbɔ* groups or among musicians at local funerals. Sometimes fights emerge over the small amount of spoils to be divided up among the funeral musicians: "Someone says give this person a bottle of alcohol, s/he is coming to take over the drumming or singing; this can lead to confusion and dispute among us" (K. Tagborlo, interview, January 7, 2013). Apart from these disagreements, rival groups often try to intimidate each other musically, verbally, and sometimes physically to boost their stature in the community.

Although interview questions for this research did not delve into the topic of jealousy/enviousness (*ŋuveve*), ethnographic studies of individual Ewe musicians have documented that competition between artists can take a more serious form, when people are (believed to be) so envious or hateful of a rival musician that they resort to *dzo* (sorcery) or *aɖi* (poison) to try to kill them (Burns, 2005a, p. 248; Cornelius, 2000; Seshie, 1991, pp. xi–xii). For this reason, artists will receive certain protections including herbal baths, sacrifices, or talismans and must be careful about drinking alcohol openly in public or with strangers.

Digital technology plays a very minor role in the life of the average musician, mainly due to the prohibitive cost of buying a recording device or going into a studio. Most musicians interviewed report that they do not own a recording of their own music. There have been a few recordings made by local and foreign producers, and these circulate as cassettes throughout the region (see discography on companion website). Sometimes an artist will own a tape/radio device that can make low-quality recordings at live events for their own personal use. I have observed some cases where musicians will hear certain drum-language patterns or songs on an audiocassette, which they use to teach their own group, but these new items form a small part of the total repertoire.

There has been a great deal of cross-cultural influence between the southern Ewe and neighboring Ewe-Fon speakers, including Ewe groups located in Northern Ghana and along the southern part of Togo, as well as various Fon, Gun, and Yoruba communities in southern Benin (Akyeampong, 2001; Asiwaju & Law, 1985). Over time, many music genres have flowed back and forth across this region, enriching the musical environment of southern Eweland. In the 1950s, for example, Ewe migrant laborers returning from Benin brought a new music form called *Gahu*, which had developed out of the *Gome* dance, a pan-Atlantic music that had been circulating for many years throughout coastal African communities from Senegal to Cameroon in West Africa, and across the Atlantic Ocean to parts of the Caribbean, Latin America, and the United States (Collins, 2007; de Aranzadi, 2010; Harrev, 1987; Ladzekpo & Eder, 1992). Southern Ewe artists have always absorbed stylistically resonant musics from the outside, localizing them through the lens of preexisting musical practice.

The Diaspora

There are several professional Ewe musicians who have migrated to Europe and the United States. Perhaps the most successful professionally is Gideon Foli Alorwoyie. Alorwoyie was a drummer in his hometown of Afiadenyigba when he was discovered playing at a festival and brought to Accra to work as a drummer in the first national folkloric dance company, the Gbeho Research Group. In 1969, he was hired as a lead drummer for the Ghana Dance Ensemble, based at the University of Ghana, where he also taught courses in African drumming for the School of Performing Arts. Alorwoyie was one of the main informants for John Chernoff's book, *African Rhythm and African Sensibility* (1979). Alorwoyie has also worked off and on with David Locke, and was a participant in Locke's PhD dissertation *The Music of Atsiagbeko* (1979). More recently, they collaborated on the book *Agbadza Music* (2007), a folio of 25 drum-language patterns and songs from an early style of *Agbadza* music. Alorwoyie is now a professor of music at the University of North Texas.

The Agbeli family has also instructed several generations of foreign students in southern Ewe music. Godwin Agbeli (1942–1998) grew up in Aflao and eventually gained a post teaching and performing Ghanaian folkloric dances with the National Folkloric Company at the Arts Council of Ghana in Accra, where he was based through much of the 1970s (Locke & Agbeli, 1992). David Locke worked extensively with Agbeli in Ghana from 1975 to 1977 on *The Music of Atsiagbeko* (1979). Locke and Agbeli later collaborated on a series of publications including the article "A Study of the Drum Language in Adzogbo" (Agbeli & Locke, 1980) and the books *Drum Gahu* (Locke & Agbeli, 1987) and *Kpegisu* (Locke & Agbeli, 1992). Agbeli also instituted the Dagbe Center of African Music and Dance in the southern Ewe town of Kopeyia (see Figure 3.1), which has facilities for room and board, meals, a performance hall, numerous rehearsal sites, and a staff of perhaps 10 artists who teach several lessons each day. Since Agbeli's death in 1998, the Dagbe Center has been directed by his sons Emmanuel, Nani, and Victor. Due to the influence of Locke and his students, as well as word of mouth, the Dagbe Center is the number one destination for foreigners looking to gain an immersion experience in Ewe traditional music.

The Ladzekpo family of Anyako has also had a tremendous impact on the dissemination of southern Ewe music at the University of Ghana and in the Ghana Dance Ensemble, as well as in American academic institutions. When the Ghana Dance Ensemble was formed in 1965, Kobla Ladzekpo and his senior brother

Husunu Afadi Adonu were the first Anlo Ewe music experts in the group, and also taught Ewe music to students at the University of Ghana (Adinku, 1994). Kobla Ladzekpo became the main informant and research assistant for the American ethnomusicologist Hewitt Pantaleoni. Together they coauthored an important article on *Takaɖa* music (1970), and Ladzekpo subsequently wrote a widely cited article about *Habɔbɔ* groups in Eweland (Ladzekpo, 1971). Kobla Ladzekpo became an adjunct instructor of African music at the University of California, Los Angeles, a position he also obtained at the California Institute of the Arts (CalArts). His brother Alfred codirected the African Music and Dance Program at CalArts and also taught at Pomona College. Another Ladzekpo brother, C. K., has been teaching African music at the University of California, Berkeley, since 1973. Many of his students have gone on to professional careers in music, including Bill Summers (percussionist, Herbie Hancock's Headhunters group), Royal Hartigan (author, percussionist, and teacher, most recently at the University of Massachusetts Dartmouth), and Vijay Iyer (internationally known jazz pianist).

A smaller but still significant contribution has been made by Fred Kwasi Dunyo, who collaborated with Canadian researcher Karen Armstrong to build a center of cultural research in Dagbamate, featuring music and cultural studies at the local Apetorku Shrine. Dunyo now works as an adjunct instructor of African music at the University of Toronto and directs many African folkloric groups in schools and institutions in the Toronto area.

Implications for Sustainability

Despite the importance of music in Ewe cultural life and the general respect given musicians, the most significant factor affecting musicians today continues to be the lack of financial support for their services. While musicians are able to find other forms of work to survive, their economic status and their association with traditional religion puts them at the margins of modern society. Fulfilling the role of a musical leader creates excessive demands on one's time and physical health, and also exposes one to spiritual attacks from jealous rivals. Although Ewe music has attained an important presence in Western academia through the work of a few Ewe musicians primarily from the Agbeli and Ladzekpo families, there has not been a concerted effort to develop institutions for musical learning in Eweland, outside of the Dagbe Center, making it difficult for communities to solicit governmental and nongovernmental organizations for grants and other forms of support.

Ewe music making continues to be associated primarily with funerals, ceremonies, and seasonal festivals. Since the colonial period, Ghanaian Eweland has been a relatively peaceful region without any major outbreaks of violence or governmental repression, a fact that has allowed Ewe music to flourish over the past 100 years. Nevertheless, today there are two major challenges to the sustainability of traditional music making: the Christian religion, proponents of which have attacked music making and other aspects of traditional culture as evil, and the changes brought by modernization in Ghana, which frame traditional music making as an antiquated activity with no career potential, and hence of limited value. The Ewe composer and intellectual Philip Gbeho summarized these hostile forces in a 1954 essay:

> This "Iron Curtain" between the educated African and his own music has been the work of missionaries. They have done many things of which I am justly proud, but their early teachings that our music was the work of the devil — in order to convert us to Christianity — has done a lot to prohibit the music that is at the center of our culture. (p. 63)

Cultural and Social Contexts

Music making forms an integral part of the daily life of an Ewe community: "Since there are a lot of deaths in the village, the drums are sounding all the time" (K. Tagborlo, interview, January 7, 2013). Grand Drummer Gideon Foli Alorwoyie has also noted, "Drumming is very important in our lifestyle. It is like a daily thing for us. Every other day we play in our hometown" (in Davis, 1994, p. 14). In most Ewe towns and villages, the sound of certain genres of music can identify the occasion, even from a distance.

Nevertheless, the rise of the Christian religion and Western education over the past century has had a major effect on Ewe traditional life. As noted earlier by Gbeho, Christianity and Western lifestyles are associated with modernity; in contrast, traditional drumming is seen as archaic by growing numbers of community members. The church initially tried to introduce Western hymnal singing, without any dancing or drumming: "In the beginning, the Christian Church said that its members should not join in traditional music making; [according to them] the Bible says that we praise God with the organ and singing [church songs], not with drumming and dancing" (P. Nudzor, interview, January 8, 2013). However, many participants describe how various Christian churches are beginning to recontextualize traditional music forms: "Christian churches have begun borrowing our traditional music and have adapted the songs and the themes to fit Christian beliefs. In a traditional song, if they reference the name of a traditional priest, they will change it to Christ" (P. Nudzor, interview, January 8, 2013). An example of this trend is a cassette produced by the Church of the Pentecost in Anloga, which contains original Christian hymns with titles like "Va nakpor Yesu fe nyonyo" (Come and see the goodness of Jesus) and "Va ne magblore na wo lo" (Come and let me tell you the good news), set to traditional *Agbadza* drumming (Church of the Pentecost-Anloga District, 2005). Since traditional music genres may contain ideas and practices from traditional religious worship, some churches have created their own drumming genres: "Other Christians do not want our drums to accompany them, but they still play their own drums. That has brought a conflict between some of us now" (D. Avaga, interview, January 18, 2013).

Many popular Ewe dances like *Agbadza, Atsiagbekor*, and *Gahu* are quite well known throughout Ghana, and Ghanaians respect the southern Ewe for maintaining deep links with their traditions: "There are many ethnic groups in Ghana that play drums, but from what I have seen, we the Ewe, our drumming has reached a place beyond the others. We have so many different types of dance-drumming that are interesting" (K. Tagborlo, interview, January 7, 2013). Like Tagborlo, many of the musicians interviewed take pride in the beauty of their music and how it has managed to persevere in contemporary Ghana. In Ghanaian cities with large Ewe migrant populations like Accra and Ashiaman, residents from different ethnic groups often come to join in *Agbadza* dances at Ewe funerals: "Many times . . . I see that when a funeral happens in our place here, our people are making music and outsiders come around, and they are happy. Our drumming makes people happy" (R. Tuwornu, interview, January 6, 2013).

Ewe music forms a significant part of dance and music curricula at the University of Ghana and in the repertoires of folkloric performance groups. Ewe music requires such specialization in singing, drumming, and dancing, however, that none of the academic or professional folkloric groups have reached the artistic level of a group in Eweland. Nevertheless, through the combined work of folkloric performance groups, ethnomusicologists, and Ewe artists in the diaspora, Ewe music has become representative of West African percussion music for many people in Europe and the United States.

Constructs

Music making in southern Eweland occurs at free public events, where community members are expected to participate as part of their general civic and family responsibilities (Burns, 2012; Gadzekpo, 1952). All of the artists interviewed reported that people from different strata of society make music together: "We all play the same music, poor and rich. When the drums start sounding, if people feel it in their bodies, they will come around" (D. Gali, interview, January 18, 2013). Since Ewe musicians are poor, they can articulate the sentiments of the average rural Ewe resident, who is also poor: "Most of the songs were composed by poor people who were lamenting on life, or on losing a relative. Later people with money came and also joined in" (K. Tagborlo, interview, January 7, 2013). Grand Drummer Richard Tuwornu echoes this sentiment: "In the beginning the song and drum leaders bring out new styles of music. People hear the music and appreciate it so the musicians become popular in the community. There are people from our town that live in Europe and America and have a lot of money, but are still in a *Habɔbɔ*" (interview, January 6, 2013). Shrine and church members are also drawn from all levels of society, and they meet and worship in the same places, so there is no separation by class or wealth in their musical activities.

There is an awareness of change in Ewe music discourse, and nearly all of the respondents acknowledge that there have been changes to the music in varying qualities and degrees. Grand Drummer Daniel Avaga, for example, reported to us: "Yes, there are small changes coming all the time. There used to be certain music genres like bravery music [warrior's music] that have gone out of fashion today" (interview, January 18, 2013). In addition to the loss of repertoire, there have also been changes in the drum language and song texts:

> Yes, today change is coming, in both the subject matter of the songs and the subject matter of the drums. Like I said, the song texts used to insult people or make fun of certain situations; now they have taken those references out. And the drumming, they also used to insult people with drum language; now they are just boasting. (P. Nudzor, interview, January 8, 2013)

Attitudes toward change vary. Some emphasize its creative aspects, and hence maintain a positive view of change, a viewpoint articulated clearly by Grand Drummer Richard Tuwornu:

> There is change. The change is that a long time ago, our grandfathers and grandmothers, how they played, they just had *Agbadza*, and they were playing it this way for a long time. Then when they started to die, we were also coming up, and the drum language began to change. Today, the new style of music that we are doing, it is also sweet for people. *Agbadza Reggae* we call

it; that is the music that is out now; it was not around before. (interview, January 6, 2013)

Others chose to emphasize the loss of repertoire, and thus maintained a negative view of change: "We are no longer looking after the ancient musics that our forefathers played like *Akpoka*, *Atrikpui*, and *Adevu*, the latter of which we played when accompanying the groom to the wedding site" (D. Avaga, interview, January 18, 2013).

There are some gender distinctions made in Ewe music discourse and practice, but in most contexts there are no *se* (laws, or religious taboos) that govern or regulate these distinctions (Burns, 2009; Hunter, 2012). The main area where gender comes into play is drumming, which is socially viewed as a male activity, much in the same way cooking is viewed as a female activity. Although one can occasionally find men who cook and women who drum, it is rather uncommon to see a woman play the drums. One notable exception is the all-female 31st of December Kpegisu Haborbor women's movement, which features female drummers. In their case, their formation and development were sponsored by the women's movement to demonstrate the potential for women to achieve in business and the arts. In southern Eweland women and men sing, and gender comes into play only when selecting someone to lead the songs for a certain genre of music. *Agbadza*, for example, came out of older war dances, so men usually lead the songs, but there are still many women in the chorus. Dancing is done equally by men and women, although the subject matter of the dance may dictate the preference for a male or female dancer.

Implications for Sustainability

As traditional religious institutions continue to decline, secular occasions like funerals have become the primary context for music making in southern Eweland. In many parts of Ghana this process has evolved to the point where DJs have replaced live music during funerals, a practice that has become more common in certain parts of Eweland as well. Nevertheless, at the present time, the southern Ewe continue to be recognized in Ghana and abroad for their vibrant music culture, and they provide a poignant example of how traditional music continues to survive in some contemporary African contexts.

INFRASTRUCTURE AND REGULATIONS

Ewe music making continues to take place outdoors in public meeting spaces, which are open to all members of society. There is no governmental support for local arts, and consequently the government has little influence on local music practice. Since southern Ewe music tends to be composed and transmitted orally, only a few groups have attempted to copyright their music or to regulate its dissemination.

Infrastructure

In Eweland, performances are generally held in public meeting spaces (*vɔnu* or *ablɔme*), which are open spaces between compound houses in each district of the town: "If we play drums, there is a meeting ground in our area; we meet to play there. When we are going to have an event, we send out a messenger, who will notify the community that we will be playing somewhere at a certain time" (R. Tuwornu, interview, January 6, 2013). Since the *vɔnu* is a free public space, most groups do not need, nor could they afford, their own performance grounds. Shrines and churches generally conduct music events at their facilities or in the homes of group members.

Rehearsals in southern Eweland, when they occur, are typically for *Habɔbɔ* groups, which have the organization and leadership to be able to manage regular meetings (Anyidoho, 1983; Burns, 2009; Fiagbedzi, 1977; Jones, 1959; Ladzekpo, 1971). When a new *Habɔbɔ* is formed, the *henɔwo* and *azagunɔwo* get together for closed meeting sessions called *havɔlu* (song meeting), where they work out the basic songs and drum accompaniment for the group. Once the group begins performing outside, members will usually meet once during the 4-day market cycle for practice sessions known as *hakpa* (song composing). In contrast, District Funeral Ensembles only meet at funerals, so they do not have regular rehearsals, although the *henɔ* and *azagunɔ* may meet privately with their support musicians to work out new songs or drum language patterns. Shrine and church members learn the liturgical music of their faith as they participate in the regular meetings of their organizations.

Ewe instruments are made by local craftspeople and are sold in some of the local markets: "We buy them in the market. The most important one is in Akatsi; if you are looking for good drums, they make them for sale, and they are there" (D. Avaga, interview, January 18, 2013). The standard Ewe drum set is composed of several sizes of barrel stave drums. The region once had a lot of hardwood trees and drums were carved in every village. These trees have since disappeared, and carpenters in Togo and Akatsi have devised a way to make the drums from barrel staves (Galeota, 1985). A complete set of instruments including *atsimevu*, *sogo*, two *kidi* response drums, and *kagan* would cost approximately $US500, a sum that is too large for most individual drummers to bear. Hence, most drum sets are owned by *Habɔbɔ* groups or shrines, or they are paid for by a share of the funeral contributions in the case of a District Funeral Ensemble. The drums have to be maintained by replacing the skins, which come from two main species of duiker that inhabit the forest belt to the north: Maxwell's duiker (*avugbe*) and the red-flanked duiker (*ese/klatsa*). These animals are becoming increasingly rare, and a skin now costs around $US20, which is very expensive in the local economy. Because of the cost of changing a skin, it is common to see drums being used in various states of disrepair and to find several shells without skins packed away in the drum room.

The iron bells (*gankogui*) are made by blacksmiths (*gbedε*), who also specialize in various ironworks including hoe blades, knives, and metal traps. The bells are moderately expensive, at around $US10 to $US15 depending on the size. The gourd rattles (*axatse*) are made by local craftspeople, who weave a net of beads around the larger end of a bottle gourd. These are usually $US3 to $US4 and are readily affordable. *Habɔbɔ* groups that feature solo dancers must also purchase *sosi* or *lasi* (dance sticks made from animal tails), which can cost $US30 for a decent pair. Sometimes a *Habɔbɔ* will also need to purchase special costumes for the solo dancers, including things like raffia skirts and more elaborate cloth wraps. These items are owned and maintained by the group.

To attend and participate in a district funeral event, a person would be expected to own or borrow two yards of dark-colored cloth, which is wrapped around the waist before entering the dance space. Shrines have their own dress regulations, usually a few yards of different-colored cloth and certain bead necklaces or bracelets. A *Habɔbɔ* will have several official outfits that must be purchased by new group members.

Laws, Regulations, and Funding

All of the participants unanimously indicated that there is no government or institutional support of any kind for their music. Kwadzo Tagborlo gives a representative response:

There are no sources of help for drummers. If you come to play the drums for someone today, and you have a wife and kids, you will not end the show and they will give you $1 or $2 for your work. They might give you some food or drink, or praise you and then send someone to thank you for helping with the funeral. We are struggling; we do not find any profit in drumming in Africa here, among the Ewe people. (interview, January 7, 2013).

Richard Tuwornu adds, "Drummers and singers do not get any help at all. But we are all here helping people (with our music)" (interview, January 6, 2013). While there are chiefs in Eweland, they never maintained a system of court music; consequently, there are no local examples of the praise poet/oral historian that features prominently among griot cultures in other areas of West Africa.

Outside of the two National Dance Ensembles in Accra, the government does not support traditional music making, and there is no governmental regulation of local arts. Through the colonial period up to today, the Ghanaian government has only intervened in local music when there was a conflict or outbreaks of violence. In Eweland during the 1950s, for example, there were some incidents of violence that occurred between rival singers during *halo* song duels, which prompted the government to outlaw the practice of *halo* in 1962 (Anyidoho, 1983; Avorgbedor, 2001; Awoonor, 1974).

Ewe music groups borrow repertoire freely and frequently from each other, often without acknowledgment. There is a copyright board in Accra that watches over commercial popular music and producers of local music that register with it, but they do not have the capacity to enforce the regulations, and there continues to be a thriving market of illegally duplicated CDs and cassettes.

Implications for Sustainability

The lack of significant government support for traditional music has had both positive and negative effects in Eweland. On one hand, there are no regulations, taxes, dues, or fees to pay, so musicians can practice their art without restriction. On the other hand, the lack of government involvement makes it impossible to enforce copyright laws and therefore to receive royalties or other residuals from one's performances or recordings. Since music making occurs at public events, it is also not possible to sell tickets, so there are no funds to build concert venues or practice facilities. At the very least, the cost of instruments and materials has remained relatively stable, and they are still affordable for most active groups.

MEDIA AND THE MUSIC INDUSTRY

Southern Ewe music has a miniscule presence in the Ghanaian commercial music industry, particularly when compared to Ewe groups living in Togo. One major difference between these countries is that Ewe and Gbe-speaking people inhabit the entire southern region of Togo, including its political and media capitol Lomé, while southern Ghana including Accra is dominated by the Akan and the Ga. Reflecting this absence of media influence, when we asked our informants the questions in this domain, there was little response. While there has been a significant international presence of Ewe music in ethnomusicology textbooks, this has not had any tangible effect on local music. All of the artists surveyed want to record their music so that it can spread outside their communities, and to be able to leave it for succeeding generations; however, they do not have the resources to fund studio time nor the technical understanding of recording processes to realize this aspiration.

Media Engagement

At present, most Ghanaians are able to access modern mass media devices including radio, TV, CD/DVD players, MP3 players, computers, and mobile phones. Regional West African pop music, particularly hip-hop-influenced musics from Ghana, Togo, Cote d'Ivoire, Benin, and Nigeria, dominate the airwaves along with imported pop music from England and the United States.

Ewe traditional music continues to live outside the media industry. Virtually none of the groups sampled in this study reported having an existent recording of their group to market. Part of this is organizational: District Funeral Ensembles and Sacred Music Ensembles do not collect dues, and therefore they have no source of capital to fund a recording session. Occasionally, a local music promoter will approach a group to sponsor a recording, offering to pay them a small recording fee, after which the promoter can market and sell the recordings on his or her own, paying little or no royalties to the group on the sales of the product. Understandably, many groups refuse to record under these arrangements.

Ewe music has had a more substantial presence in the national media, particularly through broadcasts of state events or important funerals in Accra. Ewe dances also form a large part of the repertory of the two National Dance Ensembles, as well as other private folkloric groups operating in Ghana. Grand Drummer Daniel Avaga acknowledges the impact that Ewe music has had on people of other ethnic groups:

> Yes, our music has spread outside Eweland. The Akans have also gotten into it; the Northerners have also gotten into it. Our Ewe drumming and singing is sweet for them, like how their own music is also there; our music is also performed live and people enjoy it. . . . That is why some Akans and Northerners have joined us. They see that there is something beneficial in it, and they have money to contribute. (interview, January 18, 2013)

Many of the artists interviewed believed that Ewe music had spread outside of Eweland, although they did not have much direct experience about its actual impact. Kwadzo Tagborlo's response is typical of those surveyed: "Ewe drumming, our grandfathers started it from Dahomey and its environs. From this nucleus it spread to three places: Ghana, Togo, Benin, Nigeria. . . . Ewe music has spread all throughout this region" (interview, January 7, 2013). Those that have traveled outside, like Grand Drummer Nudzor Prosper Gbeti, have observed its impact in the West: "Outsiders are playing our music. I have traveled to America to places where they are all learning our music" (interview, January 8, 2013). There some commercial media outlets that play the tracks from locally available recordings of Ewe music, including a few radio stations in Ghanaian and Togolese Eweland, but these opportunities are limited to the relatively small number of groups that have been fortunate enough to produce a recording.

Presence in the Music Industry

There are a limited number of locally produced cassette recordings of Ewe music. However, they represent the music of perhaps only 10 or so groups (see discography on companion website). Habɔbɔ groups have the capital to produce a recording, but their funds are usually tied up in paying out funeral contributions and in meeting the operating expenses of the group.

The northern Ewe have fared somewhat better with the spread of Ewe Christian music through recreational dances like Borborbor and Akpese. Since the early period of cassette recording in the 1980s up to today, Borborbor and Akpese cassettes from several popular groups have dominated local cassette markets throughout Eweland. These cassettes are often played continuously in local bars and in between performances during funerals and other public events.

Online, there are some field recordings of Ewe music that have been digitized and placed on open-access webpages including collections by A. M. Jones and James Koetting (see web discography). David Locke also has online sites devoted to Agbadza and Yewe music. There is an increasing presence of Ewe music on YouTube and other Internet sites, particularly field recordings of traditional Ewe events like funerals or ceremonies. There are also recordings of Ghanaian and international African music ensembles playing folkloric versions of popular Ewe dances.

I have been involved in an initiative to help southern Ewe groups document and promote their music. Using grant support from the Arts and Humanities Research

Council (United Kingdom) and the National Endowment for the Humanities (United States), I was able to film, edit, and produce three DVDs of music videos in collaboration with the Dzigbordi group of Dzodze and the Dunenyo group of Denu (see web discography). Presently the groups are selling these DVDs at their head-quarters and in local markets, and this has expanded their popularity in Eweland. With the support of the *Sustainable Futures* project, I have been able to extend this initiative to seven of the groups that contributed to this study: the Mawulikplim Adzogbo Group, 31st of December Kpegisu Haborbor, Donkutorwogbe Haborbor, Tsodeme Haborbor, Unity Haborbor, February Haborbor, and the Mamisi Rasta Shrine. For their participation in this research, each group received a 60-minute DVD of music videos of their own group, a 60-minute CD audio recording, and cover art and packaging materials. Like Dzigbordi and Dunenyo, these groups will be able to duplicate these materials locally and will control all of the profits and royalties from the recordings.

Implications for Sustainability

Although the Ewe have one of the most widely recognized music traditions in Ghana, they have not been able to successfully create a sustainable music industry that has the capacity to record, promote, and market local music. There are many recordings of Ewe music made by ethnomusicologists, but most of these record-ings are not available in Eweland. The lack of a sustainable and productive local music industry continues to impede the growth and sustainability of traditional music making in the region.

ISSUES AND INITIATIVES FOR SUSTAINABILITY

As discussed throughout this chapter, southern Ewe music continues to thrive at local funerals, ceremonies, and festivals, and it appears as though it will continue in the immediate future. Ewe music also has had a significant presence in the rep-ertories of folkloric groups and in the national media, and it is studied and taught as a model of traditional African music in ethnomusicology courses throughout the world.

Overall Vitality

Traditional music continues to be a vital part of southern Ewe traditional life and is one of the prime ways that people participate in community activities. Local notions of *aɖaŋu* (divine talent) and *amedzɔdzɔ* (the rebirth of ancestral abilities) at least guarantee that the next generation of Ewe artists will also be called into musical service.

One of the major problems affecting District Funeral Ensembles and Sacred Music Ensembles is that there is little provision made for musicians, instruments, and supplies in these organizations. *Habɔbɔ* groups have the leadership and organizational structure to at least maintain their costumes and instruments, and also to be able to provide some compensation to a few key artists. However, only the larger *Habɔbɔ* groups can provide enough for their lead artists to earn a modest salary.

Within the local media industry, which currently supports the production of a limited number of cassettes, CDs, DVDs, and MP3s of traditional music, there appears to be potential for local artists to promote and to earn royalties on their recordings. However, making these opportunities more widely available would require significant sponsorship and organization at the local level, which does not appear to be within reach at the present time.

Key Issues for Sustainability

Perhaps the key issue affecting the sustainability of southern Ewe music is the lack of pay and professional opportunities for local musicians. While a small number of Ewe artists have been given the opportunity to teach in Accra or abroad, for the average community musician it is not possible to earn a living from his or her talent. Although payment was never a part of traditional music making, in contemporary society artists find it difficult to balance the requirements of their art with the need to earn a living.

Up to now, there has been no sense of fraternity among Ewe musicians, most living relatively isolated lives in their local towns. There has also been a divide between Ewe musicians who are well educated and have established connections with the outside world and those who have spent much of their lives in their rural hometowns. Ewe musicians who complete secondary school and have some proficiency in English can eventually move to Accra and join folkloric groups, and from there perhaps get the chance to teach abroad. Unfortunately, apart from a few individuals like Godwin Agbeli and Fred Dunyo, those who do get a chance to pursue professional careers outside of Ghana rarely come back to develop music-making opportunities in Eweland.

Past Initiatives

Ewe music has been recorded extensively, mainly in the form of audio field recordings. Nearly all of these are located in various academic and state institutions, with limited outside access. Some important online collections include the A. M. Jones

Collection in the National Sound Archive at the British Library, items within the James Koetting Collection at Wesleyan University, and the *Agbadza* collection by David Locke and Gideon Foli Alorwoyie at Tufts University (see discography on the companion website). The University of Ghana maintains an archive of field recordings within the compound of the School of Performing Arts, which was sponsored for many years by the International Academy of African Music and Dance established by J. Kwabena Nketia. The center lost its international funding in 2006, however, so access to the archive is limited, and its condition and maintenance are presently in jeopardy.

As discussed earlier, there are some important centers for the study of Ewe music located both in the capital Accra and in Eweland itself. The two largest institutions in Accra are the School of Performing Arts at the University of Ghana and the Centre for National Culture (formerly the Arts Centre). Both institutions have Ewe drummers, singers, and dancers on staff. In addition to maintaining performing groups, these two institutions also provide classes to Ghanaian students and foreigners in the music of the main ethnic groups in Ghana including the Ewe, Akan, Dagomba, Ga, and Krobo peoples.

Within Eweland, there are two important centers for intensive professional or academic research into Ewe music. The Dagbe Centre, located in Kopeyia, is the only center that specializes in music and dance, and is developed for international students and faculty. With a few exceptions, virtually all of the books, articles, papers, and dissertations in the field of Ewe music published since the 1990s have come out of research done at least partially at the Dagbe Center. Apart from Dagbe, a broader institution is located in Klikor, the Blakhud Research Center, which facilitates research into a number of Ewe traditional arts including music, religion, *kente* weaving, and traditional medicine.

Current and Planned Initiatives

One important factor for sustainability is the current support for local music within the Ghanaian education system. Most schools have the funds to organize a folkloric group of some type and will often hire local musicians to work with the students on a particular genre of music like *Gahu* or *Atsiagbekor*.

Following the initial success of the Dzigbordi and Dunenyo recording projects, the additional groups we collaborated with for the *Sustainable Futures* project will also be able to benefit from having a marketable recording of their music. The results of these new collaborations will hopefully provide further data on how these types of projects might continue in the future, and perhaps provide a model for collaborative research within traditional communities.

ACKNOWLEDGEMENTS

I would like to thank the people of Dzodze, Denu, Aflao, Kopeyia, Klikor, Tengekope, Dagbamate, Dzita, and Ashiaman for welcoming us into your towns and for opening all the necessary doors for us, so that we could collect the field research for the project. Special thanks to our host families who took care of us in Ghana: Kwadzo and Dzatsugbi Tagborlo, "Fu Manchu" Kudawoo, Godwin and Nana Azameti, and Kwakutse and Comfort Agboku, *akpe kakaka*.

Next, I would like to acknowledge the hard work of the *Sustainable Futures* Ewe research team, including Trevor Wiggins, Godwin Azameti, Kwakutse Agboku, Michaela Pinnock, and Maritza Rodriguez, particularly the last three individuals, who toiled with me for 3 long weeks in January 2013 collecting field interviews, taking photographs, making audio recordings, and filming music videos. We would like to thank all of the groups that participated in this study: Mawulikplim Adzogbo Group, 31st of December Kpegisu Haborbor, Donkutorwogbe Haborbor, Tsodeme Haborbor, Unity Haborbor, February Haborbor, and the Mamisi Rasta Shrine.

Finally, I would like to acknowledge the contributions of the *Sustainable Futures* project, including members of the West African Percussion project advisory board: Kofi Agawu, David Locke, George Dor, Gavin Webb, Trevor Wiggins, and Kwakutse Agboku.

REFERENCES

Adinku, W. O. (1994). *African dance education in Ghana.* Accra, Ghana: Ghana Universities Press.
Afokpa, C. J. (2005). From Aflao eastwards: A coastal tour of Ewe material culture. In B. Lawrance (Ed.), *The Ewe of Togo and Benin* (pp. 270–292). Accra, Ghana: Woeli Publishing Services.
Agawu, K. (1995). *African rhythm: A Northern Ewe perspective.* Cambridge, MA: Cambridge University Press.
Agawu, K. (2003). *Representing African music: Postcolonial notes, queries, positions.* New York, NY: Routledge.
Agbeli, G., & Locke, D. (1980). A study of the drum language in Adzogbo. *African Music,* 6(1), 32–51.
Agbodeka, F. (2000). The land and its people. In K. Gavua (Ed.), *A handbook of Eweland: Vol. II: The Northern Ewes in Ghana* (pp. 1–4). Accra, Ghana: Woeli Publishing Services.
Akyeampong, E. K. (2001). *Between the sea and the lagoon: An eco-social history of the Anlo of Southeastern Ghana c.1850 to recent times.* Athens, OH: Ohio University Press.
Alorwoyie, G. (2007). *Agbadza music* (Edited and Transcribed by D. Locke). Self-published.
Alves, W. (2012). *Music of the peoples of the world* (3rd ed.). New York, NY: Cengage Learning.
Amenumey, D. E. K. (1986). *The Ewe in pre-colonial times.* Accra, Ghana: Sedco Publishing.

Amenumey, D. E. K. (1997). A brief history. In F. Agbodeka (Ed.), *A handbook of Eweland: Vol. I: The Ewes of Southeastern Ghana* (pp. 14–27). Accra, Ghana: Woeli Publishing Services.

Anyidoho, K. (1983). *Oral poetics and traditions of verbal art in Africa* (Unpublished doctoral dissertation). University of Texas, Austin, TX.

Asiwaju, A. I., & Law, R. (1985). From the Volta to the Niger, c.1600-1800. In J. F. A. Ajayi & M. Crowder (Eds.), *History of West Africa* (Vol. 1, 3rd ed., pp. 412–464). New York, NY: Longman Group.

Avorgbedor, D. (1986). The interaction of music and spoken texts in the contexts of Anlo-Ewe music. *Black Orpheus, 6*(1), 17–26.

Avorgbedor, D. (1987). The construction and manipulation of temporal structures in Yeve cult music: A multi-dimensional approach. *African Music, 6*(4), 4–18.

Avorgbedor, D. (2001). "It's a great song!" Haló performance as literary production. *Research in African Literatures, 32*(2), 17–43.

Awoonor, K. (1974). *Guardians of the sacred word: Ewe poetry.* New York, NY: Nok Publishers.

Burns, J. (2005a). *The beard cannot tell stories to the eyelash: Creative transformation in an Ewe funeral dance-drumming tradition* (Unpublished doctoral dissertation). School of Oriental and African Studies, London, UK.

Burns, J. (2005b). My mother has a television does yours? Transformation in an Ewe funeral drum tradition. *Oral Tradition, 20*(2), 300–319.

Burns, J. (2009). *Female voices from an Ewe dance-drumming community in Ghana: Our music has become a divine spirit.* SOAS Musicology series. Aldershot, UK: Ashgate Press.

Burns, J. (2011). Doing it with style: An ethnopoetic study of improvisation in Ewe dance-drumming. *African Music, 9*(1), 154–205.

Burns, J. (2012). Cooling the road: The role of music within the southern Ewe funeral ceremony. *Mortality 17*(2), 158–169.

Charry, E. (2000). *Mande music: Traditional and modern music of the Maninka and Mandinka of Western Africa.* Chicago, IL: University of Chicago Press.

Chernoff, J. M. (1979). *African rhythm and African sensibility: Aesthetics and social action in African musical idioms.* Chicago, IL: University of Chicago Press.

Church of Pentecost, Anloga District. (2005). *Megbɔna (several volumes)* [audio cassettes]. Ghana: Church of Pentecost.

Collins, J. (2007). Pan African Goombay drum-dance music, its ramifications and development in Ghana. *Legon Journal of the Humanities, 18*, 179–200.

Cornelius, S. (2000). They just need money: Goods and gods, power and truth in a West African village. In I. Monson (Ed.), *The African Diaspora: A musical perspective* (pp. 243–266). New York, NY: Garland.

Davis, A. L. (1994). *Midawo Gideon Foli Alorwoyie: The life and music of a West African drummer* (Unpublished master's thesis). University of Illinois, Urbana-Champaign, IL.

de Aranzadi, I. (2010). A drum's trans-Atlantic journey from Africa to the Americas and back after the end of slavery: Annobonese and Fernandino musical cultures. *African Sociological Review, 14*(1), 20–47.

Djedje, J. (2008). *Fiddling in West Africa: Touching the spirit in Fulbe, Hausa, and Dagbamba cultures.* Bloomington, IN: University of Indiana Press.

Ellis, A.B. (1965 [1890]). *The Ewe speaking people of the Slave Coast of West Africa.* Chicago, IL: Benin Press.

Fiagbedzi, N. (1977). *The music of the Anlo: Its historical background, cultural matrix and style* (Unpublished doctoral dissertation). University of California, Los Angeles, CA.

Fiagbedzi, N. (2009). *Form and meaning in Ewe song: A critical review*. Point Richmond, CA: Music Research Institute.

Fynn, J. K. (1971). *Asante and its neighbours 1700-1807*. London, UK: Longman Group.

Gaba, C. (1965). *Anlo traditional religion: A study of the Anlo traditional believer's conception of and communion with the "holy"* (Unpublished doctoral dissertation). University of London, London, UK.

Gaba, C. (1997). The religious life of the people. In F. Agbodeka (Ed.), *A handbook of Eweland: Vol. I: The Ewes of Southeastern Ghana* (pp. 85–104). Accra, Ghana: Woeli Publishing Services.

Gadzekpo, S. B. (1952). Making music in Eweland. *West African Review, 23*(299), 817–821.

Galeota, J. (1985). *Drum making among the Southern Ewe people of Ghana and Togo* (Unpublished master's thesis). Wesleyan University, Middletown, CT.

Gbeho, P. (1954). Music of the Gold Coast. *African Music, 1*(1), 62–64.

Gbolonyo, K. (2012). *Ewe musical texts as vehicles of indigenous knowledge and concepts: A linguistico-philosophical exposition*. Paper presented at the Fourth International Symposium on the Music of Africa, Princeton University, Princeton, NJ.

Greene, S. E. (1996). *Gender, ethnicity, and social change on the upper Slave Coast: A history of the Anlo Ewe*. Portsmouth, NH: Heinemann.

Harrev, F. (1987). *Goumbe and the development of Krio popular music in Freetown Sierra Leone*. Paper presented at the Fourth International Conference of IASPM, Accra, Ghana.

Hunter, J. (2012). *The rise of women's drumming in Africa: Performing gender and transforming community in southeastern Ghana* (Unpublished doctoral dissertation). Brown University, Providence, RI.

Jones, A. M. (1959). *Studies in African music* (Vols. I and II). London, UK: Oxford University Press.

Ladzekpo, K. (1971). The social mechanics of good music: A description of dance clubs among the Anlo Ewe speaking people of Ghana. *African Music, 5*(1), 6–13.

Ladzekpo, S. K., & Eder, A. (1992). Agahu: Music across many nations. In J. Cogdell DjeDje & W. G. Carter (Eds.), *African musicology: Current trends: A festschrift presented to J.H. Kwabena Nketia*. Atlanta, GA: Crossroads Press.

Laumann, D. (2005). The history of the Ewe of Togo and Benin from pre-colonial times. In B. Lawrance (Ed.), *The Ewe of Togo and Benin* (pp. 14–28). Accra, Ghana: Woeli Publishing Services.

Locke, D. (1979). *The music of Atsiagbeko* (Unpublished doctoral dissertation). Wesleyan University, Middletown, CT.

Locke, D. (2010). Yewevu in the metric matrix. *Music Theory Online, 16*(4). Retrieved from http://www.mtosmt.org/issues/mto.10.16.4/mto.10.16.4.locke.html

Locke, D., & Agbeli, G. (1987). *Drum Gahu: The rhythms of West African drumming*. Crown Point, AZ: White Cliffs Media.

Locke, D., & Agbeli, G. (1992). *Kpegisu: A war drum of the Ewe*. Crown Point, AZ: White Cliffs Media.

Mamattah, C. M. K. (1979). *The Eves of West Africa: Vol. I: The Anlo-Eves and their immediate neighbours*. Accra, Ghana: Advent Press.

Manoukian, M. (1952). *The Ewe-speaking people of Togoland and the Gold Coast*. London, UK: International African Institute.

May, E., & Hood, M. (1983). *Music of many cultures: An introduction*. Los Angeles, CA: University of California Press.

Meyer, B. (1999). *Translating the devil: Religion and modernity among the Ewe in Ghana*. Edinburgh, UK: Edinburgh University Press.

Nettl, B. (Ed.) (2011). *Excursions in world music* (6th ed.). Boston, MA: Pearson.

Nukunya, G. K. (1997). Social and political organization. In F. Agbodeka (Ed.), *A handbook of Eweland: Vol. I: The Ewes of Southeastern Ghana* (pp. 47–72). Accra, Ghana: Woeli Publishing Services.

Nzewi, M. (1997). *African music: Theoretical content and creative continuum.* Oldershausen, Germany: Institut für Didaktik Populärer Musik.

Okpewho, I. (1992). *African oral literature: Backgrounds, character, and continuity.* Bloomington, IN: Indiana University Press.

Pantaleoni, H. (1972a). *The rhythm of Atsia dance drumming among the Anlo (Eve) of Anyako* (PhD dissertation). Middletown, CT: Wesleyan University.

Pantaleoni, H. (1972b). 3 principles of timing in Anlo dance drumming. *African Music, 5*(2), 50–63.

Pantaleoni, H. (1972c). Towards understanding the play of atsimevu in Atsia. *African Music, 5*(2), 64–84.

Pantaleoni, H., & Ladzekpo, S. K. (1970). Takada drumming. *African Music, 4*(4), 6–31.

Pressing, J. (1983). Rhythmic design in the support drums of Agbadza. *African Music, 6*(3), 4–15.

Rosenthal, J. (1998). *Possession, ecstasy, and law in Ewe voodoo.* Charlottesville, VA: University Press of Virginia.

Seshie, L. K. M. (1991). *Akpalu fe hawo: Tata evelia.* Accra, Ghana: Sedco Publishing.

Shelemay, K. (2006). *Soundscapes: Exploring music in a changing world* (2nd ed.). New York, NY: W. W. Norton and Company.

Tang, P. (2007). *Masters of the Sabar: Wolof griot percussionists of Senegal.* Philadelphia, PA: Temple University Press.

Temperley, D. (2000). Meter and grouping in African music: A view from music theory. *Ethnomusicology, 44*(1), 65–96.

Titon, J. (2008). *Worlds of music: An introduction to the music of the world's peoples* (5th ed.). New York, NY: Cengage Learning.

Waterman, C. A. (1990). *Jùjú: A social history and ethnography of an African popular music.* Chicago, IL: University of Chicago Press.

Wiggins, T. (1999). Drumming in Ghana. In M. Floyd (Ed.), *Composing the music of Africa: Composition, interpretation, and realisation.* Aldershot, UK: Ashgate.

4

HINDUSTANI MUSIC

Resilience and Flexibility in Recontextualizing an Ancient Tradition

Huib Schippers[1]

HINDU AND MUSLIM courts and places of worship, houses of landowners and salons of courtesans, major festivals and intimate celebrations, radio and recording studios, Indian stages and Western concert halls, analog and digital formats: Hindustani music has a long history of flourishing and reinventing itself across divergent settings. In spite of a long period of colonization and considerable socioeconomic challenges, Hindustani music has emerged and maintained itself as the principal form of "art music" in the North of India (as has Karnatak music in the South), in contrast with the situation in many other countries in Asia and beyond, where European classical music has taken this position. In addition, it has interacted extensively with folk music, religious music, and popular music, including the omnipresent songs from the Bollywood film industry since its spectacular rise to popularity from the middle of the last century.

While there is a long history of elders bemoaning the state of Hindustani music, most will attest that the tradition at large is very much alive today and in no imminent danger. It appears to have a capacity for readjusting to new tastes and

---

[1] The author would like to acknowledge the input and contributions of coresearchers Joep Bor (in particular to the opening sections on the music and its history) and Shubha Chaudhuri and her team (to the sections on systems of learning music; infrastructure and regulations; and media and the music industry). I have used the most widespread spelling of Indian music terms (without diacritics) throughout this chapter.

realities in a country where over a period of 150 years, it has solidified its position as a national classical tradition, with an epicenter shifting from courts to cultural elite, mostly living in vast urban centers. In this process, Hindustani music has engaged with a world of new choices that come with a new social order, greater affluence, mobility, and an unstoppable advance of technologies that affect how music is learned, created, performed, perceived, and disseminated.

BACKGROUND

Hindustani music is a term generally used to refer to the "classical" art music of North India (and also present-day Pakistan, Bangladesh, and Nepal), the geographical region roughly bounded by the Himalayas to the north and east, and the states of Maharashtra and Orissa in the west and south. South from there is the territory of the strongly related but distinct "classical" tradition of South India, referred to as Carnatic or Karnatak music. The two are distinct but share a common history and key features. In both traditions, each performance combines two essential musical elements: melodic structures known as *raga*, and rhythmic cycles known as *tala*. These are complemented with *pada* (lyrics) in the case of vocal music.

Hindustani music encompasses two major vocal genres: the virtuoso *khyal* and its more austere forerunner *dhrupad*. With its florid style and romantic lyrics, khyal (meaning imagination, idea, or thought) developed into a genre that attracted new patrons and audiences, and challenged the preeminent position of dhrupad, particularly during the 19th century (Wade, 1984). The word *dhrupad* is derived from *dhruva* (fixed) and *pada* (song). It was the dominant tradition of courtly art music since at least the 15th century (Sanyal and Widdess, 2004, pp. 45–59).

Nowadays, instrumental styles are often considered derivative of the vocal styles. However, given their prominent place both in the ancient treatises and in contemporary practice, they should be regarded as largely autonomous, although they do share a number of elements with the two major vocal styles. In addition, there are some "light classical" genres that form part of the repertoire of many musicians in the Hindustani tradition, including *thumri, ghazal, dhun, dadra, bhajan*, and *qawwali* (Wade, 1979, pp. 177–188).

Hindustani music exists alongside a wealth of other genres, including religious music, folk music, and various forms of contemporary popular musics, of which the booming music of Bollywood, the largest film industry in the world, most emphatically provides the soundtrack to North Indian lives in the 21st century (Booth, 2008).

Hindustani classical music can be performed in principle by both males and females of all ages, ethnic groups, and major religious affiliations, including Hinduism, Islam (including Sufism), Sikhism, Jainism, Buddhism, and Christianity. In practice, male Muslims and Hindus tend to dominate the stage. Traditionally, Hindustani music was primarily handed down within families of musicians, but over the past 100 years or so, many people without strong family music backgrounds have become highly respected musicians (Bakhle, 2005, pp. 256–262). A remnant of the court and family traditions—associated with specific cities but now fading rapidly—is the *gharana*, a "school" or stylistic tradition, recognizable by its specific format and approach to the performance of raga (Ollikkala, 2000, pp. 377–379).

With a theoretical literature going back almost 2,000 years, Hindustani music is well documented in Sanskrit, Persian, Hindi, Urdu, Bengali, English, and several other languages. While in-depth studies of this music in English date back to Willard's 1834 *Treatise on the Music of Hindustan*, the last century especially saw a wealth of publications on different aspects of this tradition, with a number of key monographs over the past five decades (Bakhle, 2005; Farrell, 1997; Neuman, 1990; van der Meer, 1982; Wade, 1979; Widdess & Sanyal, 2004) and edited volumes (Arnold, 2000; Bor, Delvoye, Harvey, & Te Nijenhuis, 2010; Tagore, 1965). A selection of these is listed on the companion website to this volume.

Literally hundreds of thousands of recordings have been made since 1903 on wax roll, 78-rpm, LP, CD, DVD, and web-based formats, now documenting well over a century of a tradition in constant change. A list of 100 key recordings is included as select discography on the companion website.

Through dozens of musicological treatises and other documents, we know that continuous changes in power, patronage, and musical taste in relation to Hindustani music have had a profound effect on style and repertoire, including the Indo-Persian encounter in music, which reached its zenith during the Moghul era (1526–1739), to which much present-day Hindustani art music owes its depth and finesse (Bor et al., 2010). But in spite of the fact that major changes took place in the practice and theory of music (particularly since the second half of the second millennium), there is a remarkable continuity in Hindustani music, especially in the way musicians think about it.

While contemporary Hindustani music has sometimes been naively represented as a primarily "spiritual music," particularly in its marketing to Western audiences (cf. Shankar, 1969), and certainly has profoundly contemplative and philosophical elements that bear this out (van der Meer and Bor, 1982), it is much better understood as a refined and essentially worldly tradition that morphed into its current shape at royal courts: a *musique savante*, a practice aimed at connoisseurs. The music presupposes a highly knowledgeable audience to appreciate its full scope of legacy, creativity, timbre, intonations, variations, improvisations, and ornamentations.

Hindustani music is quite unashamedly elitist, although it has also become a powerful expression of Indian identity at large both in the country itself (Bakhle, 2005, pp. 256–258) and in the diaspora (Farrell, 1997). Today, it draws an audience not unlike that of Western classical music in Europe or the United States: from dozens of audience members at house concerts, to hundreds at mainstream classical concerts, to many thousands at festivals and events featuring star performers, a phenomenon made possible by greater ease of travel, technology, and the recording industry, amplified by the development of the media.

Features

In essence, Hindustani art music is improvised solo music, and at its core lie the concepts of raga and tala. Ragas and talas provide the melodic and rhythmic building blocks for traditional compositions and extempore elaborations of melodies and rhythms within a strict framework. Ragas and talas are not instrument dependent: At a conceptual level, music for voice and all instruments is essentially the same. In fact, many musicians have learned from artists singing or playing a different instrument, particularly in more advanced training.

The concept of raga, which has evolved over a period of almost two millennia, eludes a broadly accepted brief definition. Broadly speaking, a raga can be regarded as a melodic type (or melodic species) with a unique form, embodying a unique musical idea. But a raga is also a dynamic musical entity, a tonal framework for composition and improvisation. As well as a fixed (ascending and descending) scale, each raga has particular melodic features, such as the order and hierarchy of its tones, their relative strength and duration, and the way in which the notes are embellished (Bor, 1999, pp. 1–2). In the more abstract realm, the association of a raga with a particular emotional state (and a time of day or specific season) is considered as relevant as its melodic structure.

Tala refers to the entire system of rhythmic organization in Indian music, including the way time is manifested and regulated by means of audible and silent hand gestures. Like raga, the concept of tala has evolved over a period of 2,000 years or more, and many talas of the past have become obsolete. In today's musical parlance, tala includes both rhythm and meter, while *laya* governs the tempo and refers to timing in general. Each tala cycle has a fixed length and consists of a number of time units or beats (*matras*) of equal duration that are grouped into sections. For example, the cycle of the common 16-beat *tintal* consists of four sections of four matras each. But there are also irregular cycles, like *rupak*'s 3 + 2 + 2, and rare talas with 8½ or even 5¼ beats.

As a performance tradition, Hindustani music is both strikingly stable and continually in motion. The current performance format mostly features a melodic soloist (vocal or instrumental), supported by a percussionist providing rhythmic accompaniment and response, and one or more additional musicians providing a melodic "shadow" (like the sarangi or harmonium do with voice) and the drone against which all melodies are set. Duets, where the performers alternate as soloists are also quite common. The music simultaneously represents musical material and knowledge gathered and developed by generations preceding the present exponents, and spontaneous creativity inspired by the moment. Khyal singer Purvi Parikh sees this as one of the reasons for the sustainability of Hindustani music:

> I think one of the main reasons that I see why it has survived, and in pockets it has survived in its traditional self, is because I think the core of Indian classical music is that we are our own creative masters. We are given a certain skeleton, and a certain grammar, and a certain framework, but within that we really are able to explore our own sensibilities, our own ideas, and project them. (interview, January 26, 2010)

Most instrumentalists—sitar, sarod, bansuri, shehnai, santur, vina, guitar, violin, and sarangi players—and dhrupad singers begin their performance with a long *alap*, which is the unmeasured, improvised, and unaccompanied part of their raga recital. In the alap (literally, "discourse"), the musician typically unfolds the raga note by note, phrase by phrase, in a leisurely manner. Here, the raga's typical melodic movements, subtle ornamentations, and other salient features are methodically disclosed, and musicians display their improvisatory skills by creating a micro-universe around one tone for some time, or by creating ever-changing combinations of two, three, four, or more notes. Regardless of genre or style, the alap (called *vistar* in khyal) is considered the best medium for expressing the essence and flavor of a raga by most connoisseurs.

After the slow alap is completed, the performance often gathers momentum through use of an accelerated tempo in the second part called *jod* (literally, "joint"). Although a distinct rhythmic pulse is introduced, the jod has no regular meter and usually there is no drum accompaniment. The final section of the alap is called *jhala*. It is faster and more vigorous than the jod and can build up to a super-fast speed in instrumental music performances.

In instrumental styles, the alap section is usually followed by one or two compositions set to a particular tala, one in slow and one in fast tempo, with variations and improvisations of increasing length and complexity. In dhrupad, the compositions tend to be more austere, and the variations more predetermined. In khyal,

FIGURE 4.1 A typical ensemble for performing khayal, with Shubha Mudgal (voice and tambura), Aneesh Pradhan (tabla), and Sudhir Nayak (harmonium).
Photo: Sharka Bosokava, Brisbane, Australia, May 2013. Used with permission.

the most common performance model consists of a slow composition (*bada* "big" *khyal*) followed by a fast song (*chota* "small" *khayal*, where melodic runs called *tans* are paramount), but several other possibilities exist. A raga can be performed in 3 to 4 minutes (as the still-much-loved 78-rpm recordings of the first half of the 20th century attest), but nowadays it is more common to develop a single raga over 45 to 75 minutes as a full concert item.

A dhrupad ensemble consists of a soloist (sometimes two who share the solo line), a pakhavaj (cylindrical two-headed drum) player, and one or two disciples playing the *tanpura* to provide a drone. A khayal ensemble consists of a soloist (or two—ensembles of brothers are quite common), with rhythmic accompaniment provided by a *tabla* player, and a harmonium (or *sarangi*) player following the vocal melody like a shadow or an echo (see Figure 4.1), usually also with one or two disciples playing the *tanpura*. A typical instrumental ensemble consists of a soloist, a tabla player, and tanpura accompaniment.

SYSTEMS OF LEARNING MUSIC

Learning classical music in India is firmly based on the concept of dedicated hard work in a close association between master and disciple referred to as *ustad-shahgird* by Muslims, but best known by the Hindu term *guru-shishya-parampara*. This system of transmission is built on profound respect and even awe of the learner for the teacher as an embodiment of knowledge (Ranade, 1999). While such an approach is at odds with egalitarian approaches to learning and teaching, it makes sense in this context: The guru not only serves as the holder of the keys to skills, creativity, and innovation within the boundaries of the tradition but also holds in his or her memory the entire aural library of musical material handed down. Strikingly, there are no self-taught musicians of any significance in Hindustani music.

In its most intense form, guru-shishya-parampara is a holistic, "total immersion" approach: the student often lives with the master, becomes part of the family, and slowly absorbs not only the repertoire and technique but also the underlying values, attitudes, and behaviors that come with being a Hindustani musician (Neuman, 1990, pp. 30–58). Slawek (1987) describes the relationship as "of a spiritual nature. The guru is likened to a god, and the disciple must fully submit to him" (p. 2; cf. Slawek 2008). As a result, it is a potentially high-yield, high-risk relationship.

Guru-shishya-parampara remains *the* format for training Hindustani musicians (Schippers, 2007). Mature musicians proudly refer to the musical lineage through their gurus, while others go through great trouble to construct a venerable lineage by connecting their predecessors to a particular gharana (style school): "Whether a musician is considered great, good, or even mediocre, he will (in the absence of anyone else) establish—so to speak—his credentials as a musician on the basis of whom he has studied with and whom he is related to" (Neuman, 1990, p. 44).

This system is increasingly being criticized by younger musicians as being anachronistic, too authoritarian, and prone to power abuse, and its challenges are well documented. While court patronage, providing a stable physical and economic basis for musicians, formed a highly conducive context for the guru-shishya-parampara system, the contemporary life of musicians, who have to travel and seek out concerts and teaching engagements to survive, is much less stable. In addition, students and scholars have attributed the vulnerability of the system to careless teaching, lack of career support, or even various forms of abuse by gurus who have difficulty living up to the ideal of this rich and complex relationship. This constitutes a particular risk for students who are not part of a family tradition. Tabla player Aneesh Pradhan is well known for proclaiming that gurus are enjoying all the comforts of the 21st century but would like their students to live in the 19th century. However, he still holds the system dear: "The role of the guru is extremely important, not just as an information giver, but translating that information into knowledge, and into wisdom. People glorify this tradition a lot.

But how does it translate into practice?" (interview, January 18, 2012). Be that as it may, guru-shishya-parampara has proven effective in preparing generations of musicians for the stage, and to date no viable alternative for this system has emerged in formal educational environments.

While it is easy to overemphasize the spiritual component of practicing Hindustani music, many of the stories that students are told as part of their enculturation into the tradition highlight supernatural aspects of the music, its transmission, and the humility the music should inspire. Ravi Shankar (1969) recounts one of the most popular stories thus:

> Narada was given the task of bringing music to the world. As he met with great acclaim, his pride grew. Lord Vishnu decided to teach him a lesson and took him to the abode of the Gods, where they saw many men and women weeping over their broken limbs. On seeing this Narada asked with concern, "Why are you all crying? Who did this great injustice to you?" They replied, "We are the Ragas and Raginis of music, created by Lord Siva. Narada here, ignorant of the true knowledge of music and unskilled in performance, sang and played them recklessly. The result was the breaking of our limbs!" Narada saw the error of his ways and repented. (p. 43)

There are no a priori restrictions for anyone—Indian or non-Indian—to learn to perform Hindustani music, but reputable gurus can be selective in imparting their knowledge. Access to rare ragas and compositions, and to keys to alap and rhythmic improvisation, may be held back. This does not occur so much within families of hereditary musicians, but it certainly does with outsiders, who have to prove worthy to get the most valuable material. In this context, aural knowledge has real economic value in its potential to build reputations in a highly competitive environment.

Hindustani music does not strongly focus on the idea of "talent" in the Western sense for identifying or explaining great musical prowess (nor does it see reincarnation as an important factor, as musicians may in Karnatak music). The most quoted reason for anyone being a great performer is receiving tuition (talim) from a reputable guru in combination with relentless practice (riyaz). Late sarod maestro Ali Akbar Khan often recounted that his father, Allauddin Khan, used to tie his long hair to the ceiling so that he would be jerked awake when he dozed off during all-night practice sessions (Schippers, n.d., p. 12).

In lessons, which are typically one on one or in small groups, technique tends to be taught first through exercises, then through simple compositions (bandishes in vocal music, gats in instrumental) with basic fixed improvisations, proceeding toward highly complicated compositions and more free improvisation structures, as well as the essential alap. While teaching styles differ substantially, generally not much is explained. To a large extent, students are expected to hone their own analytical skills in distilling the essence of raga from precomposed fragments of music.

The lessons range from highly practical technical details to the esoteric. Hariprasad Chaurasia, one of the leading performers and teachers of the turn of the century, emphasized the latter when speaking of the learning needs of his advanced students of the bamboo flute bansuri:

> They also have to understand that you don't have to tune the instrument, but you have to tune yourself. The instrument itself, the flute, does not need to be tuned, but if you are not tuned [inside], then you cannot play in tune. (Chaurasia, 2003)

Located within a cultural tradition that has a history of learned treatises going back almost 2,000 years, the practical transmission of Hindustani music has remained essentially aural/oral (as has Karnatak music in the South), although it has a long practice of written music theory. In spite of various initiatives in that direction from the 1870s as part of Hindustani music's modernist and nationalist project as India moved from feudal society to nation-state (Bakhle, 2005), Western staff notation never has come to play a role of prominence in the world of professional performance (Farrell, 1997, pp. 67–76). Efforts toward notation, however, particularly those by Bhatkhande, have contributed to democratizing music by enabling access to musical material beyond the realm of the traditional masters: The written solfa system *sargam* is applied widely in training and in collections of compositions used in music schools (Bakhle, 2005, pp. 68–70). However, aural systems of transmission are still of crucial importance. A gap of a single generation in an aurally transmitted tradition can be fatal, although the wide availability of portable recording equipment and archives can be said to mitigate such threats somewhat.

As described before, the professional training of Hindustani musicians is highly formalized, even though it takes place almost completely outside of formal institutions. The choice of a guru is a serious affair, and in principle one stays with that guru until he or she passes away. Ironically, many of the (teachers of the) greatest musicians in India have had more than a single guru, thereby combining the legacies of several traditions.

Much of the teaching tends toward holistic instruction. Most teachers do not explain much, but through extensive exposure to endless examples of what works and does not work in particular ragas, talas, compositions, or improvisations, the student develops a keen analytical sense to interpret and apply what he or she hears, and can apply this independently in due course. The formalized but non-institutionalized transmission allows for the tradition to keep changing, while contexts shift and the tradition holds middle ground between perceived "authenticities" and newness. The interaction with the guru is emphatically unequal, focused on individual, long-term, independent development. This is represented in Figure 4.2 (based on Schippers, 2010, p. 163).

TWELVE CONTINUUM TRANSMISSION FRAMEWORK (TCTF)

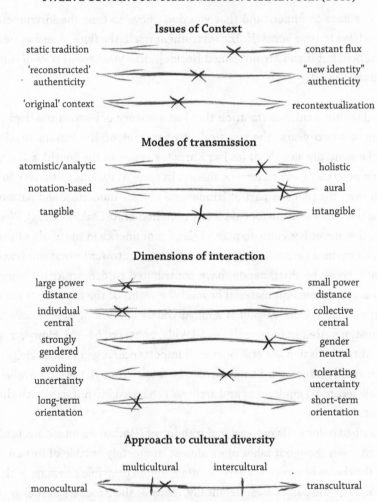

Issues of Context

static tradition ⟷ constant flux

'reconstructed' authenticity ⟷ "new identity" authenticity

'original' context ⟷ recontextualization

Modes of transmission

atomistic/analytic ⟷ holistic

notation-based ⟷ aural

tangible ⟷ intangible

Dimensions of interaction

large power distance ⟷ small power distance

individual central ⟷ collective central

strongly gendered ⟷ gender neutral

avoiding uncertainty ⟷ tolerating uncertainty

long-term orientation ⟷ short-term orientation

Approach to cultural diversity

monocultural — multicultural — intercultural — transcultural

FIGURE 4.2 An overview of choices made on the Twelve Continuum Transmission Framework during an advanced bansuri (bamboo flute) group lesson led by Hariprasad Chaurasia at the World Music Department of the Rotterdam Conservatorium.

Reproduced from Schippers, H. (2010). *Facing the music: Shaping music education from a global perspective.* New York, NY: Oxford University Press, p. 163.

Undeniably, the unequaled access to recordings of music, first through discs and now through the Internet, is changing the realities of learning Indian music. On the one hand, this has enabled hundreds of thousands of listeners and students to have access to recordings of the greatest masters of the 20th century, providing them with powerful examples of excellence at the touch of a button, which their peers 100 years ago could not even have dreamed of, as well as access to Skype learning and other digital support mechanisms. On the other hand, this has caused a reduction of diversity in approach and style, with a majority of musicians emulating the most famous, virtuoso, or trendy musicians.

While philosophically the learning and teaching systems described previously are still held in great regard, changes in society have had a major impact on guru-shishya-parampara. Globalization has changed the life of musicians but also brought institutions to a previously—and in many ways still—self-regulating environment for both the practice and learning of music.

In terms of training professional musicians, the college, school, academy, or conservatorium is perhaps the most relevant new context to consider. In North India, a large number of music schools for beginners and amateurs have been established over the past 100 years, largely on the basis of the groundbreaking work of V. N. Bhatkhande and D. V. Paluskar, such as the Gandharva Mahavidyalaya. While going back to the efforts of Maula Baksh in Baroda in the 1880s (Bakhle, 2005, pp. 39–43), music schools now abound throughout India due to the work of Bhatkhande and Paluskar, with the former working from a secular and the latter from a devotional perspective (Bakhle, 2005, pp. 175–179). This has made learning Indian classical music much more widely accessible beyond the families of hereditary musicians, and to women. However, there is a general consensus that these schools primarily cater to amateurs—who in time may turn into knowledgeable audience members.

Namitya Devidyalal emphasizes the need for educated audiences, both for the sake of music and their own sense of identity:

I think what is needed to make [Hindustani music] sustainable is by intervening and creating a whole new generation of thoughtful listeners, of discerning listeners, which does not necessarily mean they all have to be great performers or connoisseurs; they just have a sensitivity and sensibility for the arts. And for that, you have to have it in your ambient environment far more. For instance, when you turn on the radio in the morning, you should be able to hear [raga music] just so that the sound enters the bloodstream. This is part of a much larger cultural structure, which is where we all come from. (interview, January 20, 2012)

For those who have the ambition, talent, and perseverance needed for professional training, the first port of call is schools established by individual artists.
There are no Western-style conservatoires in India; the vast majority of emerging musicians still learn through a long association with a guru. Some musicians,
including leading performers such as Zakir Hussein, argue for a conservatoire-
style formal education for Hindustani music as a crucial factor in its sustainability: "Sometimes I wish universities would actually introduce professional training
with standardized teaching systems and fund it" (interview, January 24, 2010).
However, such views are still in the minority.

An interesting contemporary model for guru-shishya-parampara evolved in
Kolkata. Since 1978, the Indian Tobacco Company (ITC; formerly the Imperial
Tobacco Company) has sponsored the Sangeet Research Academy (SRA), which
replicates the guru-shishya-parampara system in a contemporary setting: an
inner-city campus with 10 gurus and 32 students (called scholars). Both gurus
and scholars are housed and fed on campus and given a stipend that enables
them to cover living expenses while they learn and teach. While the organization still has some challenges (such as the successful integration of learning
and research), it has attracted a number of prominent masters and produced
some leading vocalists of the current and emerging generation of musicians.
Speaking of the beginning of the academy, ITC/SRA Director Ravi Mathur
relates:

> In the late 1960, the board of the Indian Tobacco Company found that post-
> Independence, the maharajas and nawabs who had so far patronized musi-
> cians were no longer going to play a role. The government of India, with all
> its good intentions, was limited. The universities, music schools and colleges
> of music were gradually becoming academic institutions not related to per-
> formance. In all this emerged a niche, and that was guru-shishya-parampara.
> So ITC decided to create a fully funded, tension-free environment with a very
> favorable master–student ratio, where students can put in 6 to 8 hours of
> learning and practice every day. (interview, January 18, 2010)

Meanwhile, in the West, over the past 30 years full-degree courses in Hindustani
music have emerged. These operate in a space of continual negotiation between
North Indian traditional transmission on the one hand, and essentially 19th-cen-
tury, European ideas on education and training that characterize the conservatoire
on the other (cf. Schippers, 2004). While there were some Westerners learning Indian classical music to some extent during the first half of the twentieth

century, the phenomenon became a substantial force in the life of Hindustani music in the 1960s. This has led to many centers of teaching Hindustani music throughout the West, particularly in Europe and the United States. Most of these are single-guru undertakings, but a number of larger schools have grown from sustained work by senior musicians like the late Ali Akbar Khan in the San Francisco Bay area. Indian musicians have also been teaching in higher education settings, which has led to degree courses in Hindustani music in some conservatoires and art institutes in the West, most notably the California Institute for the Arts in Los Angeles, California, Dartington College of Arts in Totnes, Devon (UK), and the Codarts Academy for Music and Dance in Rotterdam, The Netherlands.

Implications for Sustainability

The consequences of the organization of learning and teaching Hindustani music for its ecosystem are profound. The highly organized and ritualized close relationship between master and disciple has ensured the transmission of key traditional material over many generations, while the gharana system has been a defining factor in the development and continuity of distinct styles of schools. Both are now challenged by major changes in society and technology, but high-level musicians keep emerging. The development of music schools over the past 100 years continues to help educate and maintain a knowledgeable audience. With an eye to the future, initiatives in India and abroad to organize formal professional training for Hindustani musicians show some promise to address challenges in transmission, both face to face and via the Internet.

MUSICIANS AND COMMUNITIES

Like many other music traditions, Hindustani music can be seen as linked to a number of partially overlapping communities. As mentioned before, a strong bond between professional musicians has been the gharana (or style school), mostly associated with a famous artist who belonged to a specific city or court, and often with a strong family tradition. However, bonds between musicians of a single gharana are less pronounced now than they have been. Other settings leading to a sense of community, albeit a much looser one, have been the courts, music circles, and various stations of All India Radio. Music conferences, although primarily festivals, have also contributed to a sense of community among musicians since the first All India Music Conference in 1916 in Baroda, and especially after Independence in 1947.

Musician–Community Relationships

Hindustani music has always depended on an inner circle of aficionados to support it: wealthy patrons, elite audiences, scholars of Indian music, critics, and advanced learners. Together with senior musicians, these have played a continuing role in the patronage and development of the music, embracing great traditionalists and innovators, and discarding fads and superficial displays of prowess. There are records of old masters climbing the stage to publicly hit young musicians with their cane if they felt they did not respect the tradition (Shankar, 1969, p. 57). There is concern that this senior group and its influence are waning. The vast majority of contemporary audiences do not consist of highly informed music lovers, allowing musicians with superficial knowledge and skills to come to prominence.

Widespread concerns have been expressed about the size of the audience (stratified into connoisseurs, those that primarily engage emotionally, and followers of things fashionable), their lack of motivation, and advancing age (although mature-age audiences may be the norm). There is a perceived need for audience development and even training, and a sense that young audiences have too many distractions that prevent them from engaging with classical music. The student organization SPICMACAY is doing excellent work at the university level, organizing free concerts by top-ranking musicians on university campuses throughout India (group interview, January 15, 2012). However, there is particular concern about the enculturation of young children, who still predominantly learn English songs in school and get minimal exposure to quality Hindustani music.

The online environment is offering children, musicians, and music lovers the opportunity to create virtual communities. This is occurring on an ever-increasing scale, both within India and with diasporic Indians.

Being a Musician

Although there used to be a stigma attached to some aspects of being a professional musician (see later), Hindustani musicians are well respected in contemporary Indian society at large, and there is even a media-driven star-cult around some of the leading performers. There is a clear but unformalized delineation between star performers, professionals, amateurs, and laypeople. Within the community of professional musicians, there is a strong and well-documented sense of hierarchy based on age, status, seniority, musical lineage, genre, and instrument. In the latter category, tabla, shehnai, and sarangi suffered most severely from low prestige (Bor, 1986/1987, pp. 63–70), but tabla especially has shaken off this stigma, with tabla maestro Zakir Hussein arguably the most widely revered and respected Hindustani musician today. The hierarchy among musicians is reinforced and formalized by ceremonies surrounding becoming a disciple, as well as etiquette among musicians acknowledging seniority in performances and other gatherings, which includes asking permission to perform and giving money or gifts to more senior musicians (cf. Lyberger, 2008).

The position of women in Hindustani music has changed drastically over the past hundred years, emerging from an association with the courtesan tradition of *baijis*, which was frowned upon, and leading to an "antinautch" (antidance) movement, which ultimately even criminalized these courtesans. Shubha Mudgal observes a major shift in attitudes toward women in music over three generations in her own family. After describing how the grandmother in her erudite family only allowed her children to learn the piano (from a female missionary), she then spoke of her mother, who encouraged her daughter's musical passion, even at the expense of university education after graduating from high school at age 18, which led to a successful and viable career combining khyal singing with work in popular music:

> A hundred years ago, if I had been a musician, I would have perhaps received a lot of admiration as a performer, been appreciated as a music maker, but not as a member of society. There would have been a stigma attached to my being a woman music maker. And now, I am given a great deal of respect by the state, by the public, by everyone. That means perceptions have changed about the role of women musicians in society. (interview, January 19, 2012)

One of the most striking characteristics in relation to sustainability in this domain is an almost complete lack of collaboration between musicians (outside of their own family/gharana). The court system has disintegrated and, since the 1980s, All India Radio has become insignificant as a state patron of Indian classical music, and there are no classical musicians' unions advocating government support for concerts, a prominent role of Hindustani music in schools, greater exposure in national media, or pension schemes for retired musicians, of which there are very few.

The Diaspora

Indian music has spread across the West (most notably the United States, Canada, the United Kingdom, and mainland Europe) for well over a century, quite independent of—or at least in addition to—the wide spread of Indian people across the planet. The orientalist fascination with India led to tours of *devadasis* (temple dancers) toward the end of the 19th century (Bor, 2013). Sufi Inayat Khan traveled the length and breadth of the United States and Europe to spread his music and philosophy, and Ravi Shankar's elder brother Uday celebrated successes with his dance and music troupe in the 1930s, working mainly in and from Paris. In the 1950s, a number of prominent Western classical musicians, including Yehudi Menuhin, developed a strong interest in Indian classical music. Then, in the late 1960s, Indian music broke through in Western counterculture, featuring at pop festivals like Woodstock, Monterey, and the Concert for Bangladesh (Farrell, 1997; Lavezzoli, 2009; Sangeet Research Academy, 1996).

Key figures in Western music, most notably violinist Yehudi Menuhin, Beatle George Harrison, and much later Peter Gabriel, were instrumental in introducing Western audiences to music from the Indian subcontinent. While maybe not so significant in a purely musical sense, Yehudi Menuhin sitting on the floor playing a duet with Ravi Shankar at the UN and George Harrison humbly taking sitar lessons from Shankar sent out powerful signals vis-à-vis the respect these star musicians had for Hindustani music. Other celebrated musicians, like Peter Gabriel, who promoted qawwali singer Nusrat Fateh Ali Khan through his world music festival and record label, have also made a significant impact.

Over the past 50 years, quite a refined infrastructure developed for Indian music in the West, with music schools (including a few degree courses), organizers, music critics, radio programs, and record labels dedicating themselves to the spread of this tradition. For Indian musicians, this has been an important pathway to new audiences, income, and prestige. Western interest in certain traditions—such as the passion for dhrupad by French scholar Alain Danielou—has even played an important role in their survival in India: The success of dhrupad musicians abroad rekindled an interest at home in a languishing practice (Sanyal & Widdess, 2004, p. 282).

Implications for Sustainability

There are a number of forces in this domain with significant implications for the ecosystem of Hindustani music. The first of these is a well-defined and time-honored hierarchical structure among musicians that provides stability to the tradition and its performance and transmission processes, as well as a guide to "authoritative editions" and approaches to compositions, improvisational structures, ragas, and talas. The second is a highly knowledgeable inner circle of supportive music lovers who appreciate the depth of the tradition and are not easily swayed by superficial showmanship. The third—and possibly related to the previous two—is the striking absence of organized collaboration between musicians to advocate for joint causes. The first is an unambiguous strength from the point of view of a healthy ecology for Hindustani music. The second also constitutes a strength in principle, but less so than a century ago, as the cultural elite is no longer synonymous with those in power. While the third may be seen as a strength in terms of allowing a great diversity of voices, in sum it probably works against a well-supported future for Hindustani music, and efforts to create a peak organization to advocate for Indian music and musicians at large have not yielded substantial results to date.

CONTEXTS AND CONSTRUCTS

While a decline in music cultures is commonly attributed to major social, religious, cultural, political, and technological changes, as mentioned before, Hindustani music has successfully reinvented itself in very different sociocultural contexts. It has done so by making incisive changes to some aspects of the lives of musicians (including converting to Islam, getting involved in "politicking," rebranding the art), but apparently without making major sacrifices to what most Hindustani musicians consider the essence of their art.

Cultural and Social Contexts

Unlike the music of the south of India, Hindustani music has had an extensive and fruitful interaction with cultures to India's northwest, all the way to present-day Iran. The Moghul courts were places where people and cultures mixed extensively. Names of various instruments, including the iconic sitar (from *seh tar*, three strings), ornaments and techniques are of Persian origin. Over the centuries, the music has remained open to new influences and innovation while retaining a very strong sense of its own essence.

To this day, a cultural/intellectual elite forms the strongest support base for Hindustani music. Traditionally, this group has enjoyed the music in closed communities of courtiers and music circles, who invite an artist to come and perform for a small group of connoisseurs in a setting that emulates a court. Sharad Sathe, who runs what used to be known as Dadar-Matunga Social Club, one of the oldest music circles in Mumbai, describes this as follows:

Dadar-Matunga Social Club was started in 1953 by Dr S. G. Joshi, a well-known nose and throat specialist keen on music. They used to have sittings at somebody's place, as is usually done in the initial stage. Gradually the membership increased. In 1981, we secured our own place and the name was changed to Dadar Matunga Cultural Centre. Now we have over 1,100 members and present a classical music concert every month. (interview, January 28, 2010)

Another key format is the "music conference," a multiday music festival with a range of artists, which goes back 100 years. These festivals can take place indoors but more often occur on a field with a stage. People walk in and out, and as the evening and then night progresses, more and more senior artists are presented, with the top artist often performing around dawn.

Over past decades, a more Western-style recital format featuring only a few or a single star artist has been growing, more in line with the demands of contemporary working lives. The concert season still very much focuses around the winter months (January to March), when the weather is most conducive to outside events. The concentration on a relatively brief concert season is seen as problematic by musicians, music lovers, and organizers; some argue it would help to have it spread out more throughout the year.

Constructs

Indian classical music has a clearly developed aesthetic component, going back to the Natya Shastra of Bharata (3rd century CE), one of the world's oldest treatises on performing arts. Central to the aesthetic experience are *bhava* and *rasa*, referring to the mood of specific ragas. There are nine rasas in theater, including heroism, sadness, eroticism, and peace. According to the theory, these are evoked by the action on stage and resonate in the spectator not as the emotion itself, but as a pleasurable mirror or echo of this emotion.

A key characteristic of Hindustani music is how it constructs its own past. This takes various shapes. First, there is a strong tendency to make things older than they really are, in a manner reminiscent of Hobsbawm's invented traditions (Hobsbawm & Ranger, 1983). Perhaps the most well-known example of such invented antiquity is the antedating of the invention of the sitar and tabla to the 13th century instead of the 18th century (Miner, 1993). Second, there is the tendency to edit out key factors in the history of the music, such as the long association with courtesans, as musicians and scholars tried to re-engage with respectable middle-class families in the first half of the 20th century. Third, there is the bias of Hindu versus Muslim musicians: While the latter is likely to emphasize the Muslim (especially Sufi) contributions to the tradition, the former tend to relate the history of music to its perceived main Hindu roots.

The Sanskritization of Indian music was placed center stage in the expansion to the West. A major new context arose. In fact, the constructs underlying this expansion in the late 1960s were very much based on Hindu aspects of culture: antiquity, devotion, meditation, and a close connection to God. And while most Indian musicians frequently profess links to the spiritual in both the essence and the practice of Indian music (in fact, practice is often equated to *sadhana*, a focused practice to achieve a spiritual result), it is essentially a worldly tradition, and many musicians tend to display emphatically worldly behavior both on and off stage.

Hindu and Muslim musicians share a strong conviction of the excellence (if not the superiority) of their art, supported by its association with temples and courts, and a long history of learned writing (*sangit shastras*). This may help explain why—unlike in almost all colonized nations—Western art music never got a foothold in India. While the Hindustani classical tradition is a living tradition par excellence, having embraced new ideas and influences throughout its history, there is no significant evidence of undue Western influence, not even in the classical performances of its main ambassador to the West, Ravi Shankar. Western music did enter India through marching bands, popular music, and—most evidently—elements of Indian film music, but the principal frame of musical reference of the country is still its own tradition. Only now, at the beginning of the 21st century, through efforts of the new Parsi CEO of the National Centre for the Performing Arts, does India have its own chamber orchestra, still predominantly populated by foreign musicians.

Excellence in Indian music is highly valued and carefully scrutinized. The integrity of the tradition is closely guarded by the tradition bearers. Such conservative mechanisms serve a living tradition well. Now, as the newly affluent tend to be at the front during concerts, there is a concern that such checking mechanisms no longer exist. This is exacerbated by a concern that there are fewer and fewer expert reviews in newspapers.

This leads to another striking factor in the constructs underlying Indian music: the conviction from generation to generation that the music is in decline or even dying. It is as apparent from recent interviews with senior masters as from the words of Coomaraswamy over 100 years ago that there is a strong perception that the music was better in the past, and that the younger generation does not care about the tradition. While it is difficult to gauge the future, this can be evaluated in retrospect by considering what we now see as the great generations of the first and second halves of the 20th century. Rather than taking decline as a given, the conservatism such perceptions entail possibly serves as a mechanism to ensure careful thought before changing key aspects of the tradition or adding new elements. Many would argue that this has led to a balanced development of Hindustani music over the centuries.

Still, while there is a strong sense of a music that has not changed in essence, each successive period has left its mark on the music, creating a rich and paradoxical mix of underlying constructs. Critic, administrator, poet, and playwright Ashok Vajpeyi notices a shift that he feels touches on the essence of the art, a particular quality that is lacking in contemporary performance:

> The Indian classical arts have always been delicately, almost dangerously, poised between the erotic and the sacred, between the sensuous and the spiritual. ... The sense that I have to perform, that my music is between the erotic and sacred, between the physical and the metaphysical, between the sacred and the erotic; that sense seems to have been lost. So here is a music that is now neither erotic in a deeply sensual sense nor sacred in a deeply spiritual sense. And it has not been replaced by an alternative vision. (interview, January 12, 2012)

Many senior musicians and connoisseurs share this view. Few see Hindustani music as in imminent danger, but many refer to a perceived loss of depth, which may be temporary or, some fear, permanent because of the drastically changed environment.

Implications for Sustainability

Three key features of Hindustani music in the domain of contexts and constructs have a direct impact on how it negotiates its ecosystem. First, in spite of a strong and relatively narrowly defined tradition, Hindustani music has demonstrated a striking flexibility in adapting to new contexts and environments. Second, Hindustani music has been able to reinvent itself in terms of values and history to suit the needs of its support base. Third, and most important—and somewhat paradoxical in relation to the first two—Hindustani music has been able to inspire a strong conviction of its quality, value, and consistency through the ages, safeguarding it from excessive unconsidered change due to changing tastes or foreign influences.

INFRASTRUCTURE AND REGULATIONS

While it is widely considered as one of the great classical traditions of the world and a symbol of national pride, as discussed before, Hindustani music has a striking lack of formal support and regulations governing its sustenance and development, given its size and grandeur. There is a dearth of dedicated performance venues, music schools, grants and funding opportunities, representative bodies, and local and national policies relating to classical music in North India.

Infrastructure

Hindustani music has relatively modest demands in terms of infrastructure. Intimate *mehfils* (musical soirees) are held in people's houses with the artist playing unamplified on a small dais, while public concerts are often presented in multipurpose venues with a varying degree and quality of sound amplification, and the major festivals over the winter months are generally put on outdoors in public parks, sport fields and showgrounds. Concert organizers do express concerns about certain aspects of such facilities, the quality of amplification, green rooms, and traffic (in terms of both noise and preventing people from arriving at specific venues in time in gridlocked cities). In addition, there are a number of good world-standard performance facilities, each with its own focus and concert series.

A key aspect of infrastructure is the technological support that is now widely available. This has been a major enabling factor in the shift from small elite audiences to much larger ones. Large-scale concerts of Hindustani music are reasonably common now. Amplification has made it possible for soft instruments to be heard, and for vocal music it has enabled greater diversity in the use, subtlety, and timbre of voices.

At a more "low-tech" level, most musicians have access to decent instruments, but there are some challenges. A generation of master instrument makers and repairers has just passed away. In addition, the availability of ivory, deer horn, and particular types of seasoned wood needed to make top instruments is decreasing. In accompanying instruments, the harmonium has replaced the sarangi, possibly as the result of a combination of tuning challenges and low status (Bor, 1986/1987). Increasingly, tambura has been replaced by electronic tambura or recordings of tambura on a CD, smartphone, iPod, or computer as part of a broader rise of electrically supported and e-instruments. The latter shift is partly a result of the risk of air travel for delicate instruments. Sensitivity to temperature changes and humidity is another continuing and major challenge in India, exacerbated by air conditioning and stage lights (cf. Sangeet Research Academy, 2010).

A final force worth mentioning in this field is the Sangeet Natak Akademi (SNA), founded by the Indian government but run as an independent society, which describes itself thus on its official website:

The Sangeet Natak Akademi – India's national academy for music, dance and drama – is the first National Academy of the arts set-up by the Republic of

India. It was created on 31st of May 1952. As the apex body specializing in the performing arts of the country, the Akademi also renders advice and assistance to the Government of India in the task of formulating and implementing policies and programmes in the field. Additionally, the Akademi carries a part of the responsibilities of the state for fostering cultural contacts between various regions in India, and between India and the world. (Sangeet Natak Akademi, 2016)

The most visible activity of the SNA is to bestow awards on deserving artists: visible both for the profile they create and for the controversies over who receives the awards and when. In addition, the SNA organizes concerts, festivals, and seminars; distributes (modest) grants to performing arts initiatives; promotes documentation, research, and cultural exchange; and has a small-scale Artists' Aid program to support those in need. However, the impact and turnover of the institution are rather insignificant in the face of the overall picture of the Hindustani music industry.

Laws and Regulations

In terms of the more intangible infrastructure of regulations and support structures, there is surprisingly little to either support or stifle Hindustani music. No laws are enforced that restrict music making, learning, and performance. But there are also very few laws that facilitate any of these. Corporate giants Indian Tobacco Company and Tata have received tax advantages by categorizing their music activities through the Sangeet Research Academy (SRA) and the National Centre for the Performing Arts (NCPA) as research. Increased demands on corporations for "social responsibility" may prove fruitful for Hindustani music. The government finances Doordarshan (television) and All India Radio, but it has not substantially invested in the latter since the 1980s. Through the Indian Council for Cultural Relations (ICCR), it has been supporting selected musicians to tour internationally since 1950. Finally, it confers the most prestigious (but also heavily politicized) Padma Awards every year on Republic Day.

There is a time-honored tradition of touching one's ear as a mark of respect while mentioning or thinking of a musician who composed or taught a composition, but the formal realities of rights are less ideal, as Shubha Chaudhuri observes. Hindustani music, like other forms of traditional music in India, is not covered in the Copyright Act of 1995. It is considered as part of what used to be called "expressions of folklore," now referred to as "traditional cultural expressions." This meant that the music itself, being a part of tradition, was not covered. Chaudhuri contests that issues of rights, ownership, copyright etc. remain a major concern among the practitioners of Hindustani Classical Music, which causes confusion and misunderstandings. The major issue is that few musicians are aware of what their rights are, which leads to exploitation and unfair practices at certain times, or on the other end, unrealistic ideas and expectations as to what their rights may be. (Interview January 12, 2012)

While compositions and improvisations cannot be copyrighted, performances can, under Section 38 of the Copyright Act. However, record companies tend to hold these rights. Chaudhuri explains that even so, issues of copyright, piracy, and other violations remain largely unimplemented, and royalties are often not paid. In addition, there is a free exchange of private and bootleg recordings, now more than ever because of digital downloads. Ringtones featuring excerpts from Hindustani music are also popular; artists tend not to be remunerated for these either. Therefore, in the end, intellectual property and copyright laws presently do not play a significant role in the sustainability of Hindustani classical music.

Implications for Sustainability

Many aspects of infrastructure and regulations play an important part in the ecology of Hindustani music. Hindustani music has very modest needs in terms of resources and infrastructure, reflected in the virtual absence of substantial grant regimes and dedicated spaces with appropriate acoustics/amplification. Further, Hindustani music has been able—and seems to continue to be able— to find instruments, source equipment, and set up teaching institutions without much formal help. Finally, national institutions, societies, and foundations, as well as the nation's laws, play only a minor role in sustaining Hindustani music, which is surprising for a music tradition that has contributed significantly to defining India's intangible cultural heritage.

MEDIA AND THE MUSIC INDUSTRY

From a global perspective, Hindustani music has demonstrated early uptake in its engagement with mass media and the music industry. All India Radio was established in 1936 (although its predecessors in Mumbai and Kolkata started broadcasting as early as 1927; All India Radio, 2013a). The first wax roll recordings of Hindustani music appeared in 1902, mostly recorded by a mobile studio that traversed the country in search for its greatest talent.

Media Engagement

All India Radio (AIR) is widely acknowledged for its support to Hindustani classical music in the first three decades after Independence in 1947. It effectively assumed the role of principal patron after the courts had lost their ability to support music, paying salaries to hundreds of musicians and providing a—surprisingly rarely challenged—classification system based on merit (A, B, and C class artists). It also introduced the iconic National Program of Music in 1952 at the initiative of Information and Broadcasting Minister B. V. Keskar, a long-serving and outspoken classical music supporter: This was a 90-minute "feast of Classical Music" broadcast on Saturdays from 9:30 p.m. to 11 p.m., featuring many of the leading musicians of each successive decade (All India Radio, 2013b).

Long-time AIR producer Nityanand Haldipur described the waiting rooms at AIR at the time as modern-day *durbars* (courts), where the great *ustads* discussed intricacies of ragas and talas (interview, January 20, 2010). The graded artist system provided almost unchallenged quality control for Hindustani classical music. With its 40% music commitment, most of this classical, AIR in combination with Doordarshan on television provided satisfactory access to classical music in the opinion of many (Sangeet Research Academy, 2010). People knew when to listen, as programs were well advertised in print.

Since the 1980s, due to government funding cuts, AIR has not been hiring new staff (performers, technicians, or administrators). Consequently, it is no longer a significant patron of Hindustani classical music. Since that time, the position of classical music on radio has been in decline in terms of frequency, length, time slots (now late), and its relationship vis-à-vis popular music, which provided better opportunities for sponsorship. Dissemination of information is much less successful (loss of print media, slow emergence of web-based formats). Meanwhile, commercial stations show little or no interest in classical music. Corporate sponsorship only works if a CEO happens to be interested, and is not seen as worthwhile from a marketing perspective, barring events that engage the handful of superstars of classical music.

According to some, the decline in radio exposure and rise of television has influenced the nature and quality of performance. Chaya Ganguli, a producer trained in Hindustani music who has been working with Doordarshan for several decades, asserts:

> There has been a shift.... People now want to enjoy things visually. I feel this is sometimes harming the artists because their focus is going away from tuneful singing. They are visually very good, but as one guru said (I will

not mention the name): "Their songs are to be seen, not heard." (interview, January 19, 2010)

Another factor of considerable importance is the printed press, as India contin-ues to be a country of avid newspaper readers. Shanta Gokhale misses the reviews that helped shape her musical sensitivities (interview, January 17, 2012). An age divide exacerbates the situation: Audiences tend to be over 40, while journalists are generally young without sufficient interest in and knowledge of the arts. The school education system is letting down the arts. Dileep Padgaonkar qualifies this by stating that lack of coverage is most pronounced in the English-language press (Sangeet Research Academy, 2010), which is getting more entertainment focused. He emphasizes that Indian-language newspapers are gaining circulation and influ-ence, and do devote space to culture. Others argue that the role of newspapers may be limited, and that people tend to make up their own minds. But there is a par-ticular concern for the lack of frequency and quality in press coverage, especially for upcoming artists.

In terms of the question between nurturing and catering to the market, the dichotomy between articles *on* art and articles *about* art(ists) is raised, the lat-ter increasingly focused on celebrity culture and the entertainment economy. Marketing (e.g., naming concerts) is getting more refined, and artists are increas-ingly driven to use gimmicks, both on stage and off stage. A number of them now have hired public relations consultants or agencies to ensure their names appear in the newspapers, more often than not in society columns rather than music-related articles.

Presence in the Music Industry

The Indian operations of the Gramophone Company of India (HMV) started in 1901 as the first overseas branch of Electrical & Musical Industries (EMI), London. The earliest recording made in India was that of Gauhar Jan, a *baiji*, in the year 1902:

Although the recording was made in India, the disc was manufactured in England. So, at the end of the record she announced her name, to enable the technicians abroad to fix the right label to the disc. This practice of announcing one's name at the end of a song continued until 1908, when the Gramophone Company of England set up manufacturing facilities in Sealdah, Calcutta. (retrieved June 7, 2012, from www.recordsindia.com/companies_hmv.html)

Later, a bigger factory was set up in Dum Dum, Calcutta. In 1931, the Gramophone Company, Columbia, Odeon, and some smaller companies merged to form EMI. Even after the merger, the different companies that made up EMI retained their respective labels. The first microgroove record from Gramophone Company was introduced in 1958. These were 45-rpm 7" EP records. In 1959, an LP record plant was established at the Dum Dum factory of Gramophone Company. The first LP record was released in June, and in the first year, about 125 LP records were issued (ibid.). This was 4 years after the first LP recording of Hindustani music was published in the United States, featuring Ali Akbar Khan (sarod) with Chatur Lal on tabla, introduced by Yehudi Menuhin.

LPs constituted an important step in the dissemination of Hindustani music. For all the condensed beauty of the 78 rpm, still revered by many connoisseurs, LPs allowed ragas to be developed beyond the 3-4 minute limitation of that format, creating a practice that reflected much more what took place in performance. According to Shubha Chaudhuri, they also allowed a next stage in positioning musicians in the market:

I think [in] the LP era ... the individual was very important, and somehow the LP format supported that. How many LPs someone had was kind of an indicator of how important they were as musicians. So you had this creation of ... individual followings, the creation of stars. (interview, January 14, 2012)

This effect was felt not only in India but also in the rapid spread of Hindustani music across the Western world in the late 1960s and early 1970s. Concerts drove the new Indian music aficionados to records, and records to concerts. However, records have only provided substantial income to a few star musicians: Royalties from LPs from the late 1950s and CDs from the early 1980s represented a modest contribution to the livelihood of most musicians, but constituted important markers of prestige.

Many classical artists associated themselves with the burgeoning film industry—most notably Bollywood—as a creative outlet, a source of income, or both. Leading bansuri player Pandit Hariprasad Chaurasia remembers:

I was sent to Mumbai by All India Radio as a kind of punishment. They knew the salary would not be enough to live there, so they hoped I would quit. But I wanted to be in Mumbai, to learn more. So I started to work with the film industry. I made good money, but I also learned very much there about music from the great film music directors. (interview, January 21, 2012)

The rise of the recording industry inevitably impacted the dissemination, the reception, the learning process, and indeed the very nature of Hindustani music. While it is difficult to measure, a decline in diversity of approaches to distinctive instrumental styles and vocal gharanas may be due to extensive exposure to masters through radio/recordings. In sitar, for instance, it is rare to encounter a musician who is not imitating—or at least very audibly influenced by—one of the two most renowned sitarists of the second half of the 20th century: Ustad Vilayat Khan or Pandit Ravi Shankar.

The number of original recordings published by HMV diminished greatly in the 1980s. A repackaging industry evolved, which persists to this day, regrouping recordings by "ragas of the morning," "monsoon ragas," or the "best of . . ." particular artists. Rajiv Goenka, who was responsible for this shift in focus, recalls the considerations:

We had a wonderful catalogue of recordings by great masters, but reissuing the old records was not commercially viable anymore. So we decided to repackage some of this wealth, to reach new audiences. I know some of the connoisseurs were very critical, but commercially it was a success. (interview, January 10, 2012)

A number of other Indian and international record companies are making claims on the vast Indian market. While the earnings are made through popular music (including Bollywood songs), there is interest in Hindustani music. Among those engaging with this tradition is Sony, who signed a contract with the National Centre for the Performing Arts to bring out their series of historical recordings by the masters of the second half of the 20th century (interview with Arjun Sankalia, January 16, 2012).

In recent decades, Hindustani music has taken to the Internet on a grand scale. There are many thousands of clips of skilled and less skilled musicians, performing and teaching (or offering to teach via Skype). Over the past 10 years, dozens of online file-sharing forums have come into existence. Irfan Zuberi describes an interesting phenomenon: the rise of online music circles, exchanging and discussing in great detail old and rare recordings of artists like the legendary Kesarbai Kerkar (interview, January 15, 2012). This constitutes a reinvention of one of the quality control mechanisms of Hindustani music: connoisseurs discussing the merits and demerits of particular artists and performances in detail. This development goes back to the unmoderated "Usenet" newsgroup RMIC to which sound files could be added in the late 1990s. In the 2000s, Orkut and later the "Indian Raga" BlogSpot engaged large online communities. Online streaming (e.g., http://

musicindiaonline.com) and Internet radio (e.g., Tarang) have gained ground in the past 10 years or so. YouTube has tens of thousands of clips of Hindustani music, including tutorials for learning to sing ragas or play an instrument.

Implications for Sustainability

A number of important aspects emerge from this section for the picture of the ecosystem: Hindustani music has engaged with mass media and the music industry from early on. Particularly, All India Radio has played a key role in preserving Hindustani music in India during its first crucial decades as a young republic, effectively taking over the patronage from the courts, but this has faded almost completely. The recording industry and, more recently, online formats have ensured wide dissemination of quality music. The printed press has played a major role in contributing to quality control of the tradition by publishing criticism and alerting readers to emerging artists, but in recent years this has diminished drastically and largely been replaced by celebrity gossip. Finally, while the government stays in the background, corporate sponsorship seems to be limited to a few companies that contribute significantly and many others that contribute only modestly to specific events.

ISSUES AND INITIATIVES FOR SUSTAINABILITY

Considering the discussions on the five domains influencing sustainability in the previous pages, the Hindustani case study reveals a tradition with extensive links to the history of the subcontinent, its societal and power structures, its people, its philosophies, its other arts, the media, and the rest of the world. These links have not been rigid: The music has changed orientation and allegiances drastically over the past eight centuries. Although firmly rooted in convention and tradition, the ragas and talas of Hindustani music have shown considerable flexibility and resilience. While we know that some ragas have changed over the centuries (and certainly preferences for particular ragas change every few decades), there is a strong sense of continuity regarding what insiders consider the essence of the music.

It is attractive to map the forces working for and against sustainability in Hindustani music in the terms used in SWOT (strengths, weaknesses, opportunities, and threats) analyses, where many of the strengths are also weaknesses, and many of the opportunities also present threats. Key strengths would be the profound respect and prestige Hindustani music enjoys; a strongly developed sense and broadly shared understanding of what constitutes quality; a time-honored transmission system; and relatively satisfactory representation in the media, at least until recently. Weaknesses would include its elite/niche nature, absence from formal school curricula, dependence on informal aural transmission, and lack of consistent support in terms of funding and infrastructure. Opportunities include a sense of national pride; the rise of a large, well-educated middle class in India; the fact that social responsibility is high on the agenda of many corporations; ongoing globalization of music; and the boundless possibilities of the Internet. Threats include the incursion of too many forms of other music on the educated Indian ear; shifts of interest among India's financial, intellectual, and cultural elite; and the traffic, noise, and pollution in urban centers affecting both the accessibility and audibility of major music events.

Overall Vitality

It is relatively easy to ascertain that in spite of various challenges, Hindustani music is quite vital. Not only is this the almost unanimous view of most interviewees for this project and much of the literature, but it is also supported by the 12 indicators that Grant (2014) has developed as the Music Vitality and Endangerment Framework: intergenerational transmission is strong involving all age groups; the number of proficient musicians is stable; the number of people engaged with the genre is stable; the pace and direction of change reflect little or no change in strength; the music continues to be performed in well-established contexts and some new ones (like the online environment); mass media and the music industry engage moderately with the genre; infrastructure and resources for creating, performing, rehearsing, and transmitting the genre are generally available and accessible; the community still holds the knowledge and skills required; the music is lightly supported through specific policies; community members support the maintenance of the genre strongly; relevant outsiders (such as Western audiences and promotors) support the genre; and there is abundant, high-quality documentation of the music genre.

While there are justifiable concerns for a level of depth lost in the music over the past 100 years, it seems that most key stakeholders in Hindustani music—for all their diverse opinions on the reasons—agree that it is not a tradition under threat. This confidence seems to be based largely on the intricate relationship between the music and the very core of Indian culture (interview with Zakir Hussain, January 24, 2010), its people (interview with Namitya Devidyalal, January 20, 2012), its creativity (interview with Purvi Parikh, January 26, 2010), and even its relationships to the universe (interview with Ashok Ranade, January 26, 2010).

Key Issues for Sustainability

The key issues for sustainability for Hindustani music seem to cascade down from the esteem and prestige of the music, which generates continuing engagement by India's intellectual and cultural—and to some extent financial—elite. Prestige drives young people passionate about listening to and studying the music, media exposure and attention, audiences of all ages, engaged scholars and archivists, markets for live and recorded music, instrument makers and real estate developers creating tools and space, philanthropists and corporate sponsorship, and government support through policies, prizes, and awards. All of these are of crucial importance, but none of them seems to be under imminent threat in a continuing virtuous circle.

Past Initiatives

As discussed, major initiatives to promote and maintain Hindustani music have included Indian music conferences for a century, exposure to radio and later television, music schools based on the work of D. V. Paluskar, student concerts through SPICMACAY, support for touring musicians through ICCR, and tax deductibility for research purposes that have enabled the corporate giving that has facilitated the establishment of NCPA and ITC/SRA as major cultural institutions.

Each of these initiatives has downsides: Music conferences counterintuitively only present and do not discuss the future of music in any depth; radio and television are yielding more and more to commercial interests; the music schools do not produce credible performers; SPICMACAY can be seen as primarily a pretext to underpay top-ranking musicians; and on close scrutiny, the NCPA and ITC/SRA have research as one of their last priorities. The question is whether that really matters, if the contributions these initiatives make are in fact sufficient to keep the tradition vital.

A large number of archives have been established privately, with corporate support or under government oversight. AIR holds an enormous archive but is seen to handle it very carelessly, reusing tapes of unique performances for new broadcasts. To the horror of Indian music lovers, HMV destroyed a vast amount of its shellac collection. Others are struggling with resources for maintenance and digitization, like virtually everywhere else in the world. Important archives include Archives and Research Centre for Ethnomusicology (ARCE), Sangeet Research Academy (SRA), National Centre for the Performing Arts (NCPA), and Sangeet Natak Akademi (SNA). Some of these archives are seeking to disseminate these (for listening only) online and either try to honor or continue to struggle with issues like intellectual property.

Current and Planned Initiatives

In formal school education, there have been plans to include Hindustani music in the national curriculum, but these have not yet been implemented. College and university students can access quality concerts through SPICMACAY, but rarely have access to practical training. In the domain of the training of professional musicians, there have been discussions on the potential for Western-style conservatoires to secure the future of high-level training, or an expansion of the (very expensive) ITC/SRA *gurukul* model, but none of these has advanced significantly.

As for musicians joining forces to influence government policy, the only initiative regarding this has been the establishment of the All India Musicians' Group in 2009, an advocacy body consisting of leading performers of both Hindustani and Karnatak music. It has had a series of meetings in spite of the near impossibility of gathering the busiest performers in India in a single location, but it is too early to judge whether this will yield substantial results over time.

While the lack of emphasis on Hindustani music in young people's lives is a concern that can be addressed by either education or the media or both, there is no immediate sense that the prestige of Hindustani music is on a dangerous downturn. It is important to remember that it has always been and will probably always be an elite music, needing the support of a small group of influential, entrepreneurial people rather than mass appeal.

Surprisingly little attention is given to developing music tourism. While there are many overseas music enthusiasts and students, projects that bring audiences or learners to India are strikingly absent. In terms of infrastructure and regulations, there are no concerted efforts, although more newly built concert venues with adequate acoustics and/or amplification are being used for concerts. Social responsibility, which is on the rise for corporations, may yield serious opportunities. Media and the music industry are largely self-regulating, and the access provided by radio broadcasts and LPs in the past has been replaced by empowered listeners who can curate their own experience through the Internet, where new rich sources spring up every day.

While all of this may seem meager in terms of planning, as long as there are no major upheavals, it may well be sufficient for a strong tradition that does not depend heavily on external intervention to ensure a sustainability rooted in respect and targeted engagement of overlapping circles of musicians, avid supporters and patrons, and music lovers in India and the rest of the world, creating an ecosystem that is strikingly robust for a highly abstract tradition.

ACKNOWLEDGMENTS

This chapter is based on a 3-year research collaboration between Huib Schippers (Griffith University), Joep Bor (University of Leiden), and Shubha Chaudhuri (ARCE New Delhi), who advised and contributed to sections of this chapter, with additional input from Dhruba Ghosh (Bharatiya Vidya Bhavan, Mumbai) and Suvarnalata Rao (National Centre for the Performing Arts, Mumbai). It comprised 24 individual and group interviews conducted in 2010 and 2012 (see companion website), an overview of the literature, and the lived experience of Hindustani music between the five research team members as performers, teachers, researchers, administrators, organizers, critics, producers, and lovers of Hindustani music. In total, over 100 people were generous with their support, time, ideas, and insights (see companion website). We would like to thank them all.

REFERENCES

All India Radio. (2013a). All India Radio services. Retrieved from http://allindiaradio.gov.in/Services/NSD

All India Radio. (2013b). National programs. Retrieved from http://allindiaradio.gov.in/Profile/NationalPrograms

Arnold, A. (Ed.). (2000). *The Garland encyclopedia of world music, Vol. 5: South Asia, the Indian Subcontinent.* New York, NY: Garland.

Bakhle, J. (2005). *Two men and music: Nationalism in the making of an Indian classical tradition.* New York, NY: Oxford University Press.

Booth, G. D. (2008). *Behind the curtain: Making music in Mumbai's film studios.* New York, NY: Oxford University Press.

Bor, J. (1986/87). *The Voice of the Sarangi: An Illustrated History of Bowing in India.* Mumbai: National Centre for the Performing Arts.

Bor, J. (1999). *The raga guide—A survey of 74 Hindustani ragas.* London, UK: Nimbus.

Bor, J., Delvoye, F., Harvey, J., & Te Nijenhuis, E. (Eds.). (2010). *Hindustani music: Thirteenth to twentieth centuries.* New Delhi, India: Manohar.

Bor, J. (2013). On the dancers or devadasis: Jacob Haafner's account of the 101 eighteenth-century Indian temple dancers. In Kouwenhoven, F. and J. Kippen (Eds.), *Music, Dance and the art of seduction.* Delft: Eburon Academic Publishers.

Chaurasia, H. (2003, May 8). If you are not tuned here, you cannot play in tune. Interview with H. Schippers, Rotterdam Conservatory, Rotterdam, The Netherlands.

Farrell, G. (1997). *Indian music and the West.* Oxford, UK: Clarendon Press.

Grant, C. (2014). *Music endangerment: How language maintenance can help.* New York. NY: Oxford University Press.

Hobsbawm, E., & Ranger, T. O. (Eds.). (1983). *The invention of tradition.* Cambridge, UK: Cambridge University Press.

Lavezzoli, P. (2009). *Bhairavi: The global impact of Indian music.* Delhi: Harper Collins India.

Lyberger, L. L. (2008). Ranking behaviours and gharana hierarchy: The Nazarana ritual of Pakistani Panjabi tabla players. *Journal of the Indian Musicological Society, 38,* 186–208.

Miner, A. (1993). *Sitar and sarod in the 18th and 19th century.* Wilhelmshaven, Germany: Florian Noetzel Verlag.

Neuman, D. M. (1990). *The life of music in North India* (2nd ed.). Chicago, IL: University of Chicago Press.

Ollikkala, R. (2000). The social organization of music and musicians: Northern area. In A. Arnold (Ed.), *The Garland encyclopaedia of world music, Vol. 5: South Asia: The Indian subcontinent* (pp. 372–382). New York, NY: Garland.

Ranade, A. (1999). Guru-shishya parampara: In wider perspective. In S. Rao (Ed.), *Teaching of Indian music.* Bombay, India: Sangeet Research Academy.

Sangeet Natak Akademi (2016). [Home page]. Retrieved from http://sangeetnatak.gov.in/

Sangeet Research Academy. (1996). *Indian music & the West* (Seminar paper). Bombay, India: Author.

Sanyal, R., & Widdess, R. (2004). *Dhrupad: Tradition and performance in Indian music* (SOAS musicology series). Aldershot, UK: Ashgate.

Schippers, H. (2004). Blame it on the Germans! - A cross-cultural invitation to revisit the foundations of training professional musicians. In Orlando Musumeci (Ed.), *Preparing Musicians Making New Sounds Worlds* (pp. 199-208). Barcelona: ISME/ESMUC.

Schippers, H. (2007). The guru recontextualised? Perspectives on learning North Indian classical music in shifting environments for professional training. *Asian Music, 38*(1), 123–138.

Schippers, H. (2010). *Facing the music: Shaping music education from a global perspective.* New York, NY: Oxford University Press.

Schippers, H. (n.d.). *Swara Samrat—Emperor of melody: The life and music of Ali Akbar Khan* (Unpublished manuscript).

Shankar, R. (1969). *My music, my life.* New Delhi, India: Vikas Publishing House.

Slawek, Stephen M. (1987). *Sitar Technique in Nibaddh forms.* New Delhi: Motilal Banarsidas.

Slawek, S. (2008). The classical master-disciple tradition. In A. Arnold (Ed.), *The Garland encyclopedia of world music, Vol. 5: South Asia: The Indian subcontinent.* Retrieved from Garland Online Encyclopedia.

Tagore, S. M. (Ed.). (1965 [1882]). *Hindu music.* Varanasi, India: Chowkhamba.

van der Meer, W., & Bor, J. (1982). *De Roep van de Kokila: Historische en Hedendaagse Aspecten van de Indiase Muziek.* The Hague, The Netherlands: Martinus Nijhoff.

Wade, B. (1979). *Music of India: The classical traditions.* London, UK: Prentice Hall.

Wade, B. (1984). *Khyāl: Creativity within North India's classical music tradition.* New York, NY: Oxford University Press.

Willard, N.A. (1834). *On the music of Hindustan.* Calcutta.

5

CENTRAL AUSTRALIAN WOMEN'S TRADITIONAL SONGS

Keeping Yawulyu/Awelye Strong

Linda Barwick and Myfany Turpin

AUSTRALIA'S INDIGENOUS PEOPLE produce and participate in many varieties of music, from opera to hip-hop to performance poetry to traditional ritual performance. This chapter concerns just one of many traditional ritual genres, the *yawulyu/awelye* ceremonial genre performed by women from various country-based groups in central Australia.[1] Music is only one (albeit essential) aspect of this ritual complex. In most languages of the area, there is no one word for *music* or even *song*; rather, such terms as *inma* (in the Pitjantjatjara language) cover the whole gamut of intertwined music, ceremonial action (including dance), body painting, and ritual objects (Ellis, Ellis, Tur, & McCardell, 1978). Sustaining the musical future of *yawulyu/awelye* cannot therefore be separated from maintaining all the other social practices that surround its performance.

In July 2010, the authors, together with linguist Mary Laughren, interviewed some of our long-time friends and research collaborators in central Australia about how they see the future of their ceremonies. We asked both older people (60+) and younger people (30+) about how they learned *yawulyu/awelye*; what, if any, hurdles they see to sustaining the genre; and what they see as the way forward. We used a semistructured interview technique, whereby we

---

[1] *Awelye* is the spelling of this genre name in Arrernte and Kaytetye; it is spelt *awely* in the Anmatyerr and Alyawarr languages.

aimed to garner responses to these key questions but allowed the participants to direct the topic and course of the interviews, which were conducted in the women's preferred language and in a setting where they felt comfortable. Selected portions of the interviews were later selected for transcription and, if needed, translation into English. Some of the matters discussed here have also been presented in a different framework in a published article (Barwick, Laughren, & Turpin, 2013).

The women we consulted are affiliated with eight different *yawulyu/awelye* repertories in five different languages: Warlpiri, Warumungu, Kaytetye, Anmatyerr, and Arrernte. Women now in their 70s and 80s are senior "law women" (women with responsibility to uphold and teach traditional culture, codified as "law"; Glowczewski, 1991, 1999), while younger women in their 30s and 40s are keen to learn *yawulyu/awelye* to assume the cultural responsibility of passing law on to the succeeding generations.

BACKGROUND

Yawulyu and *awelye* are cognate names for women's country-based ceremonies in central Australia. The term *yawulyu* is a genre name for land-based women's ceremonies in the Warlpiri (Ngumpin-yapa) and neighboring Pintupi and Warumungu areas, while the cognate word *awelye* (Arrernte and Kaytetye; spelled *awely* in Anmatjerr and Alyawarr) is used for the genre among speakers of Arandic languages. (In the Eastern and Central Arrernte areas, *awelye* refers to a genre of healing ceremonies that can be performed by both men and women.)

Yawulyu/awelye is not the only ceremonial genre performed by women in these areas: women may also perform alongside men in other public performance genres (such as Warlpiri *purlapa* or the Arandic *angkwerre*) and in other sacred/secret genres of women-only ceremonies such as *yilpinji/ilpentye* "love songs," or *jarrarta*, some of which can be sold or traded between neighboring groups along traditional exchange routes (Poirier, 1992). In the Western Desert area, which has a different social organization including relations to land, the several women-only songlines do not have a collective genre name but rather are classified along with other sorts of song as *inma*; nevertheless, there are clear parallels in music, dance, and text construction to *yawulyu/awelye*. *Yawulyu/awelye* and related women's ceremonial genres among neighboring language groups (such as the Pintupi, Western Desert, and Warumungu) have been discussed very widely in the literature (e.g., Barwick, 2005; Berndt, 1950; Dussart, 2000; R. M. Moyle, 1986, 1997; Poirier, 1992; Turpin, 2011; Turpin & Ross, 2013).

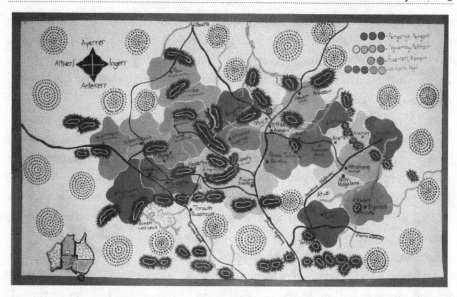

FIGURE 5.1 Map of the Anmatyerr estate groups produced by April Campbell for the Ti-Tree School Language and Culture program.
Image © April Campbell 2008. Used with permission.

The pervasiveness and lifelong significance of *yawulyu* and other ceremonial genres of the Warlpiri are encapsulated in Françoise Dussart's observation: "Long before they are born and long after they die, the Warlpiri of Yuendumu are directly and inexorably implicated in a complex repertoire of ceremonial activity" (Dussart, 2000, p. 47).

Yawulyu/awelye is the principal means by which women demonstrate their patrilineal clan identity, as belonging to a defined clan estate (Peterson & Long, 1986). As suggested in Figure 5.1, a map of the Anmatyerr estate groups produced by April Campbell for the Ti-Tree School Language and Culture program, each language area includes multiple clan estates. Each clan estate has one main *yawulyu/awelye*, usually named by the principal Dreaming (totem) of the estate (country). For example, *awelye akwelye* (water/rain) is the main *awelye* for Arnerre, a country belonging to one of the Kaytetye-speaking patrilineal clans (Turpin, 2005, 2007b). A Dreaming may cross more than one country, in which case two estates may own it (such is the case for *yawulyu ngurlu* "seed," owned by two Warlpiri-speaking clans). In such cases, however, only those segments of the Dreaming's travels that pass through their own country (equating to a sequence of song items naming places and activities of the Dreaming) are owned by clanswomen of the relevant estate.

The songs, dances, and associated stories, objects, designs, and ceremonial actions for each *yawulyu/awelye* are handed down within the clan from women to their brother's daughters (since the rights to the country and songs are inherited patrilineally, through the father's line). The songs come from eternal Dreaming law (*wirnkarra* in Warumungu; *jukurrpa* in Warlpiri; *altyerre* in Arandic languages), a time out of time in which Dreaming ancestors laid down the laws for humankind and formed the country and all beings that live upon it.

Most individual songs within a *yawulyu/awelye* series are of unknown origin, though it is clear that others have come into the repertoire in living memory, usually through revelatory dreams in which songs (and associated dances, body designs, and so on) are revealed to the dreamer by an ancestral being (Barwick, 2000; Payne, 1992). Even in such cases, the songs are regarded as having always existed and are attributed to the Dreaming ancestors rather than human agency, although those who receive the songs in dream may derive social prestige through their composition (Dussart, 2000, 2004; Wild, 1987).

Among the social functions of *yawulyu/awelye* are expression of group solidarity and identity; healing of the ill; celebration of the unique features of the relevant country; and instruction to younger generations of women about their sites, history, and cultural practices, and Aboriginal law more generally (Myers, 1986, p. 112). The use of *yawulyu/awelye* to create positive emotions to defuse conflict and build social cohesion is highlighted by the remarks of Pwerrerle, an Arrernte songwoman:

> *Wele utnenge atyenhe, wele nhakwe apeke-arle, nhakwele-arle alheme,* you know, *utnenge nhakwele aneme.* Funny you know I feel just like I'm singing out there when I sing. When you sing that song you feel real good you know, *utnwenge ngkwenhe* you *awerle-arle mwerre-arle* when you sing.
>
> When I sing, it's as if my spirit traveled over there [my country]. It's strange, but I feel like I am at that place.... When you sing that song you feel happy, your spirit feels happy when you sing. (interview, March 16, 2010)

Originally performed by women for women only, *yawulyu/awelye* ceremonies are now performed by women on a range of different public and private occasions. To mount a performance, the presence of leaders ("bosses"—i.e., women who are owners of a particular *yawulyu/awelye*) is absolutely essential, with the participation of "managers" (i.e., women who are the daughters of female owners) being highly desirable. The "boss" role is called *kirda* in Warlpiri or *apmerew-artweye* in Kaytetye, while "managers" are called *kurdungurlu* in Warlpiri or *kwertengerle* in Arandic languages. Others may join in both singing and dancing, but only bosses can explain the songs and their significance, hold custody of the ceremonial objects, direct the body painting, and decide the sequence of activities in the performance:

> *Pwetye-werne anwerne iwethe akine alhemele, re atherre anwernenhe ileke,* "All right you song *nhenhe mape,* you *atnyenerle akwete kwenhe.* Don't *impetyeke.*" Corroboree *nhenhe,* like grandfather *atyenhe,* country *atyenhe-arle apetyeke-arle.* Right up to Santa Teresa. Travel-*irreke, arelhe mape-arle* travel-*irreke* Mission-*werne. Ikwere-werne* travel-*irreke, altyerrenge re. Kele nhenge akaltye anthurre aneme ayenge irreke. Nhenge* everywhere *ikwerarle aneme anwerne alyelhetyarte ampe kweke mape-arlke aneme* teachem-*iletyarte.*

> We went out bush again and my mother and older sister said, "You must remember these songs forever, don't forget them." They explained how this ceremony was from my father's father's country, and that it goes all the way to Santa Teresa. In the Dreamtime the women traveled all the way to where Santa Teresa mission is. That's when I really started to learn about ceremony. That's when we started doing lots of singing and teaching the children. (Pwerrerle, interview, March 16, 2010)

Performances may last for many hours, or even days. A performance consists of a number of discrete song items (typically lasting from 30 seconds to 1 minute). The singing is performed by a group of women led by one or more bosses, with body percussion accompaniment (either handclapping or lap slapping by the singers). There is no limit on the size of the singing group. *Yawulyu/awelye* performances are multimodal, communicating the topics of the songs in multiple dimensions, including language, rhythm, melody, movement, and iconography (body painting, ground designs, and ceremonial objects). Each repertory has a different characteristic melodic contour, which is repeated for each item in the performance, expanding and contracting to accommodate the song texts.

Song texts are isorhythmic (i.e., they set the same text to the same rhythmic pattern, with regular beating accompaniment always aligned with the same text syllables) and are repeated strictly throughout the song item. Most texts consist of couplets (pairs of lines), frequently occurring in the repetition pattern AABB, with the string repeated over and over again throughout the item (e.g., AABBAABBAA; a characteristic often referred to as "cyclic repetition"). The song leader fits the text to the melody in the moment of performance, meaning that rather than learning songs as a rhythmic/melodic unit, the learner initially needs to follow the leader (Ellis & Barwick, 1989; Turpin, 2007a).

The song texts are typically quite cryptic and contain words difficult to discern due to modification of vowels and consonants and the use of words from different languages or registers, as well as vocables (Turpin, 2007a, 2007b, 2011). The songs are regarded as the utterances of the Dreaming ancestors concerned, and they often refer to particular places or incidents in the ancestral episodes. This is why the authoritative interpretation of the senior owners of the *yawulyu/awelye* is necessary.

For a danced performance, the sequence begins with songs performed while the dancers are being painted up with traditional designs under the direction of the bosses. Between the performance of individual songs and their accompanying dances, participants including dancers and singers may discuss the meanings of the song texts and details of the myths that are told in the song texts and re-enacted by the dancers. The body designs of the dancers and the decorations on the ceremonial objects are also related to aspects of the Dreaming ancestors being celebrated in the performance (Ellis, 1970). Some dances are for just one or two dancers, while others involve larger groups dancing in a line (usually organized on the dance ground according to their relationship to the Dreaming/ceremony in question).

SYSTEMS OF LEARNING MUSIC

Traditionally, learning of *yawulyu/awelye* songs takes place informally, through progressive immersion in performances and ongoing contact with the country and stories to which they relate. Learning the songs, dances, paintings, and meanings mostly occurs in performances, through constant repetition and (initially) imitation (see also Ellis, 1985, p. 112). There is no formal institution for instruction or named stages of learning. The teaching of songs, as with language, is primarily oral and holistic.

Learning primarily comes from paying attention and participating in the ceremonies. Learners would traditionally join in by clapping the rhythm, dancing, and humming the tune before being expected to join in the singing. The onus of learning ceremonies is very much on the learner (Hale, 1984). In Kaytetye, the verb *arit-arenke* (to pay attention to something to learn how to do it, a compound based on the verb "to see") describes specifically how ceremonies and other aspects of Aboriginal law are learned:

Awelye warle tyampe arrit-arerrantye kaltyarrerrane, kaltyinterantye kwere. Arrit-arerrantyelke mpelarte learn-*arrewethe. Arrit-arengele atyenge erlwarerrantyawe, intarerrantye apeke arrit-arengele. Arrit-arerrantye iterrtye kwerrpe anteyane tyampe,* law-*angkwarre.*

People learn women's ceremonies by paying careful attention at performances; that's how ceremonies are taught. A person watches carefully in order to learn. Someone might learn how to do something by watching me (do it), they might be staring and paying close attention (to what I am doing). A person pays close attention during a ceremony if they don't know it. (Ampetyane, Katytetye dictionary database, November 23, 2001)

Catherine Ellis conducted much research on how ceremonies are learned in the neighboring Western Desert regions of central Australia, and some of her findings apply to traditional learning throughout central Australia. In her book *Aboriginal Music: Education for Living* (1985), Ellis reported the following instructions to urban students at the University of Adelaide's Centre for Aboriginal Studies in Music (CASM) by Pitjantjatjara teachers:

> You can only master a tune by listening very carefully and concentrating while we sing for you. Then you can join in, softly at first, gradually louder. Close your eyes and do not look at the others. Your concentration will then not be distracted and you can listen more intently. You must be patient and not expect to learn a great deal in a short time. Think of learning a little properly rather than half-learning a great deal. (Ellis, 1985, p. 126)

Ellis describes how the holistic approach to learning begins with confusion (Ellis, 1985, p. 125). It is usually at a much later stage that the learner discovers how to unravel the words and structures that underlie the songs and, later still, becomes a "boss" who can lead the performance. Teaching doesn't occur unless a student "sees the need to learn and expresses interest in being taught" (p. 112). Ellis states that a "student shows his or her readiness to learn by being prepared to follow the model of the master teacher and seeking him out for help" (p. 120). Learning is at first done through imitation of a respected person and able performer (p. 123). To support holistic learning "not only were they [the Aboriginal elders] patient in repeating material as often as necessary, but they were ever ready to praise and encourage no matter how small an improvement had been made" (p. 127). We too have found that elders generally commend learners on their involvement. At CASM, Pitjantjatjara teachers stopped the lesson when learners asked questions, because this was regarded as questioning the authority and skills of the teacher. Although Ellis found that teachers do not emphasize mistakes but wait for the students themselves to observe what was wrong (p. 127), we have occasionally observed singers verbally correcting errors made by other singers, possibly after the singer fails to correct herself.

Traditionally, the individuals that one spends time with and observes to learn from them are specific categories of kin. For women's *yawulyu/awelye* songs, these are usually a woman's father's sister(s) and father's father's sister(s). Elders we consulted recalled these categories of kin as the people from whom they learned.

This is because ownership of ceremonies, like country and totems, is passed on patrilineally through one's father's father. While people own the ceremonies belonging to their father's father, people also have a relationship to the ceremonies belonging to their mother's father. This relationship is one of caretaker or manager. "Managers" are responsible for correct running of ceremonies, for placing the ritual paraphernalia in place, and for putting it away at the end of a performance (Peterson & Long, 1986). A person is expected to be able to partake in the ceremonies of their mother's father's country, though not make decisions or explain the meanings of these ceremonies, which they simply manage rather than own. People generally learn the ceremonies for which they are managers from their mother, her sister(s), and their mother's father's sister(s). Understandably, most people we spoke to talked only about the ceremonies that they own, not those that they manage.

The excerpt that follows, from an interview by linguist Mary Laughren, shows how the current generation of Yawulyu custodians at Willowra learned yawulyu:

ML: How did you learn *yawulyu* songs? Who taught you?

K. NAMPIJINPA: I was taught the songs for my Dreaming by my aunt (father's sister), Nangala (now deceased). Only one Nangala for that Dreaming is left now who knows those songs; (she is) KS Nangala. She is a younger Nangala than those old aunties who taught me the songs.

ML: Where were you living when you started learning *yawulyu*?

NANGALA AND NAMPIJINJPA: Right here at Willowra, before there was any station here or buildings.

NANGALA: We would go to Pawu (Mt. Barkly) and then come back this way.

K. NAMPIJINPA: Our mothers and grandmothers would take us around with them. We grew up here; we didn't grow up in some other far away place.

NANGALA: We were children here and we have grown old here. . . .

K. NAMPIJINPA: The Dreamings for Pawu are *ngapa* (water) and *ngurlu* (seeds.)

NANGALA: We paint the designs and then we dance.

ML: Nangala, where did you learn the songs and dances for *ngurlu*?

NANGALA: Here. I didn't move around all over the place. I just lived around here.

ML: Who taught you?

NANGALA: My elder sisters. (interview, July 13, 2010, translated from the original Warlpiri by Mary Laughren)

From this interchange, we get a picture of how *yawulyu* along with the associated knowledge of *jukurrpa* (Dreaming), country, and family relationships to country was passed on from one generation of women to the next as women went about their lives in multigenerational groups of closely related kin, or extended families. As young girls moved around the country in the company of their mothers and grandmothers, they were shown how to live off their country and were told about people and events associated with specific sites, especially waters, in their country, and also about the creative period. As they got older they were taught the songs and dances for their own patriline (their father's line) by the senior female members of that group, their paternal aunts, and their elder sisters.

In addition to the established rules of kin from whom one can learn, the skills of particular individuals no doubt also play a role in how successfully ceremonies are passed on. An aunt or grandmother who sings well, organizes performances frequently, and explains the songs in a skilled narrative fashion is likely to have more success in passing on her ceremonies than someone who does not have these skills, and the personal relationships between specific aunts and nieces no doubt further influence whether or not ceremonies are taken up.

It seems that the lack of availability of learners in the right kin category may affect the future sustainability of a repertory. Good singers and dancers are recognized as such by the community, and they are often called upon to be part of a performance, but this does not equate to them having rights to teach or make decisions about a ceremony for which they are not an owner. Two senior performers and owners of one particular song series that is very well known and relatively large (over 60 songs) are highly motivated and talented singers, equipped with detailed knowledge of the song's meanings learned from their father's sisters. Their daughters also live in the same community and as managers have learned and have rights to perform the songs, but there are no nieces (the kin category for future owners). It is unclear whether the daughters as managers will be able to pass on this ceremony in the future without the involvement of any senior owners, even though they may be the only ones still holding the knowledge of these songs.

Owners who for one reason or another do not know the songs themselves sometimes need such nonowners skilled in songs to help carry out a performance or to teach younger owners. A younger owner wishing to learn songs from a nonowner must first obtain permission from senior owners, who may deny this permission unless they have well-established relationships with the prospective teacher. Fortunately, in some cases the complex negotiations involved have been successful. Arranging such a context for learning involves great initiative, sensitivity, and negotiation skills.

Anmatyerr elder Pwerl recalls a childhood of constant exposure to her ceremonies, and this is how she learned them. As an 8- or 9-year-old, she would be painted up with her ceremonial designs by her aunts and grandmothers, thus affirming her relationship to the ceremony, country, and totems with all the rights and responsibilities that go with it:

> *Pwety-warl alhetyart map. Nheng warl-eng anetyart, iter-el alyelherl-alpetyart, arlkeny werrerl-alpetyart. werrkel pwety-el. Amarl map alhetyart. Artwang map warrk-irretyart. Kel anwern alhetyart, ayeng pwert-antey alhetyart, mother-el angetyart ayeng.*

> We used to go back out bush away from the station, to sing and paint up. The women used to go while the men worked. My mother used to take me. (Pwerl, interview, July 21, 2010)

Then, as a teenager, she gradually started joining in the singing of songs where she felt she knew the words. Crucially, her involvement was her own decision and it occurred at her own pace. Her mistaken belief that the older women were laughing at her when they were actually joking among themselves highlights the prevalent fear of making a mistake:

> *Kel awetyart 'alyelhang' kwenh ntwa tew-kwenh, ntwang alyelhay! Ayeng mother-el iletyart ntwa catchem-il-erl-alpem yanh. Kel alyelhetyart, kwek war. Kel ntert-am-arl anetyart ayeng alakenh kwek-am-akwek alyelherl-alpem. Kel inang arrken atherrem-arl, kel ayeng ntert-arl-irr-erleng, alakenh.*

> "You sing too," the older women would say. My mother used to tell me, "You know the words now," and I would be singing bit by bit. I used to be silent, but then I sang little by little. When they used to laugh amongst themselves I would go quiet [be embarrassed]. (Pwerle, interview, July 21, 2010)

People of all ages that we interviewed mentioned that as learners they were fearful of making a mistake, because elders might laugh at them. This is an issue in learning across all domains of traditional knowledge. While group participation may be an excellent strategy for minimizing mistakes and ensuring the accurate transmission of songs, one impact of this may be that only few people pluck up the courage to participate in the singing.

In Tennant Creek, Nappanangka and Napurrrurla were concerned that nowadays younger women were singing too softly, perhaps for fear of making a mistake such as singing the wrong words, whereas traditional performance practice demanded that women sing loudly and in unison. This change in performance practice was evident already in 1996 when the first performances for the *Yawulyu mungamunga* CD were recorded at the Mary Ann Dam north of

Tennant Creek (Papulu Apparr-kari Aboriginal Language and Culture Centre & Barwick, 2000):

> You can hear it on that record when we were singing at the dam; it's important to sing properly. [You can't hear anybody else singing on that recording,] only me. (Nappanangka, interview, July 15, 2010)

At Wirliyajarrayi, we also asked K. Nampijinpa and Nangala about whether the generation of women who attended school, now in their 40s and 50s, knew the *yawulyu* songs and were able to sing them:

ML: Do younger women know the *yawulyu* songs?

NANGALA: No. They don't know them. I'm the only Nangala who has these songs for Pawu (Mt. Barkly).

K. NAMPIJINPA: Pawu only has one Nangala (who knows its *yawulyu*) now. We have only one Nangala now.

NANGALA: I know the Dreaming songs and dances for the Jangala from the west who comes to Pawu to steal the rain, that Brown Falcon (*kirrkirlanji*) man.

ML: Are the young girls learning to sing the *yawulyu* songs?

NANGALA AND K. NAMPIJINPA: No.

ML: Do they know the dances?

NANGALA: Not really. They only do little bits of dancing.

K. NAMPIJINPA: A few of the young ones dance well. One young one danced with us at the opening of the new Central Land Council building in Alice Springs. There's one young Nakamarra who dances well.

[. . .]

ML: Do the young girls not like to dance?

K. NAMPIJINPA: They are too shy to dance. They feel shame. They don't carry on the ceremonies and songs belonging to their maternal grandmothers (*jaja*, "mother's mother"). Nor do they carry on the ceremonies for their paternal grandmothers (*yapirliyi*, "father's mother"). (interview, July 13, 2010)

Shaming is one of the most important methods of social control in central Australian society (Myers, 1986, pp. 120–124). In saying that the young women "feel shame" to dance in public with their painted torsos exposed, K. Nampijinpa is touching on another theme often brought up by women of her generation: the changing sensibilities of a younger generation brought up under the influence of European mores (disseminated through their schooling, television, and travels beyond their community). Some elders complain that the motivation, self-discipline, and respect for elders, all prerequisites for traditional holistic learning styles, are absent in the current generation. Although such complaints may be heard in many different contexts around the world, it should be noted that compared to previous generations, there is much more pressure on today's younger generations living in remote communities to engage in mainstream majority culture. In the past 20 years, remote communities have seen the progressive introduction of television, video/DVDs, electronic games, the Internet, mobile phones, and, in recent years, smartphones, meaning that today's younger generations have grown up with far greater engagement in mainstream culture than has ever before been possible.

Nevertheless, many younger people are highly motivated to learn about their ceremonies. At Alekarenge, M. Nampijinpa commented on the factors motivating her to document the songs known by her mother's sister Nungarrayi:

> I really want to learn that [*yawulyu*], keep it, because it's my mother's songs. I've always been interested in *yawulyu*. . . . These days everything is changing, some have lost their culture already, and by doing this [teaching and documenting *yawulyu*] we can keep it strong, our culture. . . . Because this old lady [Nungarrayi], she's the last member of our family. As the elder in our family she's the only one who knows the cultural ways, you know, our cultural knowledge. If she goes, all will be lost. (M. Nampijinpa, interview, July 18, 2010)

Many women in the older generation accept that younger generations may need the assistance of writing and audiovisual aids to learn songs (though nobody, as far as we know, uses music notation). Although literacy was first introduced in some parts of central Australia as early as the 1890s (Harris, 1990; Strehlow, 1915), widespread literacy in Aboriginal communities is relatively new and the older generation of singers tend not to use writing. Both Indigenous and non-Indigenous people have written down *yawulyu/awelye* song texts for educational purposes in recent years. In Tennant Creek, B. Napurrurla suggested involving literate language workers from the Papulu Apparr Kari Language and Culture Centre in an effort to document her songs for teaching purposes: "But we [the older generation] can still do it [sing *yawulyu*]; the language center mob can write it down" (B. Napurrurla, interview, July 15, 2010). Although Ellis (1985) herself regarded literacy as eroding the traditional oral method of learning (p. 131), she reported that elders at CASM very quickly came to rely on written versions of the song texts to help their students' learning, because this was how people who were experienced in literacy learned quickest (Ellis, 1985, p. 126), although the depth of this learning was not as great (as one student stated, "I have never forgotten what was learned when we worked without writing") (Ellis, 1985, p. 127). In the current era, where the tide of literacy is everywhere—and most

Aboriginal people use it in at least some aspects of everyday life—to insist on purely oral learning might be akin to insist on hunting with a spear instead of a gun.

Audiovisual recordings of songs have been used for many years even by older generations as part of the teaching and learning process for *yawulyu/awelye* (Barwick, 2005, p. 7; Poirier, 1992, p. 774), although in the past this type of learning was more of an adjunct than the primary means. Recordings and other documentation of traditional knowledge may be treated with the same reverence as other ceremonial objects. For example, when we visited Tennant Creek, we were told that the booklet of song texts Barwick had assembled for Nappanangka in 1999 for approval before publication of the *Yawulyu mungamunga* CD was subsequently included in the bundle of ceremonial objects Nappanangka had recently handed over to the new owner of the *yawulyu* as part of the formal transmission process (Nappanangka, interview, July 15, 2010).

In recent years, DVDs, audio recordings, and written texts of ceremonial songs and their meanings have all been embraced by younger generations who experienced schooling (people who were born approximately post-1960). These younger people are comfortable with a more individual style of learning using books and audio and video recordings, which they can pick up and learn from at their own pace and in a more private space:

> It's hard to pick up the song unless we have it written on the paper. . . . When you are telling a story it's a bit slow, and there's little spaces in the story. But when you are singing there's those sentences all together, long sentences, and it's really hard. (Pengart, interview, July 20, 2010).

For many younger people with multimedia skills, the creation of these resources offers them a chance to be meaningfully engaged during ceremonial performances without the pressure of being a learner and the responsibilities that entails. The pressure for younger women to learn in this way stems not only from a fear of making mistakes but also from greatly diminished opportunities for traditional situation-based learning.

All the older generations we consulted stressed the importance of learning "out bush," away from the distractions of town and community, and preferably at the sites being sung about. The practice of holding land claim hearings "on country" (i.e., on the traditional estate of the landowning group) arose because it was found that Aboriginal people were better able to discuss totems, songs, and affiliations to land when physically at these sites. A number of elders we spoke to believed that one of the reasons young people are not able to learn their ceremonies in the traditional way is because these people are not familiar with the country to which the songs refer, having grown up away from their own country. There is a strong relationship between knowledge of country and knowledge of songs. When singing, elders visualize the country to which the songs refer (see also Ellis, 1985, p. 130). Discussions during performances also show that the movement from site to site undertaken by the protagonists in the songs is at the forefront of the performers' minds. New songs, too, are only received when out on country, not within a community or town.

Recognizing the importance of ceremonial performances in upholding Aboriginal law, some Aboriginal organizations have sponsored bush trips for learning of *yawulyu/awelye* at various times, and other bodies such as Aboriginal health centers, language centers, libraries, and other institutions (often government funded) may also contribute on an ad hoc basis, usually depending on staff with specific interests in this area. Traditional performances may be commissioned to mark significant occasions by organizations such as the Central Land Council, a body established to act in the interests of traditional owners in managing their rights to land. The Australian Institute of Aboriginal and Torres Strait Islander Studies (AIATSIS) offers programs to disseminate knowledge about its collections and to promote community understanding of Indigenous culture, and mainstream educational institutions such as universities and schools may also create opportunities for elders to teach some traditional songs on country.

Implications for Sustainability

Yawulyu/awelye ceremonies are not explicitly taught, and there are no institutional places of learning. Learning mostly occurs holistically through participation in performance. Concern was expressed by all generations about the difficulties younger people experience in learning. Knowledge about their ceremonies can only be passed on to women by certain categories of kin (e.g., their father's sisters). Another constraint on intergenerational transmission may be the learner's shame and fear of making mistakes in this important domain of knowledge. While writing was not traditionally used, younger learners make use of written song texts in association with audio and video recordings to facilitate private study. Many elders believe that young people have difficulty in learning because they do not have regular access to the country to which the ceremonies relate.

MUSICIANS AND COMMUNITIES

There is no differentiated category of musician or performer in central Australian Aboriginal society; all people are expected to be able to sing, dance, and paint their land-based ceremonies. Performing their clan's *yawulyu/awelye* is expected of senior women traditional owners, who usually also demonstrate their knowledge in other channels and media such as narratives, sand drawings, visual arts, dancing, and upholding their cultural knowledge and traditional values in appropriate domains of public life. The roles of singer, dancer, hunter, and so on only last for the moment of that activity, and they can be taken up by anyone with the necessary rights and skills.

Although there is no distinct profession of performer, some people are recognized as being particularly skilled at singing, dancing, or painting, just as others are recognized as being a good hunter, being an intellectual, or having a particular behavioral or personality trait. A person regarded as a good singer tends to be someone who knows lots of songs, has a strong voice, and likes singing. Individuals known as good singers are often recruited by families for initiation ceremonies and *ilpentye* in return for payment (*tyenkarre* [Kaytetye], *ngijinkirri* [Warumungu]), which nowadays takes the form of cash or consumable items such as food, although traditionally *tyenkarre* involved only food and tools. The *tyenkarre* paid to singers varies, depending on the relationship between people, the need for money at the time, and what else is on offer. Sometimes no *tyenkarre* is paid at all, especially if there are perceived favors owed. Although people recognized as good singers may get *tyenkarre* in this way, the prestige does not always cross over into other domains. That is, apart from *tyenkarre*, a good singer may not receive any additional benefits, privileges, or favorable treatment from other members of the community.

Just as there is no special social category of singer, traditionally there was no concept of a nonparticipatory audience. *Ilpentye* and healing ceremonies are always performed in private with the individuals concerned. Initiation ceremonies require the participation of everyone present (although children or the sick, injured, lazy, or infirm might not be expected to perform). In the past no one was allowed to remain in the community and not participate, but this law has now been relaxed somewhat to account for the now-complex patterns of non-Indigenous and Indigenous relations. Another traditional context for land-based ceremonies was exchange between different groups, either within a community or with visitors. In this context, one group would watch while the other group performed, and then the roles would be reversed. As discussed later, in recent years, land-based ceremonies have come to be performed at intercultural gatherings where both Indigenous and non-Indigenous people are present; in these cases a clear audience–performer distinction emerges: There is no expectation of non-Indigenous people to perform in exchange.

Traditionally, everyone was expected to be able to maintain her own ceremonial responsibilities, but for social and logistical reasons the performance of ceremony has become more difficult since colonization. A community was always made up of people from several different clans (e.g., a woman's clan is different from that of her children), but nowadays there is much greater mobility and consequent social diversity within communities compared to the precolonial era, when most people lived and traveled on or close to their own country. In the 1950s, many Aboriginal people were forcibly relocated to large communities sometimes quite distant from their own country, meaning that subsequent generations have grown up no longer familiar with their own country. Since the 1980s, greater access to vehicles and opportunities to study in capital cities have meant that social networks cover even greater distances. People now marry into communities far from those in which they grew up, sometimes into areas where the ceremonies and languages are vastly different from their own. Children from such marriages often grow up not knowing the language, ceremonies, and country of the "married in" parent.

For any performance it is necessary to gather particular people, namely, the most senior owners, and sometimes others who for one reason or another know the songs well. The logistics of this can be expensive and complicated if these people live far away from each other or from the performance location. Public transport is lacking in remote Australia, as is access to private vehicles, especially for older people (this is even more the case for women than for men). Distances are vast, up to 600 kilometers, and so travel can be very costly and logistics extremely difficult. Nevertheless, the commitment to continuing performance of *yawulyu/ awelye* is strong.

Implications for Sustainability

There is no social category of specialist performers: Everyone is expected to be able to sing, dance, and paint her own land-based ceremonies. Mounting ceremonies is more difficult than in the past due to dislocation from home country and dispersion of the relevant people across wide areas. It is not uncommon for individuals to marry into communities far away, thus losing the opportunity for themselves and their children to participate regularly in learning through performance of their own ceremonies. Women's knowledge transmission suffers particularly from lack of access to vehicles and resources to teach or to learn from the right kin in distant communities.

CONTEXTS AND CONSTRUCTS

Yawulyu/awelye and other forms of ceremony have always served as a way of displaying and managing group identity within a complex social landscape involving diverse complementary groups and many gradations of social difference.

Australian Aboriginal societies display and recognize a huge range of linguistic and cultural diversity, and ceremony has always been a primary means of intergroup communication. Although a considerable proportion of Australia's estimated 250 languages are no longer spoken, today most Aboriginal communities include people from a range of different language and culture groups. As Fred Myers (1986) observed of the Pintupi: "Singing provides a salient image of sociability. Whenever large groups came together in traditional times, they would sing together at night. Ceremony—song and dance—was the real content of most intergroup relations" (p. 112).

For example, describing *yawulyu* performances of the Warlpiri people who came to live on Kaytetye country at Alekarenge in the 1950s, F. Napurrurla highlighted the various clan estates, naming the Dreamings and skin groups of their owners:

The old people brought the songs and ceremonies for Miyikampi, Jiparanpa (*ngurlu*, "seed"), Pawurrinji (*ngurlu*), and Kulpurlunu (*ngapa*, "rain"). The Nangalas and Nampijinpas danced for Rain (*ngapa*). The Napanangkas and Napangardis danced for Miyikampi. The Nakamarras and Napurrurlas danced *ngurlu* for Jiparanpa (my side) and for Pawurrinji. Also the [Kaytetye] Jarrajarra groups (Napaljarri-Nungarrayi) had their business and the women would dance for their own father's father's country and Dreaming. (Edited translation from Warlpiri by Mary Laughren; F. Napurrurla, interview, July 18, 2010)

Although the dramatic social changes since colonization have had major effects on when, where, why, and how ceremonies occur, it is notable that they have had very little effect on their details. That is, there is very little cross-cultural influence in the actual music, dance, and visual designs in ceremonies. This is no doubt partly due to the fact that ceremonies are not simply entertainment, but expressions of Aboriginal law. The details of the music, song texts, dance, and body designs of each repertory form part of an integrated social mechanism for displaying and managing social difference and identity between groups. Stability in shared conventions in music, poetics, dance, body decoration, and song texts is needed to highlight the points of difference between repertories, the markers of clan identity. Each individual *yawulyu/awelye* repertory emphasizes the particular features that distinguish it from its neighbors (e.g., body designs, place names, and mythological references that are tied to the particular country being celebrated; see Figure 5.2).

The traditional use of *yawulyu/awelye* and other ceremonial genres to show cultural identity has been extended over the previous 50 years or so to legal contexts where performance of songs naming places and Dreamings has been accepted as

FIGURE 5.2 Molly Napurrurla Presley, May Napurrurla Presley, and Clarrie Kemarr performing the *awely* from Rrkwer (Mount Denison area) at the opening of the Desert People's Centre in Alice Springs, Northern Territory, 2010.

Photo: © Margaret Carew. Used with permission.

evidence of traditional ownership. When we visited Tennant Creek in 2010, we interviewed Nampin, a community leader who has a long history of eloquent speech making and advocating for Warumungu interests. She has been a member of the Central Land Council and other community organizations and has participated in several land claims. At the time of our visit, she and other senior women were involved in various court hearings regarding potential government use of Aboriginal land. She regarded maintaining knowledge of *yawulyu* as essential for ensuring a continued voice for Aboriginal people in legal disputes:

> It's important for language and *yawulyu* to be very strong. *Yawulyu* and *pujjarli* [men's public ceremony], they're the main ones for anyone in the whole of this country. If you've got your cultural songs and your cultural dances and if you've got something coming up in whitefella way [i.e., a court hearing], you can break it up with your dancing. You can show them, you can do your challenging, and tell them what you've got for the ground.

That's the main important thing I always say to my kids. Not only to my kids, to everyone else. I tell them, "That's the main thing you have to hold, your cultural dancing, and your language." There's two kind[s] of things in your cultural way. You have to talk in language; then you have to translate it in English. Then you do your dancing; you tell them what you're dancing for. That's how you show these people, so they know, "Oh yeah, they've got the strongest ceremony," you know, "and the cultural way of showing us." (Nampin, interview, July 17, 2010).

Although the main focus of our interview was *yawulyu*, the main women's land-based ceremonial tradition, Nampin broadens the frame of her remarks here to include *pujjarli*, the men's public ceremony that is sometimes performed in similar public contexts, including land claims and native title hearings (there also exists another much larger body of men's songs that are restricted and not suitable for public occasions). Throughout Aboriginal Australia, songs and ceremony are tied to particular places and often name them and recount aspects of their foundation myths (Ellis, 1992b). As such, ceremonial performances have been accepted in court hearings under both Land Rights and Native Title legislation as evidence of attachment to country (Bell, 1993; Koch, 1994, 1997, 2004, 2013)—"you can tell them what you've got for this ground." Traditional knowledge management protocols dictate that only the senior owners of the country can elucidate their meanings, so Nampin regards the explanation of the performance in language and then translation into English as a guarantee of the authority of the owners and as an integral part of the "cultural way."

Like Nampin, B. Napurrurla was concerned that in the future her descendants might be disadvantaged by not carrying on knowledge of their *yawulyu*:

But in the future, you know government people are going to ask young people, "Do you know your culture?" What are they going to say? Nothing, they can just look at it [not perform it]. That's why I say to my family, "You're going to have to learn your culture." (B. Napurrurla, interview, July 15, 2010)

It is clear that many younger Indigenous people are not aware of the fragility of their traditions, nor of the role these ceremonies play as required evidence of Aboriginal authority and/or ownership in Aboriginal people's legal claims to land in negotiations with government and the private sector. Young people may be unaware that their own grandparents were able to secure their land in part by singing their traditional songs, with all the knowledge that entails. More broadly, there is a lack of knowledge of how traditional knowledge and practices have assisted Aboriginal people in negotiations relating to their land and culture.

Some communities that were originally established as Christian missions had a history of suppression of traditional ceremonial religious practices such as *yawulyu/awelye*, which were considered "satanic" (Carter, 1996; Harris, 1990), but in other instances Christian missions supported the continuation of traditional languages and ways of life. Today the main threats to *yawulyu/awelye* stem from disruption of traditional languages, lack of access to country, and lack of knowledgeable singers living, or able to get together, in one place. In addition, a number of government policies—such as the closure of bilingual programs in Northern Territory schools and an increased focus on mainstream employment under the Northern Territory National Emergency Response Act (2007)—have had the possibly unintended effect of encouraging people to abandon traditional practices.

Implications for Sustainability

Despite extensive social changes in the ways and means by which ceremonies occur, there is remarkably little cross-cultural influence on the actual music, dance, and visual designs used in ceremony, which are consciously preserved and revered as originating in ancestral precedent. Shared conventions in music, poetics, dance, body decoration, and song subjects allow each repertory to highlight the Dreaming stories and places that are specific to that clan's identity. This traditional use has extended in the last 40 years to legal contexts where performance of *yawulyu/awelye* has been accepted as demonstrating native title to land. Significant threats to sustainability of *yawulyu/awelye* today stem from loss of access to the traditional knowledge that lies at the heart of *yawulyu/awelye* (through disruption of traditional languages) and loss of access to the country to which songs relate, as well as from a public climate of neglect or even disrespect of traditional culture.

INFRASTRUCTURE AND REGULATIONS

Yawulyu/awelye ceremonies have developed a remarkably flexible and resilient performance practice requiring little material infrastructure, but are heavily dependent on human infrastructure (knowledgeable elders and keen learners) and the resources to bring the right people together and support them during performance.

Yawulyu/awelye is a sung genre and does not normally employ musical instruments (though wooden clapsticks manufactured from readily available woods such as mulga are sometimes used for percussion alongside body percussion such as handclapping and lap slapping). Clapsticks are sometimes made for sale to tourists. Materials for body painting (e.g., ochres) and decoration (e.g., feathers, cloth), as well as ritual paraphernalia such as *kuturu* (digging sticks, decorated and used to mark the ceremonial ground), were traditionally sourced from known sites on country and carefully looked after by senior owners (male relatives are sometimes involved in the manufacture of wooden objects). These days there is some use of modern materials such as acrylic paints instead of ochres or cardboard in place of bark, but generally traditional materials are preferred if available.

Because *yawulyu/awelye* performance (though not necessarily the audience) is restricted to women, the preferred location for performances is generally in a private location, preferably out bush, on country (within the estate of the relevant land-owning group). Dancing requires an open space, usually selected to have a windbreak provided by rocks or trees. Such bush trips require access to four-wheel-drive vehicles, firewood, food, and camping supplies.

The fundamental regulatory framework for *yawulyu/awelye* is Dreaming law (*jukurrpa* or *altjerre*), which established the precedents for human behavior, including ceremony, and which continues as the primary point of reference for ongoing replenishment of the practice through dreaming of new songs, dances, and stories and protection of the rights of the owners to display and make decisions about their *yawulyu/awelye*. Artists' rights for published materials are covered under Australian copyright legislation, which now includes moral rights, as well as mechanical and authors' copyrights. The Australia Council for the Arts has published a series of useful recommendations regarding copyright protection for traditional music (Australia Council for the Arts, 2008). The Australian Institute of Aboriginal and Torres Strait Islander Studies also covers relevant questions in their *Guidelines for Ethical Research in Australian Indigenous Studies* (Australian Institute of Aboriginal and Torres Strait Islander Studies, 2011), which provides an excellent framework to guide researchers and Indigenous communities in setting up projects that enable ethical and effective research participation by tradition holders.

The costs involved with *yawulyu/awelye* performances principally concern the cost and logistics of bringing the necessary people together and feeding and housing them through the performance. Traditionally, some women's ceremonies circulated as part of regional exchange networks, and passing on of a ceremony from one group to another was expected to be paid for in blankets and other goods (Berndt, 1950; Ellis, 1992a; Poirier, 1992). Today, costs may be covered either informally (e.g., through co-opting researchers and relevant bodies such as the land council, health center, or language center) or formally through grant applications such as those supporting Indigenous festivals in the region (Yeperenye,

DanceSite, Mbantua—see further later). *Yawulyu/awelye* performances may also be commissioned by government or commercial bodies for public events—such as art gallery openings, book launches, or the opening of new buildings—in which case performance fees are expected to be paid. Various short-lived and constantly changing Australian government schemes for supporting Indigenous culture (currently the Indigenous Languages and Arts Projects stream) have supported some groups in recent years, but the overall government budget available for support of Indigenous arts (or indeed, the arts in general) is diminishing.

Implications for Sustainability

Human and transport infrastructure are the main requirements for sustaining *yawulyu/awelye*. Material infrastructure surrounding *yawulyu/awelye* is minimal, and traditional regimes of knowledge management in combination with copyright protection and ethical guidelines developed by Australian government bodies provide adequate legal protection. Travel, food, and shelter are required to bring the right people together for performances and learning opportunities out bush and to provide access to traditional sites providing materials for ceremonial objects and body painting. Occasions for performance (and hence teaching and learning) are supported in an ad hoc way by a variety of government and commercial funding sources, but such funding is increasingly under threat from changing government policies.

MEDIA AND THE MUSIC INDUSTRY

Yawulyu/awelye is not a commercial music genre and thus has only an incidental presence in the broadcast media and little to no relevance to the music industry. The main occasions for appearance of *yawulyu/awelye* in the mainstream media concern incorporation of *yawulyu/awelye* into public events such as festivals, art openings, and other public events (see Figure 5.3). Usually there is little or no attempt to explain the significance for any outsiders, because traditionally *yawulyu/awelye* does not involve a passive audience. For today's mainstream audiences, *yawulyu/awelye* performances become iconic, marking the respect of the commissioning group for Aboriginal culture in general. Such staging of public events may nevertheless enhance the maintenance of the tradition through widening the opportunities for performance-based learning. Furthermore, it is likely that by increasing the visibility of the tradition, public displays and consequent broader public awareness assist in persuading supporting and funding bodies of the need to keep the tradition viable.

FIGURE 5.3 Alyawarr women performing their *awely* from Antarrengeny at the opening of the Central Land Council Building in Alice Springs, June 2009. Singers seated (left to right): Dorothy Pwerl Jones, Nora Kemarr Moore, Rosie Kngwarrey, Georgina Kngwarrey, Lilly Kemarr Morton, Katie Kemarr, Kathleen Kemarr, Betty Kemarr, Lucy Pwerl Dobbs, Doris Pwerl. Dancers (left to right): Mary Kemarr, Linda Pwerl Dobbs, Lena Ngal Skinner, Angeline Petyarr.

Photo: © Central Land Council, 2009, reproduced from *Antarrengeny Awely. Alyawarr Women's Songs from Antarrengeny*. Used with permission.

In some cases, documentations of *yawulyu/awelye* for the purposes of teaching and learning have been published, mostly without commercial distribution and marketing (Harrison, O'Shannessy, & Turpin, 2011; Laughren, Turpin, Morton, & Willowra Community, 2010; Turpin & Ross, 2004, 2013; Watts, Campbell, & Turpin, 2009). In 2000, the Papulu Apparr-kari Language and Culture Center in Tennant Creek facilitated the publication of a CD, *Yawulyu mungamunga* (Papulu Apparr-kari Aboriginal Language and Culture Centre & Barwick, 2000), in a release timed to coincide with the Sydney Olympic Games (see also Barwick, 2005). One reason the publication was supported by the Warumungu women elders (some of whom also participated in the Olympic Games' opening ceremony) was to raise the prestige of *yawulyu* among younger generations by demonstrating that it was valued in the commercial music market.

Some *yawulyu/awelye* recordings have also been published by ethnomusicologists in academic contexts: *yawulyu/awelye* tracks appear in published recording anthologies (A. M. Moyle, 1992), as well as in recordings published with books, such as Richard Moyle's *Alyawarra music* (R. M. Moyle, 1986). Copies of these recordings circulate in the relevant communities and are also used in teaching and learning.

Implications for Sustainability

The sustainability of *yawulyu/awelye* is only incidentally affected by its occasional public emergence in performances and publications. When ceremonies appear in events open to the general public (such as arts festivals), performers are mainly interested in educating their own future tradition holders, while commissioning bodies often include the performances as indicators of a general respect for Indigenous culture without any real interest in their significance. Nevertheless, demand for public performances of *yawulyu/awelye* contributes to the frequency of otherwise rare occasions for learning through performance, and publications may raise the prestige of the genre and involvement of media-savvy younger generations. Raising the public profile of *yawulyu/awelye* through such means may also assist in persuading external funding bodies of the value of continuing to support the tradition.

ISSUES AND INITIATIVES FOR SUSTAINABILITY

The question of the overall vitality of *yawulyu/awelye* is much on the minds of present-day tradition holders, as it has indeed been for past generations. Catherine Ellis, who worked with Aboriginal singers from the 1960s to the 1990s, was deeply concerned with the question of how to assist Aboriginal people in maintaining their traditional ceremonies. In reflecting on her fieldwork, she saw the main question for sustainability as

> whether the means were available to these performers to preserve a living tradition that, although differing from their old one, was comparable to it in terms of the processes of creating, of controlling the world through song, and of stating identity through performance. How can they go on performing creatively while adapting their traditions to the circumstances in which they now live? This is a difficult transition, which may require some outside assistance, but it is not an impossibility. (Ellis, 1992a, p. 160)

The key issues around sustainability of *yawulyu/awelye* thus relate to support for the intergenerational transmission of the ceremonies. The right people need to be educated and trained to take charge of the future of their own *yawulyu/awelye* tradition. As identified in this chapter, some of the major factors affecting this situation concern much broader cultural questions and include the following:

- Knowledge of country, Dreamings, and language
- The ability to bring together the right people to perform, teach, and learn

- The ability to access traditional country
- Understanding of the historical importance of *yawulyu/awelye* in securing and demonstrating rights to land
- Empowering younger generations to apply their own creativity and cultural understandings in adapting the *yawulyu/awelye* tradition to the modern world

While family-based learning continues, there are diminishing traditional opportunities to perform *yawulyu/awelye*, although some new avenues are emerging. Older people are anxious about the social consequences of not handing on *yawulyu/awelye* and are conscious of difficulties in gaining access to resources and time to allow learning to take place on country in the old way. Tradition holders have embraced many different opportunities for supporting intergenerational transmission of knowledge through projects that inspire people to learn, provide performance opportunities, and produce resources for learning. Projects to document *yawulyu/awelye* have been one important avenue.

Younger people desire written and recorded documentation of *yawulyu/awelye*, especially so that they can learn the difficult song words, which they find hard to pick up in the infrequent performances that take place these days. This is partly due to the difficulty of the song language itself and partly due to younger people's relative lack of experience of the traditional knowledge and lifestyles referred to in songs (such as places, hunting techniques, and ecological knowledge). M. Nampijinpa commented:

> I've wanted everything to be recorded on tape or maybe write a book or something, DVD. We've got history stories, but we need to know Dreamtime stories and traditional songs. We don't know about traditional songs. These are the ones that need to be recorded, traditional songs. (M. Nampijinpa, interview, July 18, 2010)

In addition to empowering younger people to create their own records of *yawulyu-awelye* for later private study, documentation sessions themselves can create an enjoyable social environment for both young and older people to interact around their cultural heritage. Ellis reports that documenting women's songs in northern South Australia resulted in Aboriginal women there reviving ceremonies that had not been performed for years: "My requests for songs stimulated an interest in them, so traditions were again passed from one group to another, and children began to be taught long-neglected songs" (Ellis, 1992a, p. 156).

While the first users of recording technology for documenting traditional songs may have been outsiders, today it is commonly community members who record their own songs, which are then used for learning, enjoyment, health purposes, providing backup in performances, and so on. The ready availability of digital audiovisual devices for recording songs enables almost immediate access to listening and other uses. Recently, more and more younger Indigenous people are remixing song recordings in multimedia works (a good example is the works created in Yirrkala through the Mulka project; Kral, 2012).

Although some song documentation projects have previously been funded by various Australian government funding schemes to assist Aboriginal people in research and teaching projects on Aboriginal languages (e.g., Turpin & Ross, 2013), the current "Indigenous Languages and Arts" scheme does not specifically include song within its scope. Tying Indigenous traineeships to similar projects has proved successful in the past. In the 1980s, the Aboriginal Employment Development policy gave traineeships to Indigenous people across the media in both public and private sectors, leading to the creation of the Indigenous Unit at the national television broadcasters SBS and ABC, as well as to Aboriginal people employed in remote Indigenous media centers filming many traditional songs (Rachel Perkins, interview, June 25, 2010).

Increased opportunities for intergenerational learning through performance have been supported through the development of various Indigenous-led festivals in which many different Aboriginal groups participate. The emphasis on participation in such events is more conducive to supporting traditional learning modes than staged performances for passive predominantly non-Indigenous audiences in non-Indigenous art festivals.

For example, the Yeperenye festival held in Alice Springs in 2001 was possibly the largest-ever national event of Indigenous ceremonies and the biggest performance of traditional music in Alice Springs for 100 years (it also included many other arts). Such events can reassure younger Aboriginal people that traditional music is culturally acceptable and instill them with pride in their culture. Yeperenye has been cited by some as having triggered their own desire to learn *yawulyu/awelye* (Turpin, 2011, pp. 18–19). Festival co-organizer and Arrernte filmmaker Rachel Perkins believes that Indigenous traditional performance needs to be at the center of a festival, not just an added element:

> I think you have to put Indigenous stuff at the center and build all your processes and protocols and outcomes around that. At Yeperenye ... we had the right groups represented and consulted with them properly. (interview, June 25, 2010)

Perkins describes the first day of the Yeperenye festival:

When [Aboriginal] people realized what was going to happen, that everyone was going to dance and all these people were going to watch, ... people became very proud and competitive. People started forming dance
groups on the day, because I think they saw a demonstration of culture
and pride, and the audience were really appreciative of it. (interview,
June 25, 2010)

Describing the state-by-state showcase of ceremonies at Yeperenye, Rachel
Perkins recalls the Tasmanian representatives coming on stage to say: "We don't
have any [songs and] dances and that's because of our history; and we are not
going to make them up, but we are proud to be here." At that moment she understood how important these things are in fostering the solidarity among Aboriginal
people that such a festival enables (interview, June 25, 2010).

Although calls from Aboriginal people to make Yeperenye a regular event were
ultimately unsuccessful in attracting the necessary funding and support, the
momentum the festival spurred no doubt inspired later events. A similar but
much smaller festival, the Mbantua festival, was co-convened by Perkins and co-
organizer Nigel Jamieson in Alice Springs in October 2013. Other festivals in the
region influenced by Yeperenye at which *yawulyu/awelye* was performed include
DanceSite (Tennant Creek, 2007–2012), Mobfest (Ti-Tree, 2008–2010), and
Milpirri (Lajamanu, 2006–). It is worth noting that such initiatives require considerable funding, which is increasingly difficult to secure.

Because of the popularity of Alice Springs with tourists, performing regularly
for tourists has been an opportunity for Arrernte people, but one they have
never embraced (Rachel Perkins, interview, June 25, 2010). Perhaps Arrernte
people think the economic benefits are too small or that the logistics of getting a
performance group together are too great, or perhaps the main focus of tradition
holders lies in educating their own future tradition holders rather than the general public. Similarly, at the Nyinkka Nyunyu Art and Culture Centre in Tennant
Creek, which opened in 2002, while some Warumungu people supported the idea
of performing for tourists, on the whole they did not find the enterprise worthwhile. The issues involved in developing the Nyinkka Nyunnyu Tennant Creek
Culture Centre are discussed in detail by Christen (2007), who states: "Cultural
centers are ... sites of local and national desires for material and cultural success
and historical redress" (p. 118). Despite the potential of a regional or national
culture center to offer opportunities for showcasing songs, instilling cultural
pride, and providing economic opportunities, there is no culture center in Alice

Springs; and although there have been discussions among Indigenous people about establishing one, for a variety of economic and political reasons nothing as yet has got off the ground.

Intergenerational transmission of song knowledge on country has been enabled by a number of projects. Women's Law and Culture meetings, held almost annually in various locations since the 1980s with support from the Ngaanyatjarra Pitjantjatjara Yankunytjatjara Women's Council and the Central Land Council, have provided a valuable performance opportunity for women and inspired a number of younger people to learn their ceremonies (Turpin, 2011, p. 18). Although some note that there has been deterioration in the state of ceremonies over this time, it is not possible to identify the exact nature of any change because at the performers' wishes the most of the meetings are not recorded.

Since 2007, Dancesite Artback NT has run an Indigenous traditional dance program, which involves taking Aboriginal people back out on country to learn the songs, experience the sites, and learn the stories. In 2003, the Arrernte Healing Centre Akeyularre was established in Alice Springs to promote and support traditional healing in the Arrernte region (Abbott, 2004). A holistic learning program for traditional songs and ceremonies through organized trips on country is a major focus, which has empowered new generations of performers to perform for outside audiences at public events such as the DanceSite festival (A. A. Pwerrerle, interview, March 16, 2010).

There is little opportunity to support the intergenerational transmission of learning within a formal school context. Reasons include lack of funding to pay elders to teach, elders being uncomfortable or unfamiliar with the school environment, lack of logistical support to take learning on country, and lack of knowledge on the part of many non-Indigenous teachers about Indigenous teaching processes and how they can fit in with the education system outcomes, including assessment of student learning.

Nevertheless, some schools have incorporated the teaching and learning of traditional songs in their programs. At Tennant Creek, Warumungu cultural worker Narrurlu recounted an occasion when *yawulyu mungamunga* songs were integrated into a high school performance of Shakespeare's *Romeo and Juliet*:

When I was working at the high school we used one part of it [*yawulyu mungamunga*] for that *Romeo and Juliet*, because they were lovers. We spoke to that old Nappanangka, [to ask] which one we're not allowed to use, so she told us which number to use. She said, "Nope, don't use this one, don't use that one, use this one!" (Narrurlu, interview, July 16, 2010)

In 2008, the Northern Territory (NT) government put an end to bilingual education that operated in some NT schools where English was not a first language, and insisted that the first 4 hours of all NT schools must consist of English only. At the same time, schools in New South Wales and Victoria were beginning to implement Aboriginal language programs and some sought permission to use NT language materials in their schools. Indigenous language teachers may have felt angered at requests to teach other children their language while the right for their own children to learn their language was being denied. In such a climate, it would not be conducive to intergenerational learning for a non-Indigenous person to have access to formalized learning of Indigenous traditions when Indigenous people could not. Any initiatives to teach songs should involve pathways for younger Aboriginal owners to access learning and ultimately teaching their traditions.

In 1992, Catherine Ellis (1992a) stated:

One of the most important things we can do . . . is to advise funding authorities of the importance of appointing traditional performers as the teachers of their own tradition to outsiders. In Australia in particular, there is enough money and person-power to appoint traditional performers [to teach] to every region of Australia, knowing that in doing so we are encouraging a strong sense of identity in the traditional performance (of whatever type) and are thereby encouraging the preservation of a living contemporary tradition. (p. 162)

CASM, established by Ellis at the University of Adelaide in the 1970s, was able to employ Pitjantjatjara elders as performance lecturers in an era of federal policies that recognized the importance of Aboriginal culture (e.g., NT Land Rights Act, bilingual education). In contrast, various current NT and Australian government policies seem to challenge the value of Indigenous culture. While CASM continues, at the time of writing (2015), Ellis's dream of an Australia-wide network of traditional performers/teachers is very far from being realized, and it is difficult to conceive of the current Australian government agreeing with her assessment of the availability of funding for such a program. Nor have recent years seen a large increase in the pool of qualified Indigenous people interested in participating in such teaching to outsiders, though the numbers are growing. Sustained and coordinated efforts will be required to support education and training of upcoming generations of Aboriginal people in learning and practicing their own traditions before they can be expected to interpret them to outsiders.

Motivating younger people to take up their *yawulyu/awelye*, providing the source materials for learning in situations where performance traditions are under threat, and finding a place for ongoing creativity in expression of *yawulyu/awelye* knowledge were key issues addressed in an interview held on June 25, 2010, with Arrernte filmmaker Rachel Perkins.

To redress the widespread lack of knowledge of how traditional knowledge and practices have assisted Aboriginal people in negotiations relating to their land and culture, Perkins suggested a documentary film or book showcasing the Aboriginal people and the songs they sang in various legal, political, and intercultural settings and the beneficial outcomes they brought.

Intergenerational learning could be supported in a more systematic way through a program to provide Indigenous people access to digital recording equipment and remuneration to record their relatives' songs, with the digital records created being housed in national collections to provide an ongoing resource for future generations. Similar ideas have been developed by the National Recording Project for Indigenous Performance, which advocates a grant program to nominated Indigenous organizations that are best placed to identify the areas of greatest need (Marett et al., 2006; National Recording Project for Indigenous Performance in Australia, 2011, pp. 6–7).

In some cases, Aboriginal people have revived ceremonies from early records, but for many there are simply no records. As an Indigenous person with experience in areas where there has been much cultural loss, Perkins recognizes the urgency to work with singers now: "We've got to engage with these precious living things [songs] now somehow; otherwise they will be gone in 100 years like they are in New South Wales, Victoria, and Tasmania" (interview, June 25, 2010). In 2015 Perkins initiated the Arrernte Women's Project for this purpose (Perkins, 2016).

Perkins also advocates for the ongoing renewal of *yawulyu-awelye* knowledge through regular festivals, where Indigenous performers from different areas can also participate as active audiences supporting other traditions.

CONCLUSION

Although sustaining *yawulyu/awelye* continues to encounter significant challenges, the high esteem in which the genre is held by so many practitioners and learners across a large area gives reason for some optimism. The central issue is enabling support and motivation for intergenerational transmission of the ceremonies, with the right people being trained to take charge of the future of their own tradition, including interpreting it to outsiders. Past and current initiatives that have met with success include song documentation and revitalization programs (including mobilizing younger people to participate in documentation), commissioning of performances for festivals, support for private performance events such as Women's Law and Culture meetings, trips to country facilitated by arts and health organizations, and employing performers to teach about *yawulyu/awelye* in various education projects. For various reasons, other potential points of focus for teaching and learning activities, such as cultural centers and tourism, have not provided an appropriate context. Future or suggested initiatives supported by some of our interviewees include a government-supported digital recording and archiving program for Indigenous songs, research projects to document the songs in existing archives and collections and make them available to learners, regular performance festivals, and the creation of books and films to educate various audiences about the significance of *yawulyu/awelye*.

ACKNOWLEDGMENTS

Thank you to all the practitioners of *yawulyu/awelye* at Willowra, Tennant Creek, Alekarenge, Ti-Tree, Arnerre, and Alice Springs who shared their ideas and concerns with us. Interviewees are referred to using their skin name, a marker of social identity commonly used in place of personal names. The spelling of skin names follows the standard orthography of their primary language. We are also grateful for input from Rachel Perkins (director, Blackfella Films), Mary Laughren (University of Queensland), and our colleagues listed in the advisory committee. We would particularly like to acknowledge April Campbell, the Central Land Council, and Margaret Carew (Batchelor College, Alice Springs) for allowing us to use their photographs and illustrations. Advisory committee (National Recording Project for Indigenous Performance in Australia): Codirectors: Payi Linda Ford (Charles Darwin University), Aaron Corn (Australian National University); Steering Committee Cochairs: David Manmurulu (Warruwi Community), Allan Marett (University of Sydney); Members: Marcia Langton (University of Melbourne), the late Joe Neparrnga Gumbula (University of Sydney), Wanta Patrick Jampijinpa (Lajamanu Community), Wukun Wanambi (Mulka Centre), Cathy Hilder (Northern Territory Library), Grace Koch (Australian Institute of Aboriginal and Torres Strait Islander Studies, deputy for Director Russ Taylor), Sally Treloyn (University of Melbourne), Kevin Bradley (National Library of Australia), Stephen Wild (Australian National University).

REFERENCES

Abbott, K. (2004). Return to the heart. *Aboriginal and Islander Health Worker Journal, 28*(2), 4–5.

Australia Council for the Arts. (2008). *Music: Protocols for producing Australian Indigenous music.* Sydney, Australia: Australia Council for the Arts.

Australian Institute of Aboriginal and Torres Strait Islander Studies. (2011). *Guidelines for ethical research in Australian Indigenous studies.* Retrieved from http://www.aiatsis.gov.au/research/docs/ethics.pdf

Barwick, L. (2000). Song as an Indigenous art. In M. Neale & S. Kleinert (Eds.), *Oxford companion to Aboriginal art and culture* (pp. 328–335). Melbourne, Australia: Oxford University Press.

Barwick, L. (2005). Performance, aesthetics, experience: Thoughts on Yawulyu mungamunga songs. In E. Mackinlay, S. Owens, & D. Collins (Eds.), *Aesthetics and experience in music performance* (pp. 1–18). Amersham, UK: Cambridge Scholars Press.

Barwick, L., Laughren, M., & Turpin, M. (2013). Sustaining women's yawulyu/awelye: Some practitioners' and learners' perspectives. *Musicology Australia, 35*(2), 191–220.

Bell, D. (1993). *Daughters of the dreaming* (2nd ed.). Sydney, Australia: Allen & Unwin.

Berndt, C. H. (1950). *Women's changing ceremonies in northern Australia.* Paris, France: L'Homme, Hermann et Cie.

Carter, P. (1996). *The lie of the land.* London, UK: Faber & Faber.

Christen, K. (2007). Following the Nyinkka: Relations of respect and obligations to act in the collaborative work of Aboriginal Cultural Centers. *Museum Anthropology, 30*(2), 101–124.

Dussart, F. (2000). *The politics of ritual in an Aboriginal settlement: Kinship, gender, and the currency of knowledge.* Washington, DC, and London, UK: Smithsonian Institution Press.

Dussart, F. (2004). Shown but not shared, presented but not proffered: Redefining ritual identity among Warlpiri ritual performers, 1990-2000. *Australian Journal of Anthropology, 15*(3), 253–266.

Ellis, C. (1970). The role of the ethnomusicologist in the study of Andagarinja women's ceremonies. *Miscellanea Musicologica, 5,* 76–208.

Ellis, C. (1985). *Aboriginal music: Education for living.* St. Lucia, Australia: University of Queensland Press.

Ellis, C. (1992a). Living preservation: Problems of cultural exchange with central Australian traditional performers. In A. M. Moyle (Ed.), *Music and dance in Aboriginal Australia and the South Pacific: The effects of documentation on the living tradition* (pp. 155–162). Sydney, Australia: Oceania Publications.

Ellis, C. (Ed.). (1992b). Power-laden Aboriginal songs: Who should control the research? [Special issue]. *World of Music, 36*(1).

Ellis, C., & Barwick, L. (1989). Time consciousness of Indigenous Australians. In G. F. Messner (Ed.), *Introduction to the performing arts* (pp. 1–27). Geelong, Australia: Deakin University.

Ellis, C., Ellis, A. M., Tur, M., & McCardell, A. (1978). Classification of sounds in Pitjantjatjara-speaking areas. In L. Hiatt (Ed.), *Australian Aboriginal concepts* (pp. 68–80). Canberra, Australia: Australian Institute of Aboriginal Studies.

Glowczewski, B. (1991). *Du rêve à la loi chez les aborigènes: Mythes, rites et organisation sociale en Australie.* Paris, France: Presses Universitaires Françaises.

Glowczewski, B. (1999). Dynamic cosmologies and Aboriginal heritage. *Anthropology Today, 15,* 3–9.

Hale, K. L. (1984). Remarks on creativity in Aboriginal verse. In J. C. Kassler & J. Stubington (Eds.), *Problems and solutions: Occasional essays in musicology presented to Alice M. Moyle* (pp. 254–262). Sydney, Australia: Hale & Iremonger.

Harris, J. W. (1990). *One blood: 200 years of Aboriginal encounter with Christianity. A story of hope.* Sydney, Australia: Albatross Books.

Harrison, A., O'Shannessy, C., & Turpin, M. (Eds.). (2011). *Jaru-kurlu: Traditional stories and songs by senior Warlpiri women from Wirliyajarrayi (Willowra), Yurntumu (Yuendumu), Lajamanu & Nyirrpi communities with accompanying audio CD.* Victoria, Canada: Trafford Publishing.

Koch, G. (1994). Australian Aboriginal music and the land. *Annuario degli Archivi di Etnomusicologia dell'Accademia Nazionale di Santa Cecilia, II-1994,* 109–121.

Koch, G. (1997). Songs, land rights, and archives in Australia. *Cultural Survival Quarterly, 20*(4), 38–41.

Koch, G. (2004). Voices of the past speaking to the future: Audiovisual documents and proof of native title in Australia. *International Association of Sound Archives Journal, 22,* 20–31.

Koch, G. (2013). *We have the song, so we have the land: Song and ceremony as proof of ownership in Aboriginal and Torres Strait Islander land claims.* Canberra, Australia: AIATSIS Research Publications.

Kral, I. (2012). *Talk, text and technology: Literacy and social practice in a remote Indigenous community.* Bristol, UK: Multilingual Matters.

Laughren, M., Turpin, M., Morton, H. N., & Willowra Community (Writers). (2010). *Yawulyu Wirliyajarrayi-wardingkiki: Ngatijirri, ngapa [Willowra songlines: Budgerigar and rain].* (Willowra Community, Producer). Willowra, Australia: Willowra Community.

Marett, A., Yunupiŋu, M., Langton, M., Gumbula, N., Barwick, L., & Corn, A. (2006). The National Recording Project for Indigenous Performance in Australia: Year one in review. *Backing Our Creativity: The National Education and the Arts Symposium,* 12–14 September 2005 (pp. 84–90). Surry Hills, Australia: Australia Council for the Arts.

Moyle, A. M. (1992 [1977]). *Australia: Aboriginal Music/Australia: Musique Aborigene. UNESCO collection: Music and musicians of the world/Musiques et Musiciens du Monde* [audio compact disc]. Ivry-sur-Seine, France: AUVIDIS-UNESCO-IICMSD D8040.

Moyle, R. M. (1986). *Alyawarra music: Songs and society in a Central Australian community.* Canberra, Australia: Australian Institute of Aboriginal Studies.

Moyle, R. M. (1997). *Balgo: The musical life of a desert community.* Nedlands, Australia: Callaway International Resource Centre for Music Education.

Myers, F. R. (1986). *Pintupi country, Pintupi self.* Canberra, Australia: Australian Institute of Aboriginal Studies.

National Recording Project for Indigenous Performance in Australia. (2011). *Submission in response to the National Cultural Policy discussion paper (Australian Government Department of Regional Australia, Local Government, Arts and Sport).* Retrieved from http://culture.arts. gov.au/sites/default/files/submissions/Submission 333_Redacted.pdf

Papulu Apparr-kari Aboriginal Language and Culture Centre, & Barwick, L. (2000). *Yawulyu mungamunga: Dreaming songs of Warumungu women, Tennant Creek, Central Australia* [audio compact disc with scholarly booklet]. Sydney, Australia: Festival Records D139686.

Payne, H. (1992). Claiming the rite. *Musicology Australia, 15,* 83–86.

Perkins, R. (2016). Songs to live by: The Arrernte Women's Project. *The Monthly,* July 2016, issue 124, 30–35.

Peterson, N., & Long, J. (1986). *Australian territorial organization: A band perspective/Nicolas Peterson in collaboration with Jeremy Long.* Sydney, Australia: University of Sydney.

Poirier, S. (1992). "Nomadic" rituals: Networks of ritual exchange between women of the Australian Western Desert. *Man, New Series, 27*(4), 757–776.

Strehlow, C. (1915). *Die Aranda—und Loritja-Stämme in Zentral-Australien IV (ii). Das Soziale Leben der Aranda—und Loritja-Stämme.* Frankfurt am Main, Germany: Joseph Baer & Co.

Turpin, M. (2005). *Form and meaning of Akwelye: A Kaytetye women's song series from Central Australia* (PhD thesis). University of Sydney, Sydney, Australia.

Turpin, M. (2007a). Artfully hidden: Text and rhythm in a Central Australian Aboriginal song series. *Musicology Australia, 29*(1), 93–108.

Turpin, M. (2007b). The poetics of central Australian song. *Australian Aboriginal Studies, 2*(1), 100–115.

Turpin, M. (2011). Song-poetry of Central Australia: Sustaining traditions. *Language Documentation and Description, 10*, 15–36.

Turpin, M., & Ross, A. (2004). *Kaytetye picture dictionary.* Alice Springs, Australia: IAD Press.

Turpin, M., & Ross, A. (2013). *Antarrengeny Awely. Alyawarr women's traditional ceremony of Antarrengeny country* [book with embedded audio plus 40 minute film and audio CD]. Darwin, Australia: Batchelor Press.

Watts, L., Campbell, A., & Turpin, M. (2009). *Mer Rrkwer-akert* [2 video discs (49 min)]. Alice Springs, Australia: Charles Darwin University Central Australian Research Network.

Wild, S. A. (1987). Recreating the jukurrpa: Adaptation and innovation of songs and ceremonies in Warlpiri society. In M. Clunies Ross (Ed.), *Songs of Aboriginal Australia* (pp. 97–120). Sydney, Australia: University of Sydney (Oceania Publications).

6

BALINESE GAMELAN

Continual Innovation, Community Engagement, and Links

to Spirituality as Drivers for Sustainability

Peter Dunbar-Hall

BALINESE PERFORMING ARTS exist in an climate of ongoing development. Forms of music and dance—and the corresponding instrumental ensembles—continually evolve. They also decline, and as performers die, repertoires disappear from collective memory. Often what is seen as "traditional" is in fact a relatively new type of ensemble and its repertoire. But the sense of loss causes concern for many musicians (see Ramseyer, 2009), some of whom reclaim traditions of music and dance under threat (e.g., the work of I Wayan Sinti described in Eiseman, 1990).

Gamelan can be translated as "ensemble." Researchers differ on how many types of Balinese gamelan exist. Some state there are about 25, while others claim there are up to 40. Balinese gamelans cover a range of types, each with a qualifying name. There are some regional preponderances: *gamelan jegog* in western Bali, *gamelan selonding* in eastern Bali, and *gamelan gong gede* in central and eastern Bali. These are also used in other parts of the island; it is important not to assume regional exclusivity for any type. The smallest gamelan can have as few as two players (a two-member *gamelan gender wayang*—for accompanying *wayang kulit* [shadow puppet plays]), while a three-member gamelan, called *gamelan rindik*, of two bamboo *rindik* and one *suling* (bamboo flute) is also found. From these small numbers, gamelans increase in size to the largest ensembles, such as *gamelan semar pegulingan* and *gamelan gong gede*, both of which can have more than 30 players. A full *gamelan gong kebyar*, the most common form of gamelan to be seen in Bali, numbers approximately 25 players. Numbers are flexible, and not all instruments of an ensemble need to be used if players are not available.

Types of gamelan reflect three significant aspects of Balinese music: material, function, and tuning. The cases of gamelan instruments are generally made of hard timber, with keys of wood, bamboo, iron, or bronze. Bronze-keyed gamelans are the most usual. Each type of gamelan has a dedicated role. However, in many cases one type of gamelan is used for multiple purposes, and it is not unusual for the repertoire of one type to be adapted for another. This is a mainstay of Balinese music aesthetics, and creators of new pieces of music demonstrate their abilities by referring to various gamelan styles in their *kreasi baru* (new creations) and/or

TABLE 6.1

Basic Gamelan Type-Role Framework

Gamelan Type (Shown by Qualifying Name)	Core Contexts
Angklung	Funerary/cremation rites; temple events
Arja	Accompaniment for *arja* (popular theater)
Batel gender wayang	Accompaniment to *wayang kulit* (shadow puppets), especially with stories from the *Ramayana*
Beleganjur	Processions
Gambang	Religious events
Gambuh	Accompaniment to *gambuh* (dance-dramas)
Gender wayang	Accompaniment for *wayang kulit* (shadow puppets), especially with stories from the *Mahabarata*; life cycle events
Gong kebyar	Originally for *kebyar*-style music; default gamelan for many types of music
Joged	Accompaniment to popular dance genre
Luang	Religious events
Pelegongan	Accompaniment for *legong* dance; nondance pieces in *legong* style
Selonding	Religious events
Semar pegulingan	Court music of precolonial Bali
Semaradana	Contemporary type of gamelan used across various types of Balinese music
Suara	Religious events and tourist performances of *Kecak*

moving sections of pieces of music from one type of gamelan to another. Table 6.1 shows a basic gamelan type-role framework.

Published research on Balinese music and dance has a history dating back to the 1930s. This has been an invaluable foundation for subsequent investigations of art forms and their development, popularity, and decline. The research documents revival projects and their purposes and problems, and is sometimes used by Balinese musicians in revivals of repertoires, types of instruments, and performance aesthetics. There is genuine interest among Balinese musicians in seeing and hearing material from the early/mid-20th century. Sometimes notation of pieces of music made by non-Balinese researchers, especially by Canadian composer Colin McPhee (see McPhee, 1966), are used by Balinese musicians to learn repertoires from the past.

Balinese music uses a complex theoretical system based on differences between tuning systems, and pitch subsets within these. Different types of gamelan use specific tunings and pitch subsets; thus, tuning and pitch subset are linked to different types of music and the roles and meanings ascribed to them. There are two tuning systems: *pelog* (seven tones) and *slendro* (five tones). *Pelog* appears in full on *gamelan luang, gamelan semar pegulingan, gamelan selonding*, and *gamelan semaradana*. Other *pelog* sets use only a pitch subset of *pelog*: *Gamelan gong gede, gamelan gong kebyar*, and *gamelan pelegongan* use a five-tone subset of *pelog*. *Slendro* is the tuning of *gamelan angklung* and *gamelan wayang kulit*, and other gamelan types that incorporate *gender wayang* instruments. Uniquely, *gamelan jegog* uses a four-note subset of *pelog*.

One of the issues that emerged during this research was the care taken by some musicians to ensure that gamelan distinction and tuning reflected past practices. In this way musicians avoid standardization, seen as detrimental to preservation of the complexities of Balinese music and dance as a meaning-bearing system. Alongside this is the use of a new ensemble type called *gamelan semaradana*, which has developed since the 1980s and uses the full seven-tone tuning of *pelog* (see McGraw, 1999/2000; Vitale, 2002). This type of gamelan allows reconstruction and performance of repertoires of the past (such as that of *gamelan semar pegulingan*), but at the loss of recreation of timbre and authenticity of sound that would have been heard from original *semar pegulingan* instruments.

Cultural and Social Positioning

Gamelans in Bali exhibit distinctive traits. The tuning of instruments in pairs, one of which is tuned slightly higher than the other, is one such practice. This practice (see Gold, 2004; McPhee, 1966; Tenzer, 1991, 2000) produces the typical "shimmering" sound of Balinese ensembles, due to the sound waves that are set up by a full ensemble. While a summary explanation of this tuning characteristic gives the impression of a simple element of Balinese music practice, distinctions between types of gamelan can be made through measurement of the beats per second produced by playing two instruments of a higher/lower tuned pair, and the rapidity of beats per second across a whole gamelan.

This use of partner instruments reflects the Balinese religious concept *Rhwa Bhineda* (complementary opposites), which defines the world as a system of opposites that in tandem produce the balance required for life to progress successfully. The presence of balanced opposites pervades much of Balinese life, and also many elements of Balinese performing arts. For example, life in general is perceived in Balinese Hindu cosmology as the coexistence of *sekala* (the seen) and *niskala* (the unseen; Eiseman, 1990). Some instruments in ensembles are similarly named to reflect *Rhwa Bineda*, for example, the pair of largest gongs is *gong wadon* (female— largest and lowest) and *gong lanang* (male—slightly smaller and therefore higher).

Balinese gamelan music is used across all social functions. Core uses of each type of gamelan (e.g., *gamelan gender wayang* to accompany *wayang kulit* [shadow puppet theater]) should not be seen as exclusive. Their roles in religious activities (temple events, life cycle celebrations) and village requirements are central to their ongoing uses. Tourism provides a strong outlet for gamelan and dance activity, and the importance of the tourist industry in this regard is well documented (Hatch & Hatch, 2005; Picard, 1990, 1996; Rubinstein & Connor, 1999; Vickers, 1989; Vickers, Putra, & Ford, 2000).

Balinese gamelan music covers many genres. There are purely instrumental pieces of music, some for religious events, and some for secular. Much music accompanies dance, and dance and its music are inseparable in Balinese performing arts aesthetics. Dances are of many types; many are descriptive (e.g., of animals), some depict aspects of Balinese life, and some are abstract. In addition to communal dancing at religious events, there are choreographed dances, including group dances depicting aspects of daily life (e.g., fishing, weaving, bull racing— many of these were created in the 1950s and 1960s at the request of Indonesian President Sukarno, who espoused a social-realism arts ethic). Some solo dances, such as Baris Tunggal (a stylized male warrior dance), have been derived from communal dance genres and made into exhibition dances, which are the subject of strongly contested competitions. There are also many types of *topeng* (mask) dances. Dances are used in religious contexts, and there is a Balinese system for contextualizing music and dance across settings from the purely secular to the highly religious, so that meanings and implications of performances change depending on the event and location (Bandem & deBoer, 1995; Racki, 1998). Music and dance are also strongly linked to trance states and contact with the spirit world (Rubin & Sedana, 2007; Sudyatmaka, 2000).

Formal Features

Gamelan music is highly structured texturally. Generally the highest parts move at the fastest rate, while lower parts move more slowly. This links pitch to speed of performance technique, creating a heterophonic texture. Music is punctuated by gong patterns (which exist in formulas with stylistic implications); in gamelan with drums, the music is driven by drumming.

The highest, most decorative line of gamelan texture uses a compositional technique known as *kotekan*—a combination of two independent parts to produce a third, holistic line of music (McPhee, 1966; Tenzer, 1991, 2000; Vitale, 1990). This emphasizes the *Rhwa Bineda* concept of complementary pairs. The presence of the tuned-apart instruments is linked to this technique, so that often one *kotekan* part, *polos*, is played on the *pengumbang* (lower) instruments, while its complementary part, *sangsih*, is played on the *pengisep* (higher) instruments. However, this practice is not uniform, and some groups mix *pengumbang* and *pengisep* within *polos* and *sangsih*: These different ways of assigning *pengumbang* and *pengisep* produce subtle acoustic distinctions between ensembles. This is indicative of the diverse application of theoretical and practical ideas among Balinese musicians, where terminology is not standard, and names of pieces of music and instruments need not be consistent. Standardization is actively discouraged and each gamelan group has its own style of playing, as well as versions of pieces of music that are recognized (and respected) by other players.

Performances in their Balinese uses are as long as they need to be. In temple contexts, music is played for as long as is necessary. In many examples of repertoires used for this, pieces include repeated sections to be played as many times as needed. Performances can take place at whatever time is required, and in temple events, this can be around midnight or starting from midnight and continuing for as long as appropriate. It is common for multiple forms of music to be performed at the same time in different locations within a temple during religious events; this contributes to a Balinese aesthetic of *ramai* (busyness) that will please visiting deities. For example, a *gamelan gong gede* style piece could be performed at one end of a temple complex while a performance of *wayang kulit* is given within hearing distance at the other end.

The lengths of tourist performances are highly controlled, mostly to between an hour and an hour and a half. Such performances move quickly through a range of styles of Balinese music; canonic repertoire is to be expected, although some groups introduce new pieces in contemporary styles of Balinese music. Canonic performance exemplifies the problem of standardization that is now appearing in some Balinese gamelan practice. To show a range of dance styles with their own types of gamelan accompaniment, it would be necessary to use different sets of instruments. This is impossible, so one set of instruments is used throughout. Such a "one size fits all" style is common in many cases, but this is not seen as wrong or inappropriate. There are groups that make sure that dance and gamelan repertoire match the appropriate gamelan type. Thus, different ideologies of performance coexist. The practice of moving repertoires from one type of gamelan to another is an acceptable stylistic practice, so use of one type of ensemble for the music of another need not always be seen as detrimental. Often movement of a piece of music from its original gamelan type to that of another involves restylization of the piece so that it becomes a new version of the piece in its own right. There does not seem to be a problem with this new version becoming "the piece," although older performers and audience members may note that it is not the "real" piece as they knew it. Figure 6.1 shows a typical street sign advertising a performance for tourists.

Tourist performances can involve editing of long pieces into shortened versions of them. The same happens for *wayang kulit* performances, which for Balinese audiences can last 3 to 4 hours, but for tourists last approximately 1 hour. Editing of pieces of music also relates to the size of ensembles. So in addition to the

FIGURE 6.1 Street sign advertising a *wayang kulit* performance for tourists, Pengosekan. Photo: Peter Dunbar-Hall, 2011.

number of ensembles decreasing, ensembles may be reduced in size for tourist performances. This is often at the insistence of hotel/restaurant managers keen on cutting costs. These practices are not uniform, and there are many managers keen to represent Balinese music and dance as authentically as possible, as well as groups who refuse to participate in tourist performances due to their belief that such practices undermine Balinese performing arts. This is an area of contested ideologies and varying practices; it is difficult to make definitive statements, apart from noting that these practices exist and are debated by arts practitioners.

Composition of new music and dance is an ongoing and vibrant component of Balinese performing arts. Creation of new pieces and dances are requirements of final-year students at Institut Seni Indonesia (ISI—tertiary-level college for the performing arts; Institut Seni Indonesia, 2006); the annual Pesta Kesenina Bali (PKB—Bali Arts Festival) requires performing groups to present newly created music and dance alongside older styles. Many musicians are active composers, and recordings of their groups contain selections of new pieces alongside performances of standard repertoire. In addition to composers who work within the traditional sounds of Balinese gamelan music, there is an avant-garde music scene open to all influences (McGraw, 2005). There is also a strong popular music scene with its own "Balinese-ness," often blending instruments and sounds of "tradition" with those of the popular music world, such as can be heard in the recordings of rock guitarist Balawan and his group Batuan Ethnic Fusion.

Summary

Balinese music and dance exist in a context of difference—of ensemble type, tuning systems, roles and uses of ensembles, historically situated popularity/prevalence of repertoires, performance practice, and localized aesthetics. It is accepted that types of music and dance rise to popularity and decline; it is often these types that become the object of revival projects, and these projects imply interest among Balinese musicians and audiences in knowing about, preserving, and valuing past traditions. There is a vibrant creative scene at work, with much activity in the creation of new music and dance and in investigating the possibilities of tunings, instrument development, ways of performing, and cross-cultural influences. The complexities of Balinese theoretical systems in music, especially in the tuning of instruments and manipulation of the acoustic properties of instrumental ensembles that are tuned in pairs, and the intricacies of subsets of pitches extracted from the seven-note *pelog* "scale" add to the levels of complexity faced by researchers of Balinese music. While there is a sense of the "traditional" in performances of Balinese music and dance, there is a symbiotic ethos of a tradition of ongoing change and development. In this way the concept of "tradition," particularly as it refers to cultural sustainability, is difficult to locate and define as static.

SYSTEMS OF LEARNING MUSIC

Teaching and learning of music and dance are strongly entrenched in Bali. This exists, mostly, outside the school system, and is driven by expectations that people will contribute to religious and other sociocultural events through performance. Performances for tourists and participation in festivals and contests also create a need for teaching and learning.

Philosophies of Learning and Teaching

Many Balinese children have their first learning experiences next to older children or adults during rehearsals or performances. *Jegog* musician I Ketut Suwentra, from Jembrana, stated that "I just heard my father.... [He] never taught me" (June 23, 2010). This was also mentioned by I Dewa Putu Berata, from Pengosekan: "My father would be rehearsing and I would be beside him . . . and I'd always accompany my father that way.... At that age I was still young . . . but I was sure I could do it, that I could get all the *kendang* (drum) parts right" (interview, September 21, 2010). There is an expectation that members of the community will participate in religiously contextualized performances of music and dance, so opportunities for children to learn through religious events are normal and regular. Explicit teaching of music and dance is mostly at the village level—teachers set up classes or are employed by a village or a music group. Outcomes of teaching include the ability to perform for religious events, entry in a *lomba* (contest), performance in public events (e.g., festivals), tourist performances (on a paid basis), or production of a recording (McIntosh, 2006).

Teachers are usually performers, or performers who have ceased public appearances. Cokorda Ngurah Suyadnya, from Ubud, who runs a wide range of performing groups, uses many teachers but always tries to utilize local musicians, especially those from his groups. Some teachers have academic qualifications (mostly from ISI), but these are a minority—there is a belief that academic qualifications are not necessary for being a good musician and teacher. One teacher, I Wayan Mandra, from Sanur, commented that "the desire to learn is important . . . so that the pieces of my childhood are not forgotten . . . (and) music from the past can be passed on and people can learn" (interview, February 6, 2011). While this gives the impression of robustness of teaching and learning, some musicians note that various types of Balinese music are not as easily or strongly taught/learned. For example, *dalang* I Made Gender Sukadana commented that the learning of *wayang kulit* was problematic as "just a few people [learn] ... because [this] is not popular now, not strong.... [There is] too much choice, television [and] they can choose music from another country.... Before television and satellite a long time ago *wayang* is very strong.... Now it is changed [and] it can be difficult now to find a *dalang*" (interview, June 20, 2009). Similarly, I Dewa Putu Berata commented that "[young people] might think gamelan is not modern, so by the time they are teenagers they are more interested in pop music.... In villages this is very apparent [and] pop music is even used in *odalan* (religious observance) now" (interview, September 21, 2010). There is no formal system of music teacher training. It is usual for a teacher to be able to play all the parts in a gamelan so that these can be modeled for learners. Teachers are often expected to be the creators of new pieces/dances.

Strongly reified teaching practices exist, which are learned (in what seems a subliminal way) by students through participation, and are subsequently used by them when they become teachers. Successful teaching methods are in place and perpetuated. Tangible aspects of learning and teaching, such as the ability to perform, are balanced by strong ideological systems linking music and dance intangibly to religious and social beliefs and practices, and to a sense of group ethos. I Dewa Putu Berata noted this as an outcome of teaching/learning:

> Teaching gamelan is important not only for teaching how to play a particular piece, but there are many positive aspects that I've experienced, like the feeling of unity and learning how to accept different attitudes, so that different characters, different social and educational backgrounds can all come together as one. (interview, September 21, 2010)

It is essential for Balinese people to contribute to the religious life of their community. Contribution is part of acceptable (and expected) social mores. A basis of Balinese community life is the concept of *gotong royong* (collaborative contribution), through which members of a community contribute personally as part of a group—this can be seen in membership of a gamelan or dance group, where each person performs his or her part for the beneficial effect of the whole group. Intangible aspects of music and dance are also present in ways in which structures and techniques of music composition and dance reflect aspects of Balinese Hindu religious beliefs. In this way, music and dance are one way of symbolically expressing Balinese Hindu belief systems, and music and dance are aspects of an integrated arts aesthetic (Harnish, 1991; Laskewicz, 2003).

There are clear indications that some performers are singled out, seen as talented, and accorded acclaim. *Seniman tua* (senior artists) are highly sought out as teachers and advisors, often in reclamation projects. They are honored pub-licly with awards and are invited to perform at festivals. There are clear family traditions of music and dance, in which several generations will include perform-ers. For example, in Ubud, descendants of Cokorda Mas (who taught Balinese music performance at University of California, Los Angeles for Mantle Hood in the 1960s) include his daughters, one of whom, Cokorda Sri Agung, is a highly sought-out dance teacher, and her two sons, one a dance star, the other a prodi-gious gamelan performer. Among some musicians, the existence of family tradi-tions of music and/or dance performance is made explicit, as I Gede Oka Artha Negara pointed out when referring to his own teaching and performing career in Bali and America: "I just follow my DNA." He expanded on this by explaining that his grandfather, father, and uncles were/are musicians, and that this constitutes what he calls a "musical dynasty" (interview, June 23, 2010).

Learning and Teaching Practices and Approaches

Music and dance are learned through informal (observatory, participatory) and formal (structured lessons) means. Rudimentary notation exists but is rarely used. If used, it only represents the *pokok* (skeletal pitch framework) of pieces of music. Only one musician interviewed, Cokorda Raka Swastika, from Ubud, dis-cussed using basic notation for the melodic material framework of a new piece he was creating; the highly ornamented and complex upper parts of gamelan tex-tures and intricate drumming patterns are not notated. Music is learned by rote and repetition; repertoires are memorized, and in this way music is maintained through individuals. This means that individual people "carry" repertoires and knowledge of their playing styles. In turn, this can mean loss of repertoires and performance methods as musicians die, producing interesting cases of transmis-sion. For example, before his death in 2002, Peliatan musician I Wayan Gandra taught a kebyar-style dance piece, Taruna Gandrung, to members of the group Cudamani. He had learned this piece decades before and had not taught it but kept it "in his head." His teaching of this piece led to other groups learning it, so that after his death, the piece, which is virtuosic for dancer and gamelan accompani-ment, is now regularly performed (sometimes under the title Kebyar Gandrung). Another case of a senior artist teaching repertoire from the past is that of I Wayan Mandra from Sanur, who works with the group Mekar Bhuana (Denpasar) to rec-reate music of the *pelegongan* tradition. However, Mandra's interpretation of his part in this activity is interesting—although popular as a teacher, he states that he is not explicitly a teacher, just a musician who likes to pass on pieces of music to others (see Figure 6.2).

FIGURE 6.2 Members of the group Mekar Bhuana learning from I Wayan Mandra (on left of photo).
Photo: Peter Dunbar-Hall, 2011.

Learning and teaching are based on personal interactions between teachers and learners. Digital technologies are used by musicians who can afford them as ways of reproducing repertoire. These devices are expensive, often impossibly so for many Balinese, but they are having an influence on ways of transmitting and gaining repertoires. Reading McPhee's description of teaching and learning in the 1930s (McPhee, 1947) and comparing this to what can be seen today will produce little difference in the strategies employed by teachers, the running of learning sessions, and the expectations placed on learners (Dunbar-Hall, 2008).

Nonmusical Influences on Learning and Teaching

Music and dance are inextricably linked to practice and ideology of the Balinese Hindu religion (Becker, 2004; Harnish, 1991; Herbst, 1981, 1997; Rai, 2001; Tenzer, 1991). Music and dance are also integrated into communal life, family, and village events, for expression of *banjar* (village subdivision) identity and gender politics (certain performance genres being the domain of *remaja* [young men], although this is now challenged in the ongoing developmental nature of Indonesian gender politics—see Bakan, 1997/1998; Dibia & Ballinger, 2004).

Even though they are not institutionalized, music and dance in village contexts are highly managed. Temple activity is managed by committees set up and run through village memberships. Teaching is highly organized, with regular rehearsals. The regularity of certain events keeps the necessity for performances high. Other, nonplanned events, such as funerary/cremation rites or *lomba* and festivals, create the need for music and dance to be provided, and thus taught and learned. The tourist industry adds to these expectations, providing another source of performances (in some locations run to highly organized weekly schedules, in others run by hotels, restaurants, or musicians). Maintaining instruments (making, tuning, repairing), moving instruments to and from performances, and designing and manufacturing dance costumes and masks are all implicated in the ecological system of music and dance, providing employment for artisans and adding to the number of people associated with the performing arts who benefit from the financial gains of involvement with the tourist industry.

Implications for Sustainability

There is a strong tradition of the teaching and learning of music and dance in Bali. This combines coincidental learning and structured learning. Individual learning in one-to-one situations is rare, reflecting a social practice of group participation observable in many aspects of Balinese life. Among teachers, there are common methods (modeling, teaching by rote, intense repetition of pieces, development of aural memory), and these seem to be perpetuated when a learner who has become a performer moves on to becoming a teacher. Musicians found it difficult to theorize about these methods, probably because they had learned them through enculturation and had not been taught them explicitly. Teaching music and/or dance was seen as something quite natural to do. No institutionalized teaching of teachers was identified in the project. Historical sources in the form of descriptions of teaching/learning music and dance show that methods of pedagogy have changed little over time. There is indication that the ongoing strength of teaching and learning of Balinese music and dance contributes significantly to sustainability of these performing arts.

MUSICIANS AND COMMUNITIES

Musicians have significance in Balinese communities, and performance is considered a religious offering. Alongside this, performing as a representative of one's village or region is also considered prestigious and a source of personal and collective pride.

The Musician–Community Relationship

The relationship between musician and community in Bali results from religious expectations and from a community lifestyle ethos in which individuals contribute through their own parts. This is based on a historical tradition that cannot be dated. Numerous interviewees commented that much music and dance activity is related to and driven by religious obligation. For example, Cokorda Ngurah Suyadnya stated that music will continue "because of [the] link with *upacara* (religious observance), with ceremony.... As long as we have ceremony in Bali, I'm sure that gamelan is going to be staying—*selonding, gambang, angklung*" (interview, June 26, 2010). I Made Gender Sukadana concurred: "When there is ceremony there must be *wayang*" (interview, June 20, 2009), also noting that this art form always has its religious connotations, even when it is performed for tourists. Some types of Balinese music are still only performed in religious settings. This is the case with gamelan *selonding*, as I Wayan Sudirana noted: "*Selonding* is sacred.... (It is) only for temple ceremonies ... and players must be *mawinten* (purified) to play on these instruments" (interview, July 4, 2010). Alongside religiously influenced musician–community relationships, the presence of high levels of tourist activity in parts of Bali creates another type of relationship, in which performance is seen as a way to demonstrate local pride, to present village-based versions of pieces, to attract tourists to areas, and to contribute to the financial benefit of a village. Some musicians utilize tourist performance to keep a tradition alive. This is the case with the work of I Ketut Suwentra in reclaiming and maintaining *gamelan jegog* in west Bali, as his son explained: "We are like heroes.... [My father] wants to protect *jegog*," seeing this as a means of "protecting Balinese culture" (interview, I Gede Oka Artha Negara, June 23, 2010).

The relationship between musicians and their communities can be seen in the annual Bali Arts Festival (Pesta Kesenian Bali), in which groups perform as representatives of their regency (Bali is divided into eight regencies) or village. Strong local pride is a factor in this, and intense rivalries between villages and groups exist.

Being a Musician

Many musicians work in other jobs but take part in music and dance when necessary. Numerous groups that perform for tourists have regular (usually weekly) performance schedules requiring ongoing rehearsals and learning of repertoire. Remuneration for these players is not great. There are musicians who support themselves through performing and/or teaching, but once group costs have been met (for transport, instrument maintenance, costumes, fees to managers, etc.), performers might only receive the equivalent of a few dollars per performance, sometimes less. There are cases of tourist operators undercutting accepted payment levels, charging musicians for performing, and requiring groups to perform with reduced instrumentation to cut costs. Performers are often at the mercy of such practices, despite government regulations, which are not enforced. There is a government regulation that performances of Balinese dance must be accompanied by live music, but some tourist events use recorded music. This occurs with little or no control. Some gamelan groups finance their activities by hiring themselves out for special events. Some performers support themselves entirely through performance and/or teaching—but this is a difficult life in a situation of rising living costs. Everyday realities for musicians, therefore, consist of combining daily work with the requirements of rehearsals and performances. Expectations of rehearsing to achieve the standard for performance at the Bali Arts Festival are heavy, which is similar for *lomba* between groups, villages, and regencies.

Technology is making inroads on how Balinese musicians work—for example, by providing access to repertoires—but costs for equipment remain prohibitive. Many groups and/or individual musicians make recordings (both CD and DVD/VCD), and these are marketed at performances and in shops. In tourist areas this is quite common, but these can be difficult to find in other locations. Many clips are posted on YouTube by the musicians involved and often by tourists too.

Groups move around in Bali, for religious performances, for paid performances, and for festivals and *lomba*. In this way a certain level of cross-regional influence is generated. Some groups tour internationally, and this also brings Balinese musicians into contact with music and dance from other locations. I Ketut Suwentra discussed musical influences from outside Bali on his work, mentioning *kolaborasi* (collaboration), specifically listing African drumming and Japanese music as examples of musical influences. There are also Balinese musicians living and working outside Bali, whose compositions and performances show influences from a wide range of sources (e.g., I Wayan Yudane in New Zealand and I Wayan Sudirana in Canada). Often these Balinese musicians outside Bali are employed through academic institutions or community Balinese gamelan groups to teach Balinese music; some are postgraduate students working at the master's or doctoral level. The part played by Balinese gamelan groups outside Bali in maintaining repertoires of Balinese music and dance, creating new repertoires, recording music and dance, and supporting the work of Balinese musicians in Bali should not be overlooked. Many of these groups consist of non-Balinese players, and often these groups travel to Bali for lessons and performances, or fund travel by Balinese musicians to work with them in their own countries. There are continuing examples of these groups having their own recorded outputs and ongoing concert schedules (e.g., Gita Asmara [Vancouver], Lila Cinta [London], Suara Jaya [Sydney], Sekar Jaya [San Francisco], Son of Lion [New York]). In some cases these groups preserve pieces of music and traditions of playing from the past, due to their own sources of teaching (i.e., non-Balinese teachers who have studied in Bali) having learned from Balinese teachers and recreating what they learned, while traditions in Bali have moved on. Sometimes such groups act as "time capsules" and return repertoire and performance practices to their sources. These groups also produce new Balinese music that feeds back into the repertoire of Balinese music as a whole.

Implications for Sustainability

Due to the religious implications of performance in Bali, musicians and dancers are respected for their ability to contribute to the efficacy of religious events, through contributing to collective offerings to Balinese gods. No religious observation of any kind can be complete, and successful, without music and dance. Some musicians support themselves entirely through music and/or dance, and alongside performing this usually involves teaching. However, the large majority combine being a musician with other forms of employment. Payment for musicians is not high, and in general any funds coming to a group are used first to pay costs, then distributed equally between all group members. Production of recordings, for sale locally through shops or at tourist performances, can boost group income. Balinese musicians work not only in Bali but also outside Bali, often as teachers/academics in universities. Their contacts with non-Balinese musics and musicians are one means through which cross-cultural music influences enter Balinese music and dance. Another way that this occurs is through non-Balinese performing groups (often of a community music nature) outside Bali. These sometimes act to preserve repertoires and performance aesthetics that are changing in Bali, and thus play a role in maintaining knowledge of aspects of Balinese music and dance, contributing to its sustainability as a tradition in sound and as a system of thinking about and through music.

CONTEXTS AND CONSTRUCTS

There is an ideology of the new in Balinese performing arts, and to speak of tradition is to reference practices of development and adaptation. Adaptation is both from within Balinese music and dance and by taking on influences from other locations.

Cultural and Social Contexts

When Balinese musicians discuss influences on their compositions, they often note that music from another geographic source was used in a piece (e.g., Agus Teja Sentosa indicated that he had used ideas from Thai music in his works, while I Wayan Sudirana uses rhythmic structures from Indian music in his compositions). Another important aspect of Balinese music is its cross-referencing of stylistic traits from one type of gamelan music to another—this is a significant aspect of composition of new pieces and relates to the reverence accorded members of past generations. It also draws on belief in Hindu cyclical cosmology, and thus can be used to refer to, and reify, religious ideology. Similarly to tuning systems, different types of Balinese music display traits—such as melodic motifs, rhythmic cells, gong and drumming patterns, types of ornamentation, texturing procedures, and other devices—that identify a specific type of music. This practice underpins much in the creation of new pieces and is seriously followed and acknowledged by knowledgeable performers and listeners. In their own way, these practices (of adapting ideas from non-Balinese sources and of manipulating the implications of ideas from Balinese sources) act as a cross-cultural matrix in Balinese music. To this should be added popular music, which in Bali combines elements of Balinese music with instruments and compositional styles of Western-derived popular music.

Constructs

An avowed belief in the strength of Balinese cultural identity (referred to as *ajeg Bali*—"Bali strong") drives much performing arts activity. Performance is one way to express Balinese culture, as Cokorda Ngurah Suyadnya commented: "We want to show everybody that the art in Bali is very rich. . . . I want to prove that Bali art is very rich" (interview, June 26, 2010), while a desire to "protect Balinese culture. . . . We have to be proud, standing like a *jegog*. . . . We are protecting the traditional" (interview, June 23, 2010) was the opinion of I Ketut Suwentra. The inward-looking practice of self-referencing is one way of achieving this as it reminds listeners of a tradition, the past, multiple levels and aspects of Balinese music and dance, and a strong, ongoing culture. It presents a nexus between many aspects of music and dance, involving the past and the present in a new mixture of ideas: sound, style, historical context, people associated with music and dance, regional variants, awareness of the act of creation, and awareness of a creator's own knowledge of his or her act of creation. Partly for this reason, there is strong interest in films made since the 1930s, especially if these include performances, as well as in collating old photographs of performers and using old recordings (the earliest recordings of Balinese music seem to be some 78-rpm discs made by Beka-Odeon in 1928) as the sources of repertoire and playing styles. This is one attitude that steers musical direction. As members of the group Mekar Bhuana stated: "[I] want to know what my ancestors have created . . . to understand music from the past" (interview, I Wayan Sadera, February 6, 2011); "[I] want Bali to be like it used to be" (interview, I Nyoman Sunarta, February 6, 2011); "[I] want to be involved with preserving tradition" (interview, I Putu Suwarsa, February 6, 2011).

Another is an aesthetic of the new. When *kebyar*-style music evolved in the opening decades of the 20th century, it was considered avant-garde. The same comment can be made of contemporary compositions by Balinese composers, which, as with those of composers in all parts of the world, challenge boundaries of what is considered usual. The history of Balinese music has many examples of new styles emerging or developing out of existing ones. In addition to *kebyar*, others include *gamelan angklung kebyar* (combining *gamelan angklung* and its instruments with the compositional techniques and playing styles of *gamelan gong kebyar*), *gamelan pelegongan* as a purely instrumental genre (i.e., not intended to accompany *legong* dance) in the 1920s and 1930s, and works composed for the relatively recently formulated *gamelan semaradana* and those for *gamelan wayang kulit* in seven-tone tuning (rather than its usual five-tone one). These and others demonstrate a continuing ethos of creation and rethinking as an ongoing tradition in Balinese music.

Gender issues are strong in Balinese music and dance. In the past, while both men and women were dancers, only men played instruments. I Wayan Sudirana confirmed this when he noted that in the past "women made offerings and men played. . . . Now women play gamelan [and this] spreads from village to village" (interview, July 4, 2010). Currently there is growth in *gamelan wanita* (women's gamelan groups) and in women performers taking over what were once men's performance genres. Examples of movement of performance types from the male domain to performance by women includes *kecak*, which is now presented in some parts of Bali by female groups; *dalang* (puppet masters), who were once always male but who can now be female; and dances once performed only by men, such as Baris Tunggal (solo warrior dance) and the male role in Oleg Tamulilingan (courtship dance of two bees), which are now performed by women in male costume. In some ways this extends and plays with the tradition of *bebancian* (male dancers performing female roles) and *nandir* (boys dancing female roles) of the past. These instances can be read against wider challenging of gender roles, both in the broader Indonesian polity and in line with international movements. It is now also normal to find girls learning to play gamelan—a relatively new occurrence in Balinese performing arts gender politics with the potential to alter accepted practice as the girls mature into adult performers. One such group is that of Cudamani, in Pengosekan, about which Emiko Susilo, co-artistic director of Cudamani, noted: "We've found that with the girls' group it's very influential. . . . They're very good musicians, and when they go and play somewhere it really has an impact on the people that watch them" (interview, September 21, 2010). Her fellow co–artistic director, I Dewa Putu Berata, also noted this aspect of the work of Cudamani: "My thoughts are open to challenge some of the customs that we have in Bali, like establishing a group of women from a young age. That's our experiment because I've observed that women in Bali establish groups once they are old" (interview, September 21, 2010). As with developments in arts aesthetics in types of music and instrumental ensembles, this reinforces the view of Balinese performing arts as a site of ongoing development, adaptation, challenges, and conceptual engagement, creating a view of Balinese music and dance as a self-reflexive discourse.

Implications for Sustainability

Alongside religious implications of music and dance and performance of them, cultural constructs in Balinese music and dance relate to ways in which creation of new repertoires often works through reference to earlier works. Concomitantly, Balinese musicians use influences from outside Bali in their works, and some work in ways that constitute an avant-garde movement, challenging accepted ideas of tuning and established ways of structuring music. This is also evident in forms of Balinese popular music. Other challenges to an implied status quo include changes in music gender politics. It is now common to see girls' or women's gamelan groups/performing ensembles, to locate women *dalang* (puppeteers), and to find girls being trained on gamelan, something that in the past was reserved for boys. This widening of acceptance of girls and women as instrumentalists emphasizes ongoing changes to established ideologies and implies a new means of sustaining Balinese gamelan music.

INFRASTRUCTURE AND REGULATIONS

There is no dedicated infrastructure for music and dance in Bali, and whatever space is seen as viable is used for performance. While there does not appear to be an overarching regulatory system for performances, music and dance are highly controlled by performers, expectations of the tourist industry, and community-driven means.

Infrastructure

Balinese music and dance can be performed wherever is necessary or appropriate: a village, a temple, a palace, a beach, a street. Many instances of music activity are carried out in street processions/parades, for religious purposes, or for festivals and

FIGURE 6.3 Ceremonial Baris dancers during a religious ceremony on Sanur beach.
Photo: Peter Dunbar-Hall, 2011.

celebrations. This epitomizes the concept of *desa–kala–patra* (place–time–context), which helps define the significance of an event. Through interpretation of these three ideas, music and dance take on levels of meaning. Performances in temple compounds are sacred, but in varying degrees depending on their location within a temple footprint. Music in the most sacred parts of temples is intended for the gods; that in the outermost parts, for people (although gods will be present; see Figure 6.3).

For tourist events, locations tend to be chosen for their appeal to tourist sensibilities: temple forecourts, palaces, community pavilions, parks, forests, streets, beaches, hotel gardens, and restaurants. There is often an appeal to a precolonial Balinese ethos and an attempt to recreate Bali of the past through uses of historic buildings, decoration, and lighting. Performance costumes assist, as they have changed little over time, as reference to photographs and films from the early decades of the 20th century verifies. The design and ornamentation of instruments also have changed little over time, so a gamelan set up for performance creates its own aura of tradition.

Learning, rehearsals, and performances commonly occur in public spaces, such as a *bale banjar* (community pavilion). These are situated at significant sites in the village layout and are used for many community activities. Usually the locally owned gamelan will be housed in one of these, so rehearsals and performances take place in them. Learning/teaching and rehearsing are public, and there is no restriction on people watching.

Ownership of a gamelan by an individual or family is a sign of extreme wealth. Mostly a performing group, village, or temple owns instruments, which are accessible to many people. The one set of instruments might be used by numerous groups and teachers. In poorer areas of Bali, it is necessary for sets of instruments to be lent between villages, as I Gede Oka Artha Negara explained in the case of *gamelan jegog* instruments in western Bali.

Manufacture of instruments is carried out by *pande*, a special caste who are allowed to work with metal. Often, *pande* represent generations of a family. These artisans make *kris* (religiously implicative ceremonial daggers), as well as musical instruments; there is a link between instruments, their design and manufacturing, and levels of spiritual power (DeVale & Dibia, 1991). Manufacture of musical instruments in Bali is focused in four areas: Singaraja in the north; Klungkung in the east; the villages around Blahbatuh; and Denpasar in the south of the island. Knowledgeable people can identify where instruments were made by their design, and even which *pande* made them. In discussion with one *pande*, I Wayan Pager, from Blahbatuh, it was explained that while manufacture of instruments rises and falls in line with costs and inflation in Indonesia, his foundry remains busy. He both makes new sets of instruments and restores old ones. His instruments are used outside Bali, in Australia, Europe, and the United States, and he has traveled internationally to tune and repair sets of Balinese instruments (I Wayan Pager, June 21, 2010).

Balinese performing arts require elaborate costumes and paraphernalia. *Wayang kulit* require their own equipment—puppets (of water buffalo hide), a screen, a lamp, and a box for keeping the puppets safe. Contemporary forms of *wayang kulit*, such as *wayang listrik* (electric *wayang*), utilize various forms of lighting, digital technology, and multimedia. All of these requirements lead to support for the manufacture and maintenance of performing arts accessories, adding to the ecology of music and dance in Bali. Manufacture of such artifacts is often centered in known locations. For example, making of *wayang kulit* puppets and the other necessities of this performance genre is prevalent around the southern Balinese town of Sukawati, where teaching of *gamelan gender wayang* (the gamelan specific to *wayang kulit*) and the art of the *dalang* (puppeteer) is also prevalent.

Laws, Regulations, and Funding

The concept of individual composition/composer is a novel one in Bali (many pieces of music on CDs show no "composer," but lately groups have begun showing the creator[s] of music and/or dance). Some texts by Balinese authors list the creators of music and/or dance pieces, but often sources are contradictory on this. Terms such as *komponis* (composer) have been created and introduced into music aesthetics, while the term *pencipta* (a person who makes/creates) has been adapted to describe what can be thought of as a composer. Terms such as *penyusan* (a person who organizes things) are found. The introduction of Western-derived terms is indicative of a trend to equate ideologies of Balinese music with those found in Western music. This may be the result of various influences, including contact with Western musicians and travel by Balinese musicians outside Bali for the purposes of performance or university study. There do not seem to be any copyright laws, payment of royalties, artists' rights, or restrictions on performances, and this was confirmed in discussions with musicians. As there is no published notation (except in rare instances, e.g., Dibia's 2000 book on *kecak*), issues of copyright do not apply. Many recordings are privately manufactured and sold in shops, in markets, at performances, or via Internet sites. Many recordings show no details of recording. It is not uncommon to find track listings that vary from recording to recording (i.e., one piece will appear with different names on different recordings). Sale of these recordings is one source of finance for performers. Some groups, for example, Cudamani, record and sell CDs through American production companies (in this case, Vital Records in California). Other funding sources are ambiguous. There is some funding of performing arts projects from local government agencies. However, performers tend to work to find funding for and from their own performances. Musicians were explicit that managing agents are known to undercut payments to performers, payments to groups to perform at the annual Bali Arts Festival are notoriously diverted away from performers, and accounting procedures are ambivalent. The term *korupsi* (corruption) figured strongly and regularly in discussions with musicians.

There was a feeling that government support existed, but not explicitly financially, in such areas as the granting of performing licences (for tourist events), as Cokorda Ngurah Suyandnya explained: "The government supports [us] by [granting] a licence to perform. . . . If [musicians] do not have a licence, they cannot perform, so that's the best support from the government" (interview, June 26, 2010). A similar opinion (that government support is conceptual rather than financial) was expressed by I Ketut Suwentra. In explaining the revival of *gamelan jegog* in western Bali in the 1980s, he noted that a performance request from the local government was a significant impetus in supporting his work in teaching *gamelan jegog*, and that "government support is just spirit power, not money or infrastructure" (interview, June 23, 2010). I Wayan Sudirana also stated that government support existed in these types of ways, noting that the government was committed to preserving music and dance, and that the annual Bali Arts Festival was a way of doing this, even though funding to support performers did not always reach them. On the local level, he noted that local events are funded locally, through the village or regency networks, and that these were important as they necessitated group rehearsals and provided performance outlets. At such events, he stated that people appreciate seeing the rarer types of gamelan or having the chance to see a girls' group performing. Despite these forms of support, there is a feeling that the government had little idea of the scope of the work being done by village-based musicians: "They should come sometime and see what the *sanggar* (performing groups) [are doing], the group activity, so they know exactly what the *sanggar* are doing. ... Not so many people from the government come, except [if] they have a competition or if they have an art festival" (interview, Cokorda Ngurah Suyadnya, June 26, 2010).

Some groups have used external funding to support their work. For example, in the 1970s in Denpasar, I Wayan Sinti used a Ford Foundation grant to restore and record an antique set of instruments, and in the 1990s, Italian researcher/performer Maria Cristina Formaggia had funding from the Ford Foundation to investigate, stage, and record performances of *gambuh*, ancient Balinese dance-dramas. The group Cudamani, from Pengosekan, also funded their work through a Ford Foundation grant, and this allowed them to travel in Bali to study various styles of music and dance: "We have had two field studies in north Bali. ... One of the reasons we can do this is we have a grant from the Ford Foundation ... and in addition we've brought teachers ... to come here and teach. ... There are not many organizations that have been able to do that" (interview, Emiko Susilo, September 21, 2010).

There is no overt restriction on the content of music and dance—but it must be remembered that Balinese Hindu ethics exist above activity and influence what any performer would seek to do. Restrictive laws from the Jakarta-based federal Indonesian government, while they may exert influence in other parts of Indonesia, which is for the most part Muslim, are not enforced particularly rigorously in the Hindu context of Bali.

Implications for Sustainability

Performance of music and dance takes place wherever appropriate. An overarching ideology of place–time–context helps define the intent, and outcomes, of performance. Similarly, teaching and learning take place wherever possible—often publicly. This helps reinforce and perpetuate the sense that music and dance "belong" to those surrounding their transmission and expression. Types of collaboration, within Balinese music and also involving influences and people from outside Bali, are welcome and feed into the artistic sources in creation of new works. Performing and teaching require musical instruments and other paraphernalia, and there is a network of producers of these; often these are localized, and specific villages/

areas are recognized as centers of their production. The name of a gamelan maker is often commented on, and there are debates and preferences over the work of these. There does not seem to be a system of copyright, royalty payments for performance, restrictions on performance (apart from those invoked by adherence to Balinese Hindu ideology), or imprecations for performance of any specific repertoires or styles of music. Government support for music and dance is seen as more conceptual than financially real.

MEDIA AND THE MUSIC INDUSTRY

Live performance is the mainstay of Balinese music and dance, although many performers manufacture CDs, DVDs, and VCDs for sale to supplement income from performances. Numerous commercially produced recordings also exist, and Internet resources are becoming widely used.

Media Engagement

Balinese TV and radio regularly broadcast shows that include traditional and contemporary music and dance. Traditional shows tend to consist of canonic repertoires used in tourist performances and are criticized by some musicians as examples of the lowest tastes in entertainment. Non-Balinese researchers often make documentaries and record rarer repertoires with funding from outside Bali (as with the aforementioned Formaggia). Increasingly, Balinese musicians engage with social media such as Facebook and YouTube.

There is a history of recording companies from outside Bali producing substantial recorded outputs of Balinese music. For example, in the 1990s, two companies, King Records and Celestial Harmonies, released important CD sets of Balinese music, which document music activity in Bali at that time, preserving repertoires and types of ensembles that are now considered rare and that were performed by significant musicians. Other recording projects emanate from within Bali. For example, Bali Records has a large catalog of standard repertoire recordings, although their filming and production values are not especially high. Interestingly, these discs show the names of composers of dance music and choreographers, in cases where it is possible to ascertain them. Bali Records also produces an ongoing series of CDs, *The Best of Gambelan Bali* (note the Balinese spelling), which presents pieces of music that have won the competition sections of the Bali Arts Festival for best new pieces of music each year; they provide a means for accessing a body of recently composed music for gamelan. Similar to recordings from Bali Records are the outputs of two other companies: Ricks Records and Maharani. Since the early 1990s, a performing group from Teges Kanginan, Sekehe Dharma

Purwa Jatu (http://www.goarchi.com/yp/), has produced and released their own recordings to document local performance traditions of *semar pegulingan*. The same organization has been active in recording *gamelan selonding* and music for *gambuh*, both rare types of Balinese performance. Other performing groups that contribute to this market include the Denpasar group Mekar Bhuana (http://www.balimusicanddance.com), which has begun recording their reclamation of historical repertoires project on CD, while groups such as Cudamani (http://www.cudamani.org), from Pengosekan, are recorded and released through an American label, Vital Records. Many performing groups make their own recordings and sell them on an ad hoc basis. Musicians such as I Gede Oka Artha Negara and I Wayan Sudirana specifically mentioned the value of making recordings of Balinese music (alongside teaching and performing) as a means for helping maintain repertoires. I Gede Oka Artha Negara's father, I Ketut Suwentra, also spoke about the value of recordings: "[Recording] is how we make *gamelan jegog* alive" (interview, June 23, 2010). I Wayan Sudirana noted another aspect of recordings of Balinese music when he commented that his doctoral research had been assisted by reference to recordings made by non-Balinese people.

Presence in the Music Industry

Balinese music and dance are highly visible in Bali. As the instruments for Balinese music are specific to this type of music, the island presents a closed ecosystem, with its own instrument production, pedagogic methods, performing arts outcomes, problems, and agendas. The special nature of the relationship between performing arts and the Balinese Hindu religion adds to this closed system. Outside Bali, Balinese music is learned, researched, and performed, and in academic studies of music, usually at the university level, it is a regular topic of study. This is supported by solid published research by specialists on this topic and by readily accessible recordings. The Internet has created differences in how people access Balinese performing arts: Instead of needing to travel to Bali, much research and other information can be seen and heard online. Its influence in Bali is not so clear, although some Balinese musicians use social networking and information websites to advertise/represent their work. Costs for this may be an issue in musicians' deciding whether they will use these forms for publicizing their work. A well-subscribed and ongoing email list (gamelanlistserv) connects gamelan musicians and enthusiasts worldwide. While it covers all types of gamelan from the Indonesian/Malay world, the postings on Balinese music are substantial and provide a useful source of research, information, and notification of new recordings and books on Balinese music and dance.

The annual Bali Arts Festival attracts strong audience support, as do locally organized events. Local festivals involving high levels of music and dance are a regular occurrence. Table 6.2, a tabulation of performance genres at the 2010 Bali Arts Festival, indicates the extent of participation and the range of types of music and dance presented.

TABLE 6.2

Performance Genres at the 2010 Pesta Kesenian Bali	
Genre	Number
Angklung kreasi	8
Arja	8
Balinese song	3
Beleganjur	2
Calonarang	3
Caruk	1
Choir	1
Classical music and dance	8
Contemporary dance	8
Dance drama (incl. prembon, topeng)	23
Gambang	1
Gambuh	3
Gandrung	1
Gong kebyar	26
Janger	3
Jegog	2
Joged bumbung	7
Kecak	2
Kendang mebarung	1
Legong	2
Leko dance	1
Ngelawang	2
Pesantian	2
Rindik	1
Selonding	2
Semar pegulingan	1
Wayang kulit	11
Wayang listrik	1
Wayang wong	3
Total performances	136

TABLE 6.3

Other Performance Events at the 2010 Pesta Kesenian Bali

Events	Number
Balinese modern theater	1
Documentary film	4
Ethnic fusion music	1
International collaboration	1
Jazz gamelan fusion	2
Literary recitation	1
Poetry with music	1
Non-Balinese performing groups	3
Total	14

Table 6.2 indicates the strong prevalence of *gamelan gong kebyar* and the small number of groups presenting rarer types of ensemble, such as *gamelan gambang*, *gamelan semar pegulingan*, and *gamelan selonding*. Table 6.3 lists other types of events (i.e., nontraditional), a relatively new part of the festival, which shows increasing interest in ongoing creation of new music and genre types among Balinese musicians.

Tourism has become a major source of income, especially in the major cultural tourist triangle formed in the south of the island (Denpasar–Sanur–Ubud). Within this area tourist performances are regular, though attendance numbers can vary depending on the weather and other factors, such as terrorist activity, health scares, and international financial conditions. Tourism is a double-edged sword. It creates the need for teaching and learning; provides opportunities to perform; allows presentation of Balinese cultural products; feeds into support for makers of instruments, costumes, and other paraphernalia; provides funding for local projects; and supports people in the margins of the music industry, such as ticket and program sellers. As Emiko Susilo commented: "The tourist industry's had a huge impact on the performing arts. . . . Now because of tourists there's so much demand for dancers . . . and they need [dancers] at six different places every night, so there's a lot of demand for performers" (interview, September 21, 2010).

At the same time, tourist performances often lead to replication of canonic repertoire, shortening of pieces of music, reduction of performing group size, adaptations of music and dance to fit the timetable of hotel/restaurant meal services, and representation of types of performance anchored in the past and not reflecting the vibrant nature of ongoing creative developments. Balinese musicians have their own terms for tourist performances; instead of Legong Kraton (Palace Legong) as the name of a dance type, they refer to Legong Hotel (Hotel Legong) or Legong Turis (Tourist Legong).

Patronage, almost in a medieval sense, still exists in Bali, and royal families and/ or high-caste people wield strong control over aspects of daily life. In some areas, members of royal families are heavily involved in supporting, running, managing, and financing performing arts activity. This is especially prevalent in areas where royal families have maintained vestiges of the power held by them before the onset of Dutch colonialism in Bali in the early decades of the 20th century.

Government support, at a federal level, for Balinese performing arts seems to exist—as part of pan-Indonesian policies to foster these arts and to support regional diversity that defines the Indonesian polity. How this support reaches musicians is difficult to see. Musicians openly criticize a lack of funding from high government levels, although they are told this exists. Bureaucracy, both in Bali and Jakarta, is seen as the ultimate destination for any funding programs that are publicized. Funding for the annual Bali Arts Festival exists, but the small amounts that are channeled to performers from the overall budget is criticized by musicians, who point out that being selected to represent their regency at the Bali Arts Festival (selection is by audition of groups at the regency level) might be seen more as a burden than an honor in financial terms.

Implications for Sustainability

There is a readily observable music industry in Bali: Performance, teaching and learning, recording, broadcasting, and research are ongoing. In many performances, especially in areas of high levels of tourism, there is a tendency to present a canonic repertoire of music and dance, often one that creates a sense of traditional Balinese culture (even if some of the music and dance performed are recently created). Performances for tourists require the provision of performers, and this necessitates teachers, instruments, and other forms of infrastructure; through these factors the music industry is supported; and many Balinese musicians use this tourist-derived support to fund their own agendas of creation of new repertoires and styles of music and dance, to purchase and repair gamelan instruments, and to pay for the other costs of ongoing music and dance activity. Some groups use tourist performances to fund village costs, for example, to pay for new temple buildings. Performance formats continue to reflect traditional practices (derived from culturally expected roles of music), while at the same time there are musicians who challenge these and whose work investigates new styles of performance, for example, through multimedia activity, through utilization of artistic influences from outside Bali, and through a sense of moving Balinese performing arts into new territory.

ISSUES AND INITIATIVES FOR SUSTAINABILITY

Music and dance exist in Bali in different ways, covering a range of genres and types of ensembles, for different purposes, and with varying degrees of support. In some areas, support is strong, especially those with high levels of tourism and traditions of valuing performing arts. In some areas, for example, the poorer, eastern areas of Bali, there are villages without instruments or with ones in poor condition. Alongside firm activity in the creation of new music and dance, both from within the traditional stylistic palettes of Balinese music and dance and from influences from outside Bali, there are projects to reclaim repertoires, styles, and performance practices of the past. Cokorda Ngurah Suyadnya commented on agendas of representing Balinese music and dance when he stated, "I want to prove that Balinese art is very rich" (interview, June 26, 2010), as did I Ketut Suwentra, who stated that one of his aims is "to protect Balinese culture" (interview, June 23, 2010), while his son, I Gede Oka Artha Negara, stated that "we are protecting the traditional" (interview, June 23, 2010).

Alongside concern for music and dance, there is a strong "grassroots" movement, *ajeg Bali*, in which presenting performances of historic repertoires is a way to remember Balinese history, to show the achievements of Balinese artists, and to remind that Balinese performance culture is ongoing, complex, and productive—that Balinese culture is strong. For many Balinese people, this implies criticism of federal Jakartanism, in which the central Indonesian national government (in Jakarta) is seen as opposed to Balinese individuality. The fact that many businesses in Bali are owned by non-Balinese people is a factor here, and Balinese people often comment that they work, but profits go to bank accounts in Java/Jakarta.

Systemic study of music is represented by ISI and KOKAR (an arts-dedicated secondary school). While ISI is criticized by many musicians for its teaching and administration practices and has been a continual topic of Indonesian press criticism, it provides university-level degree programs in Balinese performing arts and requires students to undertake not only performance in their chosen genres but also research into local traditions. These research projects are archived in the library of ISI and sporadically appear as articles in the ISI house journal, *Mudra*. ISI requires from its students creation of new compositions and dances. Teaching and learning of music and dance are regular and ongoing at the village level, in some schools, through privately run *sanggar* (studios), or in groups based around *banjar* (village sector) membership. There is one dedicated performing arts secondary school, KOKAR (Konservatori Kawitan), in Blahbatuh, at which students study various types of Balinese performing arts. This covers canonic repertoire and does not investigate past traditions of Balinese music. Festivals at varying levels of locale are regular events, sometimes with funding, often without.

Key Issues for Sustainability

Sustainability covers three main areas in this context. First is that of repertoires and their performance practices. Styles of music, and their dedicated ensembles, continually rise and fall in popularity. This is not unrecognized by Balinese performers, many of whom work to reclaim older forms of performance. Within this there are levels of reclamation, from groups who may use a *gamelan gong kebyar* to learn and perform music of the tradition of *gamelan gong gede* to groups who seek out antique instruments with tunings and timbral envelopes that reflect how music is thought to have sounded in the past. This raises the issue of authenticity as a spectrum of ideologies and applications, none of which is presented as a final opinion.

Second is the continuity of collective memory. In an aural/oral tradition relying on individuals remembering music and dance, as older performers die, often their knowledge dies with them: "In terms of the performing arts . . . many times we've had incredible performers and then they've passed away before they've passed on their knowledge, and then you lose that, and it's such a tragedy when that happens" (interview, Emiko Susilo, September 21, 2010). There is an attempt to controvert this by employing *seniman tua* to teach music and dance of the past, and to publish the reminiscences of and/or archival information from these people. These instances are reinforced by the honor accorded senior artists and ways in which their careers are remembered and celebrated. Reclamation projects utilizing recordings and films of the past are important, providing sources of repertoires and performing styles, costuming, and choreographies.

The third area is that of the unseen aspects of the music industry: manufacture and provision of instruments, costumes, and paraphernalia; provision and use of performance spaces; roles of broadcast media and recordings in supporting the work of performers; the personnel who teach and manage performing arts activities; the employment of people working behind the scenes to promote and run performances and sell tickets and programs; and recording producers and the industry of selling recordings and other forms of information. This infrastructure of people and their roles is unseen by many audiences, yet their contribution and financial gain are significant aspects of and outcomes of music and dance.

Existing above these three wide areas of sustainability is the influence of religion on the arts in general in Bali, and ways in which music and dance are integrated into the belief system of Balinese Hinduism, where performance is both an offering and a sacrament, providing a means for personal and group *dharma* (spiritual well-being). Issues relating to the religious meaning of the performing arts in Bali are researched and debated by various scholars (e.g., Davies, 2006; Harnish, 1991; Rubinstein & Connor, 1999).

Past Initiatives

Projects to reclaim and maintain styles of Balinese music and dance of the past have been documented since the 1930s, when Canadian composer and researcher Colin McPhee set up a *gamelan semar pegulingan* and brought in a teacher to recreate a tradition that he documented as in serious decline (McPhee, 1947, 1966). Other projects have included that of Wayan Sinti in the 1970s in *gamelan semar pegulingan* and the work of Cristina Formaggia in the 1990s in *gambuh*, documented in her two-volume publication *Gambuh: drama tari Bali* (Formaggia, 2000). There is the recording project of Sekehe Dharma Purwa Jati, in Teges Kanginan, under the management of Australian musician and researcher Doug Myers, in documenting *legong* and *semar pegulingan* traditions, and in *gambuh* and *gamelan selonding* (Davies, 2006; Myers, 2010). Also worth mentioning is a reclamation project in Ubud of Janger, leading to regular performances of this music and dance genre, and research by Balinese scholars into rarer forms of gamelan, for example, that of I Wayan Sudirana into *gamelan luang* (Sudirana, 2009). Also important is the work of I Ketut Suwentra in Jembrana (west Bali), credited with almost single-handedly saving the local tradition of *gamelan jegog* in the 1980s. Another contributing factor is the expectation of the Bali Arts Festival that older repertoires will be performed alongside current and new types of music. In the academic context, there has been research into the current state of *gamelan gong gede* in the central regions of Bali (Hood, 2010a, 2010b); publications on and recordings of *gamelan selonding* in eastern Bali (Ramseyer, 2009); and a project to record and document *gamelan trompong beruk*, found in only the village of Bangle, eastern Bali. It is a requirement of ISI that students are engaged in documenting local traditions of Balinese music and dance. The group Cudamani, in learning various styles and repertoires, for example, works on reclaiming pieces of the northern Balinese *gamelan sekatian*; and ongoing work of the group Mekar Bhuana, in Denpasar, includes documenting and recording music and dance of the *gamelan semar pegulingan* and *gamelan pelegongan* traditions using instrument sets from the early 20th century. This group has recently also begun working on documenting the repertoire of *gamelan selonding*. This list is not conclusive but is representative of proactive work by performers and researchers from within and outside Bali over a number of decades to contribute to the sustainability of a tradition through projects in repertoires and styles under threat of decline and loss.

Current and Planned Initiatives

Projects in reclamation continue to exist in Bali. An implication of them is that they engender the need for instrument manufacture (e.g., Mekar Bhuana's work and that of I Wayan Sudirana on *gamelan selonding* both involved the manufacture by *pande* of new sets of instruments). They may also involve the recording industry (it has become more usual for such projects to lead to documentation in the form of CDs, DVDs, VCDs, and websites), as well as management of events to present the work of such projects. Many projects exist in isolation and are locally driven, resourced, run, and presented; many remain unacknowledged beyond their local boundaries.

Musicians comment on these issues of preservation, often referring to teaching of music and dance as a major way to keep them alive: "If it is just studied then the next generation will lose it and it will have to be unearthed again, so it must be continuous and that's why I focus on education" (interview, I Dewa Berata, September 21, 2010). They also state that their work in keeping specific styles of music alive is important: "Our mission is to protect (gamelan) *jegog* . . . to spread the knowledge to the world . . . [and] protect [it] from globalization. We don't want *jegog* to disappear. . . . We have to protect the old songs . . . traditional, classic songs" (interview, I Ketut Suwentra, June 23, 2010). Sometimes, musicians list the processes they see as necessary for keeping Balinese music and dance as an ongoing tradition. I Wayan Sudirana, for example, listed research, locating *seniman tua*, and documenting music and dance as activities that need to be undertaken (interview, July 4, 2010). The three-part and interrelated mixture of teaching, performing, and recording is the way to achieve this, according to I Gede Oka Artha Negara (interview, June 23, 2010). In addition to these, I Wayan Mandra saw the opportunities offered through festivals and television performances as support for music and dance (interview, February 6, 2011). What seems needed, despite these opinions and exemplifications of individuals' work, however, is funding (always a problem) and clearer ways of monitoring it; personnel trained in documentation and archiving; repositories and cataloguing of materials; clearer indication of government roles, leadership, and support; and collating and evaluation of past and present projects to give a holistic overview of what has been done and what remains to be done.

ACKNOWLEDGMENTS

The author thanks Agung Rai, Agus Teja Sentosa, Cokorda Istri Sri Agung Astiti, Cokorda Ngurah Suyadnya, Cokorda Raka Swastika, I Dewa Putu Berata, Emiko Susilo, I Gede Oka Artha Negara, I Ketut Cater, I Ketut Suwentra, I Made Gender Sukadana, I Nyoman Sunarta, Putu Evie Suyadnyani, I Putu Suwarsa, Vaughan Hatch, I Wayan Mandra, I Wayan Pager, I Wayan Sadera, I Wayan Sudirana, and I Wayan Tusti Adnyana.

REFERENCES

Bakan, M. (1997/1998). From oxymoron to reality: Agendas of gender and the rise of Balinese women's gamelan beleganjur in Bali, Indonesia. *Asian Music*, 29(1), 37–86.

Bandem, I. M., & deBoer, F. (1995). *Balinese dance in transition: Haja and kelod* (2nd ed.). Oxford, UK: Oxford University Press.

Becker, J. (2004). *Deep listeners: Music, emotion and trancing*. Bloomington, IN: Indiana University Press.

Davies, S. (2006). Balinese legong: Revival or decline? *Asian Theatre Journal*, 23(2), 314–341.

DeVale, C., & Dibia, I. W. (1991). *Sekar Anyar*: An exploration of meaning in Balinese gamelan. *World of Music*, 33(1), 5–51.

Dibia, I. W. (2000). *Kecak: The vocal chant of Bali*. Denpasar, Indonesia: Hartanto Art Books Studio.

Dibia, I. W., & Ballinger, R. (2004). *Balinese dance, drama and music: A guide to the performing arts of Bali*. Singapore, Southeast Asia: Periplus.

Dunbar-Hall, P. (2008). "Good legong dancers were given an arduous program of training": Music education in Bali in the 1930s. *Journal of Historical Research in Music Education*, 30(1), 50–63.

Eiseman, F. (1990). *Bali: Sekala and niskala: Essays on religion, ritual, and art* (Vol. 1). Singapore, Southeast Asia: Periplus.

Formaggia, M. C. (2000). *Gambuh: drama tari Bali* (Vols. 1 & 2). Jakarta, Indonesia: Lontar.

Gold, L. (2004). *Music in Bali: Experiencing music, expressing culture*. New York, NY: Oxford University Press.

Harnish, D. (1991). Balinese performance as festival offering. *Asian Art*, Spring, 9–27.

Hatch, V., & Hatch, E. (2005). The music and dance of Sanur. In L. Lueras (Ed.), *Sanur: The birthplace of Bali style* (pp. 60–80). Batuan-Sukawati, Indonesia: Bali Purnati Center for the Arts.

Herbst, E. (1981). Intrinsic aesthetics in Balinese artistic and spiritual practice. *Asian Music*, 13(1), 43–52.

Herbst, E. (1997). *Voices in Bali: Energies and perceptions in vocal music and dance theater*. Hanover, NH: Wesleyan University Press.

Hood, M. M. (2010a). Gamelan gong gede: Negotiating musical diversity in Bali's highlands. *Musicology Australia*, 22(1), 69–94.

Hood, M. M. (2010b). *Triguna: A Hindu-Balinese philosophy for gamelan gong gede music*. Munster, Ireland: Lit Verlag.

Institut Seni Indonesia. (2006). *Panduan Studi*. Denpasar, Indonesia: Institut Seni Indonesia.

Laskewicz, Z. (2003). *Music as episteme, text, sign and tool: Comparative approaches to musicality as performance*. Brussels, Belgium, and Taipei, Taiwan: Saru Press.

McGraw, A. (1999/2000). The development of the "gamelan semara dana" and the expansion of the modal system in Bali. *Asian Music*, 31(1), Winter, 63–93.

McIntosh, J. (2006). How dancing, singing and playing shape the ethnographer: Research with children in a Balinese dance studio. *Anthropology Matters*, 8(2). Retrieved from http://www.anthropologymatters.com/journal/2006-2/mcintosh_2006_how.htm

McPhee, C. (1947). *A house in Bali*. Singapore, Southeast Asia: Oxford University Press.

McPhee, C. (1966). *Music in Bali: A study in form and instrumental organization in Balinese orchestral music*. New Haven, CT: Yale University Press.

Myers, D. (Ed.). (2010). *Legong*. Sayan, Bali, Indonesia: Amandari.

Picard, M. (1990). "Cultural tourism" in Bali: Cultural performances as tourist attraction. *Indonesia*, 49(April), 37–74.

Picard, M. (1996). *Bali: Cultural tourism and touristic culture*. Singapore, Southeast Asia: Archipelago Press.

Racki, C. (1998). *The sacred dances of Bali*. Denpasar, Indonesia: Buratwangi.

Rai, W. (2001). *Gong: Antologi Pemikiran*. Denpasar, Indonesia: Bali Mangsi Press.

Ramseyer, U. (2009). *The theatre of the universe: Ritual and art in Tenganan Pegeringsingan*. Basel, Switzerland: Mueum der Kulturen Basel.

Rubin, L., & Sedana, I. N. (2007). *Performance in Bali*. London, UK: Routledge.

Rubinstein, R., & Connor, L. (Eds.). (1999). *Staying local in the global village: Bali in the twentieth century*. Honolulu, HI: University of Hawai'i Press.

Sudirana, I. W. (2009). Pengawak kinda: Melody and time in a Balinese gamelan luang composition. *Mudra: Journal of Art and Culture*, 2009, 34–47.

Sudyamatka, S. (Ed.). (2000). *Nadi: Trance in the Balinese art*. Denpasar, Indonesia: Taksu Foundation.

Tenzer, M. (1991). *Balinese music*. Singapore, Southeast Asia: Periplus.

Tenzer, M. (2000). *Gamelan Gong Kebyar: The art of twentieth-century Balinese music*. Chicago, IL: University of Chicago Press.

Vickers, A. (1989). *Bali: A paradise created*. Singapore, Southeast Asia: Periplus.

Vickers, A., Putra, I. N. D., & Ford, M. (Eds.). (2000). *To change Bali: Essays in honour of I Gusti Ngurah Bagus*. Denpasar, Indonesia: Bali Post.

Vitale, W. (1990). Kotekan: The technique of interlocking parts in Balinese music. *Balungan*, 4(2), 2–15.

Vitale, W. (2002). Balinese Kebyar music breaks the five-tone barrier: New composition for seven-tone gamelan. *Perspectives of New Music*, 40(1), 5–70.

7

WESTERN OPERA

The Price of Prestige in a Globalized "Total Theater" Experience

John Drummond

ART FORMS COMBINING storytelling, theatrical presentation, and music can be found in virtually every culture (Drummond, 1980, pp. 13–37). *Opera* is the term given to the version that emerged in Europe at the end of the 16th century and is now found on almost every continent. Over the centuries it has taken different forms: While most opera has been sung throughout, some forms include spoken dialogue, and while most operas have been composed for companies of trained professionals, some are for amateur or young performers. Access has traditionally been through attendance at a live performance, but operas are now widely available through contemporary media. Its history is well documented: Thousands of books have been written about opera as an art form, its history, and its place in Western culture, as well as about particular operas, composers, singers, companies, and opera houses. There are many reliable online resources providing information about all aspects of opera. While the repertoire is largely standardized, sustainability issues for the art form are based more on changing practices in production, the possibilities and challenges offered by new media, and the changing context of funding for the arts.

Nowadays opera is formally distinguished from two allied practices: "the musical" and "contemporary music-theater," though in practice the distinction is blurred. "The musical" refers usually to works including spoken dialogue, although Schonberg's *Les Miserables*, for example, has continuous music. "Contemporary music-theater" or "New Music Theater" (see Salzman & Desi, 2008) uses sound, space, and physicality in experimental ways and often eschews narrative. Some works of this kind call themselves operas—for example, Robert Wilson and Philip Glass's *Einstein on the Beach* (1976)—and others do not.

The focus here is on the more conventional kind of opera, which forms the typical repertoire of the genre. It is presented in live performance, normally by self-defined opera companies, and usually in indoor theater spaces that are often designed for the purpose. Its content is commonly a tragic or comic narrative involving identified characters, and the story is told in words and music. The music is the most important ingredient: Opera is often performed to audiences who do not understand the language of the text, and who do not mind. While the text and even the story can often be modified without causing irreparable harm, the music is usually not tampered with in any significant way. It is usually performed by professionally trained singers accompanied by professionally trained musicians, although performances by skilled amateurs do take place. While live performances are considered the essence of the art form by many, performances may be recorded and are disseminated widely in audio and audio-visual formats.

Background

Born in Europe, Western opera expanded across the world, particularly in the 19th century, as part of European colonial processes. Like other forms of Western music, it has escaped much of the stigma attached to that process. Newer kinds of globalization in the latter part of the 20th century have made it accessible in other parts of the world in live performance, and almost everywhere through technology.

James Steichen (2011) suggests that concerns about the viability of opera have been present throughout its history. Opera began as an attempt to revive a long-dead art form, Greek tragedy, and its subsequent history includes moments when it appeared (at least to some practitioners) to be on the verge of collapse and in serious need of renewal: The reforms of Gluck and his partners in the 1760s and the rethinking of the art form by Wagner in the 1840s to 1850s provide two significant examples. Steichen notes that debate on the future of opera emerges every 40 years or so and cites authorities asking the question in 1884, 1928, and 1968. In 1986, the journal *Daedalus* published a series of conversations about "The Future of Opera" among 29 leading practitioners. In 2001, the Edinburgh Festival mounted a study day asking, "Does opera have a future?" (Higgins, 2001). In 2007, Sarah Zalfen identified the "crises" faced by opera companies in Berlin after 1989, in London in 1997–1998, and in Paris between 1986 and 1994, where in each case survival was on the agenda. This chapter asks the same question again, but from a different perspective, which seeks to place opera in a wider context of the sustainability of music genres across the world.

Opera's position in society has changed over the centuries. Originally entertainment for princes and courts, it found a place in wider European society during the 19th century: Where once its stories, structures, and musical style had appealed to educated and sophisticated connoisseurs, it now found ways that appealed to much wider audiences. This process highlighted an issue. Opera, as a powerful amalgamation of several media, is deeply affecting: To what purpose should its power be employed? Should it be regarded as entertainment or as a potentially transformational experience? Can it be both? These questions are central to an exploration of opera's future, for they have practical implications. Because it presents several art forms simultaneously, opera has always been an expensive activity. Many operatic works require large resources of personnel, equipment, and space. Who pays for this? Entertainment can be paid for by those who are entertained, but even that income may be insufficient. How are potentially transformational experiences to be funded? Is there a communal (governmental, charitable, "public good") responsibility to support them?

Funding questions are of importance not only because of the costs of opera but also because of its changing status in society. "By the mid twentieth-century," write Salzman and Desi (2008, p. 8), "due perhaps to the impact of the mass media (notably film), opera seems to have lost its keystone position at the apex of the arts." Snowman (2009) echoes this:

> Opera has always needed powerful figures prepared to embrace (and finance) it. For centuries, it could count on the sponsorship of political leaders, from princely patrons to variegated twentieth-century dictatorships and democracies. By the turn of the twenty-first, however, despite its unprecedented global popularity, opera was becoming politically marginalized: a specialist, "niche" interest that received progressively less public attention and which governments were increasingly disinclined to encourage. When Blair, Berlusconi, Bush, Chirac or Putin visited each other, they might dress up for a formal dinner at a castle or a palace. . . . But the last place that generation of foreign dignitaries or their successors normally wanted to be seen taking their counterparts to was to the opera. (p. 412)

Zalfen (2007, pp. 278–279) reports on public discussions about how the Royal Opera House London's deficit was to be funded in the late 1990s. Newspapers used phrases such as "stuffy, snobby, exclusive elite" to describe operagoers, and suggested that "it is time these rich showers of snobbish parasites were forced to pay for their own elitist hobby." The social divisiveness of such statements was only augmented when the chairman of the opera house board remarked, "We mustn't downgrade the opera house: I don't want to sit next to somebody in a singlet, a pair of shorts and a smelly pair of trainers." Such social divisiveness is not new. Lindenberger (1984) notes that opera, as the most extravagant art, has always been socially highly contested.

The situation is complicated by additional factors. Chief among them is the direction taken by Western art-music in the 20th century. A music that, in the 19th century, had been readily understood and enjoyed by large numbers of the middle-class population moved in new directions that effectively cut it off from its support base. Instead, audiences focused on the heritage, in opera and more widely in classical music. As Ross (2007, p. xvi) puts it, "Classical music is [now] stereotyped as an art of the dead, a repertory that begins with Bach and terminates with Mahler and Puccini. People are sometimes surprised to learn that composers are still writing at all."

Even within the world of classical music, opera has from time to time been regarded as moribund, famously in Pierre Boulez's suggestion in a 1966 *Der Spiegel* interview that the most elegant solution to the decay of opera was to blow up the world's opera houses. They have survived, and new ones continue to be built, largely performing a historic repertoire of 50 or so familiar classics. Of the 60 productions reviewed in the May 2011 issue of *Opera* magazine, 44 were of works from the canon. Meanwhile, "serious" art-music composers have continued to provide operatic works, ones that audiences may have found "difficult," but which are often justified with the "potentially transforming experiences" argument. Other composers have moved into New Music Theater. Still others have sought to appeal more directly to an audience whose tastes lie within the styles of the canon, working in musicals or composing film music.

While these varied art-music strands have developed, popular music and the musics of other cultures are more widely accessed than ever before, and fusions and connections between different musics are common. The rich musical diversity in society creates challenges for a cultural practice like opera. Some of the challenges are artistic and aesthetic; others are social and political. Where once it could claim to be the most sophisticated and innovative genre in a uniformly accepted musical culture, it now finds itself labeled a conservative, backward-looking genre in a minority music culture.

Opera's changing position in society and culture is reflected in the terminology people use. Where "music" was once considered in Western education, in the literature, and in the marketplace to be, exclusively, Western classical music, the term now includes other forms and styles. This causes terminological confusion.

"Twentieth-century music" might refer to all musics or only to classical music; "contemporary music" can refer to contemporary classical music or contemporary popular music. Living as we do in what Ross (2007) calls a "decentered culture," we all use the word *music* to refer to our own particular experience and taste. Opera can, in this sense, be seen as its own subculture, "centered" on itself and, despite its worldwide presence, preoccupied with its own concerns. One characteristic of this self-centeredness is a sense of entitlement, of surprise and anger that opera is not automatically supported by society. This is a prominent strand in the views shared by informants, and beneath it can be traced a sense of loss: Whatever happened to that world in which Western opera was considered to be the pinnacle of artistic achievement?

THE RESEARCH

For research into its ecology, Western opera presents particular challenges: It is a worldwide industry and cultural practice. Opera is presented by both professional and amateur groups in many countries, from Norway to New Zealand to Thailand to Brazil, in venues ranging from billion-dollar opera houses to small community halls. In some countries it is a major recipient of government arts support; in others it receives large amounts from philanthropic institutions and wealthy individuals. It also survives on modest funding as small opera groups struggle to survive from production to production. During this research, the project team found over 300 websites for opera companies, in 40 countries; over 150 companies were identified in the United States alone. We estimate that hundreds of thousands of people are involved one way or another each year in creating the live experience of opera, and that over 100,000 people are professionally involved, as singers, musicians, production staff, technicians, managers, theater employees, marketers, accountants, interns, and educators. For practical reasons, we decided to focus our research on those professionally involved in it, or seeking through training to become professionally involved. Even confining the research to the professional sphere, only a few individuals could be sampled for information through interviews, and we decided it was important to reach a wider body of participants through online surveys. During 2011, we conducted 65 interviews with 24 company or artistic directors of companies, large and small; 12 opera performers; nine teachers of opera, many of whom are also performers; six music directors; five stage directors; three composers; two répétiteurs/coaches; and four interviewees who had a wide overview of the art form as critics or managers of international opera networks. Interviews were conducted in Barcelona, Berlin, Brisbane, Chicago, Detroit, Dunedin (New Zealand), Graz, Helsinki, Hong Kong,

London, Melbourne, Milan, Minneapolis, New York, Oslo, Perth (Australia), Riga, Singapore, Sydney, Tallinn, The Hague, and Vienna.

Supplementing these were the online surveys, with 211 responses received from 78 performers, 36 composers, 41 répétiteurs/coaches, 36 directors of opera companies, and 20 teachers of opera. Analysis of the data received from these sources reveals common concerns, and while there will always be exceptions, there is also real consensus in the replies we received to most of the questions we posed about the future of opera.

SYSTEMS OF LEARNING MUSIC

Western opera requires training in a wide range of contributing musical, theater, and other activities. Performers on stage wear costumes, sing and act, and occasionally dance. An orchestra provides the accompaniment. A production requires direction and marketing, and a company needs management. Some companies run or own theaters that require maintenance and administration. In our research in this area, the focus is on the learning of skills by opera singers.

In the past, opera singers were taught, coached, and mentored by independent teachers, often opera singers themselves. This is now very rare. Typically, training for an opera singer involves attendance at a conservatorium or school of music, either an independent institution or one that is part of a wider educational institution such as a university. The training is normally a 3-year program for a first qualification (mostly a bachelor's degree, although in Europe some conservatoria still retain their own qualifications), and then at least 1 or more years for a higher qualification (honors or master's or a graduate diploma). Where the conservatorium is part of a university (and often called a school of music), professional training in musical performance sits beside other forms of musical skill and knowledge acquisition, and sometimes degree programs require study in areas outside music. Some institutions also include theater training, though this is not common. Opportunities for practical learning through performance vary from institution to institution.

The important role of an individual vocal teacher cannot be underestimated. Voice training is built around a master–apprentice relationship rare in undergraduate training in other disciplines. Students with some experience are as careful to select appropriate teachers as teachers are to select promising students. The voice is a fragile instrument, and inappropriate teaching can have a deleterious effect. One-to-one lessons are much more expensive than other forms of undergraduate teaching, and while this is accepted as a sine qua non for potential performers of Western classical music in all its forms, it creates financial challenges for institutions: Most schools of music and conservatoria are heavily dependent on support from benefactors or from their university. In the case of opera, the financial challenge is magnified when opera productions are presented. The opportunities for trainee opera singers to perform in opera may be limited by these considerations.

Singers, unlike instrumentalists, cannot begin to study and train effectively until their late teens, since the mature voice has not developed until then. By the time they graduate they may well not have reached the same level of technical security and musical communication as their instrumental colleagues. They may also not have had the opportunity—or the time—to study all the other performing aspects that opera requires. More specialized graduate study is offered by some institutions, and some opera companies offer further training opportunities.

Our interviewees disagree about the quality of training provided. "We are producing a lot of good young singers in this country [United States]. I think the training is better than it's ever been, and singers are more versatile than they've ever been" (Cheek, interview, April 22, 2011). But Lewis tells us, "They are not learning the craft properly. . . . With the university system you have to just get these kids through in 4 years. This isn't enough time to develop the voice slowly and properly" (interview, April 7, 2011). Wickham maintains, "Only one singing lesson a week is not enough for young singers. . . . The training should be as wide as possible including languages and history of opera, diction, phonetics, ballet, acting and movement, text analysis, et cetera" (interview, June 17, 2011). Zagars points out that "singers have to be well trained, [have] great bodies and excellent technique" (interview, October 1, 2011) so they can meet the requirements of contemporary productions. "Staging is very different now," Swedberg suggests. "It's quite possible to get a degree in some institutions but have never actually performed in an opera" (interview, April 20, 2011). But Evans advises, "In my experience, singers in Europe get more experience but are not as well trained, whereas the ones in the UK are better trained but don't get as many performing opportunities" (interview, January 18, 2011). The transition from training to career can be problematic, for several reasons. Three or 4 years may be insufficient preparation time. "I don't think we spend enough time developing young singers, we don't allow them to mature, we throw them out on the stage and they have one bad show and their career is over" (Johnson, interview, May 12, 2011). Matabosch echoes this:

> [You] come out of conservatory, you go and sing a very important role in a Mozart opera in, say, the Salzburg Festival, where you used to have to be a big star before you sang there. This is a lot of pressure before they are ready so careers these days are very short. . . . We have incredibly good singers,

but I think we have a system that is killing them somehow. (interview, November 7, 2011)

For many, gaining employment as an opera singer can be challenging. "I think we are producing far too many singers. The competition is outrageous—I can't imagine starting out now," says Zabala. "Of the people who are well qualified, half of them will get work, because of the competition. I think we are making mistakes by giving people degrees who don't have what it takes to be in the business" (interview, March 30, 2011). The competition for work is evident from the surveys we undertook with performers themselves. Nearly all trained at a conservatorium or school of music, most for 5 years or more. They lament the heavy costs a freelance performer bears, not only in attending auditions but also, in many cases, employing coaches privately. They note that constant upskilling is necessary because of the extravagant demands of stage directors, but that income is usually insufficient for this to take place effectively. Young singers reported finding it difficult to "break in" to the profession unless they are identified as the latest media sensation. They are concerned that employment decisions are not based solely on musical factors: Personal relationships and physical appearance count, and opera companies tend to favor the latest young media sensation whether or not he or she has the musical skills to deliver a good performance. Older singers tend to be marginalized. One survey informant suggested that, to be employed, you need "vocal quality PLUS skills PLUS looks." Another told us, "I've branched out into musical theater to try to give myself more of a chance to make it."

It might be thought that the scarcity of professional career opportunities would have an effect on the providers of training, but they are not in fact governed by the market for employment, but by four other factors. The first is the demand of young people for training, which is driven by dreams and not employment opportunities. The second is that the real potential of a singer cannot be identified when students enter training but will only emerge later. The third is an institutional requirement, related to reputation and funding, to show that degree programs are attracting students, are retaining them, and have a high percentage of graduations. The fourth is that having an opera department is likely to be driven more by prestige for the conservatorium or school of music than by a need for more opera singers. Wider questions about conservatorium training also relevant to opera training are addressed in Bennett and Hannan (2008), Carruthers (2010), Drummond (1998), Musumeci (2008), and Smilde (2009).

Implications for Sustainability

While the art form is flourishing, in that there is no shortage of ambitious and committed up-and-coming opera performers, employment opportunities are not increasing, and entering the profession and remaining in it is a real challenge for many. In general, the quality of formal training appears to be high, although it may be too short and there is no substitute for experience in productions.

MUSICIANS AND COMMUNITIES

Like Western classical music concerts, opera performances tend to appeal to an older age group. But can opera rely only on that group? Should efforts be made to attract younger audiences? These are questions of real concern to opera companies and performers worldwide. Opera director Homoki's answer is clear: "We need to prove to the public that opera is understandable. . . . We must open up to everyone . . . and not close up to become an elite enterprise" (interview, November 14, 2011). But Johnson sounds a warning: "We have a dedicated [older] audience that come to the opera, and a lot of solutions are 'Oh we have to appeal to our very young audience,' forgetting the audience that is already there and dedicated to you" (interview, April 12, 2011). Dickie suggests, "We need to demonstrate the economic impact as well as the innate value of the arts" (interview, April 7, 2011). Many companies are doing this, often to meet the requirements of state funders. Outreach programs are now an integral part of many opera companies' activities. "We are working very hard to get additional funding from the government but we were told that opera was elitist. So we decided we should go out and do our own work," says Ng Siew Eng, general manager of Singapore Lyric Opera (interview, June 20, 2011):

> I am trying a new approach to opera to go out and work with youth and all the young men who are out there getting into fights and playing the computer. . . . We want to make a difference and we are really serious about making opera popular. . . . We go out to libraries to do talks, and we have an opera cafe—anyone who is interested can go on stage and sing. You pay $30 and people come on and get a ticket and a drink. . . . I have lots of people coming to say, "I never knew opera is so exciting!" . . . The million dollar question is, do you want to be appealing to younger people and do interesting productions, or do you want to be traditional and appeal to the traditional audience? (interview, June 20, 2011)

Matabosch's productions have two casts: one of international singers of high level and the other of younger, less experienced singers. "The price of the second cast performances is very low and . . . it's a completely different audience, it's much younger, a 20-year age difference" (interview, November 7, 2011).

Many companies take opera into schools. "I think opera is in threat of dying out unless opera companies continue their education," says Kraus. "In the age of video games and technology, there is something about watching something live that is very special to these young people" (interview, April 8, 2011). Yuen tells of visiting schools in the United Kingdom, singing arias, taking her costume, and telling the story: "They were totally fascinated. I showed them pictures and they were riveted. I think education should start from a young age to get them engrossed" (interview, June 22, 2011). Mangin reports on Opera Queensland's education programs in primary/elementary schools:

> We create special productions for them that are commissioned by us and we tour them all through the state [Queensland] and into northern New South Wales [the neighboring state]. We see up to 32,000 young people in a year. These productions can employ up to 11 people for up to 40 weeks. . . . We charge about $6 a head. Our rule has always been that no child misses out. If a child can't pay then we pay for them. (interview, June 9, 2011)

The company also has a secondary/high school program, on a residency basis:

> We go into the school for a week. . . . The feedback we get from the students, parents, educators, is fantastic. Our work gives the students a window into opera in a literary sense, in a vocal sense, and using opera to discover themselves. We have a program that has been designed off this that has been directed at Indigenous people, in communities that are seen by the press as difficult communities, and we've had great success. (interview, June 9, 2011)

But to what extent are individual opera performers connecting with their communities? Are they respected? Can they make a living? According to our survey respondents, the life of an opera performer is not an easy one. Despite 5 years' professional training, over a quarter of respondents had not performed in opera at all in the year they completed the survey (2010). Half had performed in three or fewer productions, and three quarters of the respondents performed on fewer than 30 nights in the year. Those employed as performers also helped backstage and in marketing the production. It is not clear whether these activities were stipulated in performing contracts. Clearly this is not full-time employment in the usual sense of the term.

There were exceptions. One respondent performed in 14 productions in 2010 and gave over 60 performances. This performer is a rarity (at least according to the data we have assembled). Two thirds of respondents performed in 2010 with a full-time opera company, over a third with a part-time opera company, and just under a third with an occasional opera company. Three quarters of respondents performed in 2010 in a traditional opera house, and over half in a multimedia performing space. Other locales where they had performed opera included community halls, private homes, and open-air spaces.

Survey respondents were also asked about their income sources. Of those who responded to this question, only a quarter claimed 80% of their income came from performing; nearly half claimed that less than 20% of their income derived from performing. Half acknowledged they derived income from teaching, and half acknowledged significant income from activities not related to opera at all. The 36 surveyed composers told a similar story. Only one claimed to have earned over 80% of income from composing opera in the previous 12 months. A quarter worked with full-time opera companies, a quarter with part-time companies, a quarter with occasional opera companies, and a quarter with ensembles that only sing but do not stage operas.

The community for Western opera is no longer just in the West. The art form spread across the world in the 19th and early 20th centuries as a consequence of a wider process of European globalization. Noticeable in recent years has been its spread in China and other Asian countries. According to *The Economist*, "some 50 new opera houses have been completed in China or are near completion and many more are planned" ('E.H.B.', 2014). On December 20, 2010, *The New York Times* reported:

This year alone has seen the establishment of an Academy of Opera at Peking University; the second annual NCPA Opera Festival, with 12 different operas performed in 10 weeks; the premiere of Wagner's "Ring Cycle" in Shanghai; the grand opening of the $202 million Zaha Hadid-designed Guangzhou Center for the Performing Arts; the performance of three operas (Handel's "Semele," Zhou Long's "Madame White Snake" and Ye Xiaogang's "Song of Farewell") in just one week at the Beijing Music Festival; and a Sino-European Summit for the Performing Arts that brought directors of major European institutions like the Barbican (London), the Théâtre du Châtelet (Paris) and Deutsche Oper Berlin to Beijing to exchange experiences with Chinese counterparts. (Melvin, 2010)

What is the appeal of Western opera in Asian countries? Yoshihara (2007) suggests the process has had several phases. In the second half of the 19th century, it was associated with modernity, Westernization, and national progress. During the 20th century, it became "a tool for promoting Asian, rather than simply Western, cultural values and political objectives" (pp. 47–48). Later in the century, while it continued to be viewed as an elite culture, it became "a much more broad-based pursuit of the middle class," a practice through which "people with little or no background in Western culture could come to own a piece of symbolic and cultural capital and claim a class identity" (pp. 47–48). Hao Huang (2012) proposes that there is an affinity between Confucian musical aesthetics and Western classical music. Pal Christian Moe, casting director at the Bavarian State Opera in Munich, believes that three factors contribute to South Korea's impact on the world of opera: a tendency of families to sing at home, a fascination with Western music, and the fact that "singers from the Far East . . . sometimes have a better work ethic than, say, French and Italian singers" ('E.H.B', 2014). A 2011 article in *Time* magazine quoted Metropolitan Opera baritone Tian Hao Jiang as suggesting that "the future of opera may be in China" (Krich, 2011). China is cited as "the future" of a great many activities, not least because of its population size and growing economic strength. Given that China has its own indigenous opera styles, and many of them, it does not need Western opera to meet basic cultural needs for music theater. It is interesting to note, further, that the opera being adopted in China is institutionalized Western opera, based in opera houses. Meanwhile, Chinese opera continues to be performed and supported as well.

It may seem ironic that Western opera, like Western classical music, has become so enthusiastically practiced in Asian countries such as China, Korea, and Japan more so, perhaps, than in the region that gave it birth. But this is true of many Western cultural practices, from food to clothing to transport. Similarly, there may be more *djembe* players outside than inside West Africa. Cultural practices have always had the habit of migrating and of being adopted by other communities, and sometimes a practice is maintained in a migrant or adopted community while it is modified and adapted in its original one. In the case of opera, in a globalized world, it is probably quite natural that in non-European countries it should be both preserved and encouraged to move forward as it bumps into other, local cultural practices.

Implications for Sustainability

Opera can only flourish where there is support for it in the wider community. Education programs are necessary to help sustain community understanding of the art form. Efforts are being made by many companies to widen support and to find new audiences. Employment opportunities for opera performers are affected by high levels of competition. This may suggest a gloomy outlook, but opera is now a worldwide arts experience, and the growing support for it in Asian countries suggests it can have an appeal well beyond the communities for which its traditional repertoire was written.

CONTEXTS AND CONSTRUCTS

The weight of tradition sits heavily upon the shoulders of opera practitioners, whether it be the physical tradition of the opera house or the stylistic tradition of the 19th-century canon. In many cases "opera" is synonymous with a place or a company, and the great opera houses like L'Opéra de Paris, the "Met" in New York, Covent Garden in London, and La Scala in Milan have become the epitome of what opera has been and continues to be. They employ solo singers, choruses, orchestras, a legion of backstage technicians, and large management teams, and are extremely expensive to run. Söderblom describes them as "fortresses of art" (interview, November 29, 2011). Their repertoire deviates very little from the established canon, as Hagegård remarks: "I find that we play far too much of the old repertoire. We tend to turn even a newly built opera house into a museum" (interview, October 31, 2011). Larson describes opera as "a repackaging industry" (interview, June 11, 2011) and many, like Hellstenius, find this disturbing:

> There is something really troubling about the opera institutions as they seem to be the most conservative.... If you scroll through the opera houses in Europe you see mostly the same repertoire and the amount of new pieces are relatively very few. (interview, October 31, 2011)

At the same time, a new tradition has emerged in opera of presenting the works of the canon in new and often challenging ways. Born in Germany in the 1960s, *Regietheater* ("Director's Theater") or *Neue Inszenierung* ("New Production") has become widespread and causes much discussion. The impetus for this has been the idea of opera as "text" (see Till, 2012). The scenario, libretto, and music are products of their time, usually a time quite different from today. Those "texts" can be—or should be—deconstructed to have a contemporary impact (see Beyer, 2011; Cannon, 2012). Informants provided several perspectives on the phenomenon of *Regietheater*. For some, new production approaches are a way to renew the repertoire. Stephens maintains that "this is a good way to sustain opera, allow it to be relatable to the audience. . . . This is the way opera needs to move in order to stay relevant" (interview, April 22, 2011). Sobotka suggests that "productions need an up-to-date approach to be of interest to the audience of today. Some senior members of the audience don't like it too much . . . [but] another part of the audience really likes and appreciates it" (interview, January 18, 2011). Others are less enthusiastic. Frutiger is concerned that often "it's the director saying, 'this is me. . . .' It really doesn't have anything to do with the operas or the story or anything" (interview, April 27, 2011); and Cheek points out that "sometimes you can get directors that come up with brilliant concepts and amazing ideas but then by the third act it doesn't work" (interview, April 22, 2011). One survey respondent, a performer, took an extreme view, referring to "directors who seem bent on vandalizing great works of art." As Zagars points out:

> If a director is doing a new production in a new century, you have to be so strong with your interpretation so the performers can understand it. You have to work with them and you have to convince them, then together you can try and convince the audience. (interview, October 1, 2011).

Fournier-Facio offers a more balanced view:

> We try and get directors that do something new and inventive while still respecting the music and libretto. I love [to] experiment but I feel that one has to respect the drama and the score. . . . You must preserve the heritage but you must look into your own time; that's essential. (interview, November 9, 2011)

Lindenberger (2010, p. 107) points out that opera houses receiving state subsidies can more easily afford to present *Regietheater* productions than can ones more dependent on box office and private donations.

Regietheater is in some ways a substitute for presenting new works, as Hellstenius remarks. "*Regietheater* has opened up opera but it has also created some terrible productions. Why don't you just write a new opera if you are going to twist its meaning so much?" (interview, October 31, 2011). Everyone we spoke to is enthusiastic for new operas, at least in principle. "We need opera to tell us something about ourselves. We need new works; we can't just keep using operas that were written 100 years ago" (Matabosch, interview, November 7, 2011). "Opera houses have to commit to the production of new opera whether or not they are popular. . . . The form cannot survive indefinitely on a core small repertoire. It has to renew" (Hytner, interview, September 9, 2011). However, there seem to be several barriers to overcome.

The first of these arises from developments in the musical language during the 20th century and the challenges these present particularly to vocal music:

> It's obvious that the consequences of the modernist movement for classical music have been far more serious in their impact on a potential audience than the modernist movement in other art forms. It's a fact that what happened in the early part of the 20th century divorced people away from classical music. . . . An enormous amount of thriving music has been written in this period but as part of that exciting development the public has disappeared. (Hytner, interview, September 9, 2011)

The composers who responded to the survey made similar points. One referred to "the tyranny of the avant-garde," while another challenged the skills of many contemporary opera composers and wrote of struggling to "break through the noise of many composers writing operas who have no idea what they are doing." Interview informants also picked up this second point. "Some composers are wonderful and really know how the voice works. Some composers [just] look up a book which says that the tenor range is C to C so they write a part with no idea how the voice works" (Frutiger, interview, April 27, 2011). Frutiger's comments are echoed by Yurisich: "The big problem for new works is the voice is being asked to do things it simply can't do. . . . Some of these new works could be really good if they were put together properly" (interview, June 17, 2011). "Almost everyone wants to write an opera," says Gjevang, "but few of them understand the complexity of opera" (interview, December 6, 2011; and see Reekie's comments in Higgins, 2001).

Even those composers with an instinct for the theater, or some experience of it, will face challenges. Hanson points out that it takes 2 years to compose an opera (interview, September 6, 2011). Sobotka suggests that it is difficult to sell new operas to the public, or at least to the traditional opera public (interview, January 18, 2011). Aldridge maintains that "people are interested in the premières of new works but repeat productions are difficult" (interview, April 29, 2011). Neu points out that "companies see them as risks: With the economic downturn people are still spending money on the arts but . . . they would rather go to a third-rate *La Boheme* than . . . to something they don't know" (interview, March 31, 2011). Nonetheless, new operas can be successful. "I think if something has a good libretto and good basic story and the music is halfway decent it can have a good impact," says Fiore (interview, October 24, 2011), adding, "Opera is about the human voice and making it express something to the public. I am all for things that can reach you on an emotional level that open up your intellect and spirit." Evans seems to speak for many of our informants in remarking:

> New work is vital. We have to expose traditional opera audiences to the music of today more. I think every opera center in the world has a responsibility to produce modern opera. It can be sing-able and accessible. There's enough going on in the world in the last 25 years—there's plenty of subject matter to write on. (interview, January 18, 2011)

For some companies, the institutional opera house is recognized as an impediment to new work. "New works really need a smaller venue than the big opera house, and, here in Graz, we don't have such a venue at present" (Sobotka, interview, January 18, 2011). "For us it would help a lot to have a second smaller theater so we wouldn't have to sell so many tickets every night. . . . It's not realistic to sell huge numbers of tickets to lesser known works" (Matabosch, interview, November 7, 2011). Indeed, the smaller independent opera companies are more flexible than the "great houses." Often run by performers themselves and often without a permanent performing base, these companies usually focus on particular styles of opera, particular composers, or new work. They operate with much lower budgets and often have a gathering of loyal supporters. "There are loads of small groups doing opera on a shoestring," reports Evans. "[They] are getting more and more common in the UK now. . . . People can go touring around with a small ensemble, doing operas without chorus" (interview, January 18, 2011). An example is Pinchgut Opera in Sydney, Australia, which focuses on performing rare works from the Baroque and Classical repertoire. Anna Cernaez, general manager of the company, remarks:

> We try and use singers and orchestral players from Australia who are very much at the cutting edge of their careers. . . . We don't want to perform at the [Sydney] Opera House. We want a very small intimate space so we perform in a 1,000-seat hall. . . . We get the usual opera-going crowd but we also get a lot of younger people and lots of younger women. We worked out the average age of our audience is 33. (Cernaez, interview, June 13, 2011)

John Allison, editor of *Opera* magazine, sees this as a worldwide trend. "We haven't got to the situation where smaller companies have taken over, but they are getting more popular," he says. "I'm in favor of these things because they give a lot of work for artists. They can give opportunities to composers too, learning their trade by writing works for smaller forces than are required in the traditional opera house" (interview, September 9, 2011).

Implications for Sustainability

Renewal is essential for almost any art form to flourish. For opera, the construct of the opera house reinforces the canon and leads to attempts to renew the genre through inventive productions that meet mixed receptions. Musical language issues have an impact on the acceptability of new work, and there is little room for failure. Small companies have more flexibility and are finding a significant niche in the market.

INFRASTRUCTURE AND REGULATIONS

Probably no art form in the world needs infrastructure like opera performed by traditional opera companies, including a hall with excellent acoustics, an orchestra pit, a large stage, and a flight tower. In addition, opera is subject to a range of government regulations: health and safety in opera houses, copyright in media distribution, taxation laws with respect to public and corporate donations, and employment laws in relation to personnel. In European and some other countries, government, whether national, regional, or local, gives generous support to the art form, conditional on what is available in the public purse. Training in opera is undertaken in institutions, most of which receive government funding support, and such training takes place within a framework of quality control. Our informants seem largely optimistic about opera's ability to continue and flourish within these contexts, although there are challenges. The infrastructure costs of large opera houses, and related issues of union agreements, are clearly a potential threat to the sustainability of opera. One solution is to find alternative places to perform. "People need to find ways that are economically viable to keep performances going," says Aldridge. "I think companies may be better served if they move to smaller halls" (interview, April 29, 2011). Conway suggests, "We need to stage opera in different locations, get out of the theater to the people" (interview, June 9, 2011). Johnson sees here the possibility of presenting "riskier repertoire without the kind of fixed costs that our opera houses present" (interview, June 12, 2011). The successful use of a different location depends on matching the infrastructure requirements of the works to be performed with the infrastructure of the venue, acoustically, theatrically, and in terms of audience support. Wherever one performs opera, however, funding is a critical issue.

Various authorities have studied the economics of the performing arts in Western culture. In *Performing Arts, The Economic Dilemma* (1966), Baumol and Bowen already suggested 50 years ago that arts productivity does not operate according to classic laws of economics. They indicate that the number of people required to perform a piece of music (a string quartet, symphony, or opera) remains constant over time, and the product remains essentially the same, but that since salaries and wages and other costs do not remain constant, the costs of presenting the musical experience will continually increase. (Normally, providing more and more of the same product makes it cheaper, as computer hardware and software clearly attests.) Unless new modes of performance that reduce human costs or other ancillary costs can be introduced, opera will continue to become ever more expensive; in consequence, income will always need to increase.

Given this theory, another way some economists look at the situation for arts practices is through the lens of "market failure." This unfortunate term reflects that in certain activities—health and education, as well as the arts, for instance—the supply of a product cannot be directly funded by those who consume it. In the performing arts, the real cost of a live performance is greater than ticket purchasers are able or willing to pay. In market terms (though hopefully not in artistic ones), the performance may consequently be considered a failure. The question arises, then, of how to meet the funding gap. Economists have introduced the concept of "merit goods," where the benefit to be gained from consuming the goods is deemed to be sufficient to justify external support. The benefit may be defined as a personal one, which would lead to an individual providing external support; a commercial one, which would lead to a company providing support; or a public benefit, which would lead to the state providing support. Across the world, arguments continue about whether the greater merits in health, education, and the arts accrue to individuals or to the community as a whole. Are the community benefits enough to justify whole-community funding? Economists agree, however, that it is difficult to define and quantify what exactly are the benefits provided by arts practice, and this is what gives arts organizations like opera companies a real challenge in their search for external support. (For further discussion of these matters, see Drummond, Kearsley, & Lawson, 2008; Galloway & Dunlop, 2007; Hesmondhalgh, 2002; Holden, 2004; O'Connor, 2002; Reeves, 2002; and Throsby, 2003.) In this context, it is not surprising that funding issues should loom large in the minds of our informants. In the United States and some other countries, support for opera comes largely from foundations and corporations providing charitable donations, and from commercial sponsorship. In Europe, opera is widely supported by the state as a public benefit, important to the creation and maintenance of a well-rounded society. The challenges faced under these two systems have much in common.

In the United States, the events of 9/11 and the global financial crisis of 2008 created successive funding challenges for opera companies, as corporations grew nervous about the financial future. Many opera companies closed down, and others had to reduce their commitments. "We used to produce six operas a year; now we have four. I used to have adult education programs; now I don't" (DiChiera, interview, April 23, 2011). Mosteller points out that "philanthropic giving isn't what is used to be.... A lot of corporations are moving into funding for education and schools. It's hard to argue for the arts when the social needs are huge these days" (interview, April 7, 2011). In Europe, despite a historic belief in the arts as a public good, it was the global financial crisis that led to governments having to reconsider their funding priorities. Very few opera companies were spared. "I am very lucky that during these last years where the economy was quite bad in Estonia we haven't had the budget reduced" (Mikk, interview, September 30, 2011).

In both Europe and the United States, as well as elsewhere, the larger opera companies arguably face the biggest challenges, not only because they have the biggest budgets, but also because plans and financial commitments are made for several years ahead. William Mason, then general director of Chicago's Lyric Opera, famously stated in 2004, "I'm not running an opera, I'm running a fifty million dollar business" (quoted in Payne, 2005, p. 317). A sudden change in income, from whatever source, threatens the ability to carry out commitments. Companies have to campaign for funds. Sobotka puts forward the public-good argument: "It needs to be understood that opera is part of building and sustaining the welfare of society. It helps people understand the world" (interview, January 18, 2011), while DiChiera points to comparisons with other government subsidies for music: "The largest funded musical group in this country [the United States] is the military bands. Millions and millions of dollars are invested in this, they fund those, so shouldn't the rest of the country have music funded too?" (interview, April 23, 2011). Payne looks to a mixed economy solution:

> When I was young, I sort of believed in the socialist model that a benevolent state would take taxes from its inhabitants and provide a decent level of education, health care, transport, and culture for its citizens. I would say it was a pretty successful model from 1955 to 1995 ... and a society that has those things in balance is probably a more contented society than one that doesn't. I suppose as I got older I saw more of the benefits of a competitive market economy.... Now with the benefit of old age I have really become an

advocate of a mixed economy. I think that well-directed state investment is a good thing. I think that in successfully run opera institutions, in the next 5 to 10 years there will be a kind of balance between those forces. (interview, September 8, 2011)

Funding issues matter to the large, institutionalized companies more than they do to the smaller companies, which usually have fewer fixed costs, can more easily adjust their expenditure to suit their income, and may not need to plan so far ahead. Because they tend to have a lower profile, however, they may find it equally difficult to find funding sources. Our informants from smaller companies had less to say about money from their own perspective but were staunch in their advocacy of opera as a public good, as were those we surveyed. The term *market failure* is rejected by some, on the grounds that it humiliates the practitioners of opera. Reeves (2002, p. 28), borrowing from the report of the European Task Force on Culture and Development, itemizes seven direct and indirect economic impacts for "the arts": They provide content for the culture industries, create jobs, have local economic impact through multipliers, have their own value-adding markers, create cultural credit and esteem, create international stocks of ideas and images, and can enhance the built environment. Given these factors, opera and its fellow practices are often unjustifiably put on the back foot by some economists and politicians. The complexity of the situation faced by opera is summed up by Payne (2005):

> Opera is a social service. It sits alongside education and healthcare as something owed by responsible citizens to the rest of an identifiable society. . . . At the same time, the opera aspires beyond social service. Its loftiest examples set ideals for eternity, but it also holds a licence to criticize and satirize contemporary society. It is an entertainment with a moral force. (p. 307)

While opera is dependent on an infrastructure of public funding support, it also depends on the infrastructure of education to inform the public about what it is. Traditionally this was to be found in school curricula, but over the past 20 years, this has changed. Not only has music education in many places given way to a more generic arts education, but also within music itself a wider range of genres is studied as a consequence of a reappraisal of the relevance of *all* music practices to school-age children. In some cases, the introduction of new subjects like information technology into the curriculum and a focus on literacy and numeracy skills have pushed arts, including music, to the margins. "The lack of arts education in schools is a disaster in the UK and the US" (Dickie, interview, April 7,

2011). Fournier-Facio laments, "In this country [Italy] there is no music education at school. Primary and high schools do not have music education. . . . If you don't make these children love classical music, it is terrible" (interview, November 9, 2011). Neu tells us that "Ancient Rome [and Greece] is not remembered for their banking practices, it's for their art works and their stories. . . . We need to invest in our souls and our imaginations" (interview, March 31, 2011). Survey respondents reflected the same views, mentioning the "low level of cultural education" in society. This is a situation that goes beyond opera, and opera on its own is not likely to change it. Perhaps future curricula will return to the importance of including "souls and imaginations"; in the meantime, the need is for adaptability.

Opera's survival within a constantly changing social, political, economic, and cultural infrastructure over the past 400 years has been due to its ability to adapt. In the present changing world, this quality is called upon again. "I think the challenge for opera is to modify itself a bit, to find new ways to present itself" (Evans, interview, January 18, 2011). "I like [the idea of] 'sustainable art' because we talk about the sustainable environment. We might be forced to do sustainable opera" (Hagegård, interview, October 31, 2011).

Implications for Sustainability

Opera's position in the infrastructure of society is a little uncertain. Declining arts education and the noticeable reduction in funding by many governments and corporations create serious challenges, particularly for the large opera companies. From the data collected through this research, it seems that the healthy survival of a full-scale professional opera company depends on two factors: a local population of around two million including a significantly well-off middle class, and a tradition in that location of public and private support for the arts. Without that infrastructure, large companies are likely to struggle. Smaller opera companies have lower requirements and can flourish in less demanding environments.

MEDIA AND THE MUSIC INDUSTRY

The opera industry has used technology in stage productions since its earliest days, with spectacular stage effects aiming to match, or even exceed, the spectacular sounds of the singing. Further, the marketing and promotion of opera has always used whatever communications media may be available at the time. But recent developments in technology are having a profound impact on opera, as they are throughout contemporary society. The impact is felt in three areas: the marketing of live productions, access to recorded productions, and opera production.

We asked the companies we surveyed about marketing their productions. Printed materials are twice as favored as promotion through other media, perhaps because the traditional audience is less familiar with contemporary technologies. Yet many opera companies and opera houses do use new media to promote themselves and their productions, and even the most traditional ones have adopted media like Twitter in recent years. A small company like Pinchgut Opera in Sydney is very dependent on new media: "[Online] technology is fantastic in getting the word out and marketing.... We couldn't survive without the Internet" (Cernaez, interview, June 13, 2011).

Media also provide access to opera. Enrico Caruso's first sound recordings of opera arias were made in 1902, and since then complete operas and operatic excerpts have been made available in all the audio formats: 78-rpm discs, LP discs, cassettes, CDs, and mp3s. Opera on radio, either recordings or live broadcasts, has been widely accessible. This mediated version of opera turns it into a sound-only experience and inevitably privileges the music over the visual aspects of the work. After a century, this may well have created an audience of opera listeners rather than operagoers, affecting the way people respond to contemporary productions in the opera house. They may, for example, be tolerant of *Regietheater* so long as the music remains intact, and may be aroused to fury if the music is tampered with.

Many opera films, either location movies or ones based on theater productions, have been made available in the cinema or on DVDs for home viewing. Opera productions have been shown on television, and operas specially written for television have been around since the 1950s. Digitization has made filming easier and less complex. Marcia Citron (2000) suggests that "live and screen opera do not compete with each other but enhance each other," but points out that there are incompatibilities:

> Opera consists of reflective numbers that are relatively static. Cinema and television depend much more on movement and action, and thrive on a faster pace. When these media combine with opera, the reconciliation of differences creates a formidable challenge. (p. 8)

This does not seem to have prevented opera being accessed through the screen. DVDs can be watched on laptop computers, so an opera can be experienced privately on a commuter train or a mountaintop. On one level, the mediation places opera in the same space as anything else accessed through a private screen—an advertisement for McDonald's, a Monty Python episode, a news item about Palestine, or a pornographic movie. It increases the commodification of the practice and may reduce its impact as a "potentially transformational experience." At the same time, it enormously increases the accessibility of opera.

The issue of opera on the public screen has become much discussed in recent years with the dissemination of New York's Metropolitan Opera season in a high-definition movie format to cinemas across the world. One of our informants with involvement in the productions wonders about its impact on live local opera: "Is it going to excite people enough to want to go to the Minnesota Opera to see a live production, or is it going to be, 'Why should I pay $70 to go to the Minnesota Opera when I can pay $20 and eat my popcorn and my soda and watch the very best on the movie screen?'" (Frutiger, interview, April 27, 2011). Conway shares this anxiety: "Unfortunately . . . there are a number of people who like opera who haven't got much money and there's a film version coming up for only $25, so they are going to that instead of the live show, which is $100" (interview, June 9, 2011). Homoki warns, "It can also be a dangerous thing for local companies. Some politicians could say, 'Why do we need our local company when we have the Met here now at the cinema?'" (interview, November 14, 2011). But Aldridge takes a contrary view: "I think the Met broadcasts get people more excited about opera and will make them go and see more live opera" (interview, April 29, 2011). Fournier-Facio sees cinema opera as a way to attract new audiences: "We have realized that there are people, youngsters especially, who wouldn't dream of buying an opera ticket but would go to the movies with their popcorn and wearing jeans" (interview, November 9, 2011). Matabosch sees advantages for funding: "We are doing every year three international broadcasts in cinemas. . . . It is a very important way of promoting the house and also good for the sponsorship side of things" (interview, November 7, 2011). Steichen (2011, p. 446) suggests that the Met's inclusion in its screenings of scenes from backstage, and interviews with not only singers but also designers and costume makers, has the effect of making "a fiscal virtue out of the costly apparatus of opera production," helping potential funders realize why opera costs so much.

About a quarter of the companies we surveyed issue DVDs or sound recordings or offer TV access; half provide access to their productions through radio. Reflecting more recent developments in screen technology, a third offer access to their productions through the Internet. To more traditional live sound broadcasts on radio, and live audio-visual broadcasts on television or in the cinema, is now added live streaming of performances through the Internet, a service offered by, among many others, the Metropolitan Opera, the Glyndebourne Opera, the Vienna State Opera, the Bavarian State Opera, La Monnaie Opera, and the Royal Opera House Covent Garden. Sites like http://www.operacast.com provide information about what is available.

Contemporary media in the form of video, video projection, computer-generated imaging (CGI), and computer-controlled visual effects are all available as tools for the presentation of opera. The complexity can have its downside: "We had three or four performances that got cancelled because the computers broke down that controlled the set" (Evans, interview, January 18, 2011). But contemporary technology offers two benefits: an enhanced visual experience for the audience and a potential saving in costs. "Video projections are great. I think that's one way to do operas more cheaply without losing a huge amount of quality. Expensive sets become less necessary when you have video projection" (Aldridge, interview, April 29, 2011). "[In 5 to 10 years' time] I think an opera singer in London will sing a duet with an opera singer in New York, with all the technology that is happening, and it will look real" (Zabala, interview, March 30, 2011). "Live streaming, great idea! It's also perfectly possible to have an orchestra in one place [and] the production in another, an extraordinary thing to be able to do" (Conway, interview, June 9, 2011). Larson sees the potential for composers. "I envision, if someone will let me, writing a piece that is performed in several venues. . . . It all comes into the hall and on screens" (interview, May 11, 2011).

Implications for Sustainability

Contemporary technology has significantly changed the ecosystem for opera. As a marketing tool it spreads the opera world to new, younger audiences. In the form of high definition cinema experiences and via live streaming, it provides new access to the art form, with positive and perhaps some negative effects. As a tool for the performance of opera, it allows new spectacle. At the same time, opera at its heart will always be about the live experience of performance, and there is no reason to suppose that tradition will disappear.

ISSUES AND INITIATIVES FOR SUSTAINABILITY

In 1986, Ann Getty lamented:

> We cannot pretend that opera is in a healthy state today. There are still composers dauntless enough to try their hands, but it is increasingly hard to find open-handed patrons and open-minded audiences. Costs have escalated, and education has plummeted. We must concede that opera, especially new opera, cannot be self-supporting. . . . There is a gap between the development of the art form and the development of the audience; this gap is greater in opera than in any other art form. If the gap becomes a chasm, opera may well follow the epic and pastoral into extinction. (in Graubard, 1986, p. 2)

That gloomy prognostication of a generation ago seems not to have transpired. Indeed, those decades have seen, on the one hand, financial challenges facing the nations that opera inhabits, some as great as those of the 1920s and 1930s, and, on the other, the development of media through which opera has become more accessible than ever before. Lindenberger (2010) maintains:

Opera's been exploding all over the place: new audiences, new companies (and in towns where you could never have imagined opera before), new approaches to how one stages the thing, and to top it off ... a whole new area of inquiry that people are calling opera studies. (p. 1)

This may be slightly optimistic, although it can be said that Western opera is flourishing in terms of the richness of the experiences it offers to the public. While financial constraints have had their impact, and from 2005 to 2015 there have been closures of large and small companies, there remain hundreds of companies and individuals involved in ongoing productions of opera. At the same time, there is evidence to indicate that, in the context of the institutionalized opera house, it has become something of a museum culture, focused on the presentation of a small core of traditional works, but there does not seem to be any weakening of audience desire to see these works. The largest companies continue to base their work around the canon, in some places presenting opera in new and challenging productions but with new operas performed only occasionally, while many smaller companies offer audiences different experiences. In many of the larger metropolitan centers of the world, a range of live operatic experiences is available, and there is widespread access to opera in high definition, on DVD, and, increasingly, through the Internet.

While the future of Western opera does not seem, therefore, to be under immediate threat, informants for this research identified four issues that have a real impact on its sustainability: funding, audience development, renewing the repertoire, and adapting to the new media world.

The opera business is not about making profits, but about trying to find enough funds to pay for the next season, or even the next production (Payne, 2005 p. 53). Given the nature of the cultural practice of opera and the context in which it operates, the greatest challenge identified by those surveyed and interviewed was money. Neoliberal economics, now widely accepted across the world, favor "personal benefits" over "public benefit," and this has an impact on all arts and culture funding. "Market failure" as discussed earlier is seen as a reason for closure, not for support. Large companies and small companies alike find it difficult to balance their books if they are to continue, and a deficit of $25,000 for a small company may be as threatening to its future as a deficit of \$25 million is for a large one. Opera can no longer rely on a commonly accepted understanding of its importance, but must use the power of the experiences it provides to persuade funders to support it.

Audience development is therefore vitally important, given what some see as public ignorance and lack of appreciation of culture. Education programs are rated as highly as gaining loyal financial support. Those we surveyed seek to counter the stereotypes of opera as elitist and inaccessible and find ways to encourage younger generations to attend operas.

Renewing the repertoire, in one way or another, is a challenge everyone seems aware of. Opera companies can present the canon in a traditional way (old wine in old bottles) or in innovative ways (old wine in new bottles), or new works in a traditional model (new wine in old bottles) or in a new way (new wine in new bottles). Each of these will appeal differently to audiences, and possibly to funders too. The last three are all ways to renew the repertoire, or at least to re-present it. Informants are aware of shifting cultural perceptions and of the need "to keep ourselves relevant." They want to see new work developed but also recognize a lack of interest from traditional audiences who may be cautious about what they will hear and see. Companies can find themselves in a bind over this. While rethought productions continue to attract audiences—the traditional audience members still come for the music, and controversy attracts others—new works do not have the same impact, which means they bring greater financial challenges. In many cases, opera companies believe their survival relies on their continuing to perform the canon. In other, perhaps more adventurous ones, financial pressure becomes an incentive to doing things differently. The question as to whether opera can survive by merely reproducing the works of the past (in whatever guise) is a recurring one (see Cannon, 2012).

The new media technologies are having an impact on opera, in terms of access, marketing, and production. The Met's high-definition productions, seen in cinemas around the world, bring opera to a wider public, but it is "opera house" opera (what else could it be from the Met?), and by establishing or confirming in the audience's mind what opera is "all about," this may be stifling creative developments within the genre. But technology brings opportunity, as Nicholas Till (2012) points out: "All of these developments suggest that the future of opera may involve very different concepts of the performance space of opera, and of what constitutes an operatic audience or an operatic event" (p. 89).

One of the factors emerging from this research has been the "glut" of performers. While this is heartbreaking for many individuals whose dreams and aspirations seem destined to be unfulfilled and tragic for those individuals who are used up and spat out by the system, paradoxically, it may suggest a rosy future for opera, which depends on a continuing supply of skilled and well-trained performers.

The way forward for opera lies in the hands of the opera companies themselves. The large companies, often with their own opera houses, provide the common public image of opera, and they are continuing to be built in Asia. They preserve the image of opera as an expensive, institutionalized cultural practice focused on a canon of traditional works, and they require significant financial input from non-consumers of the product. They communicate prestige and elitism, even though they can now provide wider access to their products through cinema showings and live streaming. Classified in the last century as museums, they might better be called temples. Their contribution to the renewal of the art form comes more through innovative productions of familiar works than through newly composed works, partly because they have themselves presented opera as a canon of works. They are not well equipped to adapt quickly to changing social, political, and economic contexts. The smaller companies are more nimble. Often they have little if any overhead: They can employ singers and musicians per production, they can use contemporary online marketing techniques with websites and social media, and they can develop niche market followers. The wider reaches of the opera repertoire offer works that do not demand the full resources of the professional opera house, and they can commission new works to fit their particular infrastructure and image.

The question of the sustainability of opera comes, therefore, in two parts. First, how can the traditional, 19th-century opera houses and their large-scale companies and productions sustain themselves? They represent the tradition and the popular image of Western opera. As so-called market failures, they need to maintain and develop new external funding sources. Where the "public benefit" argument prevails, state administrations and governments may be able to help, depending on their resources and their priorities. But in continuing to present the canon they are faced with the challenge of renewing the repertoire: The two options of deconstructed presentations and commissioning new work are both risky for them. In other words, the longer they continue in their present mode, the more they may be adding to the museum image of opera, and making its sustainability questionable. The second question is a wider one: How can the cultural practice of Western opera sustain itself? Here the question is not just tied to the traditional companies and traditional opera houses: The nimble smaller companies have an important part to play, and it may well be that the longer-term sustainability of the art lies with them.

Within this challenging context, all of our interviewees and informants were clear about one thing: their passion for the art form. It may be hard to find employment, it may be hard to balance budgets, it may be hard to organize reper-toire in an effective way, and it may be hard to get new operas performed, but no one wants to walk away or give up. All have shared the extraordinary experience of what can happen when music and theater come together in live performance—that "potentially transformational experience"—and that surely will be enough motivation to sustain opera in the future.

ACKNOWLEDGMENTS

Thanks are due to Emma Fraser, Kristin Kenning, and Einar Solbu for their contri-butions and insights. I would also like to acknowledge all the opera practitioners with whom I've worked over the past 50 years and who have helped form my own understanding of this amazing art form.

REFERENCES

Baumol, W., & Bowen, W. (1966). *Performing arts, the economic dilemma: A study of problems com-mon to theater, opera, music, and dance*. New York, NY: Twentieth Century Fund.

Bennett, D., & Hannan, M. (Eds.). (2008). *Inside, outside, downside up: Conservatoire training and musicians' work*. Perth, Australia: Black Swan Press.

Beyer, B. (2011). Interviews with contemporary opera directors, selected from Barbara Beyer's Warum Oper? Gespräche mit Opernregisseuren. *Opera Quarterly, 27*(2–3), 307–317.

'E.H.B.' (2014, February 6). Opera: the new superpowers. *Economist*. Retrieved from www. economist.com/blogs/prospero/2014/02/opera

Cannon, R. (2012). *Cambridge introduction to music: Opera*. Cambridge, UK: Cambridge University Press.

Carruthers, G. (2010). Identity matters: Goals and values of intending and practicing profes-sional musicians. In M. Hannan (Ed.), *The musician in creative and educational spaces of the 21st century* (pp. 39–44). Retrieved from http://www.isme.org/publications/36-commissions-forum-documents-and-publications/66-ceprom-documents-and-publications 39–44

Citron, M. (2000). *Opera on screen*. New Haven, CT: Yale University Press.

Drummond, J. (1980). *Opera in perspective*. Minneapolis, MN: University of Minnesota Press.

Drummond, J. (1998). A change in the orders: Training the performers of the future. In H. Lundström (Ed.), *The musician in new and changing contexts* (pp. 51–62). Lund, Sweden: Malmö Academy of Music.

Drummond, J., Kearsley, G., & Lawson, R. (2008). *Culture matters: A report for the [New Zealand] Ministry of Research, Science and Technology*. Retrieved from http://www.mch.govt. nz/research-publications/our-research-reports/culture-matters-june-2008

Galloway, S., & Dunlop, S. (2007). *What's cultural about the cultural industries?* Retrieved from http://www.regional-studies-assoc.ac.uk/events/lisbon07/papers/Galloway/pdf

Graubard, S. (Ed.). (1986). The future of opera. *Daedalus, 115*(4). Cambridge, MA: MIT Press on behalf of American Academy of Arts and Sciences.

Hesmondhalgh, D. (2002). *The cultural industries*. London, UK: Sage.

Higgins, C. (2001, August 29). Arts: All change: How do you ensure opera has a future? Sack the singers? Get rid of the opera houses? *Guardian*. Retrieved from http://www.theguardian.com/profile/charlottehiggins?page=74

Holden, J. (2004). *Capturing cultural value*. London, UK: Demos.

Huang, H. (2012). Why Chinese people play Western classical music: Transcultural roots of music philosophy. *International Journal of Music Education, 30*(2), 161–176.

Krich, J. (2011, August 15). As opera struggles in the west, an art form flourishes in China. *Time*. Retrieved from content.time.com/time/world/article/0,8599,2086143,00.html

Lindenberger, H. (1984). *Opera: The extravagant art*. Ithaca, NY: Cornell University Press.

Lindenberger, H. (2010). *Situating opera: Period, genre, reception*. Cambridge, UK: Cambridge University Press.

Melvin, S. (2010, December 21). Boom Times for Opera in China, *New York Times*. Retrieved from www.nytimes.com/2010/12/21/arts/21iht-chinopera21.html

Musumeci, O. (1998). Should we change conservatory to "renovatory"? Towards a model of conservatories' idiosyncrasy. In H. Lundström (Ed.), *The musician in new and changing contexts* (pp. 29–40). Lund, Sweden: Malmö Academy of Music.

O'Connor, J. (2002). Public and private in the cultural industries. In T. Johansson & O. Sernhede (Eds.), *Lifestyles, desire and politics: Contemporary identities* (pp. 15–33). Gothenburg, Sweden: Centre for Cultural Studies: University of Gothenburg.

Payne, N. (2005). Opera in the marketplace. In M. Cooke (Ed.), *The Cambridge companion to twentieth-century opera* (pp. 306–320). Cambridge, UK: Cambridge University Press.

Reeves, M. (2002). *Measuring the economic and social impact of the arts: A review*. Retrieved from www.artscouncil.org.uk/documents/publications/340.pdf

Ross, A. (2007). *The rest is noise*. New York, NY: Picador.

Salzman, E., & Desi, T. (2008). *The new music theater: Seeing the voice, hearing the body*. Oxford, UK: Oxford University Press.

Smilde, R. (2009). *Musicians as lifelong learners: Discovery through biography*. Delft, The Netherlands: Eburon.

Snowman, D. (2009). *The gilded stage, a social history of opera*. London, UK: Atlantic Books.

Steichen, J. (2011). HD opera: A love/hate story. *Opera Quarterly, 27*(4), 443–459.

Throsby, D. (2003). Cultural sustainability. In R. Towse (Ed.), *A handbook of cultural economics* (pp. 183–186). London, UK: Edward Elgar Publishing.

Till, N. (2012). The operatic work: Texts, performances, receptions and repertoires. In N. Till (Ed.), *The Cambridge companion to opera studies* (pp. 225–253). Cambridge, UK: Cambridge University Press.

Yoshihara, M. (2007). *Musicians from a different shore: Asian and Asian Americans in classical music*. Philadelphia, PA: Temple University Press.

Zalfen, S. (2007). The crisis of culture and the culture of crisis: The case of opera in Berlin, London and Paris in the late twentieth century revisited. *International Journal of Cultural Policy, 13*(3), 273–286.

8

AMAMI SHIMA-UTA

Sustaining a Vernacular Popular Island Music

in the Shadow of Mainstream Japanese Culture

Philip Hayward and Sueo Kuwahara

OVER THE PAST 70 years, the Amami Islands have been increasingly integrated into the hegemony of standard Japanese culture. Despite this, the regional song form known as *shima-uta* (literally, "island songs") has persisted and, indeed, flourished as a result of local interest in and commitment to the form. The support for *shima-uta* reflects regional pride in the Amami Islands' heritage but also goes further in establishing *shima-uta* as an icon of Amami's difference from both main island Japan and from its southern neighbor, Okinawa. While a number of elements of traditional Amami culture, such as distinct local dialects, have diminished, *shima-uta* has consolidated as a vibrant thread in the Amami Islands' 21st-century identity.

BACKGROUND

The Amami Islands are located to the southwest of Kyushu (the southernmost major island of Japan). They form the southern portion of the Satsunan islands and a central portion of the Nansei islands and the so-called Ryukyu arc that runs southwest from Kyushu to Okinawa and on to Taiwan (Figures 8.1 and 8.2). Located along a thin chain of islands that stretches between the main islands of Japan and Okinawa, Amami has historically been both a cultural and socioeconomic "interzone" between the two regions. Until the 15th century, Amami consisted of a semiautonomous group of communities that engaged in various trade relations with

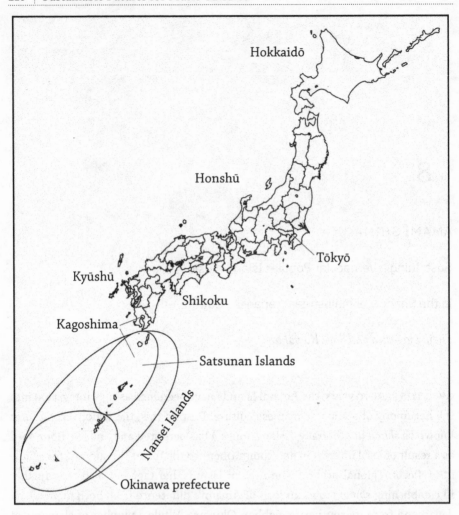

FIGURE 8.1 Map of Japan showing location of Nansei Islands; see Figure 8.2 for the exact location of Amami (derived from http://www.kabipan.com/geography/whitemap/index.html).

the Ryukyu kingdom (in present-day Okinawa) and Japan. These communities possessed marked dialectical variations within a general Amamian language that was related to—but distinctly different from—Okinawan and main island Japanese, and a range of distinct folkloric and cultural forms, including music and dance.

During the 16th century, the islands came under the control of Ryukyu until the southern influence was displaced by that of the Satsuma clan (based in present-day Kagoshima) in the early 17th century. Satsuma dominated the region until more central national control was extended to the Satsunan Islands under Japan's Meiji restoration government from 1868. During these two periods of external domination, the Amami Islands absorbed elements of adjacent cultures but substantially retained their indigenous culture, due to factors such as the region's highly dispersed communities and main island Japanese neglect of the region until the mid-20th century. Concerted development activities only began in the region following the withdrawal of US forces after 8 years of occupation in the immediate postwar period (1946–1953). Processes of modernization and integration with main island Japanese economy and society only gathered significant momentum from the 1980s. As a result, the Amami Islands have retained their distinct regional culture to a far greater extent than almost any other area of Japan (the Okinawa and Ainu regions of northern Hokkaido being the other most distinct cultural community).

Cultural and Social Positioning

The Amami Islands comprise the main island, Amami Ōshima, and five other main inhabited islands, Kikaijima, Kakeromajima, Tokunoshima, Okinoerabujima, and Yoronjima (Figure 8.2). The current population of the islands is around 120,000, with 65,000 concentrated on Amami Ōshima and with a significant number of Amamians now residing in the Kansai and Tokyo metropolitan areas of main island Japan (reflecting the islands' significant depopulation since the early 1950s). Amami Ōshima and Kakeromajima, in particular, have mountainous terrains that have served to isolate both inland and coastal communities, thereby assisting the maintenance of cultural differences between communities within short (direct) distances of each other. Reflecting this, the concept/word *shima* (also rendered as *jima*) is of particular importance in Amami. As researchers such as Haring (1952, 1954), Johnson and Kuwahara (2013), and Suwa (2007) have emphasized, *shima* refers to discrete, bounded locations with distinct attributes of various kinds. The term is usually translated as "island" and is often present as a suffix in place names to indicate their status as islands, but it is also used to refer to discrete, bounded inland locations, effectively "land islands" that are separated from neighboring locales and communities by land barriers (such as mountains, valleys, or rivers) that limit easy communication and access. *Shima* also has a further association, being taken to describe the character and/or "spirit" of place.

As American anthropologist Douglas Haring (1954) wrote after researching in Amami in the immediate postwar period, "each tiny hamlet—often out of touch with the hamlet across the mountain—preserves its dialect, its special folklore, songs, dances, festivals, technology, poetry, and economic organization; no single village is typical" (pp. 256–257). Moreover, the physical inaccessibility of some of the villages is also related to social difference. As Haring continues: "my native helpers at first were reluctant to venture into villages where they had no kin"

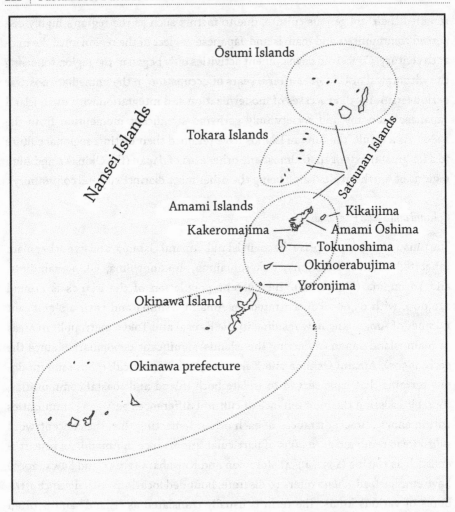

FIGURE 8.2 Map of Nansei Islands (derived from http://www.kabipan.com/geography/whitemap/index.html).

(p. 257). Japanese anthropologists have also emphasized the isolation caused by the island's terrain. For example: "villages, whose foresides were located in front of the vast sea and also whose hinterlands were hampered by 200-300m high mountains, had little contact with the outside and thus were heavily isolated" (Mizuno, 1974, p. 93, translated by the authors; see also Kagoshima Minzoku Gakkai, 1970). It is these (previously) difficult-to-access settlements that created "a land of islands." Their physical location was analogous to reaching an island by sea, with the sea acting as a network system to other coastal villages, as well as nearby and more distant islands. This environment of near isolation among settlements helps in understanding how a village or community can act as a metaphorical island.

Today, however, the mountainous islands of Amami and Kakeroma have a network of tunnels that connect many previously difficult-to-access villages. There is also reclaimed land in some of the urban areas, and an infrastructure and services provided by national and prefectural governments that the island would not otherwise be able to afford on its own. These and related factors have led to the development of a more "pan-Amamian" identity in the postwar era, which is explored further later with regard to local music culture.

Formal Features

Since the 1950s, when first external and then local folklorists began to collect the local vernacular songs of particular areas, there developed a perception that these examples of *shima-uta* (island/local songs) collectively constituted a corpus of premodern vernacular song materials that could be collectively identified as *shima-uta* and that composed a distinct cultural heritage asset for the islands. As with many bodies of vernacular song primarily communicated through oral transmission, the materials within such a corpus are of varying ages and share differing degrees of linkage with other songs (spanning single, unique songs and ones that either exist in multiple variants or can be seen to belong to song "families"). Songs are typically 2 to 4 minutes in duration (although some are considerably longer), and there is some flexibility for singers to select verses they wish to perform, often omitting verses to compress song duration. The location of the origins of specific songs is often clearly indicated in the particular dialect terms and/or topical or circumstantial references within song lyrics. Since collecting began, Amami *shima-uta* has been observed to be a song form that is habitually accompanied by rhythmic melodic motifs plucked on the three-string, banjo-like *sanshin*. The *sanshin* is similar to (but smaller than) the Japanese *shamisen* and is widely used throughout Amami and Okinawa. Although the *sanshin* has traditionally used snakeskin for its resonator cover, fabric has increasingly replaced this over the last 15 to 20 years. The Amami *sanshin* is distinct from its southern neighbor in that its strings are lighter in gauge, allowing players to use a smaller plectrum, usually in the form of a split bamboo stalk.

The singer often accompanies him- or herself on *sanshin* and may on occasion be accompanied by a *hayashi* (vocal harmonist), most often of the opposite gender. As discussed later, duetting and multiple vocal performances also occur in certain contexts. Musicologist Henry Johnson has provided a concise summary of Amami *shima-uta* in comparison to its sister song form in Okinawa:

The vocal qualities frequently range from a very low voice to falsetto. While the syllable structure of *shima-uta* is often thought of as having a Ryūkyūan influence from *ryūka* (ancient Ryūkyūan poetry), with its 8-8-8-6 classical form, *shima-uta* in Amami do not generally follow this structure, and instead have much more freedom. In terms of the scales used in Amami *shima-uta*, rather than using the Ryūkyūan (Okinawan) scale, songs tend to include other Japanese scales such as *ritsu* or *miya-kobushi*. (personal communication, June 2013; see further Koizumi, 1977; Yamamoto, 1980)

Shima-uta singers are formally and informally assessed and appreciated with regard to two criteria. The first is primarily applicable to the context of *uta-gake* (social performance) and requires evaluation by an audience conversant with the language and meaning of *shima-uta* lyrics. A singer adjudged to demonstrate a sound knowledge of the meaning of *shima-uta* lyrics and an ability to improvise lyrics that extend *shima-uta* material in an appropriate, inventive, and entertaining manner is regarded as a (competent) *uta-sha* performer. Vocal prowess, the second assessment criterion, is also adjudged as important for *uta-sha* performers but is not paramount. There are a number of vocal attributes that are prized in *shima-uta* performance: One is the "grain" (or "character") of the voice, and another is the performer's use of *guin* (an Amami term for emotive, upper-register vibrato), which can be combined with abrupt melodic leaps and/or (accommodated) register breaks (where the voice briefly "cracks" as it flips up). A singer who is vocally adept but limited in his or her understanding of *shima-uta* lyrics and/or who does not participate in *ute-gake* improvisation (or shows little competence in its performance) is referred to as a *kui-sha* (Ogawa, 1999, pp. 125–126; Tuboyama & Yanagawa, 2008, pp. 55–56).

Shima-uta is an umbrella term that includes a number of subtypes. Researcher Hisao Ogawa has identified that *shima-uta* includes three genres: *kami-uta* (literally, "god's songs"—i.e., those with an address to divine themes); *warabe-uta* ("children's songs"); and *min'yō*, a broad term that equates to the (equally broad) English language term *folk songs*. Further subdivisions are also possible. *Kami-uta* can be divided into the songs of *noro* (female ritualists) and *yuta* (female shamans). *Warabe-uta* can be divided into *yobikake-uta* (calling songs), various playing songs, and *komori-uta* (nursery rhymes/songs). The category of *min'yō* includes work songs, event songs, playing songs, songs not falling into either of the previous categories (Ogawa, 1999, p. 22), and new compositions written in similar musical style (although often with lyrics in standard Japanese or mixed Amamian phrases and standard Japanese) usually referred to as *shin min'yō* (literally, "new folk songs"). *Shima-uta* exists in several performance contexts, which are further described later in this chapter.

SYSTEMS OF LEARNING MUSIC

As a form of traditional vernacular music that circulated in a predominantly oral culture prior to the modernization of Amami from the early 1950s on, *shima-uta* repertoire and performance skills were communicated through processes of performance, familiarization, imitation, and feedback (between performers and between performers and listeners) in social/familial contexts. Developments of the form emerge from subsequent performer refinement, embellishment, and/or innovation.

Philosophies of Learning and Teaching

While written accounts documenting the social practice of music making in the prewar era are minimal, semiformal tutelage appears to have occurred either in (extended) family contexts or between accomplished and promising aspirant performers. There is no evidence that such tutelage was in any way systematized, nor that any forms of notation were used to transmit repertoire and styles and techniques of performance. Rote learning appears to have been prevalent. Due to the difficult nature of internal mobility in Amami (outlined earlier), prewar performers tended to be confined to particular localities and to have performed highly localized repertoires. This situation changed significantly during World War II. The initial impact derived from the militarization of the Japanese economy and the departure of a substantial number of young men to serve in the military in overseas campaigns. The final year of the war led to an increasing militarization of areas of the islands as they were located in the anticipated path of the US military invasion. In addition to disrupting social and familial systems, the upheavals brought members of previously isolated communities into contact with each other. After 1945, the imposition of Western styles of administration and education during the 8-year period of US occupation further disrupted cultural transmission and created a strong sense of social uncertainty. Following Amami's reincorporation into Japan in 1953, further changes occurred. In particular, there was a significant movement of population to both main island Japan and to Amami's capital city that depleted the islands' overall population and, particularly, the viability of smaller settlement areas. The improvement of road networks in the islands, and related cross-regional economic development patterns, caused an increasingly integrated Amami society in which regional differences eroded and regional elements entered into broader cultural practices.

This triple-stage disruption and reconfiguration of Amami society both weakened regional cultural transmission patterns and created elements of a pan-locational Amami cultural heritage that provided Amamians with a simultaneously broader and less regionally inscribed repertoire of song material and performance styles. It also brought in other factors. For some (particularly younger) Amamians, the modern culture of main island Japan constituted an appealing alternative to the solid traditions of their home islands and was embraced, particularly by those who relocated to main island Japan for either education or employment opportunities. This further weakened patterns of intergenerational transmission that had previously characterized *shima-uta* practice. At the same time, a better-connected and modernizing Amami also allowed for new initiatives in culture and cultural identity that inaugurated a new phase in regional culture, which included systematic research and repertoire collection, the advent of local music recording, and the initiation of song contests and festivals (discussed later).

Repertoire collection was unnecessary in a premodern context in which *shima-uta* repertoire was transmitted by oral/musical culture that was fundamentally embedded within everyday vernacular experience. Local communities were the repositories of local repertoire information. However, as these stable and discrete social aggregations became weakened by population movement and modernization, written documentation of *shima-uta* repertoire grew in importance as an archival/preservation practice. Written accounts of various Amamian folkloric practices (including details of song repertoire) commenced in the 1920s when main island Japanese scholar Kunio Yanagita published a detailed study (1925). The most significant work on *shima-uta* was produced by two amateur Amamian scholars, Eikichi Kazari and Ken'o Kubo. Kazari collected and classified many *shima-uta* lyrics in his book *Amami Ōshima Min'yō Taikan (A Grand View of Folk Songs in Amami Oshima)* (1933). Kazari's work was succeeded by Kubo (1960), who added further *shima-uta* lyrics and attempted to systematize them, and main island scholars Ogawa (1979, 1989, 1999) and Sakai (1996, 2005) uncovered more *shima-uta* lyrics, based on their long-term field research in Amami Oshima and Tokunoshima. The most recent contribution to this corpus was published by Central Gakki (Ibusuki, Ibusuki, & Ogawa, 2011), a comprehensive collection of *shima-uta* material reproduced together with Japanese translations of the song's lyrics and accompanying notes.

Learning and Teaching Practices and Approaches

The combined effect of the initiatives described earlier and discussed in detail later in this chapter created a situation in both Amami and among Amami communities in main island Japan whereby individuals who had acquired little or no skills in *shima-uta* performance from social and/or family contexts actively sought instruction from respected older *shima-uta* performers. Resultant tuition relationships combined elements of a traditional respectful musical "apprenticeship" with a paying client role. In Amami, and particularly around the capital Amami city (formerly known as Naze) itself, young aspirant performers have developed a number of loose tutelage arrangements with veteran performers who have tended to help intermediate-level *shima-uta* singers perfect their techniques and achieve individual characteristics and accomplishments within the idiom (rather than attempting to train aspirants to replicate their own idiosyncratic styles). A notable example in this regard is Yutaka Tsuboyama, who has taught and mentored highly regarded performers such as Kazumi Nishi, Shunzo Tsukiji, and Yasuo Kijima. Kōgi Fukushima, one of the first performers to record in Amami in the immediate postwar period, is commonly credited as the first performer to run regular classes for paying pupils in Amami, delivering these from the Central Gakki music company's premises in Naze from 1976. His educational activities later expanded to classes at a community center in the city, allowing a range of local people to gain familiarity with *shima-uta* performance (and related familiarity with its aesthetics).

Outside of Naze, one of the most well-known *shima-uta* classes is Takahide Yasuda's class (known as Yasuda *Min'yō Kyōshitsu*) in Kikaijima. Yasuda was born and raised on Tokunoshima, but in the 1960s he moved to Kikaijima to work, where he continued to perform *shima-uta* in family and festive contexts. Awareness of his abilities, combined with an absence of accomplished local performers, led local families to ask him to teach *shima-uta* to their children. At the time of writing, he continues to teach *shima-uta* to young people on Kikaijima; it is estimated that he has had in excess of 500 pupils since 1968. Among these have been Nami Makioka, Shiho Nagai, and Saori Kawabata, who have won Amami folk song contests and made recordings. In northern Amami Ōshima, Mitsuyo Tohara, winner of the Japan Folksong Grand Prize in 1989, opened a *shima-uta* class in 1998 at her local community hall in Kasari-chō and, since then, has been involved in various aspects of teaching and preserving *shima-uta* for younger local people. Also in the north of the island, the *Ogasari-warabe shima-uta* club, which started in August 1983, has provided long-term training for primary school children in Ogasari, supported by teachers, parents, former members, and local volunteers. This club has produced many successful young *shima-uta* singers such as Mizuki Nakamura and Marika Yoshihara, and performers from the club also regularly participate in concerts, workshops, and exchange events around Amami.

Outside Amami itself, one of the most celebrated teachers has been Kazuhira Takeshita, commonly regarded as one of the most gifted *utashas* of the mid- to late 20th century. Based in the Kansai area of Honshu, a region with a concentration of migrants and second- and third-generation Amamians, he differs from Tsuboyama and Fukushima in that he has been credited with creating a distinct "school" of *shima-uta* performers around Kansai, modeled on his distinct performance styles (particularly in terms of *sanshin* accompaniment) and philosophy. Some of his pupils have returned to Amami and promulgated his approach through their subsequent performances and teaching.

The previously mentioned music clubs for children reflect the situation of *shima-uta* performance as a practice that has not been introduced into the formal education system of Kagoshima prefecture at any level (primary, secondary, or tertiary). The few opportunities for learning *shima-uta* within the formal education system that have manifested themselves have been basic introductions that have been offered within the (limited) curriculum slot for local studies that has been present since the 1980s. Instruction is heavily reliant on the availability of staff with sufficient skills to teach. In this regard, it is notable that several principals, vice principals, and teachers from mainland Kagoshima have attempted to learn *shima-uta* to train their pupils in performing it in areas where local teachers are not readily available (H. Sakamoto, personal communication, March 14, 2011).

Younger teachers working outside of the state education system, particularly those who are alert to the financial opportunities offered by *shima-uta* teaching, have begun to provide a more modern, systematic approach to learning *shima-uta* through basic types of notation and/or tablature that they can easily reproduce with a series of pupils and/or train other trainers to utilize. This tablature indicates the single-note patterns of *sanshin* accompaniments through marks that indicate the points on which the string should be pressed to produce the correct note, together with similar notation that enables performers to hear and imitate the vocal melody. These tend to differ significantly from teacher to teacher, and no standard form—nor instructional book, DVD, or website—has been used in *shima-uta* education. This lack of formalization has resulted in *shima-uta* education in schools and (some) kindergartens being undertaken by *shima-uta* performers as essentially a voluntary activity, using instruction via imitative methods.

Nonmusical Influences on Learning and Teaching

Another issue for *shima-uta* educators concerns language and dialect. *Shima-uta* songs feature lyrics written in (various dialects of) Amami language that are unintelligible to postwar generations of locals who grew up in an educational system delivered in Japanese and in a public environment in which Japanese language dominated media and official channels of communication. Even for those who have some residual local language competence, many *shima-uta* lyrics include archaic dialect forms that make comprehension difficult. Added to this is a tendency of singers to learn *shima-uta* song lyrics and melodies (in combination) by effectively treating the songs as aggregations of vocable elements rendered with sung pronunciation that derives from and approximates that of elements of standard Japanese, making the songs difficult to comprehend (and/or "alien" sounding) for native Amami speakers. In a move meant to address both aspects of this situation, the Amami subprefectural authority funded the production and publication of a book and accompanying CD entitled *Shima-uta kara manabu Amami no kotoba* (*Learning Amami Dialect from Shima-uta*), which was distributed to all the elementary and junior high schools in Amami in 2009. The authors of this book divided Amami into six regions: northern Amami Ōshima, southern Amami Ōshima, Tokunoshima, Okinoerabujima, Kikaijima, and Yoronjima. The book features popular *shima-uta* songs translated into the *shima guchi* (dialect) of each region, so that children from each region can sing *shima-uta* songs in their regional dialect. The administration intended the book to be used as part of community activities and as material for schoolchildren's integrated learning (T. Seki, personal communication, March 14, 2011), and there is evidence that this is becoming established.

One crucial element in music education programs is the willingness of students to learn, continue learning, and graduate to performing and teaching the styles and skills they have acquired. Along with the possibilities of success and acclaim in song contests (described in greater detail later), the mainstream Japanese "J Pop" success of a small group of performers who trained in *shima-uta* over the last decade appears to have been a major factor in inspiring male and female schoolchildren to emulate the skills acquisition path of these individuals and aspire to national success in music. In this regard, self-initiated learning through emulation of recordings also appears to have become an increasingly significant aspect of local music education (often leading to and/or combining with club and class learning).

Implications for Sustainability

Traditionally, *shima-uta* performance skills and repertoire were transmitted and developed in local community contexts. In recent decades this pattern has been replaced almost entirely by formal educational operations ranging from voluntary tuition in (some) local contexts to prestigious private training operations based in metropolitan centers run by renowned (and usually veteran) performers. This has led to a degree of standardization of musical approaches and repertoire that has significantly shifted the music ecosystem, supporting a less fluid and less diverse set of musical practices.

MUSICIANS AND COMMUNITIES

The Musician–Community Relationship

Prior to the US occupation of Amami in 1945 to 1953 and the disruptions the war years and subsequent administration caused to established patterns of social interaction and community autonomy, *shima-uta* singers were largely socially embedded within particular locales and exercised their musical skills as a separate activity from their means of generating livelihood (which was usually through subsistence activities and/or engagement in commerce). *Shima-uta* performance brought prestige to individuals, families, and communities. While this prestige could be used as leverage in particular social/familial circumstances, it was not directly remunerative in a monetary sense. This situation began to shift in the postwar years. The pioneers of a switch to both earning money from performance and securing audiences outside of Amami were Fujie Kan'mura and Masagoro Minami from Kasari-chō (in northern Amami Ōshima), who built reputations as accomplished *utasha* by touring around the Amami Islands during the period of US military occupation, a time of poverty and austerity when entertainment options were limited. Minami, in particular, attracted attention by performing *shima-uta* in Okinawa and was invited to the Japanese National Folk Performing Art Festival organized by the Ministry of Education in 1961.

Being a Musician

Since the 1960s, a number of performers have begun to secure some income from performing, teaching, and/or recording activities. However, the earning opportunities are limited and unpredictable, and other professional careers offer far more reliable avenues for financial security and advancement. *Shima-uta* skills acquisition and performance retains much of the sense of a vocational calling within a strong sense of regional heritage. It continues to carry a cultural cachet that is reinforced by contemporary media coverage and the modern inscriptions of success represented by song contest awards and recording contracts. *Shima-uta* music is considered less a career choice and more an opportunity to be a tradition bearer, albeit one in new and diversifying contexts.

Shima-uta song contests have come to perform an important social function in creating a combined forum and network in various regions of Japan for Amamian amateur performers and their families and social circles, who take an interest in the contest and particular performers' progress in them. The song contests are a mechanism through which community-based *shima-uta* education and performance can be presented and adjudged through a system of evaluation and awards, essentially similar to that of the Western competition or eisteddfod. The first formal song contest appears to have been the Jikkyo Rokuon Amami Min'yō Taikai (Live Recording Amami Folksong Contest), which was organized in September 1972 by Central Gakki together with a local newspaper company (Nankai Nichinichi Shinbun), with the aim to identify new performing talent. This contest "discovered" Yutaka Tsuboyama, a 42-year-old ship carpenter from Uken village, who was a talented and versatile interpreter of traditional repertoire and who went on to become Amami's most influential contemporary songwriter.

The first regular contest was the Amami Min'yō Shinjin Taikai (Amami Folksong New Face Award), which was initially organized by Nankai Nichi-nichi Shinbun together with Central Gakki. The contest commenced in 1975 and has been held annually since then. The contest's original purpose was to provide a means to promote a cultural practice that elder members of the community perceived to be threatened by modernization and migration of young people away from the island. Prizes are offered on an annual basis to the best performer in any age category (the grand prize itself), with individual prizes also awarded to the best entrants in the children's (younger than 14 years old), youth (15 to 39 years old), middle-aged (40 to 59 years old) and seniors' (over 60 years old) sections.

The competition's first edition attracted 31 entrants and was a modest and relatively easily managed affair. Along with a range of other associated phenomena, such as the rise in availability of *shima-uta* recordings and consequent creation of a "purchasing public" for the genre, as well as the successes of Amami performers in national contexts, the average numbers of entrants has risen over the decades to around 200 per annum, with heats in various locations (illustrating the dispersal of Amamians to main island Japan) causing logistical difficulties for its organizers. The 30th contest, held in 2009, was typical of 21st-century ones and had preliminary heats in the following locations (numbers indicate entrants per site):

Kagoshima City: 22
Amami Oshima: 146
Kikaijima: 5
Tokunoshima: 35
The Kanto region (Tokyo and its surrounding area): 18
The Kansai region (Osaka and its surrounding area): 18

From this total of 244 entrants, 80 were selected for participation in the final, held in the Amami Cultural Center in Naze. The age diversity in the 2009 event was also typical, with 38 entrants in the children's section, 63 in the youth, 67 in middle aged, and 76 in the seniors'.

One illustration of the traction the New Face Award could give to winners is provided by the competition's first winner, in 1975, (then) 41-year-old Shunzo Tsukiji from Kasari-cho in northern Amami Ōshima. While Tuskiji became familiarized with *shima-uta* in a traditional manner, hearing it around him performed by family members and fellow villagers as a vernacular cultural form, he only attempted to learn performance techniques himself in his early 30s, attending classes offered by Kōgi Fukushima at Central Gakki and studying with Yutaka Tsuboyama after that. His first public performance was in the first Amami Folksong New Face Award in 1975. His success in the award led him to enter the second National Folksong Grand Championship organized by a Japanese TV company (Nihon Terebi or Nippon Television Network Corporation) 3 years later. Performing the *shima-uta* "Mankoi-bushi" in front of an audience of 37,000, he won the championship. This was a remarkable accomplishment for him and a watershed moment for Amami traditional culture, in that it increased awareness of *shima-uta* in main island Japan. It is significant that despite this success, Tsukiji has continued to work in construction management and has performed at and run a music venue in Naze as a supplementary activity to his main occupation.

The Amami Folksong New Face Award was renamed the Amami Folksong Grand Prize in 1980 and became linked to the Japanese National Folksong Grand Championship via the preliminary folk song contest in Kagoshima City. This linkage became a stepping stone for a dramatic development of Amami *shima-uta*. Tsukiji's victory was followed by Mitsuyo Tohara in 1989 and Rikki Nakano in 1990, attracting further national attention to Amami *shima-uta*. As a result of these artists' success, the number of contest entrants swelled until 1991, when Japan TV (Nihon Terebi) cut its coverage of the championship due to declining audience figures (Ibusuki, 2004, pp. 166–167). But while numbers of entrants dropped, they revived again following the success of teenage performer Hajime Chitose, who won an Amami New Face Award in 1994 and Amami Grand Prize in 1996 before going on to achieve national success in the early 2000s. Despite this resurgence in popularity as a performance form, veteran *shima-uta* virtuosi such as Yutaka Tsuboyama have contended that

> recently *shima-uta* contests have become very popular and, thereby, *shima-uta* has become very popular. Some of the young *shima-uta* singers have even gone "mainstream." But the *shima-uta* songs that are sung by them are not traditional *shima-uta*. I would like to emphasize this. If this goes on, I am afraid that traditional *shima-uta* will disappear in the future. (Tuboyama & Yanagawa, 2008, p. 29)

The issues that Tuboyama and Yanagawa raise in the case of *shima-uta* contests and mainstream crossovers concern the contextual position and function of the song form and are addressed in detail in the next section.

Implications for Sustainability

One of the most significant innovations in this domain in recent decades has been the potential for a select number of individual performers to earn a livelihood (or, at least, a partial one) for some duration. Whereas *shima-uta* performers have always possessed local "cultural capital" that has been to their advantage in various ways, potential careers in *shima-uta* performance and training (not to mention potential mainstream entertainment industry "cross-over") have been influential in attracting young performers into music making. The financial support for *shima-uta* performance is provided by a local community that has shown a proclivity to support local cultural forms during a period when Amami has been opened up to a range of other musical forms. The high profile of *shima-uta* contests in the community results from similar factors and provides a valuable channel for aspirant performers to gain exposure. In these manners the music ecosystem is actively nurtured in a manner advantageous to the continued prominence of the form.

CONTEXTS AND CONSTRUCTS
Cultural and Social Contexts

Shima-uta exists in four main performance contexts: traditional, formal, recorded, and karaoke. First, *Uta ashibi* is a traditional practice that consists of everyday singing in family, social, and/or festival contexts. This can involve individuals singing *shima-uta* in company (sometimes with extemporaneous accompaniment in the form of singing along on choruses and/or cherished passages, and impromptu percussion and/or whistling). There are also occasions on which two or more vocalists are deliberately involved in performance. This is referred to as *uta-gake*, a term that describes vocal performance of *shima-uta* in which singers are involved in *kakeai* (essentially, "dialogue"). *Uta-gake* involves two or more vocalists improvising lyrics around lyrical and melodic motifs present in established *shima-uta* repertoire. There are two main subsets of this: The first is a dialogue between male and female vocalists, which is often humorous and/or flirtatious; the second involves larger groups of vocalists. The latter form is traditionally performed by a group of singers sitting in a circle with stanzas being "passed around" the group in semiformal order. (A third form also exists but is only performed occasionally, a group-to-group variant in which a group of men and a group of women sing by turns, a practice that is traditionally a feature of annual *hachigatsu-odori* ancestral veneration festivities.) *Uta-gake* performances can be far more protracted than standard performances of *shima-uta* songs (which usually—at least in the postwar era—last 3 to 4 minutes), depending on the success of the singers in "sparking off" each other and thereby being motivated to continue the improvised dialogue.

Formal performance is a more modern practice that usually involves a single singer performing a set in a concert context, either at a live music venue as part of a festival in which performers appear on stage or as part of *shima-uta* performance contests. The performance of *shima-uta* at bars and restaurants can be located along a spectrum from social to formal depending on the venue and/or the interactive behavior of the patrons on any given night.

Shima-uta repertoire has been recorded in substantial volume since the 1950s, and songs are widely played in social and commercial contexts in Amami and among Amami communities in main island Japan. The overwhelming majority of albums are recorded by single singer/*sanshin* players. Finally, a number of *shima-uta* have been produced in karaoke versions and are performed (along with other established Japanese song genres such as *enka*, J-Pop, and Western pop–rock and balladry) in karaoke parlors. A variety of performance practices exist in parlors, but the standard karaoke set-up whereby singers sing along to lyrics on screen produces relatively uniform renditions of songs (unless singers deviate from the lyrics printed and/or have impromptu accompanists).

Like many traditional music forms internationally, *shima-uta* music now circulates in a variety of manners and contexts besides that of its original social performance context. Since the 1950s—and even more since the 1970s—*shima-uta* is performed in commercially and/or institutionally mediated contexts as both a live music form and a recorded commodity. With regard to live music performance, *shima-uta* occurs in social and/or familial contexts; ritual contexts (such as weddings and funerals); traditional festive contexts (such as summer festivals); contemporary festive contexts (such as anniversaries of Amami's reversion to Japan); dedicated music festivals and music components of broader cultural festivals (organized as both profit- and non-profit-making enterprises); restaurants and bars (where it forms an added attraction to the main business function); and live houses (where it is the prime attraction). With regard to recorded and otherwise extended and/or mediated contexts, it can be found on cassette and CD albums; online as mp3 files; as content on local (and occasionally national) radio broadcasts; for instrumental backing tracks on karaoke systems; on DVDs (both dedicated *shima-uta* performance DVDs and other DVDs about Amami that include *shima-uta* material on their soundtracks); on TV (occasional coverage of *shima-uta* performances or use of *shima-uta* music as a soundtrack element in items about Amami more generally); and as audio-visual files uploaded to services such as YouTube. Musicians also increasingly use other online media such as Facebook and personal websites to promote their material.

Constructs

In the variety of contexts detailed previously, *shima-uta* performance is, over-whelmingly, neo-traditional in form, in that it uses traditional instrumentation, arrangements, and performance styles. This is deliberate in that many enthusiasts, adherents, and/or "heritage bearers" of the form prize authenticity (i.e., perceived resemblance to a remembered earlier socioculturally "organic" music style and form) as a key element. Modernization is actively discouraged by key individuals and institutions, who largely discount the value of mediating traditional *shima-uta* to attract younger people to the genre. Interviewed by the authors in 2007, for instance, Masaki Ibusuki, head of Central Gakki Records, stated that his label was not interested in assisting the production of and/or releasing modernized/fusion projects involving *shima-uta* material (a policy that still persists in the company at the time of writing). Those Amami artists who have initiated such modernizations have met with mixed success. Noted traditional performer Shunzo Tsukiji, for instance, pioneered such approaches. As he recalled:

I made recordings together with an Okinawan jazz band around 1992. The music [was] recorded in concert at a live house called Shibuya Janjan in Tokyo and was released on CD [as *Utasha Tasukiji Shunzo Live*]. I was very pleased with the outcome, so I organized a nationwide tour with the band to promote my CD. The tour started in Hokkaido and continued down to Kagoshima with the last concert being held in Amami. I sang *shima-uta* and played *sanshin* with my backup band. I felt so good because I could sing *shima-uta* to my satisfaction backed with a beautiful melodic arrangement provided by my backup band. However, I saw many of the audience leave the hall in Amami because they were disappointed. They said that this was not the sort of *shima-uta* that they really expected to hear. Instead of the melancholy tones of Shunzo Tsukiji's *shima-uta* sung confidently with my *sanshin*, they heard the more shrill sounds of a jazz band. From the beginning, I had expected such criticism. I thought that if I held this kind of concert in Amami, *shima-uta* lovers might turn their backs on me. But I had the faith to do this, even if they rejected me. I thought that it was important that *shima-uta* should penetrate young people's minds. That['s] why I took a risk to do it, but it was a complete failure. It was too early. Since then I have not made an attempt to do anything similar. (personal communication, March 12, 2011)

More recently, another senior and revered vocalist, Ikue Asazaki, has attempted fusion/modernization for similar reasons. In an interview on Amamijin.com in 2011, she explained her motivation for expanding accompaniment and arrangement with various nontraditional instruments in the following terms:

I thought that if we keep *shima-uta* all to ourselves, it won't spread. I thought myself that I have to act to familiarize *shima-uta* to a broader public from now on. . . . I came to think that *shima-uta* could be a world-class song form, and then I started to collaborate with western and Japanese musical instruments ten years ago. (Asazaki, 2011, authors' translation)

Referring to perceptions that the *sanshin* was only adopted by *shima-uta* performers as an accompanying instrument some 300 years ago (a contention that requires further investigation), she has argued that

I sing *shima-uta* in its original form and I try not to deform it. I have stuck to this (traditional form) because of affinity for my ancestors [but] in the beginning, handclaps were the only accompaniment. Therefore I thought *shima-uta* could be matched to any musical instruments. I found that piano matched very well, which gave me the confidence that *shima-uta* could be matched with all kinds of instruments. (Asazaki, 2011, authors' translation)

Her *Uta ashibi* album (2003) includes some highly contemporary arrangements, including ones featuring prominent reggae rhythms. Asazaki's mature voice differs from younger local singers in its pronounced grain and in her use of (what appears in this context as) retarded timing. It sits slightly awkwardly with the industrial norm of the arrangements featured on the album, evidencing the compromises necessary to modernize traditional singers within mainstream popular music.

Recent local attempts to develop (very different) modernization/fusion styles have been made by artists, such as the short-lived young band Pinponzu and female duo Maricamizki. The former pursued a combination of classic American 1960s surf pop sounds and aspects *of shima-uta* on their (sole) recording, a six-track EP entitled *Okagesan desu—Live desu* (*Thank You for Your Support—This Is Live*; 2003), recorded live at Naze's Asivi venue (discussed further later). The recording begins with an essentially traditional rendition of the well-known "Yoisura Bushi" before moving through progressively more fusion-orientated material to its final track, a version of the highly popular contemporary Tokunoshima bull-fighting anthem "Waido Bushi." This track opens with a bass, drums, guitar, and trumpet sequence from the "Peter Gunn Theme" (a vintage US rock-and-roll guitar instrumental originally recorded by Duane Eddy in 1958) that gives way after around 1 minute 20 seconds to a short solo up-tempo *sanshin* riff. It then shifts to a fast-paced number that again mixes festive style (with whistles) and rock accents and a series of instrumental breaks, and eventually comes to end on an adapted version of the opening "Peter Gunn" riff. Despite the band's popularity as a live act with young audiences in Naze in the early 2000s, it didn't achieve any breakthrough to a broader regional or national marketplace (for further discussion of the EP, see Hayward & Kuwahara, 2008). By contrast, the work of Amami female duo Maricamiizki on their recording *Shimauta Bum Bung* (2006) dispenses with *sanshins* and accompanies its *shima-uta* material with Balinese *joged bum bung* gamelans (a tuned bamboo instrument played with mallets), allowing an exploration of the cross-cultural possibilities inherent in the similarity between the traditional Amami scale and the Balinese *slendro*. Despite its accomplishment and novelty, the album did not succeed in accessing a broad audience.

The most high-profile modernization/fusion projects involving *shima-uta* material and performers schooled in *shima-uta* performance have been largely produced outside of Amami, and have involved collaborations between main island producers and Amami artists keen to reach wider audiences by mixing elements of *shima-uta* and other repertoire. One aspect in which these engagements have had a direct effect in boosting young people's awareness of and interest in *shima-uta* is that a number of Amami performers have managed to draw on their skills as accomplished *shima-uta* singers to access a broad and lucrative Japanese national market, offering young Amamians a distinct incentive for learning the repertoire and related performance skills.

The "national break-out" route was first achieved by teenage singer Ritsuki (also known as Rikki) Nakano who won the national folk song ("All Japan Min'yo") award in 1990 at the age of 15, singing in the traditional style that she had learned from early childhood. Since her debut release of *Mucha Kana* in 1991, her albums have featured Amami songs along with more contemporary compositions in various styles, depending on the direction of her producers. Her work with noted Japanese-Asian musical fusionist Makoto Kubota attracted particular attention with her well-received third album *Rikki*, and she also guest starred on The Boom's successful album *Tropicalism-o* (1996). Her high, pure-toned vocal style drew the attention of the producers of the "Final Fantasy" computer game and they employed her to record "Final Fantasy X's" popular theme song "Suteki Da Ne" in 2002.

Significant as Nakano's success was, another young female singer, Hajime Chitose, had an even more dramatic career rise. Hailing from Setouchi in southern Amami Ōshima, Chitose learned *shima-uta* from an early age and went on to win two Amami *shima-uta* contests and record two cassette albums for Central Records (*Higya Merabe*, 1994, and *Shima Kyora Umui*, 1997) while still at school, attracting considerable attention in Amami. Following this early success, she relocated to Tokyo and in 2002 released an album in collaboration with Tokyo-based musicians entitled *Hainumikaz*. A single from the album, "Wadatsumi no Ki" ("Ocean Tree"), written by Japanese keyboard player Gen Ueda, established Hajime as a major recording artist by reaching number one in the Japanese singles charts and staying there for over 2 months. Sung with a gentle ("liquid") vocal vibrato, "Wadatsumi no Ki" drew on traditional Amami *shima-uta* lyrics and vocal style, expressed through a mainstream Japanese pop sensibility. The exotic wistfulness of her *shima-uta*-derived vocal technique and the restrained arrangement not only attracted the attention of Japanese consumers but also appealed to renowned (and often controversial) Belgian world music artists Deep Forest, who invited her to provide guest vocals on their 2003 album *Music Detected*. While her 2002 releases marked the peak of her career, her involvement with Deep Forest, widely covered in local Amami media, made her a local celebrity and inspired schoolchildren to follow her example and learn traditional music forms.

Another inspirational local performer has been male singer Atari Kōsuke, who began recording albums of *shima-uta* material in traditional style in 1999 before exploring a modernized style of *shima-uta* fusion music (incorporating rock, jazz, funk, and Latin influences) in 2004 on his fourth album, *Notus*, produced by Junichi Morita. This venture led to his shift toward mainstream Japanese pop–rock style and a subsequent image "makeover" on subsequent releases. His talents and photogeneity attracted the attention of Taiwanese film producers, who cast him as a Japanese school teacher in World War II Taiwan in Wei Te-Sheng's comedy–romance feature *Cape No. 7* (2008), which went on to become the third highest grossing film of all time in Taiwan. His profile in this production landed him a role in a second Taiwanese comedy, *Taipei Exchanges*, directed by Ya-chuan Hsiao in 2010, further boosting his profile in both Taiwan and Japan.

Implications for Sustainability

Whereas adaptation and modernization are sometimes seen as useful devices through which the appeal of traditional forms can be refreshed and enhanced, the opposite applies within Amami, where the continued local disdain for innovations in the musical accompaniment for *shima-uta* is notable. In this regard, the community has determined a cultural context for the form where close similarity to tradition is prioritized. At the same time, metropolitan Japan has provided a context for Amami performers to experiment with musical fusion and innovation, often to the acclaim of local audiences (particularly younger demographics). This duality of interior conservatism and external experimentation is relatively unusual in international contexts but appears to work for all concerned.

INFRASTRUCTURE AND REGULATIONS
Infrastructure

Each of the five main contexts of *shima-uta*—social, commercial entertainment, concerts, festivals, and song contests—has distinct infrastructural aspects. Social music making exists in informal contexts that do not require amplification or purpose-built stages or venues. Its infrastructural elements, such as they are, are provided by domestic and public spaces utilized for impromptu or preplanned performances. There is an overlap between these and *shima-uta* performances at local cafes or bars, although larger bars and restaurants (such as the Arahobana in Amami's capital) are distinct by virtue of having designed stage spaces and public address (PA) systems. Investment in these facilities is part of the business strategy of venue owners, who attempt to gain a market advantage by attracting customers from businesses that do not offer live music.

The only venue specifically established for music in Amami is the Asivi "live house" in Naze, which is set up as a performance venue at which alcohol and snacks are also available. Asivi's venue is part of a small complex that also includes recording and rehearsal spaces and the local radio station Amami FM (discussed later). Asivi was established by Kengo Fumoto, who was born and attended school in Naze before working in Tokyo in the mid-1980s, when he became familiar with main island Japanese live houses and their operation. Trained as a carpenter/builder, he built Asivi with friends as Naze's first modern music venue. Asivi showcases local *shima-uta* performers and other visiting acts and provides a relaxed and lively environment for music patrons.

Formal concerts at venues not providing food and beverages are held occasionally, but are a minor form compared to annual festivals (such as summer *bon* festivals) and village fairs, at which refreshments are also available. Depending on the size of a village fair, formal stage spaces and/or amplification may be provided. Larger festivals held outdoor on formal stages with PA and lighting systems are few in number, but notable ones in the last decade have included the Hana Hana festivals held in 2006 and 2007. These merit discussion here as they provide a particularly ambitious presentation of local music. The festivals were held in Hana Hana West, a large and versatile space spanning two coves and adjacent land outside Yamato village on Amami's northwestern coast, and which opened in May 2005 as a community resource for young Amamians supported by commercial sponsorship. Three music festivals were held in the venue, one in 2006 and two in 2007. These were significant large-scale events that attracted audiences to a mixture of *shima-uta* performers and retro and contemporary J-Pop acts in comfortable, outdoor beachside locations. The second festival, held in July 2007, was notable for featuring an *uta ashibi* event on the northern cove that included *uta-gake* performances by a group of veteran performers seated on stage in a semicircle facing the audience and culminated in traditional ensemble dancing. But however successful the event was at showcasing a traditional form in a well-facilitated and modern outdoor context, the high levels of sponsorship required and complex logistical issues contributed to the festivals' discontinuance after 2007.

In terms of provision of musical instruments for *shima-uta* performance, *sanshins* are widely available in Amami, with the manufacturing and repair sector based in Naze and with instruments being retailed throughout the islands at both specialist music shops and other outlets (including *shima-uta* schools and some supermarkets). The retail business is dominated by the Central Gakki store in Naze, which stocks a range of *sanshins*, with prices ranging from 15,000 yen (approximately USD $125) for a basic model to 35,000 yen (approximately USD $290) for a more elaborate one. These are available to visiting customers, as well as via mail order and, increasingly, through online retail. Unlike instruments in other regional music cultures, Amamian *sanshins* have traditionally been plain and functional rather than subject to elaborate material inlays and high-value material options. The resonator body is made of hard woods such as rosewood or red sandalwood, with ebony as the most expensive option. While snakeskin was used in the past as the material stretched across the resonator box, this was replaced with plastic during the 1980s. Snakeskin resonator membranes are now rare in Amami.

Laws, Regulations, and Funding

With the exception of services provided by Central Gakki in Naze, *shima-uta* education in Amami is decentralized and not subject to licensing or regulation, either internally or by governmental/educational bureaucracies. Local government has recently begun to involve itself in local cultural activity, through avenues such as moving to establish *shima-uta* databases and to provide materials for schools, outlined earlier this chapter. To date, there has been no government, nongovernmental organization, or external commercial financial support for *shima-uta* through educational, cultural, or heritage schemes or institutions. As a traditional song form, *shima-uta* songs are not restricted by copyright issues, and while copyright applies to specific recordings, there does not appear to have been any commercial piracy of recorded *shima-uta* material.

Implications for Sustainability

As a form reliant on voice and limited, low-cost analog instrumentation, *shima-uta* music making has very modest infrastructural needs and has neither sought nor been awarded significant resources by regional or national funding bodies. There is a ready and relatively low-cost supply of instruments in the Amami archipelago, and individuals and families appear ready to pay for tuition to learn the form. In these regards, *shima-uta* music making is essentially autonomous of governmental support or determination.

MEDIA AND THE MUSIC INDUSTRY
Media Engagement

The music industry in Amami is a small-scale operation whose principal components are commercial music schools, *sanshin* manufacturers, retail operations (selling instruments and recordings), the Central Gakki recording studio and recording label, music venues, and individual performers who have multiple income streams (in the former areas and/or have nonmusical employment). The population base of the islands and its relatively low socioeconomic status within Japan (see Nishimura, 2013) are insufficient to support full-time musicians working in the region and more than a handful of related commercial operations. The music sector therefore combines a number of artisanal/preindustrial elements with more contemporary industrial and technological practices. Central Gakki's integrated operation (combining teaching, retail, and recording) is the most modern in industrial terms and represents the company's concerted strategic development following its early entry into regional musical recording.

Presence in the Music Industry

Music recording in Amami began in 1928, when Otojo Nakayama, a female *uta-sha* from Uken village in southwestern Amami Ōshima, was recorded with *sanshin* accompaniment by Denjiro Sunao by a recording company in Kansai. The recording was commissioned by the owner of the Yamaji souvenir store in Naze. Local music recording took off in a more concerted manner in the immediate postwar period when Yonezo Yamada from Uken made a number of tape recordings of *uta-sha*, some of which were issued on vinyl. In 1951, Naze general store operator Takeo Tokuyama financed the recording and pressing of 13 *shima-uta* records by performers such as Fujie Kan'mura and Masagoro Minami. These were bought en masse by the Central Gakki music store in Naze (which had opened in 1949), a business run by Tokunoshima-born entrepreneur Yoshihiko Ibusuki, whose main activity was selling dancehall records (imported from main island Japan) and musical instruments. Having been brought up in a family familiar with *shima-uta*, Ibusuki was supportive of local music and in 1956 began to record *shima-uta*. The first two performers asked to record for the new Central Gakki label were two Kakeroma islanders who were exponents of the Southern Amami *higyauta* style of *shima-uta*, 51-year-old Kougi Fukushima and 20-year-old Ikue Asazaki. One of the label's most significant recordings took place 6 years later when renowned *shima-uta* singer Kazuhira Takeshita (also from Kakeroma) visited Naze to perform a concert. His performances and recordings for Central Gakki established him as a leader of the *higyauta* style.

One noteworthy recording of the 1970s was the 1973 recording debut of Yutaka Tsuboyama, who was the pioneer of modern *shima-uta* performance and composer of many popular *shinsaku-shimauta* (a term meaning "new *shima-uta*," because his songs were written in Amami dialect, unlike *shi-min'yo* songs, which are written in standard Japanese), including the well-known "Waido Bushi." Cowritten with Tamiro Nakamura, the title and theme of the song "Waido Bushi" are derived from the form of bullfighting popular on Tokunoshima (where bulls fight each other rather than matadors—see Kuwahara, Ozaki, & Nishimura, 2006) and, in particular, the victor's cry of "Waido Waido" ("We've done it"). When released on a cassette with other originals, the album became one of Central Gakki's biggest sellers to date. Indeed, the song has become so established in local repertoire—and on local karaoke systems—that even studiously traditional *shima-uta* performers such as Yamato Tokuhara have allowed it into their repertoire as a modern addition, and its performances have been (affectionately) parodied by local humorists Salmon and Garlic in their live shows.

Until the mid-1990s, Central Gakki continued to issue albums in cassette form only, perceiving its primary audience to be older Amamians who had not upgraded to CD technology. However, with the increasing spread of lower-cost CD systems, together with an increase in younger purchasers following the success of local song competitions, the company moved into CD production in 1991. The company's first CD release, Mitsuyo Tohara's debut album, remains the label's best seller to date, shifting 20,000 copies. The CD format proved so successful that the company switched to CD entirely by the mid-1990s (although retaining its back catalog of cassettes, which continues to sell). To date, Central Gakki has released 162 albums of *shima-uta* music (together with 53 albums of *shi-min'yō*), the vast majority of which have been sold through retail outlets in Amami or through mail order to Amamians living on main island Japan.

Central Gakki also performed an important role in making *shima-uta* available in karaoke formats, where it is available alongside J-Pop, Western pop, and other Japanese music forms (such as the nostalgic ballad form *enka*). The company first released cassette-format karaoke tapes in 1983, featuring material recorded by Shunzo Tsukiji and Yutaka Tsuboyama, and then a CD karaoke album of Tsuboyama in 1989. In 2008, the company entered into agreements with national online karaoke companies (including the majors Joysound and Daiichikosho) that allow a range of *shima-uta* tracks recorded for Central Gakki to be accessed across Japan. This material has proved highly popular with dispersed Amamian communities and has represented an important means of maintaining *shima-uta* in a (reconfigured) social space with affinities to that of its original performance context.

The increase in Amami recordings (of various kinds) in the 1980s and early 1990s made local product available for tourist souvenir purchase. A rise in interest in Amami music was also a subset of a fashion for southern island—and principally Okinawan—music that was accelerated and popularized through the success of (main island) Japanese band The Boom in the 1990s. Despite the opportunity to exploit this market, Central Gakki has maintained a distinct character by explicitly addressing its operation to an internal constituency, rather than attempting to access the main Japanese market for Amami talent that majors such as Epic have capitalized on. Central Gakki owner-manager Masaki Ibusuki has frequently reiterated his company philosophy as concerned with local cultural heritage, and as adept at managing and profiting from that in a specifically local environment. The company's only success in the broader Japanese market has been "collateral." Contacted by main island Japanese fans eager to obtain Hajime Chitose's earlier material, the company re-released the singer's *Shima, Kyora, Umui* in 2002 and sold over 6,000 copies (more than triple the usual average CD sales of Amami music).

In addition to the profile accorded to the form by *shima-uta* contests, local exposure to *shima-uta* has been boosted in recent years by the introduction of Amami FM in 2007, an initiative formulated by Kengo Fumoto that grew out of the Asivi live house's performance and recording activities. The radio service offers a combination of community news, weather, sports reports, and cultural programs. The station has a number of programs that include spoken items in various Amami dialects. *Shima-uta* tracks are widely played, usually in the form of songs from commercially available CDs, but also from in-concert recordings made at the Asivi live house located adjacent to the station. The FM station has a limited range, covering Naze and its immediate surroundings, but since 2012 it has been complemented by another local-radius FM station established by Fumoto, Setouchi Town FM, serving the far south of Amami Ōshima (with some signal coverage in Kakeroma) and providing a similar schedule of material. As in other locations, the Internet has become an increasingly important medium for exposure to music; Amami FM's web site (http://www.npo-d.org/index.html) also provides various items and links, including musical ones. The website Amami Ongaku Jōhō (Amami Music Information) (http://homepage2.nifty.com/~m_oohashi/ shimauta/) also provides detailed information on *shima-uta* singers and their CDs and concerts. Central Gakki's website (http://www.simauta.net) similarly provides detailed information on *shima-uta* recordings, concerts, and resources. The Asivi live house's website (http://www.a-mp.co.jp/index.html) also caters to a younger audience of the kind that patronizes the venue. In terms of print media, along with items in the local daily press, the monthly magazine *Horizon* published in Naze since 1995 has been significant for its regular illustrated coverage of *shima-uta* singers and recordings. In addition to its market among the local population, its prominence at airport kiosks illustrates its target market as substantially consisting of visitors to the island. Its considerable subscription base includes many Amamians living in main island Japan.

Implications for Sustainability

The Amami music industry is a small-scale one heavily based on a single company, Central Gakki, which operates with a particular cultural agenda. Although a commercial entity, the company forms a nurturing and supportive core to the local music scene. While reliance on a single entity is necessarily risky, prudent management has maintained the company as an enduring local institution. More recent ventures provide useful extensions and diversifications that, nevertheless, complement this orientation.

ISSUES AND INITIATIVES FOR SUSTAINABILITY
Overall Vitality

Shima-uta performance and teaching have proved resilient—and, in many ways, resurgent—in Amami over the last three decades, supported by a network of performers, teachers, facilitators, advocates, and audiences within Amami itself (and extending to centers of Amamian expatriates in main island Japan). In this manner, its sustainability has been organic to the community rather than being substantially dependent on external initiatives. At the same time, the nature of *shima-uta* performance, education, and promotion has shifted and now occurs within a regional space—rather than within Amami's individual *shimas*—in which voluntary organizations and commercial operations have taken on a promotional role that was not necessary at its previous grassroots level of operation. Similarly, exposure to and consumption of *shima-uta* material is increasingly technologically mediated (via recordings and broadcast and/or digital media) rather than forming part of the vernacular soundscape of individual *shima*. These contextual changes have also affected the nature of song texts, performance practices, evaluations of performer competence, and consumption of *shima-uta* material.

Key Issues for Sustainability

In their original forms, *shima-uta* compositions recorded and represented aspects of local folklore and/or historical incidents through the language of the lyrics and through the melodies that realized these, and performers interpreted these aspects through appropriate vocalization. By contrast, contemporary performers usually learn and perform *shima-uta* songs primarily as melodic texts. They may have insight into the themes of lyrics, but this insight may often be scant (indeed, during our research we encountered performers who had a more limited awareness of the nature of particular *shima-uta* lyrics than we did). In this manner, contemporary *shima-uta* performance aligns itself to *kui-sha* accomplishment (i.e., vocal skill) rather than the interpretative and lyrically improvisatory ability that characterizes *uta-sha* performance. While comprehensive use of publications such as Ibusuki et al. (2011) might modify performer knowledge of song material to some extent, as yet no programmatic attempts have been made to encourage *shima-uta* performers to modify classic repertoire through adding topical elements, as was commonplace during the form's circulation within a primarily oral culture. Language competence is obviously key here. Unless there is a significant revival in speaking Amamian dialects (which seems distinctly unlikely), lyrical improvisation is unlikely to return to *shima-uta* performance in any meaningful manner—unless the practice could be recast into a song form performed in standard Japanese.

Past Initiatives

In one sense, *shima-uta* resembles those forms of Western "folk music" transcribed, edited, and published by collectors in the 19th and early 20th centuries that are now predominantly known to regional communities through recordings and performances that derive from the collected versions (albeit second or third hand). But there is a marked linguistic difference, as many of the Western folk songs were collected in a form of national language fairly intelligible to contemporary performers. *Shima-uta* material, written in dialect forms of Amami language (which is itself little spoken within Amami today), invites comparison to other song repertoires sung in archaic languages. In another sense, we might perceive *shima-uta* to have become a form of "art song," recontextualized from a vernacular context to one in which it is fixed, canonized, and appraised by various stakeholders who exert influence over (their perceptions of) its "proper" performance.

Current and Planned Initiatives

Transformation of the kind described earlier necessarily diminishes one level of textual signification—that is, the lyric's denotative and connotative linguistic function—prioritizing traditions of musical rendition that may have been informed by lyrical content but which are increasingly distant from (and unable to access) those linguistic cues for vocal interpretation. In this regard, there exists something of a generational rupture between the elder generation of *shima-uta* performers (born before the reversion to Japan in 1952), many of whom are still teaching and performing, and younger performers. But acknowledgment of this rupture does not amount to a definitive critique of the contemporary form of *shima-uta* as a "pale shadow" of previous song forms, but rather notes the difference of the contemporary form from its predecessors.

Similarly, there are rupture points concerning accompaniment. A number of veteran performers regard the combination of vocal and *sanshin* as, effectively, the *essence* of *shima-uta* performance and the key to maintaining the integrity of the form; conversely, younger practitioners have argued that more modern interpretations are vital. Shunzo Tsukiji, for example, has contended that

> I don't think that it is good to only sing traditional *shima-uta* songs with *sanshin* accompaniment. Therefore, I think I can exert a positive influence by putting a contemporary inflection on *shima-uta* performance. (personal communication, March 21, 2011)

While there may be significant differences of opinion, our research indicates that what is most important for Amami audiences is their affective engagement and identification with *shima-uta* as a referent for place, culture, history, and heritage. *Shima-uta's* performance traditions and linguistic bases underpin the legitimacy of the form, provide a deep connection with Amami identity, and symbolize the resilience of Amami's community. Similarly, while *shima-uta* may have disappeared as a performed element of the everyday life of communities, its presence in mediated forms has secured it a different prominence in public and technological soundscapes, where it functions as an aural icon of the islands and their people. Research uncovered strong and often passionate views on ideal performance practices and learning techniques, and a substantial emotional investment by younger performers and facilitators in the form's perpetuation, two significant indicators of its future viability.

ACKNOWLEDGMENTS

Thanks to Taiki Machi, Megumi Takarabe, Purnamawati, and Ayako Shiinoki for assisting us with research for this chapter and to Rebecca Coyle and the various individuals in Amami who encouraged and facilitated our research in various ways. Additional research funding and facilitation were provided by the Division of Research at Southern Cross University and the University of Technology Sydney, Australia, and by Kagoshima University, Japan.

REFERENCES

Asazaki, I. (2011). Ikue Asazaki's homepage [Interview]. Retrieved from http://amaminchu. com/entertainment/interview001.html

Haring, D. (1952). *The island of Amami Oshima in the Northern Ryukyus, scientific investigation in the Ryukyu Islands, report no. 2*. Washington, DC: Pacific Science Board, National Research Council.

Haring, D. (1954). Comment on field techniques in ethnography illustrated by a survey in the Ryūkyū Islands. *Southwestern Journal of Anthropology, 10*(3), 255–267.

Hayward, P., & Kuwahara, S. (2008). Transcience and durability: Music industry initiatives, shima uta and the maintenance of Amami culture. *Perfect Beat—The Pacific Journal of Research into Contemporary Music and Popular Culture, 8*(4), 44–63.

Ibusuki, Y. (2004). *Fucchu Nise* [An eternal youth]. Naze, Japan: Central Gakki.

Ibusuki, M., Ibusuki, K., & Ogawa, H. (Eds.). (2011). *Amami Min'yo Souran: Amami Shimauta Zen-kashi, Kyoutsuugo-yaku, Zen-kyokumoku Kaisetsu* [A comprehensive list of Amami folk-songs: All lyrics of Amami Island-songs, their standard translation and comments on the all songs]. Kagoshima, Japan: Nanpoushinsha.

Johnson, H., & Kuwahara, S. (2013). Locating Shima in island drumming: Amami Ōshima and its archipelagic drum groups. *Shima: The International Journal of Research into Island Cultures, 7*(1), 14–38.

Kagoshima Minzoku Gakkai. (Ed.). (1970). *Amami no Shima: Kakeroma no Minzoku* [The Island of Amami: The folk culture of Kakeroma Island]. Tōkyō, Japan: Daiichi Hōki Shuppan.

Kazari, E. (1933). *Amami Oshima Min'yo Taikan* [An overview of folk songs in Amami Oshima]. Kagoshima, Japan: Nanto Bunka Kenkyusha.

Koizumi, F. (1977). Musical scales in Japanese music. In K. Fumio, T. Yoshihiko, & Y. Osamu (Eds.), R. Emmert (Assistant Ed.), *Asian musics in an Asian perspective: Report of Asian traditional performing arts 1976*. Tokyo, Japan: Heibonsha.

Kubo, K. (1960). *Minami Nihon Min'yo Kyokushu* [Collection of the folksongs of southern Japan]. Tokyo, Japan: Ongakunotomosha.

Kuwahara, S., Ozaki, T., & Nishimura, A. (2006). Transperipheral networks: Bullfighting and cattle culture in Japan's outer islands. *Shima: The International Journal of Research into Island Cultures, 1*(2), 1–13.

Mizuno, O. (1974). Sonraku Kōzō [Village structure]. In K. Nagasawa (Ed.), *Amami Bunkashi: Nantō no Rekishi to Minzoku* [A history of Amami culture: The history and folk culture of the South Islands] (pp. 93–102). Fukuoka, Japan: Nishi-Nihon Shinbunsha.

Nishimura, S. (2013). Economy in the islands of Kagoshima. In K. Kawai, R. Terada, & S. Kuwahara (Eds.), *The islands of Kagoshima* (pp. 62–67). Kagoshima, Japan: Kagoshima University Research Centre for the Pacific Islands.

Ogawa, H. (1979). *Amami Min'yo-shi* [A monograph of Amami folk music]. Tokyo, Japan: House Daigaku Shuppannkyoku.

Ogawa, H. (1989). *Kayo no Minzoku: Amami no Utagake* [The folklore of songs: Amami dialogue songs]. Tokyo, Japan: Dai-ichi Shobo.

Ogawa, H. (1999). *Amami Shimauta he no Shoutai* [Introduction to Amami Shimauta]. Kagoshima, Japan: Shunendo.

Sakai, M. (1996). *Amami Utakake no Diarogu* [Dialogue songs of Amami]. Tokyo, Japan: Dai-ichi Shobo.

Sakai, M. (2005). *Amami Okinawa Nakiuta no Minzokushi* [An ethnography of the mourning songs in Amami and Okinawa]. Tokyo, Japan: Shougakukan.

Suwa, J. (2007). The space of Shima. *Shima: The International Journal of Research into Island Cultures*, 1(1), 6–14.

Tuboyama, Y., & Yanagawa, H. (2008). Dialogue: Amami Min'you no Keishou to Hozon [Succession and preservation of Amami Folksongs]. In *Joshibi no Mukei Bunka Isan Purojekuto Gijiroku* [Conference minutes on an intangible cultural heritage project in Joshibi University of Art and Design] (pp. 52–57). Tokyo, Japan: Joshibijutsu Daigaku.

Yamamoto, H. (1980). Characteristics of Amami folk songs. In R. Emmert & M. Yuki (Eds.), *Musical voices of Asia: Report of Asian traditional performing arts 1978*. Tōkyō, Japan: Heibonsha.

Yanagita, K. (1925) *Kainan Shouki* [Short Sketch on Southern Sea]. Tokyo, Japan: Ookayama Shoten.

9

SAMULNORI

Sustaining an Emerging Korean Percussion Tradition

Keith Howard[1]

GLOBAL EFFORTS TO sustain and preserve "traditional" music tend to reflect performance practices that survive among aging musicians or in archived recordings, photographs, and other documents. Reconstructions may be attempted as systems enshrine ahistorical forms as representative archetypes, but preservation is always situated at a specific point in time. As time passes, new competing musical forms emerge, gain popularity, and, inevitably, decline: How can new traditions be sustained where older musical traditions have already been embraced by a preservation system? How can creativity and development be accommodated? This chapter explores these issues, focusing on a Korean percussion genre, *samulnori*, developed by a celebrated quartet, SamulNori, which in recent decades has arguably been Korea's most successful "traditional" music.

---

[1] This chapter assembles material treated more fully in my book (Howard, 2015). As with most publications by foreign scholars on Korea, I use the McCune-Reischauer Romanization system for Korean terms, as modified by the Korean Ministry of Education in 1988 (*shi* rather than *si*, to reflect pronunciation). However, I retain the Romanized spelling and capitalization favored by members of the original quartet, *SamulNori*, but refer to the genre, using small case, as *samulnori* (rather than the McCune-Reischauer *samullori*). I employ the standard East Asian definition of "folk" as the "little" tradition, in contrast to the court and literati "great" tradition.

SAMULNORI, THE QUARTET; SAMULNORI, THE GENRE

SamulNori is a quartet of Korean percussionists that first performed on stage in February 1978. The name, coined a few months later by the folklorist Shim Usŏng, means "four things play"; it was once used for four typical percussion instruments encountered at Buddhist temples but now indicates the four core instruments of local bands and itinerant troupes: small and large hand-held gongs (*kkwaenggwari* and *ching*), an hourglass-shaped double-headed drum (*changgo*), and a squashed barrel drum (*puk*). SamulNori rapidly gained considerable popularity, so much so that many other groups emerged, and the distinct repertory and style of performance became a genre, samulnori. Today, there are many dozens of amateur and professional samulnori groups. The genre is taught in dedicated institutes, it features in the state-sanctioned school curriculum, and there are a number of workbooks dedicated to helping aspiring "samulnorians." Abroad, samulnori is a familiar part of Korean performance troupes and Korean diasporic activities, and groups exist in many universities.

BACKGROUND

Samulnori is actually a recent evolution of something much older. Its antecedents are local percussion bands, known under the umbrella terms of *nongak* or *p'ungmul* and preserved as icons from Korea's past within Important Intangible Cultural Property (*Chungyo muhyŏng munhwajae*) 11, and itinerant percussion troupes, notably Namsadang, are preserved as Important Intangible Cultural Property 3. Local bands have long since been eponymous with the Korean soundscape. Popular opinion associates percussion with premodern Korea. This is common in contemporary takes on mythology, such as the following, written by the folklorist Zo Zayong (1926–2000) to celebrate the 10th anniversary of that first SamulNori performance: "A long, long time ago there lived deep in the mountains . . . goblins who loved to play uproariously on drums and gongs every night" (Zo, 1988, pp. 38–39).

In November 2014, *nongak* was inscribed on the UNESCO *Representative List of the Intangible Cultural Heritage of Humanity*. Korea's submission to UNESCO highlighted the six nationally recognized local bands under Important Intangible Cultural Property 11, and 25 bands appointed at provincial and city levels. Korea's percussion bands have iconicity. Domestic and foreign Korean concerts routinely end with a full company dance to drums and gongs. Demonstrations by Korean workers and students have since the 1970s been routinely choreographed to drums and gongs (see, e.g., Lee, 2012). The iconicity of percussion bands, however, has in recent decades shifted from *nongak* to samulnori. For example, 1,100 drummers performing as *Big Bang SamulNori* created aural mayhem at the 1993 Taejŏn EXPO.

This was an evolution of the massive samulnori display at the opening ceremony of the 1988 Seoul Olympics (Dilling, 2007, pp. 29–31), which in turn evolved from the multiple samulnori forces deployed for Paik Nam June's *Bye Bye Kipling* at the 1986 Beijing Asian Games. Percussion bands and troupes date from a time when the majority of the population lived and worked in the countryside, but the samulnori genre is essentially urban—and Koreans today are one of the most urbanized populations in the world. I pose the question in this chapter, then, why *nongak*, as a distant memory of a time long gone, should be preserved and sustained for future generations rather than samulnori.

Just as the decline of rural bands and itinerant troupes can be mapped onto modernization and urbanization, samulnori evolved initially as part of a concert culture intended to appeal to the growing population of Seoul, a population that was increasingly affluent and increasingly nostalgic. New ways to present folklore on stage were needed, and samulnori proved an excellent fit. As samulnori grew in popularity, it was promoted through festivals and workshops, and in the production of recordings and notation books. It was taken up by schools and by groups, particularly where the local bands of old had died out. Abroad, it became part of the burgeoning international concert scene for non-Western music and proved approachable in a way that other genres of Korean music were not. However, as much as it was readily appreciable, samulnori was considered by local musicians and by students, who associated themselves with the *minjung munhwa* culture-of-the-masses movement of the 1970s and 1980s, to stand at a considerable remove from local bands. This distancing was exacerbated because much journalism and scholarship allied the original quartet, SamulNori, to itinerant troupes (see, e.g., Hesselink, 2012). This set up a paradox in which the very popularity of samulnori was challenged by questions about its authenticity, a legacy that today, in turn, challenges its sustainability.

The flexibility of samulnori added to the paradox. Quartets collaborated with jazz musicians, pop musicians, singers, and shaman ritualists. They entered the Korean pop charts accompanying rappers. They adapted repertoire developed for other ensembles or instruments for the four percussion instruments, and premiered compositions for samulnori and orchestras of Western or Korean instruments. An intriguing example of adaptation is the samulnori canonic piece "*Samdo sŏl changgo*," which, played on four hourglass drums, substantially differs in structure from drum dances previously part of the repertoires of local bands and itinerant troupes, but is closely allied to another traditional genre entirely, the solo melodic instrumental genre of *sanjo* (Howard, 2006b, pp. 51–52). This adaptation, then, was from one traditional genre but was glossed through reference to another, very different traditional genre: This challenges understandings of preservation, and, I will argue here, is indicative of the need to allow creativity and development.

Most samulnori is performed seated. This contrasts local bands and itinerant troupes, who in previous times (as well as nowadays when performing preserved forms as intangible properties) stood and danced. For most of the samulnori repertory one of each instrument is played, although in specific pieces the quartet takes four hourglass drums or two players take small gongs. In the local bands and itinerant troupes of previous times, larger groups of performers participated. The small gong players gave rhythmic models, the large gongs the underpinning foundations, and the barrel drums accented and expanded on the large gong foundations. Hourglass drum players used two sticks to echo both small gong and large gong structures. Samulnori tends to foreground the hourglass drum and its player rather than the small hand-held gong and its player, which in part reflects the drum's potential for complex, virtuosic patterning—a matter pertinent to staged performances.

Each samulnori piece is compact in the sense that each consists of a fixed and tightly controlled series of discrete episodes and motifs. Each episode or motif derives from local or itinerant repertoires of the past and is juxtaposed with other episodes or motifs from the same repertory or from different sources. In other words, each samulnori piece juxtaposes discrete patterns that may once have had different uses, in, for example, ritual, entertainment, or work activities, or may have once been typical of different localities. Each piece is virtuosic, requiring players to develop fluency, speed, and a shared aesthetic that moves beyond instrumental technique to incorporate breathing and body movement. In contrast, local percussion bands and itinerant troupes had (and have) larger memberships, accommodating performers with different skill levels, and presenting music that was more expansive, less fast, less complex, and, in terms of both movement and music, less fixed and more variable.

SYSTEMS OF LEARNING

Samulnori practitioners, teachers, and students refer to elements inherited from the two core antecedents but tend to emphasize one over the other. These two, and their respective systems of training, are known through competing histories that make any single picture of learning in the past inherently problematic. While local percussion bands typically espoused a benign teaching agency through egalitarianism (Howard, 1990) or communitarianism (adopting, via Kyung-soo Chun [1984, p. 168], a contested idea from John Bennett), itinerant troupes are reported to have had more formalized apprenticeship and adoption-based training (Hesselink, 2012, pp. 22–24; Shim Usŏng, 1974a, 1974b). But SamulNori's emergence in 1978 came after much music training had been institutionalized, and more than a decade after local bands and itinerant troupes had been appointed as Important Intangible Cultural Properties.

The Korean Properties system itself has influenced contemporary systems of teaching and learning. The system is a top-down effort to preserve, teach, and promote performance arts and crafts that establishes notions of lineage, practice, and style—notions that may or may not have existed in earlier times—and validates specific repertoires and musicians. Institutionalization has also involved universities and schools, again validating specific repertoires and musicians, but through a need for notations, standardized repertoires, and authorized teaching and examination processes. In the post-1945 era, two pretertiary schools have been central to training in traditional Korean music (*kugak*): the Gugak High School (Kungnip Kugak Kodŭng Hakkyo) and the Traditional Music Arts School (Chŏnt'ong Yesul Hakkyo). The first was set up by the National Gugak Center (Kungnip Kugagwŏn) and reflected its concerns with court and literati traditions. SamulNori emerged from the second, a school established by musicians who specialized in folk music. Their aesthetic reflected their background and training but soon responded to demands for teaching. SamulNori gave their first workshops on Wando Island off Korea's southern coast in 1981 but began to focus on teaching only later, as their audiences (in Percy Grainger's terms, the "hearer host") switched from passive receivers to active learners. In 1987, and again in 1988, they were invited to run summer camps in Miasamura in Japan, where the popularity of percussion was running high due to the success of *taiko* groups. Camps in Korea followed, culminating with the establishment of a training institute in 1994—the SamulNori Hanullim Puyŏ Kyoyugwŏn (a translation would be the SamulNori Foundation Study Institute in Puyŏ).

By 1989, photocopied notations, developed with the musicologist, pianist, and composer Lim Dong Chang, were introduced for samulnori classes at the Chungang Daily News Cultural Center (Chungang Ilbo Munhwawŏn). The chosen notation met nationalistic requirements, fitting the need to fix Korean identity at the center of practice. "Koreanness" was imparted by revisiting court notation, *chŏngganbo*, a system devised in the 15th century for ritual music. Now, SamulNori and Lim turned its vertical columns through 90 degrees, to become horizontal systems. They removed what they perceived to be Eurocentric metric indicators (3/4, 4/4, etc.) and substituted a Taoist-derived tripartite idea that divided a single rhythmic pattern (*changdan*) length into units and subunit beats: A 12/8 pattern was thus rendered as 1, 4, and 12. They also replaced Chinese-derived pitch indicators with circles of different sizes to represent different gong and drum strikes. The notation was published in a set of workbooks (Korean Conservatorium of Performing Arts, 1990, 1992, 1993, 1995).

SamulNori also developed an aesthetic based on breathing and movement that became key both to teaching and to performance. This was rooted within a Korean dance concept, "motion in stillness" (*chŏngjungdong*). Although with deep roots, the articulation of this appears to have much to do with the early 20th century, when dance was put on Western-style proscenium stages. Motion in stillness is a way of positioning each element as part of a continuous flow, avoiding the pointing of ballet, and emphasizing cyclical movements—alternations of bending and extending to lower and lift the body, shoulder movements that rise with apparent breath inhalation, a stretch of the back that releases as the shoulders and back relax, and so on. The link is, as with one aspect of the notation system, to Taoism, rather than, for instance, a Czikszentmihalian management of optimal experience (see, e.g., Czikszentmihaly, 1990). Kim Duk Soo (1992) has written that motion in stillness was one of the first things he learned as a child (p. 22), and it may be pertinent that both Kim and a second early member of the quartet, Ch'oe Chongshil (b. 1953), began their professional lives as child dancers. As the aesthetic was embedded within samulnori teaching, the term *hana-a*, which at its most basic level derives from *han/hana*, "one," was incorporated, indicating how the aesthetic is designed to impart unity across a performance group. Articulated as a down/up bending movement in dance, the aesthetic consists— using brackets to give the elements of *hana-a*—of a bend of the knees (*ha-*), a rise (*-na-*), and a rebound (*-a*). Samulnori students first learn this as a "walking dance" (Kim Dong Won, 1999, pp. 6–11), but samulnori is primarily performed seated. So, when seated with instruments, students practice from a relaxed posture with chin slightly downward (*ha-*), inhale while raising both head and torso (*-na-*), then keep raising the head up and back (*-a*), falling back to start again. The fall seamlessly joins the relaxed start, creating a circle—a Taoist loop, with continuity created by interlocking *yin/yang* commas—joining one *hana-a* to the next and avoiding any sense of premature completion. The samulnori aesthetic is known as the *hohŭp*.

To *hohŭp* unity, SamulNori adds a notion of balance. This, too, is critical in the system of learning. Each sound is considered—moving from tripartite Taoism back to the binary—*yin* (Korean: *ŭm*) or *yang*, the former dark, negative, the receptive female, and the latter light, positive, the penetrating male. *Yang* sounds tend to have higher pitches and thinner timbres; on the drum, they may be damped, whereas *yin* sounds are open. Rhythmic detailing balances *yin* and *yang*, working from the smallest to the largest element: Beats are grouped into units comprising trochaic and iambic strong + weak (*yin + yang*) or weak + strong (*yang + yin*) feet; units are grouped into rhythmic cycle lengths; cycle lengths are paired; and so on. Further, the double-headed hourglass drum is considered to produce *yin* strikes on its lower-pitched head and *yang* on its higher-pitched head; strikes of the lower-pitched head typically mark the beats, and therefore link within the *hohŭp* conception to the inhaling phase, while strikes on the higher-pitched head match exhalations. Taken one stage further, the hourglass drum is considered to encapsulate the rhythms played on the other three samulnori instruments, both *yin* and *yang*, and is therefore central to the group. Indeed, the drum embodies the universe: The lower head is considered to represent earth and the higher heaven, with the player, as man, sitting in between.

The aesthetic totality is presented in textbooks designed for international students. Here, I will briefly mention just three. The first, written by Kim Dong Won in 1999 and published by the Overseas Koreans Foundation through the Korea National University of Arts, effectively summarizes the approach to teaching, allotting much of its space to the aesthetic. The second, written by Lee Young-Gwang and published by the Ministry of Culture, Sports, and Tourism in 2009, builds on samulnori teaching and learning at the National Gugak Center—where, as I will outline later, a second samulnori group was established in 1984. Lee's text details posture and instrument playing techniques, but also includes much more notation of samulnori pieces, in a manner suggesting two earlier volumes by the center's samulnori maestro Ch'oe Pyŏngsam (Ch'oe, 2000; Ch'oe & Ch'oe, 1992). The third, by No Suhwan (2011), promotes itself as a textbook for the hourglass drum in local percussion bands but divides into three sections, each based on samulnori repertory. First comes a discussion of the samulnori seated drum piece, second, a drum dance (as part of the samulnori danced piece, "*P'an'gut*"), and third, notation for the drum in three canonic samulnori pieces.

Starting in 1989, SamulNori organized a regular festival, the *Samulnori kyŏrugi*, that reflected the standardization of their system of learning. Attracting groups from around Korea and abroad, the *kyŏrugi* made—much as had government-sponsored National Folk Arts Festivals and National Percussion Band Contests before it—judicious choices of judges to measure appropriate performances of appropriate repertory maintaining appropriate aesthetics. While the requirements of individual *kyŏrugi* have differed, the 1995 festival coined the term *samulnorian* for those taking part. The 2008 festivities celebrated 30 years of the genre and were coupled to a symposium in January 2009 at which the three surviving members of the first quartet reunited. The 2010 festival, held in Nonsan (the birthplace of the fourth early member, the late Kim Yongbae [1953–1986]) as the "World SamulNori Great Festival," underlined how a vibrant and vital musical genre had been created: Over 3 packed days, 86 performances by 840 performers in 77 groups took place.

There are implications for sustainability in the way that festivals, combined with the teaching and learning strategies that sit behind them, have created a fixed repertoire, the performances of which clone aesthetics and musical content. As time passes, these become virtual frozen artifacts that upcoming percussions are wary of changing or developing. As the early samulnori musicians who established the repertoire come to be celebrated for achievements in the past, it is likely to become increasingly difficult to retain the vitality that the genre had in its first years of existence.

MUSICIANS AND COMMUNITIES

As in much of the world, Korean musicians have in the past customarily occupied low-status positions when performing for money or payment in kind. Itinerant bands consisted of professional musicians and were, by definition, low status; local bands, populated by rural farmers, were not. Until the 1890s, musicians who performed for payment belonged to a virtually outcast group known as the *ch'ŏnmin*, along with shamans, butchers, tanners, and executioners. They were not allowed to own land, and hence were unable to accrue significant wealth. However, many musicians enjoyed the patronage of the wealthy and knew how to behave in the company of social superiors. Again, some of the best musicians were always aficionados hailing from high social groups, who would never accept payment for performance, and much of whose music was associated with self-cultivation (see Sung Hee Park, 2011, Chapter 2). In the 1890s, reforms to the hierarchical system began. These were part of Korea's opening to the world and, as a consequence, high-status Western art music began to be introduced.

The long-time SamulNori associate Chu Chaeyŏn writes that the genre the first quartet created and its performance style reflect the time in which they grew up (Chu, 2010, pp. 20–22). In the post–Korean War years, itinerant troupes were in terminal decline and local band styles had been modified for staged performances at festivals as Korea began to treasure its traditional culture. Many percussionists occupied a border area, organizing semiprofessional rather than itinerant troupes for defined periods. These included Kim Duk Soo's father, and Ch'oe Chongshil's seniors in the Samch'ŏnp'o band on the southwestern coast; they no longer attracted a low-status tag, and winning prizes at national and regional festivals served to elevate their prestige. Again, professional musicians had become part of celebrated performance groups used to promote Korea at home and abroad, and were senior teachers at the Traditional Arts School. SamulNori, thus, embraced both the modified local bands and itinerant troupes. Not unexpectedly, they blurred the same distinctions Helen Rees (2009) refers to in respect to the many different potential types of musicians in China (p. 9); their music and their identity were, and are, both urban and rural, professional and amateur, traditional and popular, national and local.

Nonetheless, some samulnori musicians struggle with status. This also has to do with the genre's instruments: In Korea, drums and gongs do not have the prestige or versatility of melodic instruments. As confirmed by the Seoul National University professor Kim Snggn, a hierarchy of instruments operates, based on Western art music, in which strings are ranked at the top, above wind and brass; percussion languishes at the bottom (interview, May 30, 2011). Comments made in interviews for this chapter corroborate this opinion:

> Most performers get little respect and can't generate an income from playing the drum or from any other part of samulnori. (Chang Chaehyo, hourglass drum player, Hongik University, December 20, 2010)

> Our samulnori masters get little support despite their musicianship. It seems that although samulnori descends from *p'ungmul*, and *p'ungmul* is one part of Korean traditional music, it is disregarded simply because it does not have the supposed high merit of aristocratic or court music. (An Taech'on and Yi Ch'anghun, members of The Gwangdae, December 20, 2010)

Pak Ŭnha, a founding member of the National Gugak Center Samulnori, was particularly eloquent in explaining the situation:

> Samulnori is looked down upon as third-rate. There is a tendency to regard instruments that you hit with disdain. Yet, the basis of music is essentially rhythm; hence, percussion instruments are important. Also, professional musicians and academics in Korean universities don't want to promote samulnori; the only reason they tolerate it is because of the attention it continues to enjoy overseas. (interview, November 2, 2010)

The first SamulNori quartet to perform, in February 1978, comprised Kim Yongbae on *kkwaenggwari*, the small hand-held gong; Kim Duk Soo on *changgo*, the double-headed hourglass drum; Yi Chongdae on *puk*, the barrel drum; and Ch'oe T'aehyŏn on *ching*, the large hand-held gong. The line-up was adjusted for a performance on April 18, when Ch'oe, primarily known as a *haegŭm* (two-stringed fiddle) player, and Yi, known more as a *p'iri* (oboe) and *taegŭm* (flute player), were replaced by Ch'oe Chongshil and his older brother Ch'oe Chongshik. In that performance, Kim Yongbae played *puk* and Ch'oe Chongshik *kkwaenggwari*. Ch'oe Chongshik was replaced by Yi Kwangsu (b. 1952) for an April 1979 performance (Chu Chaeyŏn, 2010, pp. 27–33). A period of stability followed, but when Kim Yongbae left to front a new quartet at the National Gugak Center in 1984, Kang Minsŏk was drafted in. Then, when Ch'oe Chongshil left in 1989, Kim Ŭnt'ae joined. Yi moved on to new projects in 1993, leaving Kim Duk Soo as the sole original quartet member. Kim remains the person most closely associated with SamulNori (Figure 9.1).

In the early 1980s, the National Gugak Center expanded its concertizing and to do so needed to broaden its repertoire. It established a second samulnori quartet, persuading Kim Yongbae to join Pak Ŭnha (b. 1960) and existing center staff

FIGURE 9.1 Kim Duk Soo, SamulNori member and *changgo* hourglass drum player, performing in Chilgok, October 2014.
Photo: Keith Howard.

members. But the new group failed to gel. Two new members were drafted in, both with strong backgrounds in itinerant troupes and semi-itinerant bands: Nam Kimun (b. 1958) from the Namsadang itinerant troupe as Important Intangible Cultural Property 3 and Ch'oe Pyŏngsam (b. 1957) from the Pusan-based Ami Nongak, a provincial Property. Still, when the group's first domestic album was released on the Jigu label in April 1986, it was critically reviewed. Members of Namsadang argued with Kim Yongbae, visiting his apartment on May 1, and 2 days later, though reportedly because of an argument with his girlfriend, Kim committed suicide (Kim Ŭnjŏng, 1986; Kim Hŏnsŏn, 1991, pp. 313–323, 1998, pp. 313–314). With Nam and Ch'oe now at its helm, the quartet finally began to meet expectations.

In 1985, a third samulnori group took to the stage: the unashamedly populist Durae Pae. Durae Pae launched as a sextet, doubling instruments, introducing dance, and adding an extra instrument in the form of a massive barrel drum. Reflecting the fact that the average length of a pop song is somewhere between 3 and 4 minutes, Durae Pae shoehorned samulnori pieces into this time frame. Samulnori was also adopted as part of a multifaceted performance group, Dulsori, founded in 1984, combining with *minyo* (folk songs) and *p'ansori* (epic storytelling through song, art, calligraphy, and dance). Dulsori have toured the world, proving to be particularly popular at WOMAD, the multisited world music and dance festival set up in 1982 by former Genesis progressive rock member Peter Gabriel— in earlier years, the first SamulNori appeared at the festival and recorded a track for Gabriel's record label (*A Week in the Real World*, Real World/Virgin CDRW25, 1992). Dulsori developed the massive drum of Durae Pae into a drum set, *modŭm puk*—"various" barrel drums. Such sets soon became common, but since sets of this sort were not part of the first SamulNori, and since they had no place in local band or itinerant troupe traditions, they continue to be criticized by some. Kim Kich'ang, for instance, a member of the Ch'ŏngbae Chŏnt'ong Yesultan (Cheongbae Traditional Art Troupe), told us that

> the primary threat to samulnori right now is that performers can only do a limited amount with the four instruments. To be creative, they add additional instruments, without thinking deeply about what they are doing. So, they add what we call *modŭm puk*, drums that are ultimately copied from Japanese *taiko*. (interview, November 8, 2010)

A plethora of samulnori groups soon populated Korea's performance stages. One that I visited in 1991 was Tasŭrŭm, established in March 1986 and featuring four young blind musicians who were students at Inch'ŏn Hyegwang School.

Another was Poong Mool Nori, which, following a residency at the Lotte World entertainment complex, was recruited as an international ambassador team for the Korean government. Over a 6-year period, it gave some 300 foreign concerts in this role. Later, the group Kwang Myung, formed in 2004, adopted samulnori rhythms for massive Japanese-style drums plus oil drums and assemblages of other percussion. In fact, Kwang Myung evokes the combination of samulnori and anything that makes noise from the kitchen—pots, pans, and knives—that is best known through Korea's most successful musical to date, "Nant'a/Cooking."

In 1993, the SamulNori quartet became a foundation, SamulNori Hanullim. This brought together various activities and allowed for an extended membership. Offshoots have included an instrument retail operation, an arts organization that since 2003 has run a concert hall, and additional groups whose names and personnel continuously change. According to one account, at the turn of the millennium the number of events put on by the foundation was second only to the sum of events featuring the many performance groups of the National Gugak Center (Shingil Park, 2000, p. 181). At the same time, as the initial quartet gradually disbanded, its remnants began to be called the "Kim Duk Soo SamulNori"; Kim became a brand, appearing in countless adverts and on a multitude of media programs both at home and abroad (Chu Chaeyŏn, 2010, pp. 82–85).

In the mid-1990s, Kim was appointed professor at Korea National University of Arts, where he set about training up-and-coming percussionists. While this multiplied the number of musicians he could call on, it also expanded the ranks of excellent Korean percussionists, so much so that Yi Kwangsu turned to me at a samulnori festival in Yesan in September 2014, remarking (here, I paraphrase): "When I was young, I was known as a child prodigy. But there's nothing special about being a child prodigy anymore. Just look at all these hundreds of amazing kids performing samulnori!" Figure 9.2 shows one of the 50 groups that performed at Yesan in 2014.

Many samulnori musicians abroad have Korean heritage. Groups are often based at universities where there is, of necessity given the transient nature of the Korean student diaspora, a rapid turnover of members, as a glance at some of the available websites confirms.[2] Elsewhere, in Japan, Central Asia, China, and North America, many groups consist of diasporic Koreans. Two of the most prominent teachers and performers are the British-based Nami Morris (at the University of Cambridge) and the Vancouver-based professor Nathan Hesselink (University of British Columbia). Hesselink, alone to my knowledge, has developed new

---

[2] See, for example, http://www.indiana.edu/~samul/samul.html, http://www.its.caltech.edu/~godong/, http://shinparam.org/zbxe/?mid=pungmul, http://music.emory.edu/performance/documents/samulnori. html, http://www.mit.edu/~oori/, and https://ulife.utoronto.ca/organizations/view/id/2973

FIGURE 9.2 A student samulnori group performing at the Yesan Samulnori Festival, September 2014.
Photo: Keith Howard.

repertoire pieces—one based on East Coast local band practice, one adding guitars and Indonesian gongs, and one that fuses little-known local band rhythms with European rock constructs. Notwithstanding the visibility of samulnori in the national and international arena, however, control of the genre remains firmly in Korea. This is illustrated in the samulnori festivals, which, although welcoming and encouraging foreign teams, perpetuate the elements of control, as we were told in late 2010 by somebody I will here cite anonymously:

> We renamed our festival as the "World SamulNori Festival" to encourage foreign musicians not just to visit Korea briefly, but to come to Korea for a few weeks, so we could have a look at what samulnori they had learned in order to check they had grasped the basics and to correct them.

Keeping control in Korea impacts the promotion of samulnori abroad. Too often, Koreans still consider that foreign audiences must be introduced to Korea. Reflecting this, those who dispense funding expect artists to mix repertoires, favoring potpourri programs or multiart presentations. On one side, this discourages any development of samulnori beyond the core canon of pieces. On the other side, though, recent years have seen a tendency to blend Korean traditional forms with Western elements in an attempt to add familiarity. This is evident in the genre of *kugak fusion*, a genre that became prominent in the first decade of the new millennium and that mixes Western and Korean instruments, often including samulnori percussion. As we see more globally, however, fusions do not entice foreign audiences in the way that regional traditions do. Foreign audiences expect the traditionesque—using this term to allow for more recent interpretations—and foreign samulnori teams therefore tend to maintain the established samulnori repertoire. This, though, increasingly runs counter to what is expected and funded at home, in Korea. And, with validity and support in Korea measured at least in part in terms of success abroad, there is likely to be a question about the sustainability of samulnori both at home and abroad unless the local and foreign can be squared.

CONTEXTS AND CONSTRUCTS: THE SAMULNORI CANON

The first quartet, SamulNori, established a genre, samulnori: a set of discrete pieces that were shared among emerging groups as a canon. Three pieces descending from local percussion bands and itinerant troupes were premiered within an initial 15-month period. The pieces were regionally distinct, using rhythmic structures from troupes that had once operated in the central Kyŏnggi and Ch'ungch'ŏng provinces ("*Uttari kut*" or "*Uttari nongak*" or "*Uttari p'ungmul*"), and bands from the southeastern South Kyŏngsang province ("*Yŏngnam nongak*") and the southwestern Chŏlla provinces ("*Honam udo nongak*"). Taken together, these three comprise what I call the inner canon. To these, four further pieces were added by 1982—an outer canon—to give a total repertoire more than large enough to sustain interest over a whole concert. The first of these four additional pieces, "*Samdo nongak*" (*samdo* = three provinces), blended rhythmic structures from different regions and was intended to substitute for the individual pieces of the inner canon. Three sections within it lifted, in the order in which they appear, the processional *Och'ae chil kut* episode that opens the third piece, an episode known as *Pyŏl tal kŏri* ("Bright moon scene") from the second piece, and the characteristic hocketing episode known as *Tchaksoe* from the first. The second of the four additional pieces, "*Pinari*," evolves from a prayer for blessings long known to itinerant troupes and continues to function as an opening piece in samulnori concerts. The third, "*P'an'gut*," provided a danced second half to concerts, constructing a tightly choreographed four-man version of similarly named former local band entertainment performances. The fourth, "*Samdo sŏl changgo*," created a seated version of many existing local band and itinerant troupe drum dances, with all four samulnori musicians playing hourglass drums rather than the quartet of mixed drums and gongs. Today, several versions of "*Samdo sŏl changgo*" coexist. An eighth piece can be added, representing the second common southwestern style, "*Honam chwado nongak*," but a version of this appears on only one samulnori recording (King SYNCD-114, 1995).

As new quartets formed, they retained the inner and outer canon, seeking distinction by extending or compressing each piece. It is not unreasonable to ask whether sustaining a genre is possible with such a small and restricted repertoire. Unlike samulnori, the comparable Japanese *taiko* percussion repertoire continuously grows, allowing a blend of Japanese and foreign materials to emerge both inside and outside East Asia. But, I note that Korea tends to favor short periods of intense creativity followed by extended periods of stasis. In terms of traditional music, this can be seen in *kagok*, the set of 26 lyric songs in male and female versions that is today Important Intangible Cultural Property 30: All *kagok* are built on frames derived from a single melody, the first surviving notation of which dates to 1572. Or consider *shijo*, three-line poems associated with the artistic preferences of the educated middle classes, all set to a single basic melody in a tritonic mode. Similarly, there are just six widely recognized "schools" (*ryu*, but in this context, effectively, pieces) of *kayagŭm sanjo*, Property 23, and just five *p'ansori* (epic storytelling) through song stories within Property 5. It may be Western centric to assume that sustaining a genre over time requires either a broad and extensive canon or the constant development of new repertory. But it is because of the canon, and because it is recognized that it is assembled from older percussion music, that samulnori has begun to replace local bands and itinerant troupes. To quote one distinguished scholar, who places responsibility squarely on the first quartet:

> For those whose sensibilities have become somewhat jaded, SamulNori has provided a fresh and startling impulse. . . . For an older generation, the music created a most poignant nostalgia. . . . We are drawn slowly, bit by bit back to an original hometown that we all shared in our collective memories. . . . It is exactly these memories and the energy of our people which has been recreated to such perfection by SamulNori. (Hahn Myung-hee, 1992, pp. 5–6)

Nonetheless, samulnori faced much criticism from folklorists who documented music in the countryside and older musicians who saw in the genre a challenge to what they remembered from the past. Students, at the time caught up in an attempt to challenge dictatorship through the culture-of-the-masses *minjung munhwa*, rejected its highly structured stagecraft. The folk music specialist Yi Pohyŏng (1985, p. 146) wrote how samulnori should not be considered traditional (*chŏnt'ong*), and other senior academics challenged the link to tradition (Yi Sŏngch'ŏn, 1994, pp. 180–181; Yi Sŏngjae, 1994, pp. 96–101; Ch'oe Chongmin, 2002, p. 12). Many others were equally critical: In August 1990, Park Yongt'ae, now a "holder" (*poyuuja*) for Namsadang itinerant troupes as Property 3, described samulnori to me as "inauthentic" (*pijongmok*); later, in September 1997, I watched older audience members stand up and leave when a samulnori group took to the stage at one concert. And yet:

> Samulnori pieces carried over existing rhythmic patterns from *p'ungmul*, and can be claimed to be traditional. But even though we enjoy watching *p'ungmul*, we don't live as the farmers of old. When we play samulnori, we don't think about the lives of farmers. (Chang Chaehyo, Hongik University, interview, December 20, 2010)

A number of percussionists began by regarding samulnori as something inferior but changed their opinions as they learned to perform it, as revealed in the following interview comments:

> When I was at college, I participated in the mass culture movement. We used to perform *p'ungmul*, but we had a negative feeling towards samulnori. This was because *p'ungmul* was rooted in a sense of solidarity and communal consciousness, but samulnori was about a few individuals showing off their virtuosity on stage. I came to think differently when I learnt to perform samulnori, and began to recognize the accumulated skills of its performers, their artistic aesthetic, their attitudes and discipline on stage. (Yi Muyang, member of Han'guk Ŭmak Hakhoe [Academy of Korean Music] and school teacher at Kangsŏ Haksŭptang, interview, November 25, 2010)

> Samulnori is modern music. It is an indoor version of *p'ungmul* developed by the first quartet. When I was young, we tended not to use the word *samul*, and in fact our teachers hated the word, using instead the old name for bands, *p'ungmul*. (Ch'oe Yunsang, founder of group Gongmyeong and member of group Puri, interview, December 16, 2010)

Some musicians continue to distinguish the communitarian nature of local bands from the spectacle-driven samulnori, critiquing the fixed nature of the samulnori canon. Here is an excerpt from a discussion between Hwang Hŭi, Chŏng Ch'anul, and Kim Chiyŏng, members of the Yonsei University *P'ungmul* Club, responding to our question about the relationship between *p'ungmul* and samulnori:

> *P'ungmul* is what our elders used to do in their villages. When my university *p'ungmul* club performs, some older people come up and dance with us, so

that the audience and the performers become as one.... In *p'ungmul*, the important thing is for performers to enjoy themselves, to be excited by what they are doing. You can substitute rhythmic variants, as many as you like. You can put new variants in to appeal to the audience; you can even add different instruments. The more you do so, the more varied a performance will be, and the more it will appeal to a Korean audience. You should maintain the same basic repertoire, and create new variants to keep interest. If you don't do this, the music will bore listeners, and this [sameness] is really the crisis of identity evident in samulnori today. (interview, November 1, 2010)

Ultimately, samulnori repackages the music of local bands and itinerant troupes, but, in contrast to the older forms, it is ideally suited to contemporary concert culture. It reflects the Korean state's investment in public performance infrastructure and provides a Korean counterpart to the Western art music that Korea's new stages were designed to accommodate. Much as Western music is identified with a canon of "great works" (Goehr, 1992; Samson, 2001; Weber, 1992), so is samulnori. Samulnori, then, can function as a flag bearer for Korea's performance culture both at home and abroad. The repackaging has involved the development of a system of learning that includes a new notation system and an elaborate aesthetic for performance, and which links musical structures to philosophy and to folklore. In respect to the latter, samulnori has a nationalistic function.

By the 10th anniversary of the first performance, in 1988, the four core instruments were allied to wind, lightning, clouds, and rain, these four elements serving as titles for overarching sections in one of the anniversary books (Art Space, 1988a). In 1994, SamulNori were central to performances of "*Yŏnggo*/Sacred Drum" at the Opera House of Seoul Arts Center, featuring goblins and lords of the underworld. By the start of the new century, children's books appeared, such as Kwak Young-kwon and Kim Dong-won's *Samulnori iyagi/The Story of SamulNori* (2001/2003). In this, we read how Ash Monster takes over the prehistoric bright land, covering it with a layer of ash that blots out the sun. He forces the king to flee to Paektu Mountain, on the border between today's North Korea and China, a place associated with Korea's long-lived mythical founder, Tan'gun. The king prays for deliverance and is granted four treasures: the four samulnori instruments.

The constructs of samulnori have proved irresistible, to the extent that samulnori has begun to replace local percussion bands and itinerant troupes, even though those genres, and not samulnori, remain as Important Intangible Cultural Properties. School textbooks have for several decades included basic rhythmic cycles, discussed within a consideration of *minyo* folk songs and local bands. Today, samulnori is used to show both the cycles and how they link together. Indeed, research by the educator and scholar Kim In Suk (2012) reveals that samulnori is now the authorized form of percussion band music taught in schools, although it features more prominently when schools are situated distant from where local band practice survives. In the Korean countryside, Simon Mills (2014) has shown how samulnori has begun to substitute for local bands in revivals. He takes the example of the island of Ullŭngdo, where, starting in 1995, the Usan Cultural Festival marked a revival of folkloric music, replacing a local band tradition lost some decades earlier with samulnori. To explain the process, Mills adapts a perspective from the folk music scholar Yi Pohyŏng that argues declining music genres are revived in urban centers and, in new forms, are then projected back to the locales in which they once thrived. To this, he adds Agehanada Bharati's so-called pizza effect (in which pizza was taken from rural Italy to America by Italian émigrés, developed into modern pizzas, and then returned to Italy).

The implications for the musical ecosystem are considerable. The regional variety inherent in local bands and itinerant troupes is today being replaced by a defined samulnori canon shared both across the Korean peninsula and by percussionists further afield. This canon recontextualizes rhythmic structures that once functioned for differing ritual, entertainment, and work activities, and juxtaposes them in a way that prioritizes musical integrity over social function. The loss of regional variety may be inevitable, but the loss of knowledge about the function of musical structures impacts on identity, denies communitarianism, and removes long-established relationships between music and place.

INFRASTRUCTURE AND REGULATIONS
Performing SamulNori in Korea

The performance context of folk music in the past was not that of concert music today. Local bands and itinerant troupes were—and are, in their preserved Property forms—associated with outdoor spaces, combining loud and at times raucous music with dance and movement maneuvers that had much in common with military training (forming camp, breaking camp, forming lines and squares) and which required large spaces and large manpower. Samulnori is, broadly, more suited to indoor stages. The normative line taken by Korean scholars is that the country had no theater and no stage until the 20th century. Traditional venues for performance included village meeting places (*madang*), farmers' dugouts (*umjip/ kip'ŭn sarang*), dry fields (*pat*), clubs such as song societies, the gentlemen's rooms of private houses (*sarang pang*), courtesan institutes and rooms (*kibang*, etc.), and, for the aristocracy, parties held at scenic places such as mountains, waterfalls, and rivers, as well as in royal palaces (Park Sung Hee, 2014). The development of the first theaters date to the beginning of the 20th century, a few decades after Western music was introduced, and these early stages did not serve local traditions of music well.

Jumping ahead to the decade in which SamulNori premiered, Korea built a number of performance venues before, during, and after the 1970s, including the Sejong Cultural Center (Sejong Munhwa Hoegwan) in downtown Seoul; the National Theater (Kungnip Kŭkch'ang) on one flank of Seoul's geomantic protective mountain, Namsan; and the Munye Theater (Munye Kŭkch'ang) in Hyehwa-dong to Seoul's east. These were spaces for the grandiose: Western theater, ballet, and opera, with Korean equivalents such as *ch'anggŭk* opera and its relations as evolutions of *p'ansori*, and new orchestras of traditional instruments. Each grand complex incorporated smaller, intimate halls adjacent to their central spaces, and these were arguably better suited for Korean traditional music, particularly for the equivalent of Western recital and ensemble genres, from *sanjo* (scattered melodies) for solo melodic instrument and drum to midsized ensembles for, say, the literati-oriented "*Yŏngsan hoesang*" suite.

Whether large or small, theaters featured proscenium stages, with the result that concerts of Korean music began to copy the rituals of Western art music. The stages were hardly suitable for local bands and itinerant troupes, but they encouraged the emergence of new genres based on the old—including samulnori. A further, particularly important indoor performance space opened in the 1970s, where SamulNori first performed: the Space Theater (*Konggan sarang*, literally Love of Space). Citing Yi Hyŏngyŏng (2004) and Yi Haerang (1985), Hesselink (2012) introduces it as such: "The roughly 120-seat box-style space was striking in its simplicity and intimacy.... The hall was of tremendous consequence for the development of Korean traditional performance arts culture in the later twentieth century" (pp. 50–51). In many ways, it recreated the dugouts of farmers from former times. It had no raised stage, and its stepped floor made do with cushions for audiences to sit on. Developed by the architect Kim Sugŭn (1931–1986), it operated between 1977 and the late 1980s; Kim was renowned in his work for blending tradition with modernity, the Korean with the Western.

Performances of music relating to folk traditions were still limited when SamulNori took to the stage in 1978. Korea's concert scene was, however, rapidly developing. Where the National Gugak Center had promoted just 55 concerts between 1956 and 1960, 130 during the next decade, and 109 the next, it put on 81 events in 1981 alone. By the 1990s, according to their respective yearbooks, the Korean Culture and Arts Foundation counted 621 traditional music concerts in 1991, while the National Center figures for 1992 counted even larger numbers: 445

chŏngak (court music) and 858 *minsok ŭmak* (folk music) performances, plus 745 events that incorporated *ch'angjak kugak* (creative traditional music). Samulnori was included in the latter two categories. Clearly, samulnori benefited from the rapid development of venues and performance opportunities. Through to 1989, and excluding repeat performances, SamulNori could list 278 domestic and 275 foreign concerts (Art Space, 1988b). A brochure from 1994 stated that SamulNori had by then given more than 1,500 performances in total; by 2003, one website claimed that the quartet had performed nearly 5,500 times on "more than 3,000" stages (http://www.culturebase.net/artist.php?1209, now deleted; this figure is repeated in liner notes to a 2007 SamulNori CD written by Kim Tongwŏn and Chu Chaeyŏn).

The availability of rehearsal spaces was a further element in the genre's popularization. Small studios, where drum dances (*changgo ch'um, puk ch'um,* etc.) could be taught and rehearsed, proliferated in the 1970s and 1980s. Many were sited near universities, and as the student-led *minjung munhwa* mass culture movement bedded in, many a university campus hosted folk music clubs as part of an agenda to reclaim the local heritage. A number of formal societies and organizations flourished that provided arenas for teaching. These included Hŭngsadan, known in English as the Institute for the Advancement of Individuals, which, by the 1980s, from premises in Hyehwa-dong, offered lessons in masked dance dramas, folk songs, and percussion bands. P'ungnyu Hoe (Association for Elegant Music), established in 1976 for music lovers, promoted workshops, camps, and concerts across the spectrum of traditional music. Hansori Hoe (Association with One Sound), founded in 1980, was a large operation near Ewha Women's University offering instrumental and vocal lessons. Others, such as Uri Madang (Our Plaza) and Uri Munhwa Yŏn'guwŏn (Our Culture Study Institute), offered group performance workshops.

In its early years, SamulNori was based in a small studio in a building shared with a Chinese restaurant in Ahyŏn-dong, a western suburb. Cardboard egg cartons lined the walls to provide basic sound insulation. From 1987, and after the quartet appeared at student rallies for democracy, thereby distancing itself from the low-status itinerant troupe tradition and allying itself firmly to the mass culture movement, SamulNori began to offer workshops at the Chungang Daily News Cultural Center near Piwŏn, close to the Space Theater. The quartet soon moved across town, to the Live House Nanjang studio in Shinch'on, at the center of a diamond formed by four universities. Meanwhile, Kang Chunhyŏk, the former manager of the Space Theater, decamped to Hyehwa-dong, up the hill from the Munye Theater, where he built a new studio for his organization, Metaa. SamulNori migrated there as the quartet morphed into SamulNori Hanullim. This provided offices and rehearsal studios in an area that was rapidly becoming home to hundreds of small theaters. In 2003, the foundation took over Kwanghwamun Art Hall, to the north of Sejong Cultural Centre.

SamulNori and the Preservation Agenda

Samulnori forms just one part of the 20th-century development of Korean concert culture. Where local bands and itinerant troupes usually performed in open spaces lacking a stage and where audiences surrounded the performers, samulnori is best served by proscenium stages. The ecosystem has changed, but concert culture is, at its root, a part of Korea's Westernization process. Hence, Korean performing arts must compete with, and in some ways match, Western performance arts. Samulnori succeeds in doing so, but it does so less on the terms of Korean tradition than by responding to the challenges of Westernization. This introduces a further problematic element: How can samulnori fit with a music tradition that is supported by a state preservation system? That system has, since the 1960s, supported local bands and itinerant troupes, the former as Important Intangible Cultural Property 11 and the latter as Property 3. Samulnori has not been appointed within the system, but many performers consider that the genre should now receive support.

As I have explored elsewhere (Howard, 2006a, 2006b), Korean Properties are appointed based on supposedly archetypal forms known as the *wŏnhyŏng*. These are researched and confirmed prior to appointment through the Cumulative Research Reports on Intangible Cultural Properties (*Chungyo muhyŏng munhwajae chosa pogosŏ*; see Howard, 2006a, pp. 50–51). The appointment is designed to protect a Property at a time of endangerment and possible loss, and needs to maintain intangible skills by supporting individuals as "holders" (*poyuja*). The system fits what Richard Dorson once termed folklore's "historical-reconstructionism" (cited in Janelli, 1986, pp. 24–25). It utilizes scholarly research to demonstrate authenticity. Expertise has been, for court and literati music, largely vested in senior musicians and musicologists working at the National Gugak Center or Seoul National University, among them Sŏng Kyŏngnin (1911–2008), Kim Kisu (1917–1986), Chang Sahun (1916–1993), and Kim Ch'ŏnhŭng (1909–2008)—all four of whom had trained as musicians at the court music institute during the Japanese colonial period. It fell to those in a second camp, allied to the Traditional Arts School, and to folklorists to compile reports for folk music and dance. In the 1960s, though, reports were compiled as folk music began to be presented on urban stages, and the result was that aspects of presentation were accommodated in the authenticated archetypes. Lines were therefore drawn in imaginary sand to set down supposedly correct forms, and individuals and groups were given responsibility—and funding—to maintain and preserve these as intangible properties.

What, then, constitutes Properties 3 and 11? Namsadang, as Property 3, represents the practices of one of a myriad itinerant troupes, and the genre was in terminal decline by the time of its appointment in 1964. The historical record was scant, and the official report largely matched other publications by a single scholar. *Nongak*, as Property 11, appointed in 1966, stretched back into the mists of a largely uncharted history, but the regional distinctiveness set out as authoritative in the Property largely reflects presentations at mid-20th-century festivals and competitions rather than older, more local (and locally diverse) practices. If either genre were to be appointed a Property today, 50 years after the initial appointments but at a time when scholarship has advanced and methods of historical documentation have improved, or if either had been appointed 50 years earlier, at the beginning of the 20th century and as Korea began to open to the world, the archetype forms, the *wŏnhyŏng*, would have been markedly different.

Sustainability must, inevitably, challenge the freezing of cultural production at a specific point in time. Today, however, many scholars and officials find it problematic to accept that samulnori has either a sufficient historicity or faces a sufficient decline to merit support within the system. Forty years since its inception, though, much of what justified the appointment of Properties 3 and 11 applies to samulnori. Samulnori retains a core repertory, and this, as a canon, fits the authenticity and originality requirements of Properties. Albeit highly creative, this canon was put in place during a known period, 1978–1982, and its continued performance constitutes a faithful transmission of archetypal forms. Sustainability requires (as, it has been argued, does conservation; Loomis, 1983, p. iv) both preservation and promotion, and each samulnori piece offers updated versions of material from local band and itinerant troupe repertoires while functioning as a core part of many Korean performance events at home and abroad. Samulnori has become iconic, and it would not be an overstatement to say that the individual canonic pieces have given samulnori a role as an essential part of Korea's concert culture, much as, or more than, have the individual items prescribed as archetypes within Properties.

But, as with the prescribed archetypes designated as Properties, the canon has become *too* traditional. Some musicians we talked to explicitly felt that the genre should receive government funding to preserve and promote it. Chang Chaehyo, for instance (interview, December 20, 2010), remarked: "Samulnori needs government support to help engender respect from people and reflect the fact that it has been Korea's most significant traditional music for four decades." Again,

Im Sobin, a member of Han'guk Ŭmak Hakhoe (Academy of Korean Music), commented (interview, November 25, 2010): "The canonic samulnori pieces are no longer played as they were originally, and so authentic forms need to be preserved and promoted."

Because the canon is now *too* traditional, new creativity with samulnori has become commonplace. Chu Chaeyŏn (2010), in his master's dissertation, lists productions in Seoul involving samulnori during April 2010: "*Nant'a*" at Nant'a Ch'ŏnyong Theater; "*Jump*" at Cine Core Theater combining with *taekwŏndo* martial arts; "*Miso*" at Chŏngdong Theater combining with traditional dance; "*P'an*" at SamulNori Hanullim's Kwanghwamun Art Hall, combined with *p'ansori*, masked dance drama and music inspired by shamanism; "*Drawing Show*" at Chŏnyong Theater with live art; "*Baby*" at B-Boy Theater; "*Traditional Salon*" at Korea House, juxtaposing samulnori with traditional music and dance; "*Sach'um*" at Sach'um Theater with dance, ballet, and B-boys; "*Fantastic*" at 63 Art Hall on Yŏŭido Island with traditional music and B-boys; and "*Drumkit*" at Myŏngbo Art Hall mixing samulnori with other percussion traditions (p. 90). This list is impressive, particularly when compared to the limited number of traditional music performances given in earlier decades; and it is informative, because it indicates how samulnori is increasingly used in conjunction with other forms of performance rather than as a stand-alone genre. In this, samulnori is no different from other traditional Korean music: The canons of traditional genres—and samulnori—have not disappeared, but have been taken up with new creativity, blurring the boundaries between tradition and modernity. This is much as it should be if we accept that revival, and through it sustainability, should allow us to witness "a past that is alive" (after Bharucha, 1993, p. 15). This, though, challenges the concepts of repertoire and genre sustainability.

Without the safety net of state support, samulnori may soon be caught in a place built on quicksand, with the canonic repertoire neither sufficiently traditional to qualify as a Property nor sufficiently contemporary to retain an audience. Koreans are one of the most rapidly shifting populations in the world today, keen to experience ever-changing novelty and to consume the newest products. As a result, it is no surprise that musicians working with samulnori feel a need to develop their materials. Old-fashioned theories still have applicability: Contemporary cultures are in flux (Clifford, 1988; Marcus & Fischer, 1986) and foster synthesis and syncretism through the "cultural traffic" of importation and exchange (Alvesson, 1996, p. 80). Or, "there are only cultural sets of practices and ideas, put into play by determinate human actors under determinate circumstances. In the course of action, these cultural sets are forever assembled, dismantled, and reassembled" (Wolf, 1982, pp. 390–391). If I had written this chapter three decades ago, samulnori would have featured as a central example of the expansion of the concept and practice of *kugak*, Korean traditional music; it was then new music of the time. Today, it has become part of a tradition, but, as with *kugak* proper, performances of the canon continue while new repertoire develops around it. Samulnori has evolved, taking on the batteries of drums known as *modŭm puk*, and modifying every aspect of presentation.

MEDIA AND THE MUSIC INDUSTRY: BEYOND THE SAMULNORI CANON

The central, key recordings of key samulnori musicians are the 1995 CDs by Kim Duk Soo and SamulNori Hanullim (King SYNCD-114–115) and the 1992 CDs by the National Gugak Center's samulnori (Jigu JCDS-0319–0320). Other recordings of the canon by SamulNori and the National Gugak Center group include *Samul-Nori: Drums and Voices of Korea* (Nonesuch Explorer Series 72093, 1984; Oasis ORC-1041, 1991), *Samulnori* (Jigu JCDS-0050, 1986), *SamulNori* (Sony 32DG64, 1986), *SamulNori* (SKC, SKCD-K-0326, 1987 and 1988), and *National Classical Music Institute Samulnori/Samulnori: 93-iryo myŏngin myŏngch'angjŏn 3* (Cantabile SRCD-1186, 1994). These are used as yardsticks, as the models for learning each piece, and as the models through which to judge any samulnori performance.

Samulnori, though, stretches beyond the repertoire featured in such recordings. Although *kugak* is celebrated both nationally and internationally as a potent sonic symbol of identity, since the 1980s, many *kugak* specialists have begun to merge the worlds of East and West in what Hilary Finchum-Sung (2012) described as "*kugak* teams." Many fuse materials as they seek to popularize traditional music: Young *kugak* musicians have grown up surrounded by Western music soundworlds, but fusions also reflect the marketing of recording companies and concert promoters. I would suggest that the concept of *kugak* teams can be backdated to the inception of samulnori. The first quartet, for instance, gave three celebratory concerts to mark its 10th anniversary in 1988, one devoted to the canon but two moving beyond it. One of these latter, "SamulNori vs Mu," used the Sino-Korean character for things shamanic but extended the meaning to a meeting between East and West as SamulNori joined four jazz musicians, the Austrian saxophonist Wolfgang Puschnig, American scat vocalist Linda Sharrock, Brazilian percussionist Dudu Tucci, and Japanese free jazz pianist Yamashita Yosuke. The other, "SamulNori vs New Korean Music," added rock musicians playing guitars, keyboards, drums, and saxophones.

With jazz, SamulNori stretched its boundaries. The quartet first worked alongside the saxophonist Kang Tae Hwan in 1980. In 1985, Kang joined SamulNori in the first of what became annual multifaceted music and dance extravaganzas, *Ult'arigut*, organized by the then manager of the Space Theater, Kang Chunhyŏk. SamulNori toured Japan with Kang Tae Hwan and with the Japanese free jazz pianist Yamashita

Yosuke; they even shared the stage with Herbie Hancock. In 1987, the quartet recorded a video at the Suntory Hall in Tokyo and toured with international jazz musicians as SXL (Kim Hŏnsŏn, 1995, pp. 210–211). SXL added Bill Laswell's bass, L. Shankar's double-necked violin, Ronald Shannon Jackson's funk drums, and Aiyb Dieng's Senegalese percussion to SamulNori's Korean percussion. They recorded two albums, *SXL Live in Japan* (Terrapin 32DH824, 1987) and *SXL Into the Outlands* (Celluloid CELD5017, 1987; also released as Enemy Records 0350608). Next came a collaboration that lasted more than a decade with a jazz quartet, "Red Sun," featuring Puschnig, Sharrock, and others. Four albums resulted, two issued in Europe and two in Korea: *Red Sun—SamulNori* (Amadeo 841 222-1, 1989, remastered on CD as Polygram DZ-2433, 1997), *Then Comes the White Tiger* (ECM ECM-1499, 1994), *Nanjang: A New Horizon* (King Records KSC-4150A, 1995), and *From the Earth, to the Sky* (Samsung Music SCO-123ABN, 1997 and 1998). The four move from hierarchy—Red Sun above SamulNori—to equality, as the samulnori canon is celebrated.

The breadth of creativity now commonplace is illustrated in recent recordings by other groups. Kim Dong-won's *Kirŭl kara/On the Road* (Sony BMG SB70195C/88697160042, 2008), for example, intersperses four solo percussion tracks and a track of onomatopoeia for the hourglass drum between mixes of East and West featuring the Austrian group Coming and Going—*sitar, didjeridu,* Brazilian *berim-bau,* saxophone, and more. Kim is the disciple of Kim Duk Soo. *GongMyoung 10th Anniversary* (Company Gongmyoung, 2008) is by a group (GongMyoung) that began as a samulnori quartet linked to the early SamulNori member Yi Kwangsu but which invested heavily in fusion; all traces of samulnori are hidden below the surface as they balance percussion forces with the Kang Mijŏng Tonic Ensemble and the keyboardist Yi Pyŏnghun. In contrast, Yi Yŏnggwang and Samulnori Molgae's *time-blend* (Audioguy Records, AGCD0019, 2009), although again featuring a jazz pianist, foregrounds samulnori. Finally, the title of Dulsori's *Well-Wishing: Binari* (Dulsori DA110001SP, 2010, and ARC Music, EUCD2366, 2011) refers to one canonic samulnori piece but, apart from using the samulnori instruments, takes samulnori out of the mix. Elvis, if you like, has left the building.

Contrasting new creations, samulnori proper, as a quartet of musicians play-ing the two drums and two gongs, has begun to decline. This is seen in the way that a number of its musicians argue for government support, as Nam Kimun, Namsadang holder and former member of the National Gugak Center Samulnori, told us: "The market for samulnori is too small and local, and needs financial sup-port to avoid it withering and dying" (interview, October 25, 2010). The decline is linked to samulnori's position as an established part of tradition. But, if tradition can claim support from the state, in a sort of museumization of a performance art and as an essentialization of what it means to be Korean, new creativity cannot.

Hence, the marriage of tradition and modernity (or creativity) struggles to promote sustainability. In thinking about this, I need to introduce the Korean discourse of identity, which promotes "ways of thinking which dominate and determine every behaviour and feature of Koreans who are different from foreigners" (Yi Kyut'ae, 1983, cited in Kweon Sug-In, 2003, p. 46). Rather than a nationalism of difference, in today's globalized world Koreans have become content with the juxtapositions of old and new, local and foreign. Indeed, these juxtapositions are evident in the commercial recordings sampled earlier. Tradition itself, the canon of samulnori pieces, has less commercial value.

Seoul's contemporary soundscape mixes old and new, local and foreign. To give an illustration, in October 2012, I watched a performance of the Kyŏnggi Provincial Dance Ensemble at the Seoul Outdoor Performance Space (Sŏul Nori Madang). The first piece on the program featured a quintet of percussionists. Ranks of *modŭm puk* drums were joined by a set of hourglass drums set skin upward; a further *changgo* hourglass drum was positioned center stage, and musicians held *kkwaenggwari* and *ching*, small and large gongs. All four constituent samulnori instruments were present, and the performance related to samulnori: the hocketing *Tchaksoe* from "*Uttari kut*" and a solo drum episode reminiscent of "*Samdo sŏl changgo*." The third piece was announced as "*P'an'gut*" and joined a central quintet wearing samulnori costumes (black waistcoat over white trousers and jacket, with three colored sashes) with a large company of dancers with drums and gongs. The quintet matched the samulnori canonic "*P'an'gut*," performing in the center as the company of dancers stood in an arc around them. Then individual quintet musicians led groups of dancers in choreographed dances for each instrument—much as would be given as solo episodes in samulnori's "*P'an'gut*."

ISSUES AND INITIATIVES FOR SUSTAINABILITY

Samulnori musicians accept the need for new repertoire, as the following two comments indicate:

> The hourglass drum has gained tremendous popularity, but because many consider it noisy, composers give it the cold shoulder, preferring to use African *djembe* or Indian *tabla*. The fact that the samulnori repertory is largely the same and lacks dynamic or other contrasts is a key problem. (Chang Chaehyo, interview, December 20, 2010)

> When it was created, the samulnori repertory was big news. But, for 30 years it has remained the same while public tastes have shifted. The samulnori

repertory needs to evolve to meet the requirements of today's public. (Yi Pona, hourglass drum student, Hongik University, interview, December 20, 2010)

However, the canon is enshrined, as a set of fixed pieces celebrated by musicians, audiences, and educators alike. Im Subin commented how one of the first SamulNori members, Yi Kwangsu, "once said that diamonds are beautiful because they never change. The samulnori pieces are, to an extent, complete" (interview, November 25, 2010). In a similar vein, Pak Ch'angbae, president of Yongin Traditional Arts Center, remarked, "I think the repertory was created too perfectly in the first place, and this makes it meaningless to change anything" (interview, November 17, 2010), while Yi Chunu and Han Chaesuk, Namdo Gugak Center SamulNori members, told us, "Kim Duk Soo made the samulnori pieces well—it is appropriate to consider each a new piece of creative music. . . . Musicians today should polish and complement the existing rhythmic patterns of each piece, enriching them" (interview, October 29, 2010).

Today, performances of canonic pieces are measured against key recordings that feature key musicians (as listed earlier). The sustainability of samulnori requires finding a balance between the canon and new creativity. It may not, however, require that complete canonic pieces be retained. At this point, I depart from how Korea (and, more broadly, UNESCO) views the preservation of intangible cultural heritage, since I believe that the iconicity of samulnori resides not in complete pieces but in specific motifs and episodes. Motifs and episodes are what audiences and musicians alike recognize as the legacy of samulnori beyond the canon. Motifs and episodes offer kernels for new creativity, allowing the genre to transform as it is sustained, or, in Bharucha's terms, allowing the past to remain alive.

To explain, I need to briefly outline the grammar of Korean percussion, as I analyzed it 25 years ago, and as has recently been taken further by the Australian jazz percussionist Simon Barker (Barker, 2015; Howard, 1991/1992). I identified binary (e.g., 2♩) or ternary (iambic, trochaic; e.g., 3♪) archetypal *cells* at a root level that in samulnori repertoire group into compound *units*. Barker identifies these units as *rhythm/sticking cells*, because they are repeated, end to end, modifying and adjusting them (typically adding more complexity; Barker, 2015, pp. 21–30). The repeated sets of units or cells group to form *motifs*. Reflecting the way that units are repeated, Barker refers to *archetype streams*. Either motifs or sets of motifs create *episodes*. Ch'ilch'ae (seven strikes), from the samulnori canonic piece "*Uttari p'ungmul,*" for instance, has seven *units* each marked by an initial large gong strike (accent): 5♪ + 5♪ + 3♩ + 3♩ + 5♪ + 5♪ + 10♪. Each unit is a compound of binary and ternary *cells*: 3♩ + 2♪, 3♩ + 2♪, 3♩, 3♩, 3♩ + 2♪, 3♩ + 2♪, 2♪ + 3♩ + 3♩ + 2♪. The seven units, taken together, form a *motif*. As ornamentation and additional complexity are added to each repeat of the motif, we hear *archetype streams*, and joining the streams together creates the full *episode: Ch'ilch'ae*.[3]

As a second example, *Tasŭrŭm*, the introduction to the canonic "*Samdo sŏl changgo*" "evolves from a recurring embryonic dotted crotchet [quarter note] (a statement of the primary 12/8 pulsation) to a collection of dense compound rhythm sticking cell variants" (Barker, 2015, p. 35). Four *cells* (each 3♪) form a *unit* (12♪). A characteristic skip, given by a final strike on the last semiquaver/16th note of each *cell*, compresses the upbeat and flows to the downbeat of the next *unit* in a way that embraces the circular *hohŭp* aesthetic. Joining units end to end gives the *episode*. Again, *Tchaksoe* from the canonic "*Uttari p'ungmul*" matches a rapid-fire metronomic 4/4 on the two drums to hocketing between two small gong players. The hocketing becomes increasingly complex before subsiding back onto an elongated cadenza. Equally well known is *Och'ae chil kut* from the canonic "*Honam udo nongak*." Originally a local band processional, "*och'ae*" means "five strikes," and hence the pattern divides down into five *units*, each built from a sequence of binary and ternary *cells*. The downbeat of each unit is marked by a large gong strike, which SamulNori's 1989 notation renders as (10♪) 2 + 3 + 3 + 2, (11♪) 2 + 2 + 2 + 2 + 3, (10♪) 3 + 2 + 2 + 3, (9♪) 3 + 3 + 3, (9♪) 3 + 3 + 3. Repeats add additional ornamentation in the form of acciaccatura to "fill in the spaces" as the density increases, creating the *archetype stream*. Joining the streams together gives the total *episode*. Finally, *Pyŏl tal kŏri* is the most iconic episode of all. The central part of the canonic "*Yŏngnam nongak*," and given in a duple-subdivided meter sandwiched between triplet-subdivided episodes, this contains the eponymous chant familiar to virtually every Korean alive today:

> *Hanŭl pogo pyŏrŭl ttago, ttangŭl pogo nongsa chikko.*

> Look at the sky and pick out a star, look at the earth and till the ground.

> *Olhaedo taep'ungiyo, naenyŏnedo p'ungnyŏn ilse.*

> This year the harvest was bountiful, next year we will also have a good harvest.

---

[3] There is also a second process at work in *Ch'ilch'ae* that binds together aesthetic concepts. In this, the seven-unit motif is slotted into the circular *hohŭp* aesthetic. But, because *hohŭp* needs a uniform and measured breathing and movement phrasing, it is difficult to accommodate the different unit lengths within the motif, so the seven units tend to be compressed into four: 5♪ + 5♪, 3♪ + 3♪ + 5♪, 5♪, and 10♪. This matches a common fourfold progression that Korean musicologists tend to sequence as follows: to hold (*ki*), lift/connect (*kyŏng*), tighten/bind (*kyŏl*), and release (*hae*). Performers often use a slightly different sequence: to produce (*naego*), heat up (*tara*), tense (*p'undal*), and release (*iwan*).

Tara, tara, palgŭn tara, tae nakkachi palgŭn tara.

Moon, moon, bright moon, moon, bright as daylight.

Ŏdum soge pulbich'wi, uri naerŭl pich'wijune!

The light in the darkness, the light shines our way!

It is these motifs and episodes that inspire novel and increasingly complex iterations in new creativity. It is these that are heard throughout Korea, referenced by musicians even where the totality of a samulnori piece disappears from the mix. They form, to reprise an image I have previously used (Howard, 2006a, 2006b), a toolbox. They function as cues and symbols from canonic samulnori pieces and provide a common narrative based on updated local band and itinerant troupe repertoires of old. That narrative is, however, imagined in a Hobsbawmian (Hobsbawm & Ranger, 1983) manner rather than real, and it evolves over time, influenced by social trends and changing habits of consumption, and as the elements move from new to established. In other words, while samulnori was once novel, it is now a part of Korean musical identity, and musicians must both embrace and deconstruct its repertoire as they seek ways forward.

For the moment, the samulnori canon does remain. It is still closely associated with the genre's founders, and this leaves a question mark over how and even whether transmission across generations can be achieved. But it is also performed by professional and amateur groups, heard on urban stages and at competitions and festivals in Korea and around the world. It has become part of Korean education and features within school textbooks. It has its workbooks and recordings, preaching systematized aesthetics and a performance style that must be followed. Ever-increasing numbers of musicians are highly proficient in the canonic samulnori, and many use their deep understandings to embed motifs and episodes in new repertoire. Credible new music emerges when the grammar of samulnori is maintained, and particularly when motifs and episodes remain identifiable. But unless samulnori can be elevated to Important Intangible Cultural Property status, it will be up to the multitude of Koreans and foreigners who are happy to be described as "samulnorians" to determine the future of the genre.

ACKNOWLEDGMENTS

Hyelim Kim and Hyunseok Kwon worked as field researchers for the *Sustainable Futures for Music Cultures* report on which this chapter is based, conducting many of the interviews I have cited. I have also benefited greatly from the input of a number of colleagues, chiefly Nathan Hesselink, Kim In Suk, Simon Mills, and Nami Morris. I met the first SamulNori musicians in 1982 and have worked, talked, and played with many samulnorians ever since. To one and all, thank you.

REFERENCES

Alvesson, M. (1996). *Cultural perspectives on organizations.* New York, NY: Cambridge University Press.

Art Space. (Ed.). (1988a). *SamulNori. Photographs by Ichiro Shimizu.* Seoul, South Korea: Art Space Publications.

Art Space. (Ed.). (1988b). *SamulNori 10-nyŏn.* Seoul, Korea: Art Space Publications.

Barker, S. (2015). *Korea and the Western drumset: Scattering rhythms.* Farnham, UK: Ashgate.

Bharucha, R. (1993). *Theatre and the world: Performance and the politics of culture.* London, UK: Routledge.

Ch'oe Chongmin. (2002). P'ungmul ŭi hyŏndaejŏk chŏn'gae yangsang. In *Saeroun chŏnt'ong ŭmagŭrosŏ ŭi p'ungmul* (pp. 11–20). Yesan, South Korea: Yesan kukche p'ungmulche chojik wiowŏnhoe.

Ch'oe Pyŏngsam. (2000). *Samulmori paeugi: wŏlliesŏ yŏnju kkaji.* Seoul, South Korea: Hangminsa.

Ch'oe Pyŏngsam & Ch'oe Hŏn. (1992). *Samulnori. Han'guk ŭmak 27/Selections of Korean music 27.* Seoul, South Korea: Kungnip kugagwŏn.

Chu Chaeyŏn. (2010). *Samullori ŭi yŏksajŏk chŏn'gaewa munhwa sanŏpchŏk sŏnggwa* (Master's thesis). Koryŏ taehakkyo, Seoul, Korea.

Chun, Kyung Soo. (1984). *Reciprocity and Korean society: An ethnography of Hasami.* Seoul, South Korea: Seoul National University Press.

Clifford, J. (1988). *The predicament of culture: Twentieth century ethnography, literature, and art.* Cambridge, MA: Harvard University Press.

Czikszentmihaly, M. (1990). *Flow: The psychology of optimal experience.* New York, NY: Harper and Row.

Dilling, M. W. (2007). *Stories inside stories: Music in the making of the Korean Olympic ceremonies. Korea Research Monograph 29.* Berkeley, CA: Institute of East Asian Studies, University of California.

Finchum-Sung, H. V. (2012). Designing a fresh tradition: Young kugak and sonic imaginings for a progressive Korea. *World of Music, 1*(1), 121–144.

Goehr, L. (1992). *The imaginary museum of musical works.* Oxford, UK: Oxford University Press.

Hahn, Myong-hee. (1992). What is SamulNori? In Korean Conservatorium of Performing Arts, SamulNori Academy of Music/Han'guk chŏnt'ong yesul yŏnju pojonhoe, (Ed.), *Korean traditional percussion: SamulNori rhythm workbook 1, basic changgo* (pp. 5–6). Seoul, South Korea: Sam-Ho Music Publishing.

Hesselink, N. (2012). *SamulNori: Contemporary Korean drumming and the rebirth of itinerant performance culture.* Chicago, IL: University of Chicago Press.

Hobsbawm, E., & Ranger, T. (Eds.). (1983). *The invention of tradition.* Cambridge, UK: Cambridge University Press.

Howard, K. (1990). *Bands, songs, and shamanistic rituals: Folk music in Korean society* (2nd ed.). Seoul, South Korea: Korea Branch of the Royal Asiatic Society.

Howard, K. (1991/1992). Why do it that way? Rhythmic models and motifs in Korean percussion bands. *Asian Music, 23*(1), 1–59.

Howard, K. (2006a). *Preserving Korean music: Intangible cultural properties as icons of identity.* Aldershot, UK: Ashgate.

Howard, K. (2006b). *Creating Korean music: Tradition, innovation and the discourse of identity.* Aldershot, UK: Ashgate.

Howard, K. (2015). *SamulNori: Korean percussion for a contemporary world.* Farnham, UK: Ashgate.

Janelli, R. L. (1986). The origins of Korean folklore scholarship. *Journal of American Folklore, 99*, 24–49.

Kim, Dong-Won. (1999). What is SamulNori. In Kim, Duk Soo (Ed.), *SamulNori textbook* (pp. 1–5). Seoul, South Korea: Overseas Koreans Foundation/Korea National University of Arts.

Kim, Duk Soo. (1992). Author's introduction, and preliminaries. In Korean Conservatorium of Performing Arts/Han'guk chŏnt'ong yesul yŏnju pojonhoe, SamulNori Academy of Music (Eds.), *Korean traditional percussion: SamulNori rhythm workbook 1, basic changgo* (pp. 7–11 and 15–28). Seoul, South Korea: Sam-Ho Music Publishing.

Kim Hŏnsŏn. (1991). *P'ungmul kudesŏ samulnorikkaji.* Seoul, South Korea: Kwiinsa.

Kim Hŏnsŏn. (1995). *Kim Hŏnsŏn ŭi samulnori iyagi.* Seoul, South Korea: P'ulpit.

Kim Hŏnsŏn. (1998). *Kim Yongbae ŭi salmgwa yesul: kŭ widaehan samulnori ŭi sŏsashi.* Seoul, South Korea: Pulbit.

Kim, In Suk. (2012). Research on Samullori education in schools. *SOAS-AKS Working Papers in Korean Studies, 26.* Retrieved from http://www.soas.ac.uk/koreanstudies/overseas-leading-university-programmes/ soas-aks-working-papers-in-korean-studies-ii/file83333.pdf

Kim Ŭnjŏng. (1986). Kungnip kugagwŏn sangsoenŭn we chasarŭl haennŭn'ga. *Chŏnt'ong munhwa, 6*, 54–59.

Korean Conservatorium of Performing Arts/Han'guk chŏnt'ong yesul yŏnju pojonhoe. (Ed.) (1990). *SamulNori: Kim Tŏksu p'ae SamulNoriga yŏnju hanŭn changgo karak haksŭp p'yŏn 1.* Seoul, South Korea: Samho ch'ulp'ansa.

Korean Conservatorium of Performing Arts. (Ed.) (1992). *SamulNori. Korean traditional percussion SamulNori rhythm workbook 1: Basic changgo.* Seoul, South Korea: Sam-ho Music Publishing.

Korean Conservatorium of Performing Arts. (Ed.) (1993). *SamulNori: Korean traditional percussion SamulNori rhythm workbook 2: Samdo sul changgo karak/Kim Tŏksu p'ae SamulNoriga yŏnju hanŭn samdo sŏl changgo karak haksŭp p'yŏn 2.* Seoul, South Korea: Samho ch'ulp'ansa.

Korean Conservatorium of Performing Arts. (Ed.) (1995). *SamulNori: Korean traditional percussion SamulNori rhythm workbook 3: Samdo sul changgo karak/Kim Tŏksu p'ae SamulNoriga yŏnju hanŭn samdo sŏl changgo karak yŏnju p'yŏn 3.* Seoul, South Korea: Samho ch'ulp'ansa.

Kwak, Young-kwon, & Kim Dong-Won (2001/2003). *SamulNori iyagi [The story of SamulNori].* Seoul, South Korea: Sagyejŏl ch'ulp'ansa.

Kweon, Sug-In. (2003). Popular discourses on Korean culture: From the late 1980s to the present. *Korea Journal, 43*(1), 32–57.

Lee, C. In-young (2012). The drumming of dissent during South Korea's democratization movement. *Ethnomusicology, 56*(2), 179–205.

Lee, Young-Gwang. (2009). *Samulnori percussion ensemble: Encounters with Korean traditional music 1* (Ha Ju-Yong, Trans. and Ed.). Seoul, South Korea: Ministry of Culture, Sports and Tourism.

Loomis, O. H. (1983). *Cultural conservation: The protection of cultural heritage in the US*. Washington, DC: Library of Congress.

Marcus, G., & Fischer, M. (1986). *Anthropology as cultural critique*. Chicago, IL: University of Chicago Press.

Mills, S. (2014). Local heroes: Re-establishing drums and gongs in Ulleungdo's musical life. In Kinyŏm nonjiphaeng wiwŏnhoe (Ed.), *Han'guk ŭmakhak ŭi chip'yŏng: Hwang Chunyŏn kyosu chŏngnyŏntwiim kinyŏm* (pp. 419–432). Seoul, South Korea: Minsokwŏn.

No Suhwan. (2011). *Changgu. No Suhwan ŭi p'ungmul killajabi*. P'aju, South Korea: Choyul.

Park, Shingil. (2000). *Negotiating identities in a performance genre: The case of p'ungmul and samulnori in contemporary Seoul* (PhD dissertation). University of Pittsburgh, Pittsburgh, PA.

Park, Sung Hee. (2011). *Patronage and creativity in Seoul: The late 18th to late 19th century urban middle class and its vocal music* (PhD dissertation). SOAS, University of London, London, UK.

Park, Sung Hee. (2014). 1910–1911: Years that changed Seoul's music. In A. D. Jackson (Ed.), *Key papers on Korea: Essays celebrating 25 years of the Centre of Korean Studies, SOAS, University of London*, (pp. 241–252). Leiden, The Netherlands: Global Oriental.

Rees, H. (2009). Use and ownership: Folk music in the People's Republic of China. In A. N. Weintraub & B. Yung (Eds.), *Music and cultural rights* (pp. 42–85). Urbana and Chicago, IL: University of Illinois Press.

Samson, J. (2001). Canon (iii). In S. Sadie & J. Tyrrell (Eds.), *The New Grove dictionary of music and musicians* (2nd ed., Vol. 5, pp. 6–7). Oxford, UK: Oxford University Press.

Shim Usŏng. (1974a). Namsadang. *Survey of traditional arts: Folk arts* (pp. 455–472). Seoul, South Korea: National Academy of Arts.

Shim Usŏng. (1974b). *Namsadang p'ae yŏn'gu*. Seoul, South Korea: Tonghwa ch'ulp'ansa.

Weber, W. (1992). *The rise of musical classics in eighteenth-century England: A study in canon, ritual, and ideology*. Oxford, UK: Clarendon Press.

Wolf, E. (1982). *Europe and the people without history*. Berkeley and Los Angeles, CA: University of California Press.

Yi Haerang. (Ed.). (1985). *Han'guk ŭmaksa*. Seoul, South Korea: Taehan min'guk yesulwŏn.

Yi Hyŏngyŏng. (2004). *Shwipke paeunŭn samulnori*. Seoul, South Korea: Hangminsa.

Yi Kyut'ae. (1983). *Han'gugin ŭi ŭishik kujo*. Seoul, South Korea: Shinwŏn ch'ulp'ansa.

Yi Pohyŏng. (1985). Chŏnt'ongjŏgin tchimsae pujokhan samulnoriwa tchaejŭ. *Chŏnt'ong munhwa*, 10, 146.

Yi Sŏngch'ŏn, Kwŏn Tŏgwŏn, Paek Ilhyŏng, & Hwang Hyŏnjang (1994). *Algi shwiun kugak kaeron*. Seoul, South Korea: P'ungnam.

Yi Sŏngjae. (1994). *Chaemi innŭn kugak killajabi*. Seoul, South Korea: Seoul Media.

Zo Zayong. (1988). The old woman and her "duduri." In Art Space (Ed.), *SamulNori* (pp. 38–39). Seoul, South Korea: Art Space Publications.

10

MARIACHI MUSIC

Pathways to Expressing Mexican Musical Identity

Patricia Shehan Campbell and Leticia Soto Flores

MARIACHI MUSIC IS rooted in Mexican identity. As an ensemble with that name, mariachi dates back to the 19th century in western Mexico. It is an instrumental and vocal genre that encompasses traditional, folkloric, and popular Mexican expressions, the result of a process of cultural and musical *mestizaje* in New Spain, with diverse groups that emerged in rural communities during the colonial period (1521–1810). Over the past century, its reality as a diasporic genre has generated widening audiences, but also prompts questions regarding its sustainability. Despite the fact that mariachi ensembles and their music spread north to the United States and elsewhere in the world, local traditional groups in Mexico continued to perform their particular style for community festivities. With the changing needs of modernizing societies, the mariachi tradition has been constantly recreated by its diverse and growing communities, in response both to the shifting aesthetics of time and place and to how musicians and communities have interacted with their own history.

Documents from the early 19th century reveal that the word *mariachi* has a variety of meanings: a *fandango*, where singing, music, and dance come together; a *tarima*, a foot drum used to dance upon; the name of a group of musicians; the music played by these musicians; and place names. Mariachi repertoire includes *sones* and *jarabes*, as the primary secular musical forms, and *minuetes* for the sacred performative spaces.

In the early 20th century, mariachi groups from Jalisco traveled to Mexico City, where they participated in the first national radio programs in 1925 and the first Mexican sound film *Santa* in 1931. Mariachi groups later appeared in the most widely distributed Mexican films, where they wore the widely recognized *traje de charro* (suit of the horseman), already in itself a visual symbol of Mexico, and standardized the instrumentation of the genre in a form that included trumpets, such that the mariachi ensemble was no longer composed of only string instruments.

Mariachi music today is a symbol of cultural identity for many Mexicans, Mexican Americans, and people of Mexican heritage who reside in other parts of the world. In its musical appeal, mariachi music draws non-Mexicans as well, even as it functions as an important way to represent Mexican identity. Like many other musical expressions across the globe, mariachi music is largely connected to traditional religious gatherings, local festivities that celebrate rites of passage, and a variety of community social events.

The traditional groups in Mexico, when compared to the more popularized, standard, and widely identifiable version, share only the name *mariachi* and few other formal features. In general, these traditional groups tend to approach the music in a way that is far removed from the entertainment stage associated with modernization, and do not embrace the standardized instrumentation. The popular ensemble, on the other hand, is an evolution of the traditional mariachi expression in Mexico that adopted a standard instrumentation that generally consists of three to five violins, two trumpets, a *guitarrón*, a *vihuela*, a guitar, and a harp. These groups generally perform folkloric and popular Mexican musical genres, as well as art music adapted to their instrumentation.

This chapter seeks to explore the sustainability of the mariachi tradition as a whole. It covers important historiographic documentation, historical and commercial recordings, and the perspectives of key people whose experience has shaped our view of an expanding mariachi tradition that is sustained, preserved intact or in modified form, within and beyond Mexico. In doing so, the chapter also aims to unveil vital issues regarding its institutionalization in formal education and its sustainability in both traditional and popular forms.

BACKGROUND

Despite the increasing research publications on mariachi, locating a mariachi music history has been problematic, primarily due to two factors. First, like many aurally transmitted musical traditions across the world, mariachi music faces the historiographic challenge of a scarcity of published sources and audio recordings. Documents referring to mariachi music before the 1920s are few, fragmented, and widely scattered (Jáuregui, 2012, p. 210). Second, since the 1940s, two kinds of mariachi musical expressions in Mexico have coexisted: the popularized stage ensemble widely known throughout the world, and the traditional ensembles that remained in the countryside, tending to maintain an aural transmission, and preserving its characteristics against the impact of globalization. The popular groups, on the other hand, are an evolution of the traditional style but have easily adapted to the changing needs of a globalizing society.

The presence of these two musical manifestations poses a problem in constructing a linear mariachi history, so that it is important to conceive of mariachi music's historical past in terms of the elemental features that define the tradition, and which originated at distinctive moments in its history. To add to the polysemy, the traditional groups of this tradition were not always called *mariachi* and the word did not always refer to the ensemble. Brief mention is made of the formal features in the following pages, nonchronologically and only as they relate to the principal domains of this study of musical sustainability.

Cultural Meaning and Function

As musicians of the mariachi tradition emanate from diverse backgrounds, so too do the many cultural meanings that are associated with the genre. Today, mariachi music's cultural meaning stems from its regional origins, its national symbolism, and its diasporic pertinence and purpose. Referring to its regional origins, anthropologist Jesús Jáuregui refers to both a nuclear and an extended region as the geographical roots of the mariachi tradition. The nuclear region includes the states of Colima, Jalisco, Nayarit, and Michoacán, whereas the extended region spreads north and south throughout Aguascalientes, Durango, Guanajuato, Guerrero, Oaxaca, Sinaloa, Sonora, and Zacatecas (Jáuregui, 2007, pp. 212–215). Combining both these nuclear and extended regions would reach across more than half of Mexico.

In reference to the national symbolism of the mariachi tradition, from the time of the Mexican Revolution (1910–1920) to the recent globalization of the music, there has been a nationalist tendency contributing to the evolution of Mexican music. A government mission led by philosopher José Vasconcelos successfully implemented a national cultural movement that would result in a revalorization of the popular arts, elevating them to the ranks of representative creations of a national identity (Florescano, as cited in Jáuregui, 2007, p. 68). The increase in the demand for "folklore" by the urban elite in the 1920s led a growing number of mariachi ensembles to travel to Mexico City, where they could make their living as artists, later fostering a Mexican cultural identity through mariachi music.

In an era of emerging national consciousness, popular mariachi ensembles began to participate in nationally hosted competitions in popular music (for song-writers and singers), in recording albums for commercial labels, in political campaigns, and in traveling to other countries to represent Mexico's typical folkloric music (Clark, 1993; Jáuregui, 2007). As a result, from the 1930s mariachi music gained popularity as an urban popular music through radio programs, and by the late 1940s, with the growing Mexican film industry, it quickly achieved its status as a musical emblem of Mexican nationalism (Henriques, 2006; Jáuregui, 1999; Moreno Rivas, 1979). What was once a rural tradition came to be transformed into Mexico's most popular music and wide-reaching musical export. This new musical symbol of Mexico led to the genre representing in some way not only the diverse regions from which it originated but also the Mexican nation in relationship to the rest of the world.

Mariachi music thus expanded not only into Mexico City and other parts of the country but also north of its border and into Mexican American communities. By the second half of the 20th century, Los Angeles had become a major focal point for mariachi performance in the United States (Sheehy, 2006, p. 4). With the growing Mexican diaspora in Los Angeles and other parts of the United States, it was not surprising that many found in mariachi music a way to express their regional and national identity through the music performed by mariachi ensembles (Clark 2005; Madrid 2013). While cultural meaning of mariachi music undoubtedly originates as Mexican, one can find people of all cultures and backgrounds desiring to learn how to play this music, a remarkable number of whom are not of Mexican heritage.

Formal Features

The central features that define the mariachi tradition include (a) mariachi instrumentation, (b) performance methods or styles, (c) literary sung forms, (d) sub-genres, (e) dance styles, (f) performative spaces, (g) performance clothing, and finally (h) the word *mariachi* (Soto Flores, 2015). The first formal feature constitutes the diverse instrumentation that composes a mariachi ensemble (Chamorro Escalante, 1999; Saldivar, 1938; Stanford, 1972). Ethnomusicologist Thomas Stanford (1972) warned that although one cannot describe mariachi instrumentation for each of the regional variants, there was a general standard that included one or two violins (for the melody), one or various instruments of the family of guitars (for the rhythmic and harmonic aspects), and a harp (for the melody and the bass). Despite the long history of instrumental experimentation within this genre, there have been polemic discussions among performers and scholars concerning whether certain instruments should be used in groups that call themselves mariachi ensembles.

The second feature refers to the performance methods for the aforementioned instruments, both individually and part of the group. The melodic instruments (harp, violin, and trumpet) are of European origin but are performed in a manner unique to mariachi. For example, the *guitarrón* and the *vihuela* are instruments invented in Mexico and are exclusive to the mariachi ensemble. The deep-arched back of their physical structure, their tuning, and the technical practice of these instruments contribute to the particular sound and performance style of mariachi music. Finally, when the melody instruments do in fact play harmony, it generally consists of chords performed in either the first or second inversion, and rarely in a triad root position, depending on the timbre desired.

The third formal feature that characterizes the mariachi tradition is the literary sung styles and forms from various regions in Mexico. While much of the sung literature is tied to a particular melody and rhythm, there are some verses that are loosely adaptable to other melodies from other regions. The thematic content provides an overall essence of what is sung and what is meant, which can be observed in *rancheras* (García, 2004; Jáquez, 2003), *corridos* (Herrera-Sobek, 1990; Mendoza, 1954), and *sones* (González, 2009; R. V. Sánchez, 2007; Stanford, 1972).

The fourth formal feature describes the diverse mariachi subgenres from the oral tradition, popular tradition, and, more recently, classical repertory (Fogelquist, 1975; Nevin 2002; Sheehy, 2006). The most representative subgenres of the oral mariachi tradition include *corridos, valonas,* and traditional *sones,* many of which have remained in the community's collective memory. Traditional *sones* emerge from various regions in Mexico, broadly grouped into a category called the *son mexicano.* They include, but are not limited to, the *son jaliscience, son huasteco/ huapango, son jarocho, son planeco,* and *son calentano* (Mendoza, 1984; Reuter, 1981; Stanford, 1972).

Those originating from the popular tradition include the *canción ranchera, boleros, cumbias,* and *danzones.* In addition to the oral and popular styles, mariachi ensembles have also integrated art music and folk genres from Western Europe. Nineteenth-century European salon-style dance music arrived in Latin America in various waves through European migration (Vega, 1944). Dance genres such as the waltz, the *schottische,* the *danza,* the minuet, the polka, and the march arrived in Mexico and were either adapted to mariachi instrumentation or used as the basis for newly composed pieces.

The fifth feature refers to the dance styles that cannot always be separated from the musical practice (Sheehy, 2006; Stanford, 1972). In traditional *sones*, dances over the *tarima* (wooden platform) are indispensable since the stamped foot patterns are considered part of the music, percussively performing the rhythms that distinguish or reinforce the music's meter and character. In the popular mariachi tradition, ensembles play for organized dance troupes called *ballet folklórico*, where both musicians and dancers attempt to emulate on a stage the music and dance of the local rural festivities.

The sixth feature considers the performative space in which the music takes place. In rural regions of western Mexico, the *fandango* is a festive space in which music, singing, and dance are joined together in a community gathering, which has traditionally extended for 2 or 3 days at a time (Ochoa Serrano, 1994). A *fandango* is generally an impromptu gathering of open-ended duration that includes a variety of traditional music. However, with the arrival of media communication (such as radio, television, and commercial recordings), the festive space expanded for mariachi communities all over Mexico, in the United States, and abroad to include traveling caravans, large theaters, concert halls, recording studios, restaurants and clubs, warm-weather outdoor plazas, churches of various religious beliefs, and universities and schools with considerable student populations of Mexican descent. While these contexts do not all feature impromptu or open-ended performances, they do foster an important festive space necessary for mariachi music to happen within a community.

The seventh feature refers to the performance clothing used by mariachi musicians. Traditional ensembles did not generally have a uniform in which they performed; rather, they gathered with community musicians in their quotidian work clothes such as a *traje de manta*. The *traje de charro* inherited its name and style from the Spanish horsemen who came to settle in Mexico, and has been a symbol of a Mexican ranch identity since the 19th century. Maximilian the First understood this symbol upon his arrival in 1864, when he intended to legitimate his position as crowned emperor of Mexico by appearing Mexican, as he designed a royal version of the uniform, ennobling the attire. When the culmination of Mexico's independence from Spain in 1910 created the need for national symbols that differentiated Mexico from its colonizing country, the *charro* image quickly extended from horsemanship to patriotism and nationalism.

The eighth and final formal feature concerns the meaning of the word *mariachi*. Unfortunately, in the musicians' collective memory, the origin of this word was not passed on through generations, as the music was. Since scholars have not yet found historical evidence that would clearly identify the meaning of *mariachi*, their definitions and etymological approaches have resulted in ideological disputes over whether this Mexican musical symbol has French, indigenous, or mestizo origins. The association between the word *mariachi* and the French word *mariage* was, at first, an important political and ideological tool, for postindependent Mexico looked toward the elite French culture, meanwhile turning away from the Spanish crown after three centuries of Spanish colonization.

In resistance to this colonial association, scholars later associated the word with indigenous traditions, such as the Coca group from Cocula (Dávila Garibi, 1935), the Nahuatl language (Stanford, 1972), and the Pinutl language (Castillo Romero, 1973). Yet the task does not end with either French or indigenous association, as we also find scholars who deem it important to draw upon mestizo legitimation, locating the mariachi tradition as a local patriotism used primarily for claiming cultural or regional legitimation (an issue unrelated to the music itself; Meyer, 1981). While etymological research can lead to an understanding of how the form and meaning of words developed, the etymology of a word does not necessarily parallel the history of its tradition.

SYSTEMS OF LEARNING MUSIC

Musical knowledge in the mariachi tradition had been historically transmitted through the generations in an informal, aural context, independent from formal educational activities in schools. These informal educational settings have involved important nonmusical motivations for learning, such as the expression of a community's identity and cultural knowledge. Yet with the recent institutionalization of mariachi music in Mexico and in the United States, along with the powers of globalization, the teaching–learning process has entered new domains of education that include formal and nonformal methods of transmission and teaching, which are best considered as supplements to the vital informal learning processes.

Philosophies of Learning and Teaching

Mariachi musicians historically learned their music in an informal learning-by-doing context, generally with family members, in a close community setting, and independent of formal education. Without any form of written music, the only way to learn mariachi repertory before the mid-20th century was by listening to it live or playing it repeatedly. This process required a keen listening ear for picking up and recreating the nuances of the mariachi repertory. Despite the increasing opportunities for learning this music through formal education (described later), this aural means of musical acquisition continues today.

As mariachi music gained its national presence on live radio programs like XEW, mariachi groups such as Mariachi Tapatío de José Marmolejo and Mariachi Vargas de Tecalitlán, in addition to performing their own music, were invited to accompany singers. Before the use of written music for mariachi orchestration, musical producers or directors often played the different parts on piano or a mariachi instrument so that the musicians could pick them up and commit them to memory. Yet by the mid-1940s, the growing repertory and the increasing complexity of the musical arrangements meant that the aural learning-by-doing process consumed too much preparation time. As a result, aural transmission was considered inefficient, and in many instances, it became impossible. Music directors found themselves having to learn to write music in modern notation, as well as seeking musicians who could read it (Soto Flores, 2014, pp. 5–6).

The demand for multiskilled mariachi musicians in Mexico's professional ensembles after the mid-20th century fueled the need for nonformal and formal mariachi music education. To compete on a professional level, musicians were encouraged to know music theory, sing a broad repertoire in ways that were vocally strong and musically accurate, and have high-quality performance skills on their instrument. Los Angeles–based mariachi educator Claudia Zuñiga supplemented her own independent studies of instruction books by obtaining the assistance of experienced musicians. She argues that self-teaching can be limiting, and at a certain point in one's musical education, it is important to turn to a professional for guidance (Claudia Zuñiga, interview, December 10, 2012). Musicians thus complement the learning-by-doing transmission with nonformal music education, such as private lessons on their instrument, music theory, and vocal training. Others sought formal music education in academies such as music conservatories and universities.

The changing landscape of mariachi music transmission has offered opportunities for new learners. In many cases, one may learn to perform the genre outside the nuclear and extended regions in which it originated. For example, ethnomusicologist Steven Loza traces the appearance of formalized mariachi programs in the United States—as well as a shift from enculturation to education—to the late 1970s, when the development of festivals and an increasing openness toward mariachi performance arose among youth (Steven Loza, interview, November 5, 2012). The wide array of learning experiences of contemporary mariachi musicians is echoed in the varied systems for learning the genre, which are rooted in what Loza refers to as a very informal process of learning and enculturation of people who experience it in their environment, for example, in western-central Mexico.

Schools and Extracurricular Learning

Formal education, as opposed to informal and nonformal education, follows a continuous educational path that is recognized by institutional authorities in schools at the primary, secondary, and tertiary levels. In formal learning, a systematic and methodical music curriculum offers theoretical and practical tools. However, not all mariachi music learning on school campuses constitutes formal education. In the United States, for example, there are opportunities for students to join after-school and weekend social organizations where mariachi music and other Mexican cultural traditions are practiced, and where a Mexican identity is celebrated. A nonformal university mariachi experience is typically an ensemble course for students who already know the basics of their mariachi instrument; this is similar to many school bands and orchestras composed of students who have learned their instrument in private lessons, through experimentation, and through guided practice. The ensemble classes offer the students a place in which they can expand their repertoire and hone their mariachi performance skills.

While there are a growing number of educational mariachi programs offered in universities in the United States, only a few offer a degree that certifies their specialized education in mariachi music. The Associate Degree in Arts program at Southwestern College, Chula Vista, designed by Jeff Nevin, is one example of a formal curriculum that offers music education in a 2-year program, with a specialization in mariachi music. Another example is the Master of Arts in Latin Music, also with a specialization in mariachi music, offered by Texas State University. Both programs seek to offer mariachi music students a more comprehensive mariachi music education (Soto Flores, 2014, p. 6).

In Mexico, the first school to offer a formal mariachi music curriculum is the Escuela de Mariachi Ollin Yoliztli en Garibaldi, of Mexico City's Secretariat of Culture, which consists of a 3-year program that, at the time of writing, intends to offer a Professional Technical Degree in Mariachi Music Performance. The program encompasses a holistic approach to mariachi music education by offering its students, in addition to their instrument technique specialization, courses that include Mariachi Ensemble, Music Theory, Vocal Technique, Choir, and Harmony. In addition, the curriculum stipulates courses in Western Music History (which includes Mexico), Mariachi History, and Musical Cultures of Mexico. The objective is to acquire what is possible from a formal teaching and learning context, always focusing on transmitting the mariachi style.

When the school opened its doors to the first generation of students on October 15, 2012, there were mixed reactions from scholars, political authorities, and traditional musicians: Some unconditionally supported the new educational endeavor, while others severely critiqued its existence. Critics deemed its institutionalization as a threat to the natural aural teaching and learning methods that were historically in evidence and rejected the uniformity that sheet music and standardized methods of grading would bring to the music's traditional aesthetics. Supporters, on the other hand, claimed that this school was half a century overdue, and believed that institutionalizing mariachi music would give it the cultural value and academic status it needed in Mexican society.

Pedagogical Approaches

Aural learning has not been lost to the practice. Rather, it is complemented by formal and nonformal music education. Most of the musicians interviewed for this research referred to a balanced approach to aural learning and notation-based transmission, such that they are both often evident. In discussing changes in contemporary modes of mariachi learning and the shifts brought about by notation-based learning, Laura Sobrino stressed that not everything vital to the musical quality can be included in written transcriptions (interview, December 5, 2011). Numerous interviewees made the point that the decoding of print notation alone does not make for a definitive mariachi sound, but that the stylistic nuances require listening attentively so that they might be successfully portrayed in performance. Similarly, Jeff Nevin advocates for teachers to utilize both aural and notation-based teaching strategies to maximize the progress and performance of students (interview, February 16, 2013).

The teaching and learning of mariachi music has changed with the growth of a music notation industry, but access to recordings of mariachi music has preserved an aural component, both in Mexico and abroad. Online instructional videos, including YouTube clips, are assisting aspiring musicians in their listening and private practice as well, although many are limited to imitation and tend to lack the instructor's pedagogical guide necessary through an apprenticeship. Thus, the aural transmission of the genre is still important today, even with readily available musical scores generally used as a guide. Mariachi musician Julián Magaña Barajas reiterated the importance of recordings and aural learning in his development as a musician, suggesting that educators and students can learn the technique and repertoire thoroughly from albums and good recordings (interview, July 26, 2011). Despite the development of notation (and its use in formal programs of instruction), musicians continue to depend on informal aural transmission for elements of expression and style that cannot be captured in a musical score.

Implications for Sustainability

In a world where a wide variety of musical styles, genres, and songs, as well as instruments, ensembles, spaces, and meanings, have emerged and disappeared, a key issue is what and how to sustain a musical culture, without taking on a static approach to preservation. A dialogue between traditional and popular mariachi supporters, musicians, and scholars has recently emerged, which calls into question the "essence" of the mariachi tradition and whether it is being transmitted authentically. Thus, learning mariachi music is more than gaining the technical skills required to play the instruments, but also knowing something of the sonic and social features that surround the genre.

MUSICIANS AND COMMUNITIES

With the effects of globalization, traditional music genres everywhere are tending to undergo patterns of change, and responses of musicians and communities to change are not uniform. The mariachi musicians who continue to perform traditional versions of the music in their rural communities in Mexico have a separate means of income and do not generally make a living as musicians. The urban musicians who have dedicated their lives to learning to perform mariachi music can earn enough to call this their full-time career.

Perhaps as a consequence of mariachi music's global popularity, the media and the populus at large have unfairly identified mariachi musicians as overweight, illiterate, undisciplined drunks and womanizers, uninterested in applying themselves with full disciplinary intent to know the music well. Such attitudes toward mariachi musicians have contributed to the denigration and delegitimation of mariachi music as a representative cultural practice in Mexico, which is complicated by the fact that this tradition has been promoted as iconic music of that country. The disdain endured by such stereotypes has impeded opportunities in Mexico for first-rate groups like Mariachi Vargas de Tecalitlán or Mariachi de América, who are more in demand as performers outside Mexico than in their own country. Musicians and some scholars have responded to this negative reputation by beginning to demand that those at the forefront of policymaking and mariachi education in Mexico take responsibility for changing such attitudes toward this musical expression.

Musician–Community Relationship

Musicians and communities give a musical tradition its meaning. According to Daniel Sheehy, ethnomusicologist and former director-curator of Smithsonian Folkways Recordings, meaning is derived from different sources, such as culture, its people, and the society that constructs musical sounds. In genres like maria-chi that have strong connections to specific communities, the meaning derives from how people use the music and the values they attach to it (interview, November 2, 2012).

Musicians' identification with mariachi music begins with the role and signifi-cance it plays in their individual lives, and how each individual decides to appropri-ate and apply his musical knowledge. Most musicians come from musical families who have inherited the genre from previous generations (e.g., fathers, uncles, and grandfathers), while others were drawn to the opportunity to learn mariachi for economic reasons (and because they were attracted to the sound and lifestyle of a mariachi player).

Beyond the individual motives for performing this music, there is also a broader kind of identification that involves national identity and representation. By the 1950s, the aforementioned national cultural movement that revalorized mariachi music as a representation of a national identity played an important role in forg-ing new opportunities for many musicians, opening doors to new performance spaces mentioned earlier. However, while the mariachi community found a sense of belonging in these promising fields and functions, the popular mariachi tradi-tion began to suffer from a series of negative stereotypes that have proved to be challenging to overcome.

Some traditional musicians today critique the popular musicians for disap-pearing some of the communal elements that define the mariachi tradition, not entirely understanding that since the advent of the mass media, these elements were in fact not abandoned but rather modified. Traditional mariachi musician Gerardo Lerma, in providing his interpretation of the difference between the tra-ditional and popular mariachi music, suggests that traditional mariachi perfor-mance involves a festive space, called a *fandango*, that combines music, poetry, and dance, which needs to be preserved; the popular and modern mariachi per-formance, on the other hand, involves a stage group that plays popular genres and a limited selection of familiar and frequently requested *sones* (interview, August 2, 2011).

Expressions of Life as a Musician

Mariachi musicians play a variety of roles that shift depending on experience, geography, and economics. Many individuals and groups have paved the road for contemporary mariachi history and Mexican popular music in general. These include composers, solo performers, ensembles, music arrangers, and other mari-achi musicians. The popular music composers that contributed so greatly to the mariachi repertory, especially during the Golden Era of Mexican Film (1936–1959), include Agustín Lara, Lorenzo Barcelata, Salvador Quiroz, Ricardo Palmerín, María Grever, Jorge del Moral, Guty Cárdenas, Joaquín Pardavé, Pepe Guizar, Tomás Mendez, Manuel Esperón, and Ernesto Cortázar.

Performers who popularized the mariachi repertoire through Mexican film and full-length album recordings in this same period included Tito Guízar, Jorge Negrete, Lucha Reyes, Pedro Vargas, Pedro Infante, La Torcasita, Javier Solís, Miguel Aceves Mejía, Lola Beltrán, Lucha Villa, Amalia Mendoza, and Flor Silvestre. Mariachi ensembles that accompanied these artists and recorded their own independent albums have also left a lasting legacy in the history and evolution of mariachi music. These ensembles include the Cuarteto Coculense, Mariachi Coculense de Cirilo Marmolejo, Mariachi Tapatío de José Marmolejo, Mariachi Vargas de Tecalitlán, Mariachi México de Pepe Villa, Mariachi Los Mensajeros, Mariachi Perla de Occidente, and Mariachi Mariachi Oro y Plata de Pepe Chávez.

Behind the scenes, and unbeknownst to most followers of the genre, mariachi music arrangers are key to the brilliance of the mariachi sound. These figures were mariachi musicians first, not originally trained to arrange mariachi music, but with their talent and musical education, they earned the opportunity to practice this new trade. Although not much recognized by the public at large, their sense of formal features of melody, rhythm, texture, instrumentation, and expressive nuance are central to the ultimate mariachi sound that may come to be associated with a particular group of musicians. Leading arrangers have included Rubén Fuentes, Jesús Rodríguez de Hijar, Gustavo A. Santiago, Rigoberto Alfaro, and Pepe Martínez.

Notable mariachi musicians themselves are too many to name; their musical technique, and often their charismatic stage presence, have contributed in significant ways to the popularization of the genre. Musicians are well aware of their roles in the balance of composers and arrangers who, together, shape the mariachi aesthetic.

Mariachi Music Outside Mexico

The connection between mariachi music and its community of avid and appreciative listeners has had powerful effects on both sides of the US–Mexico border. For many musicians in Mexico, this genre has been an important means of expressing identity in ways both musical and cultural, as well as regional and national. For many Mexican Americans in the United States, mariachi music serves as an important means of embracing and connecting with their

Mexican roots. Ethnomusicologist Alejandro Madrid asserted that through mariachi music, Mexican Americans may reconnect with their heritage, such that although they reside in the United States as American citizens, they are keyed to mariachi music as a style expressive of their heritage (interview, November 2, 2012).

Being Mexican is not a homogenous identity due to the diversity of race, ethnicity, religion, and socioeconomic circumstance, and yet the various regional mariachi songs have formed a recognized canon for many Mexican Americans. Sheehy recalls his experience of having witnessed cultural differences between Mexican Americans and Mexican immigrants during the 1960s Chicano Movement in the United States. Compared to Mexico, a different set of vectors is present in communicating in a multicultural American diasporic society, including different attitudes, functions, and goals in performing the music (interview, November 2, 2012). The concept of mariachi as a marker of identity is dependent on qualities noted earlier, along with the player's age, gender, place of residence, family composite, and community influences.

Three social movements in the United States in the 1960s influenced the strong reception mariachi music was to have among Mexican Americans. First, the Chicano Movement in the United States, a civil rights movement that sought to confront discrimination, racism, and exploitation against Mexican Americans, created awareness for cultural pride, such that people of Mexican descent no longer had to assimilate into the United States by turning away from their cultural roots. Second, the Chicano Movement coincided with the women's liberation movement, characterized as second-wave feminism, which campaigned for legal rights and social equity for women. Both movements offered women the right to feel cultural pride, as well as the freedom to enter new avenues of belonging, which included their participation as musicians in mariachi music ensembles. Finally, an academic mariachi movement began to take hold in the early 1960s at the University of California at Los Angeles (UCLA), when ethnomusicology graduate student Donald Borcherdt took the initiative to implement the first mariachi classes in an educational setting. This led to the formation of the first university mariachi ensemble: Mariachi Uclatlán (Koetting, 1977; Loza, 1993; Sheehy, 2000). As a result of this initial effort to bring mariachi music into academia, educational mariachi programs today are found on many university campuses in the United States, as well as in many more elementary and secondary schools, specialized schools, and community colleges. As a regional, national, and cultural expression, mariachi music has served to celebrate cultural identity at home in Mexico, in Mexican America, and in other places in the world.

Implications for Sustainability

Despite the changing needs of modernizing societies and a lack of governmental support, mariachi music arguably has been kept alive because of its exceptional relevance to its community of both performers and listeners, within and beyond the Mexican borders. In Mexico, a growth in the number of traditional mariachi musicians, most of them academics or schoolteachers who are not originally from the tradition, illustrates the importance of a recent traditional mariachi revival movement. These participants consider it important to contribute to the transmission of this lesser known musical expression because they believe they are continuing the tradition. Despite the importance of contributing to its sustainability through a revival movement, the social forms in which the music had existed are not the same. Merely having these groups perform on a stage, with microphones, and getting paid for an hour of their time poses a rupture with the original performance contexts of traditional mariachi groups. Outside Mexico, a growth in the number of modern mariachi musicians would have a similar purpose: to continue a tradition. Both the traditional and the popular mariachi expression promote a sense of cultural pride for both tradition bearers and new additions of all cultures to the mariachi tradition. Despite differences in both expressions, these two sustainability options in mariachi music are not exclusive since they musically feed off each other and other traditions as well.

CONTEXTS AND CONSTRUCTS

Performance contexts and meanings in mariachi music have transformed significantly throughout its history. Shifts in the genre's cultural meaning and functions, as well as the new performance spaces that have arisen through its geographical dispersion, have generated strong views among musicians and the community concerning tradition and authenticity. This is particularly true of the relationship between popular mariachi known through commercial channels and the revival movement involving more traditional ensembles. This section examines the varied and changing contexts that both support and hinder the sustainability of the genre.

Public Spaces

Various public spaces have emerged as locations of mariachi performance. Where the principal performative setting historically had been the *fandango* gathering, today this space is being recreated outside its original context with the traditional mariachi revival movement, and into various kinds of public spaces. For example, since the turn of the 20th century, major cities have seen the growth of public mariachi plazas at the center of a community or neighborhood. In the expansive and populous Mexico City, one can listen to mariachi music at Plaza Garibaldi, a hub for tourists, as well as Iztapalapa and Cabeza de Juárez, among other plazas and locales in other parts of Mexico and beyond (notably the mariachi plazas in Guadalajara, Jalisco, and Boyle Heights in Los Angeles).

In the historic center of Mexico City, Plaza Garibaldi first earned its reputation as the "mecca" of mariachi musicians in 1927, when Salón Tenampa permanently hired Mariachi Coculense de Concho Andrade to perform. Those who yearned for a taste of Jalisco came to Plaza Garibaldi to listen to mariachi music inside Salón Tenampa. On the plaza, one can visit the renowned *Mercado de San Camilito* (San Camilito Market); stop at the local bars, cafes, and restaurants; and imbibe the famous *pulque* (an indigenous fermented alcoholic beverage with a milky texture). Mariachi musicians have long been drawn to this plaza, outside Salón Tenampa, as a gathering place where they would wait to perform for visitors or hope to be hired away by private citizens to play at family celebrations.

At Plaza Garibaldi, private citizens can seek out a mariachi group to travel to their homes and neighborhoods, perhaps to perform only one song, or for an hour, or for a full evening's social events. Musicians arrive at the plaza at all hours, either individually or as organized groups, waiting for customers. Freelance mariachi musicians who do not belong to a group also arrive at the plaza and wait for a group leader to select his players, spontaneously. In recent years, this plaza has suffered many changes imposed by government authorities, such as the replacement of the neo-Greek-style columns at the main entrance with a modern-style tequila museum, and a recently passed law that prohibits drinking alcohol in the open plaza. These changes reduced the amount of visitors to the plaza and thus the amount of earnings for mariachi musicians.

Work Stability

Of the various performance spaces, restaurants have emerged over the last half century to offer mariachi groups an important opportunity for steady income, especially on weekends and holidays. Like many other popular music ensembles, the work is dependent on the demand for the music at public and private events. Having restaurants that feature mariachi music has not only brought their businesses new customers but also given mariachi musicians the opportunity to work regularly at one location.

In Mexico, important historic venues for mariachi performance are slowly disappearing, while others are emerging. One of the most notable venues of mariachi

music was Restaurant Amanecer Tapatío in Mexico City, where the most prominent mariachi groups performed, and where important singers such as Pedro
Infante and Vicente Fernández began their singing careers. This location included
five banquet spaces, each of which featured a mariachi ensemble. When the owners passed away in the early 1980s, the restaurant closed its business. Today, one
may listen to live mariachi music at El Lugar de Mariachi (The Place of Mariachi)
in the Zona Rosa, where a mariachi group will play a song or two on its own and
dedicate the rest of the show to accompanying solo singers.

In the United States, many Mexican restaurants offer live mariachi music. The
development of this new space for the genre can be attributed to Nati Cano's opening of the Los Angeles–based dinner theater, which aimed to feature high-quality
mariachi music. In 1969, La Fonda de Los Camperos not only opened its doors to
mariachi fans (and fans of Mexican cuisine) but also drew tourists from some of
the most remote parts of the world to Los Angeles to have access to nightly performances by Mariachi Los Camperos. Soon thereafter, Pedro Rey opened up El Rey
Restaurant in Montebello, California, which featured his Mariachi Los Galleros.
Subsequently, in 1986, José Hernández inaugurated Cielito Lindo Restaurant,
home of Mariachi Sol de México. Since then, restaurants across the United States
have featured a variety of mariachi groups. These restaurant performance spaces
have offered musicians work stability that working in other public spaces could
not offer.

Sacred and Religious Spaces

The church as a performance context is an aspect of mariachi music that is largely
ignored. In part, the Catholic Church provides a space that is rich in history, culture, and tradition, and a mariachi mass offers a fresh and exuberant dimension
to devotional practices. As an effect of the liturgical changes implemented after
the Vatican's Second Ecumenical Council (1961–1965), which stated that local musical traditions in mission lands should be incorporated into Christian worship,
on April 17, 1966, Canadian priest John Mark Leclerc implemented the first *Misa
Panamericana* (Pan-American Mass), under the auspice of Bishop Sergio Méndez
Arceo. It was inaugurated in a small chapel in Cuernavaca and quickly became
so popular that the small chapel could not contain the many people who wanted
to attend, and the *Misa Panamerica* began to be celebrated in the Cuernavaca
Cathedral (Suárez, 1970). The mass soon reached other parts of Mexico and the
United States, and with this transition, mariachi groups came to be widely influen-
tial in the popularization of the *Misa Panamericana*. With the advent of this mass,
Catholic churches from many parts of the Americas since the 1970s opened their

doors to popular music ensembles, which also offered mariachi ensembles the opportunity to perform liturgical musical pieces, such as *Señor Ten Piedad* (Kyrie), Gloria, Credo, Sanctus, the Offertory, the Our Father, the Communion, and a variety of hymns.

Yet the Catholic Church is not the only space in which mariachi music plays an important part in celebrating spiritual growth. Individuals sometimes hire a mariachi group to perform more general Christian songs that celebrate, praise, and serve God. Social networks such as YouTube host a growing number of mariachi clips that present these songs of praise in rhythms such as *rancheras* (along with the singing style), cumbias, boleros, and others. Beyond Mexico and Catholicism, mariachi groups have also been invited to perform for religious and cultural ceremonies of the Jewish, Buddhist, and Muslim beliefs. Saint Augustine of Hippo once wrote: "He who sings, prays twice," and many have found it in their hearts to sing devotionally with mariachi music.

Outside the church, many traditional ensembles in Mexico participated in religious and spiritual ceremonies long before 1966. Considered sacred, the music in this context includes several instrumental subgenres, namely, *sones, jarabes*, polkas, and waltzes. These came to be grouped under the umbrella name *minuetes*, which should not be confused with the French-derived *minuet* (salon dance music that dates back to the 18th century). According to anthropologist Jesús Jáuregui, *minuetes* are musical prayers performed during the vigil of the saints, in chapels, hermitages, and domestic altars, and during the *velada de angelitos* (vigil of an infant's passing), and they constitute a vehicle of communication between the living and the world of the saints and the deceased (Jáuregui, 1987, 2006).

Although one might listen to the *minuetes* and consider them pieces with the same musical form and style as *sones, jarabes*, polkas, and waltzes, their intention is what distinguishes them from their secular equivalents: They are not associated with a festive context that involves communal *fiestas*, singing, dance, or serenades of love. In a sacred context, this instrumental music is important because it does not have texts that could signify or communicate nonreligious ideas.

Schools

The rise of mariachi music education in schools in the United States has raised the question of *who* is qualified to teach the genre, given that most formal education institutions require degrees and certifications to teach. Since this music was historically transmitted orally, it did not fit naturally into programs that are notation based and aimed at the achievement of music literacy.

The growing opportunities to include mariachi music in the school curriculum, as well as state curricular policies, local district interests, and even commercial instrument companies, are supportive of efforts to develop mariachi as an in-school offering and after-school engagement. In Mexico, arts are not included as required study in public grade school education, as defined by the *Secretaría de Educación Pública* (Department of Education). Those students who wish to obtain education and training in the arts attend schools or cultural centers that specialize in it, over and beyond their regular and required classes during the school day. The Escuela de Mariachi Ollin Yoliztli en Garibaldi is the first arts education school to specialize in mariachi music. The majority of the students enrolled, in addition to completing courses in a typical middle or high school, must complete their coursework in both institutions to receive accreditations in standard courses and in mariachi music.

Gender

Mariachi music evolved as a predominantly male-centered tradition in 19th-century western Mexico; however, historical evidence and ethnographic accounts reveal that women have performed as instrumentalists with mariachi ensembles since at least the turn of the 20th century (Soto Flores, 2015). Prior to the emergence of the earliest all-female mariachi groups, individual women performed this music since the late 19th century: Doña Rosa Quirino from Nayarit, an anonymous woman from Zacatecas, and Carmen Moreno from Los Angeles. While these may not have been the only women mariachi musicians, they do represent women who gained access to a tradition that only later became male dominated, when it gained international recognition as a musical symbol of Mexico.

In Mexico City, three all-female mariachi ensembles emerged with the artistic caravans in the 1950s: Mariachi Las Adelitas de Adela Chávez, Mariachi Las Coronelas de Carlota Noriega, and Mariachi Estrellas de México de Lupita Morales. Unfortunately, toward the end of the 1970s, when the artistic caravans ceased to operate, these all-female mariachi groups disbanded. In Brownsville, Texas, by July 1964, Mariachi Las Rancheritas was already performing as an all-female mariachi group for public social events. A year later, Mariachi Las Generalas was founded in Los Angeles, and in 1977, Mariachi Estrella Topeka in Kansas. In Mexico, two groups initiated in the 1980s have been able to sustain their presence in the mariachi performance scene: Mariachi Xóchitl, since 1982, and Mariachi Las Perlitas, since 1989. By 1994, José Hernández, director of Mariachi Sol de México, founded the all-female Mariachi Reyna de Los Angeles. Other groups quickly followed, such as Mariachi Las Adelitas de José Luis Salinas, Mariachi Mujer 2000 de Marisa Orduño, Mariachi Divas de Cindy Shea, and Mariachi Flor de Toloache from New York City.

In the United States, four women had the opportunity to perform with renowned mariachi ensembles from the late 1970s to the early 1990s: Rebecca Gonzalez with Mariachi Los Camperos de Nati Cano and Mariachi Cobre, Laura Sobrino with Mariachi Los Galleros and Mariachi Sol de México, Catherine Baeza with Mariachi Los Camperos and Mariachi Los Galleros, and Mónica Treviño with Mariachi los Camperos. Today, these groups do not have women performing with them.

Expectations of Professionals Versus Amateurs

There is a powerful social element that is expending effort to legitimate mariachi music by having top groups perform with symphony orchestras. While mariachi music has not achieved the intellectual or aesthetic credibility enjoyed by high-art music, its relatively lower status is now being countered. Some of the musicians interviewed for this research confirmed their sense of the importance of changing the public perception of mariachi musicians. The rise of formal mariachi schools in Mexico seems set to advance the recognition of mariachi musicians as the excellent musicians they are, with musical skills unique to the mariachi tradition.

Implications for Sustainability

Performing mariachi music entails a wide variety of social, cultural, and musical meanings and interpretations. With given contexts and constructs, the implications for sustainability involve musicians' decisions, which impact the interpretation of their musical experience and its relationship with their own culture and identity. Mariachi musicians today have the opportunity to perform in a wide variety of contexts, full time or as a hobby. Furthermore, with emerging educational spaces, women who did not historically have access to the tradition are developing the knowledge and skills to perform the music, while necessarily also negotiating their gender identity as mariachi musicians. Despite the growing diversity in the way mariachi music is performed, which enriches the way in which it is continually revitalized, certain repertory and subgenres are endangered and arguably need intervention.

REGULATIONS AND INFRASTRUCTURE

Throughout its centuries-old history as an aural tradition, mariachi music's survival and vitality have not depended at all on government intervention, public funding, or civic valuing. Yet, while mariachi music is widely considered a national symbol, also endorsed by UNESCO's inscription of the tradition on the *Representative List of the Intangible Cultural Heritage of Humanity*, it ironically suffers a lack of formal support and regulations that would govern its sustenance and development.

Civic Valuing and Funding Sources

In 2002, the Mexican government took the initiative to organize the *Grupo de Trabajo para la Promoción y Salvaguarda del Patrimonio Cultura Inmaterial de México* (Work Group for the Promotion and Safeguarding of the Intangible Cultural Heritage of Mexico). In 2005, Mexico became a State Party to UNESCO's 2003 *Convention for the Safeguarding of Intangible Cultural Heritage* and, in 2008, presented its preliminary draft for the *Inventory of Intangible Cultural Heritage*. This first draft already included mariachi music as one of the cultural elements in need of safeguarding (although originally the entry was for the more specific *Mariachi Tradicional: Pequeños Conjuntos de Cuerdas* [Traditional Mariachi: Small Stringed Ensembles]).

The work group's definition of a traditional mariachi ensemble legitimated the "traditional" as opposed to "modern" mariachi as the genre to be preserved and safeguarded, and the group suggested there were serious obstacles for traditional ensembles attempting to regain the identity status they once had. The safeguarding measures proposed for protecting and promoting "traditional mariachi" included (a) strengthening and supporting the *Encuentro Nacional de Mariachi Tradicional*, which takes place in Guadalajara, Jalisco, and expanding it to other states; (b) supporting instrument makers; (c) establishing music and dance workshops in mariachi performance regions; and (d) promoting and documenting discographic, print, and videographic publications.

On November 27, 2011, UNESCO inscribed *El mariachi: música de cuerdas, canto y trompeta* (Mariachi: string music, song, and trumpet) onto its *Representative List of the Intangible Cultural Heritage of Humanity*. While the procedures and cultural legislation that led to this international recognition initially only considered the traditional form of the genre as worthy of preservation, the accepted proposal finally took into consideration the popular tradition. In fact, in the Nomination File No. 00575 "For Inscription on the Representative List of the Intangible Cultural Heritage of Humanity in 2011," one of the safeguarding strategies is the creation of a mariachi school on Plaza Garibaldi, which would aim to recover, conserve, and promote the mariachi heritage by training interested musicians. Opening in the fall of 2012, the Escuela de Mariachi Ollin Yoliztli en Garibaldi constitutes the first institution to offer formal "modern" mariachi education in Mexico.

Since UNESCO's recognition, confrontations have grown increasingly between the modern/popular and traditional mariachi performance practices, underscoring inevitable differences between these two traditions. Many traditional musicians define their identity and space within the revival movement (of traditional mariachi), yet they do so by disdaining the popular tradition. This has resulted in the evolution of two sociocultural contexts that have received very little ethnomusicological attention in Mexico; these could prove of considerable future interest to scholars of the genre, and for understanding issues of sustainability.

Instrument Makers

The instrument makers that were interviewed for this research described their craft as a lifelong and family-centered occupation that sometimes brings them broad attention. Rubén Morales Anguiano from Guadalajara, Jalisco, was born a luthier and his family has dedicated their lives to building *vihuelas, guitarrones*, and harps (interview, July 25, 2011). Morales worked closely with Víctor "El Pato" Cárdenas, former *vihuela* player for Mariachi Vargas de Tecalitlán, who had commissioned Morales to make his instruments. In the early years, he worked with Morales in achieving the precise sound he wanted from his instrument. Morales explained the importance and availability of the proper wood for building mariachi instruments and underscored the importance of acquiring the proper materials, to which he then applies his impeccable craftsmanship.

In the United States, luthier Tomás Delgado spoke of the growth of his business into new markets in the United States and internationally. He began making instruments in Topeka, Kansas, in the late 1980s, when there were few mariachi groups. With the growth in mariachi education programs, the demand for *vihuelas* and *guitarrones* has also increased. It is common to find violins, trumpets, and guitars in many music stores across the nation, but *vihuelas* and *guitarrones* were originally only made in Mexico. According to Delgado, his business started to pick up in the late '70s and '80s, when schools began purchasing mariachi instruments (interview, December 15, 2012). Delgado is one of the top luthiers in the United States and, from Los Angeles, supplies instruments to mariachi, *conjunto*, and *música norteña* ensembles. He is protective of the details of his craft, and his workshop is closed to people outside his company to guard what he views as his family's artistic instrument-making secrets.

Traje de Charro

As previously mentioned, a *traje de charro* is the traditional attire worn by mariachi musicians and serves as a visual symbol of a Mexican national identity, though most are personalized for individuals or groups, who turn to tailors to have theirs made. Currently, five different kinds of *trajes de charro* are in use. The most common is the *traje de faena* (work), though its simplicity does not undervalue its elaboration or meaning. Another is the *traje de media gala*, which is a bit more elaborate and has only a few silver buttons on each side of the pants. The *traje de gala*, in contrast, has a full set of buttons and is generally black. Then there are the *trajes de etiqueta* and *de gran gala*, which are still more elaborate, and the kind of uniforms most popular groups will have made today.

Tailor Jorge Tello, owner of La Casa del Mariachi in the Boyle Heights neighborhood of Los Angeles, refers to the *traje de gala*, which he compares to a kind of Mexican tuxedo (interview, December 8, 2012). While popular mariachi groups wear the *traje de charro*, the traditional groups in Mexico continue to wear the *traje de manta*, a white cotton outfit that mariachi groups used to wear prior to the popularization of the *traje de charro*.

Laws Relevant to Public Performance

Although Plaza Garibaldi in Mexico City has attracted mariachi musicians to perform in since the turn of the 20th century, the genre experienced a mild shift in the 1960s, when there were debates about whether mariachi musicians could stand on the major avenue crossing Plaza Garibaldi, El Eje Central. Instead of limiting their space to the plaza itself, many musicians began to slip into the avenue to be among the first musicians to make contact with potential customers. Yet not all of the passing cars or pedestrians were potential customers. Their complaints about mariachi musicians "harassing" them prompted government authorities to attempt to prohibit musicians from that main avenue. This action created immediate conflict with the musicians, and as a result, the Mariachi Union was formed, with the aim of offering membership to those who would then be permitted to perform on Plaza Garibaldi, but not stand on the Eje Central.

Former General Secretary of the Mexican Mariachi Union Antonio Covarrubias explained the need for unionization. Since musicians at the time of the founding were having problems, especially in regards to playing in the streets of Mexico City, the union was created precisely to coordinate with the authorities to ensure that musicians could perform in these open spaces. Today it is very common to find mariachi musicians on any corner, but at that time, it was difficult to go out into the street without getting arrested by the police. The local regulations didn't see playing music as a type of work; instead, they saw it as an administrative infraction (Antonio Covarrubias, interview, September 9, 2012). The Mariachi Union was re-established and continues to enable musicians to play at Plaza Garibaldi. Much effort has been expended by the union to argue to government officials for the dignity of performing mariachi music, but it has had a limited impact to date. While many musicians have become union members, there continue to be non–union members who stand on the main avenue or surrounding streets, with the aim of obtaining work, and many are hired despite the efforts of the union.

Implications for Sustainability

A growing number of musical cultures across the world have submitted proposals to UNESCO in order to earn international recognition, either on the *Representative List of the Intangible Cultural Heritage of Humanity* or the *List of Intangible Cultural Heritage in Need of Urgent Safeguarding*. In 2011, when mariachi music finally succeeded in earning recognition on the first of these lists, the proposal included the popular mariachi expression along with the traditional. Earning this legitimation has had a major impact on government support particularly in Jalisco, but also in Colima and Nayarit, where mariachi events, publications, and educational programs are funded each year. In addition to government funding for educational support, there is also a growing need for academic colloquiums that would decrease the knowledge gap between educators and researchers. Despite the reality that mariachi music has evolved throughout its history, it is arguably in need of strategies that continuously promote and sustain its musical heritage.

MEDIA AND THE MUSIC INDUSTRY

As with other popular musics, mariachi music evolved alongside the globalizing cultural industries. In the early 20th century, certain groups from western Mexico began to travel to Mexico City to secure their space in a promising performance scene. Mariachi music also began to feature in emerging media formats and in the music industry. Radio broadcasts featured live mariachi music and popular groups appeared in important Mexican films, and these were fundamental in popularizing and standardizing the genre. However, since the 1980s, the mass media has offered little space for new mariachi music, and the last decade has seen an enormous decline in the number of commercial records produced that feature the genre.

Mexico City's first radio program went on air on September 27, 1921, and by 1930, 32 radio stations had been established, among them the renowned XEB *El Buen Tono* and XEW, now *Radio Televisa*, which featured live musical presentations, spoken entertainment, and local news. Diverse musical styles and performers not only filled national radio waves in large cities but also carried music and news to the most rural, remote, and forgotten parts of the country. Live radio programs became a vital way for many potential mariachi musicians who did not come from a family of musicians to gain access to this tradition.

Mexican film history documents a similar path. Particularly during the *Epoca de oro del cine mexicano* (Golden Era of Mexican Film; 1936–1969), mariachi music was often featured on soundtracks, thus underscoring its sound in the ears of the viewers. Certainly, the use of film to present (and create) national and local interests necessarily involves cinematographic decisions that may promote or subvert ideologies, and mariachi's prominence was ensured by its frequent inclusion in films of the period. To fulfill the growing demands of their public (often fans of Mexican film), mariachi groups began to perform the songs featured in these films, which seeped into the popular mariachi repertory.

With the growth of mariachi music in recordings that became widely available, the listening and learning experience was no longer localized to communities within Mexico's national borders. Mariachi developed into a transnational music. In fact, the consumption of recordings was often only a first point of departure for many mariachi musicians, especially for those living abroad. For several generations, musicians in locations far outside of Mexico have bought recordings by Mariachi Vargas de Tecalitlán and others.

If mariachi music had not been so prevalent in Mexican films, it might never have been dispersed across the globe as has happened, capturing the ears of prospective singers and players, as well as avid listeners. Many listen and strive to closely imitate the instrumental timbres and techniques, and the nuances of the melodies and rhythms that they hear on these recordings. The mariachi sound has traveled far and wide; one case in point is Mariachi Los Caballeros, a group in Croatia that at times has a sound that could be considered Mexican.

As the Internet has enabled greater access to mariachi music, international consumption of the genre has grown exponentially. While it is still important for many musicians to have the multiple versions of the *son* "El Palmero" on their iPhone, many also refer to videos on YouTube for a different way of learning the mariachi style on their instrument. Such media offer alternative ways of experiencing the tradition in its diaspora and also create new teaching-learning environments. Regardless of nationality, musicians far from Mexico can succeed in their attempts to imitate and reproduce the particularities of the mariachi sound.

While the music industry gained from the wide dissemination of mariachi record-ings from the 1940s to the mid-1980s, mariachi music today is not as lucrative for the industry as it once was. Where groups such as Mariachi Vargas de Tecalitlán were previously signed with influential and powerful RCA México, most albums today are released independently. Recordings sell in local shops that specialize in Mexican music, but piracy and the lack of an influential producer and distributer limit the number of records sold and just how far from home they can be dissemi-nated. Now, with the availability of low-cost digital distribution avenues, many mariachi groups are finding an important space on online music stores iTunes and CD Baby, where they can sell their music at relatively low prices without having to produce the physical album. Unlike many other popular music genres, mariachi music has survived (and in some places and times, even thrived) because there is still a demand for musicians to continue performing the music live for private celebrations.

Implications for Sustainability

While the media and the Mexican culture industry highly influenced the evolu-tion from the traditional mariachi expression to the popular one, they are also responsible for having documented traditional repertory and the process of change. In fact, aside from the first journalistic reviews on the first mariachi groups featured on public radio in the mid-1920s, there are only a handful of 19th-century historical documents that refer to mariachi as a musical ensemble (Jáuregui 1999). While some traditionalists might criticize the media for nega-tively impacting the mariachi tradition, they too need this form of promotion to offer a basis for sustainability, in addition to educational efforts and govern-ment intervention.

ISSUES AND INITIATIVES FOR SUSTAINABILITY

Mariachi continues its long legacy in Mexico, the United States, and elsewhere in the world as an important expressive musical practice. While only one of Mexico's many music genres, it has taken its place as a vibrant form that evolved from regional tradition to cultural emblem. Particularly for Mexicans traveling abroad, or for those of Mexican heritage who are living elsewhere in the world (as in the case of Mexican Americans living in the United States), mariachi music often defines them. The instrumentation, the voluminous "golden" voices, the melodic flair and flourishes, and the rhythmic vitality are features of mariachi that draw listeners to its spirited sound. It is immediately identifiable, energetic and conta-gious, and expressive of a range of emotions. For many who play, sing, and listen to mariachi, it is a life-giving phenomenon. In its popular form, the genre con-tinues to be performed in Mexico even as it maintains a significant international presence. The traditional Mexican mariachi style continues to thrive in a variety of local sociocultural contexts, such as in worship, at public outdoor events, and in private family celebrations.

Even as Mexicans are drawn to other musical genres and forms, both Mexican rooted and forms from outside Mexico, mariachi continues to have a special place in the musical "pantheon" of respected practices. In Mexico, mariachi music survives and is sustained through learning experiences that happen outside the formal curriculum of schools. Those who are drawn to perform mariachi are still learning it from family members or friends, by listening (to recordings and Internet sources) or by seeking training in the few specialized schools for aspiring players of all ages. The mariachi tradition survives and is sustained in these ways, and while fine musicians have emerged over a cen-tury of practice, absent is a strong civic infrastructure or government sup-port for furthering the genre through education. Without financial support for schools that teach the repertoire, instruments, and singing, the future of mariachi music in Mexico presents an uncertain and unpredictable trajectory, particularly if the aim is to preserve intact this musical practice through direct transmission of technique and repertoire in its every nuance. Whether a part of the formal curriculum or in a nonformal context, there are model mariachi programs in the United States, on the other hand, that are successfully pre-serving and passing on a canonized set of mariachi repertoire within classes that are supported by a public tax base. Much to the delight of enrolled school-children and their families, many of whom claim Mexican heritage, mariachi is occasionally offered as one of the curricular options alongside band, choir, and orchestra.

Sustainability Issues

For many generations, mariachi music has manifested itself among individuals, families, groups, and communities as an oral expression that transmits knowl-edge, traditions, and identity to current and future generations. Social factors, such as increasing migration, cultural diversity, globalization, and its own versatil-ity, have affected the sustainability of the mariachi tradition due to the changes that these social factors tend to have on intangible heritage.

The popular mariachi groups of Mexico that have become known internationally have been called into question by scholars and musicians of the traditional groups, who claim that the musical changes absorbed by mariachi ensembles threaten their preservation intact and thus move the genre ever further from its origin. These critics point to noncommercial groups as better able to preserve the original ways of living and performing the mariachi tradition. While many of the traditional-style musicians are participating in a mariachi revival movement, there are still some traditional expressions in the *sierras* (mountains) of western Mexico that sustain historically earlier stages of mariachi development but are not officially recognized. These mariachi groups need to be documented, as they are passing away. A vexing question concerning sustainability is this one: Whose mariachi music shall be continued?

Past Initiatives

The state of Jalisco has been one of the main promoters of mariachi music, in all of its variations. Since 2002, the *Secretaría Cultural del Gobierno del Estado de Jalisco* (Department of Culture of the State of Jalisco) organized the first *Encuentro Nacional de Mariachi Tradicional* (National Festival of the Traditional Mariachi) in an effort to create awareness in the Mexican community that traditional ensembles are not merely a "precursor" to the popular mariachi groups, nor a thing of the past, but continue to be a musical expression well worthy of recognition at the national level. These activities provide a forum for musical expression and dialogue among musicians from various regions of Mexico.

In the United States, mariachi festivals have been developing for several decades as important encounters for both musical excellence and dialogue about the music as emblematic of Mexico though filtered through a US experience. In 1979, Belle San Miguel and Juan Ortiz organized the first mariachi festival in San Antonio, Texas, which offered short-term educational workshops and a concert hosted by Mariachi Vargas de Tecalitlán (Clark, 1980). Since then, this festival–workshop format has permeated into other parts of the United States, including Arizona, California, Colorado, Illinois, Nevada, New Mexico, and New York.

Current and Future Initiatives

In the Nomination Form File No. 00575, submitted to UNESCO in 2011 for the inscription of mariachi music on the *Representative List of the Intangible Cultural Heritage of Humanity*, the safeguarding measures proposed include a variety of projects, most of which have already been initiated and/or completed. Many have been described earlier in this chapter; they include a compilation of documentary records; support for luthier crafts; a regional mariachi school in the municipality of San Martín Hidalgo, Jalisco; an Academic Mariachi Symposium; education workshops during festivals; CD productions; book publishing; a series of social events; and a mariachi school on Plaza Garibaldi. Overall, the UNESCO inscription has been largely celebrated by mariachi musicians and institutions. This recognition has reconceptualized the mariachi tradition as a whole by promoting both its traditional and popular expressions. Furthermore, it has also encouraged respect and dignity, which has countered the negative stereotypes that dominated the mariachi image.

The outcomes of these projects span a continuum from the documentation and preservation of mariachi to an enlivening and deepening understanding of its place in history and heritage, to pathways in honoring tradition while also allowing changes to instrumentation, repertoire, technique, contexts, functions, and means by which it is performed, taught, and learned. Future initiatives could involve further historical and ethnographic research on regional mariachi ensembles and artists in large and small communities in Mexico, among Mexican Americans, and elsewhere in the world, and the cultural promotion of mariachi via current media and social networks. With government support could also come an honoring of mariachi musicians as cultural treasures; expanded opportunities for learning mariachi in school and community spaces; cross-arts experimentation that may feature mariachi in juxtaposition with dance, drama, and other musical expressions; and the development of performance spaces that do justice to the appeal, the vibrancy, and the scope of this genre.

ACKNOWLEDGMENTS

Our research team included Cameron Quevedo, whose on-the-ground documentation was important in the early period of the research; our advisors Steven Loza, Jesús Jaúregui, and Daniel Sheehy; and our assistants James B. Morford and Leah Pogwizd. We would like to thank the professors at the Escuela de Mariachi Ollin Yoliztli en Garibaldi, from whom we learned much about the growing importance of mariachi music and its transmission. In particular, thanks to Professor Erick Mora, who has been key in systematizing mariachi music education through his transcriptions, lesson plans, and insight into the future of its education. Others in Guadalajara, Cocula, Tecalitlán, Mexico City, and Los Angeles were instrumental in developing our understanding of regional, national, and export styles of mariachi. Please visit the companion website for a full list of interviewees.

REFERENCES

Castillo Romero, P. (1973). *Santiago Ixcuintla, Nayarit: Cuna del Mariachi Mexicano*. Mexico City, Mexico: Bartolomeu Costa-Amie.

Chamorro Escalante, J. A. (1999). Organografía de los mariachis tradicionales. *Estudios Jaliscienses*, 36(May), 23–38.

Clark, J. (1980). Report: First International Mariachi Conference. San Antonio, Texas. September 27–30, 1979. *Asociación Nacional de Grupos Folklóricos: ANGF Journal*, 4(1), 21–23.

Clark, J. (1992). Mariachi Vargas. *Mexico's pioneer mariachis, Vol. 3: Mariachi Vargas de Tecalitlán, their first recordings 1937-1947* (produced by Chris Strachwitz). El Cerrito, CA: Arhoolie Records, CD7015.

Clark, J. (1993). Cuarteto Coculense. *Mariachi Coculense "Rodríguez" de Cirilo Marmolejo 1926-1936* (produced by Chris Strachwitz). El Cerrito, CA: Arhoolie Records, CD7036.

Clark, S. (2005). Mariachi music as a symbol of Mexican culture in the United States. *International Journal of Music Education*, 23(3), 227–237.

Dávila Garibi, J. I. (1935). Recopilación de Datos Acerca del Idioma Coca y de su Posible Influencia en el Lenguaje Folklórico de Jalisco. In *Investigaciones Lingüísticas* (Vol. 3, 248302). Mexico City, Mexico: Instituto Mexicano de Investigaciones lingüísticas.

Fogelquist, M. S. (1975). *Rhythm and form in the contemporary Son Jalisciense* (Master's thesis). University of California, Los Angeles, CA.

García, Peter J. 2004. "Ranchera." In *Encyclopedia of Latino popular culture*, Vol.2 (M-X), edited by Cordelia Chávez Candelaria, Peter J. García and Arturo J. Aldama, pp. 665–666. Westport, CT: Greenwood Publishing Group.

González, R. E. (2009). *Cancionero Tradicional de la Tierra Caliente de Michoacán*. Morelia, Mexico: Universidad Michoacana de San Nicolás de Hidalgo.

Henriques, D. A. (2006). *Performing nationalism: Mariachi, media and the transformation of a tradition (1920-1942)* (PhD dissertation). University of Texas, Austin, TX.

Herrera Sobek, M. (1990). *The Mexican corrido: A feminist analysis*. Bloomington, IN: Indiana University Press.

Jáquez, C. F. (2003). El Mariachi: Musical repertoire and sociocultural investment. In F. R. Aparici & C. Jacquez (Eds.), *Musical migrations: Transnationalism and cultural hybridity in Latin/o America* (pp. 162–181). New York, NY: Palgrave Macmillan.

Jáuregui, J. (1987). El Mariachi Como Elemento de un Sistema Folklórico. In J. Jáuregui & Y-M. Gourio (Eds.), *Palabras devueltas, homenaje a Claude Levi—Strauss* (pp. 93–126). Mexico City, Mexico: Instituto Nacional de Antropología e Historia/Instituto Francés de América Latina.

Jáuregui, J. (1999). *Los Mariachis de Mi Tierra ... Noticias, Cuentos, Testimonios y Conjeturas: 1925-1994*. Mexico City, Mexico: Consejo Nacional para la Cultura y las Artes, Dirección General de Culturas Populares.

Jáuregui, J. (2006). *La Plegaria Musical del Mariachi. Velada de Minuetes en la catedral de Guadalajara* (Vol. 47 del Testimonio Musical de México). Mexico City, Mexico: Instituto Nacional de Antropología e Historia.

Jáuregui, J. (2007). *El Mariachi: Símbolo Musical de México*. Mexico City, Mexico: Instituto Nacional de Antropología e Historia.

Jáuregui, J. (2012). El Mariachi. Símbolo Músical de México. *Música Oral del Sur*, 9, 220–240.

Koetting, J. (1977). The *Son Jalisciense*: Structural variety in relation to a Mexican mestizo forme fixe. In *Essays for a humanist. An offering to Klaus Wachsmann* (pp. 162–168). New York, NY: Town House Press.

Loza, S. J. (1993). *Barrio rhythm*. Urbana, IL: University of Illinois Press.

Madrid, A. L. (2013). *Music in Mexico: Experiencing music, expressing culture*. New York, NY: Oxford University Press.

Méndez Rodríguez, H. R. (1983). *Origen e Historia del Mariachi*. Mexico City, Mexico: Editorial Katún.

Mendoza, V. T. (1954). *El Corrido mexicano*. Mexico City, Mexico: Fondo de Cultura Económica.

Mendoza, V. T. (1984). *Panorama de la Música Tradicional de México*. Mexico City, Mexico: Universidad Nacional Autónoma de México.

Meyer, J. (1981). El Origen del Mariachi. *Vuelta*, 59, 41–44.

Nevin, J. (2002). *Virtuoso mariachi*. Lanham, MD: University Press of America.

Ochoa Serrano, Á. (1994). *Mitote, Fandango y Mariacheros*. Zamora, Mexico: El Colegio de Michoacán.

Reuter, J. (1981). *La Música Popular de México*. México D.F.: Panorama.

Saldívar, G. (1938). "El Origen de los Sones." *Hoy 45*, 26–47.

Sánchez, R. V. (2007). Paralelismos y Otros Recursos Limitantes en el Canto de las Coplas en los Sones de México. In A. Gonzalez (Ed.), *La Copla en México/The song in Mexico* (pp. 309–321). Mexico City, Mexico: El Colegio de México.

Sheehy, D. (2000). Mexican mariachi music: Made in the U.S.A. In K. Lornell & A. K. Rasmussen (Eds.), *Musics of multicultural America: A study of twelve musical communities* (pp. 131–154). New York, NY: Schirmer Books.

Sheehy, D. (2006). *Mariachi music in America: Experiencing music, expressing culture*. New York, NY: Oxford University Press.

Soto Flores, L. (2014). La Enseñanza de la Música de Mariachi en Diversos Contextos Educativos. In *Memorias del Coloquio: Aprendizajes y relaciones* (pp. 307–315). Guadalajara, Mexico: Secretaría de Cultural del Gobierno de Jalisco.

Soto Flores, L. (2015). *How musical is woman?: Performing gender in mariachi music* (PhD dissertation). University of California, Los Angeles, CA.

Stanford, T. E. (1972). The Mexican son. *Yearbook of the International Folk Music Council, 4*, 66–86.

Suárez, L. (1970). *Cuernavaca Ante el Vaticano*. Mexico City, Mexico: Grijalbo.

Vega, C. (1944). *Panorama de la música popular argentina: con un ensayo sobre la ciencia del folklore*. Buenos Aires, Argentina: Centurión.

11

CA TRÙ

The Revival and Repositioning of a Vietnamese Music Tradition

Esbjörn Wettermark and Håkan Lundström

CA TRÙ IS a vocal music genre in north and central Vietnam. Its core ensemble consists of a female singer and a lute player, generally a male. In addition to her voice, the singer uses a wooden clapper played with two sticks. A small drum is played by a third person, traditionally an audience member who knows the music well. The name *ca trù* literally means singing (*ca*) for sticks or tokens (*trù*), and refers to a practice of giving the singer bamboo sticks that could be exchanged for money after the performance (Đ. M. Nguyễn, 2010). Older sources often use the name *hát ả đào*—"songs of miss *đào*"—instead of *ca trù*, but the two can be used interchangeably. Although scholars and artists often claim that *ca trù* practices originated in the Lý dynasty (CE 1010–1225), recent historical scholarship suggests that *ca trù*, in a form recognizable as such today, came into existence during the later Lê dynasty in the 15th century (X. D. Nguyễn, 2010).

BACKGROUND

Through its history, *ca trù* has been associated with ritual music, as well as courtesan entertainment. *Ca trù* performers were organized into local music guilds, *giáo phường*, which had performance rights for ceremonies at the village communal house, the *đình*. The move of *ca trù* toward a courtesan art form began in the 17th and 18th centuries, when some guilds sold their performance rights and struck up new alliances with local male elites (Tran, 2013). This connected *ca trù* to an educated social elite where singers were hired to entertain at private functions rather than in community ceremonies. There were a number of different *ca trù* performance styles and repertoires, the most common being ceremonial, *hát cửa đình*, "singing at the door of the *đình*," and *hát chơi*, "singing for entertainment" (Bùi, 2008). Into the 20th century, *ca trù* groups were also hired to perform at the imperial court in the old capital of Huế (Đỗ & Đỗ, 2003, p. 173).

During the French colonial era (1858–1954), *ca trù* guilds began to move from the countryside into the cities of northern Vietnam—especially Hanoi—where they set up singing houses, *ca quán*. These were places where male patrons could go and listen to *ca trù* in the *hát chơi* style while being served alcohol, tobacco, and sometimes opium by young female waitresses. By the late 1930s, Hanoi alone was home to hundreds of singing houses, some of which were no more than glorified brothels (Dimick, 2013, p. 83), and extensive drinking and debauchery gave the genre an increasingly bad reputation. The reputation of *ca trù* as music for brothels gave the honorary title of the *ca trù* singer, *cô đầu*, increasingly derogatory connotations (Dimick, 2013).

The emerging socialist and nationalist movements considered *ca trù* tainted by colonial decadence and feudal romanticism in the cities, as well as by superstitious worship on the village level (Anisensel, 2013; Norton, 2005). After the August Revolution in 1945 and the Communists' final victory over the French colonial authorities in 1954, *ca trù* was discouraged, and according to some sources even banned, by the new Socialist government (Anisensel, 2013; T. H. Lê, 1997; Norton, 2005). With the advent of civil war, public *ca trù* activities came to a standstill, and only a few musicians and families kept the tradition alive into the present day (T. B. V. Lê, 2008; Norton, 2005). The social stigma that *ca trù* and its musicians experienced after the revolution could have been the beginning of the end for *ca trù*. However, since the early 1990s, *ca trù* has undergone a revival driven by a major reappraisal by the Vietnamese government, which has moved from considering *ca trù* a decadent, feudal, and superstitious activity to an important national heritage (Norton, 2014).

Cultural and Social Positioning

The public structures that once supported *ca trù* had all but collapsed by the late 1950s. A few artists and families secretly held on to their *ca trù* traditions, but few were willing to admit knowing the genre. Although this was still an issue at the beginning of the revival movement, many singers who had been hiding their art eventually dared to come forward, on encouragement from a handful of cultural activists (T. B. V. Lê, 2008). Today the remaining singers from this period are highly regarded for their role in teaching a new generation of *ca trù* artists.

Thanks to changing policies on religious activities, *ca trù* has even regained some of its importance as a focal point for village rituals (Anisensel, 2009). In 2009, *ca trù* was recognized by UNESCO as Intangible Heritage in need of safeguarding. However, although singers are no longer persecuted and shamed by society, there has been little increase in highly skilled performers, and the future for the genre is still uncertain.

Formal Features

Ca trù performance (see Figure 11.1) is based on sung poetry, where the singer's art is to adapt the words of the poem to its modal music system and the right musical "form," or *thể* (Norton, 2005). Old *ca trù* poetry often uses archaic language, making it difficult to understand for uninitiated listeners. However, during the first half of the 20th century, many new poems were composed in the popular *hát nói* style, using modern Vietnamese (Addiss, 1992; Đ. M. Nguyễn, 2010). While poems can be performed as separate pieces, songs are generally performed as a suite in which different performance styles are showcased (Jähnichen, 2014). The central figure of the ensemble is the female singer, who also

FIGURE 11.1 Phạm Thị Huệ (*đàn đáy*) and her daughter Nguyễn Huệ Phương (*phác*) performing with *Ca trù Thăng Long* at Đình Giảng Võ, Hanoi. The praise drum (*trống chầu*) can be seen in the foreground. *Ca trù* master Nguyễn Thị Chúc is seated behind them.
Photo: Esbjörn Wettermark, January 2, 2010.

plays *phách*. The *phách* is a struck idiophone consisting of a short piece of rectangular bamboo or hard wood lying on the ground in front of the seated singer and beaten with two sticks, one of which is split in two to create a distinct sound. The singer is accompanied by a *đàn đáy*, a three-stringed, long-necked lute, generally played by a male musician. The lute follows and supports the sung melody and performs short instrumental interludes between sung phrases. The final instrument, the *trống chầu*—often referred to as the "praise drum"—is a small double-headed drum, beaten on one side only with a thin, long stick to create a loud cracking sound. It is not played continuously, but used to start or end the performance, to articulate phrase endings in the singing, and to express appreciation of the performance. In the past, an audience member played the drum, but today, due to a lack of audience members well versed in the *ca trù* performance aesthetics, the drummer is generally a member of the ensemble. In ceremonial *ca trù*, such as *hát cửa đình*, additional stringed instruments have occasionally been used, although still with the *đàn đáy* as the main instrument (Vũ, 2008). *Ca trù* developed in a context of literary connoisseurs, and in addition to beating the drum, knowledgeable people in the audience might present a newly composed poem to the singer, who was then required to perform it on the spot. Today the *hát chơi* style is by far the most performed, although other repertoires have been revived in recent years.

SYSTEMS OF LEARNING MUSIC

Within the now-defunct *giáo phường* system of training and performance, the guild's rights to perform at ceremonies and festivals were closely monitored by senior musicians and the guild leader, *ông trùm*. These guilds were hierarchically structured and had rules of conduct and strict moral codes for its musicians, especially for female singers and students. A musician's right to perform publicly was evaluated and formalized through singing competitions, *hát thi*, and initiation ceremonies, *lễ mở xiêm áo* (Bùi, 2008; Đ. P. Nguyễn, 2003). After the breakdown of the guild system in the early 20th century, *ca trù* transmission still retained some formal elements, and learning typically involved an apprenticeship of several years with a master musician. However, after the 1950s, this method of transmission was largely broken. Since the 1990s, in addition to a handful remaining family traditions, *ca trù* clubs (discussed at length later in this chapter) have become the most important educational structure for genre.

Philosophies of Learning and Teaching

One of the few remaining artists, who performed *ca trù* for a living before the closure of the singing houses, is Phó Thị Kim Đức (b. 1931). At the time of our research (2007–2015), Kim Đức was one of the most famous *ca trù* singers in Hanoi, and she has been a significant inspiration for the next generation of artists and learners. This is how she described the beginning of her *ca trù* career:

> As my family has a traditional *ca trù* lineage I had a responsibility. If I didn't have talent for music I would have had to change to another job, but when I had a talent I had to continue the family tradition. It was my responsibility. . . . I started when I was 7 years old and I studied with my family. My grandmother, father, uncle, and my brother and me all learnt in the family from 7 to 13 years old. The old people taught me the main things . . . and I learnt to sing poems. Then I finished [studying] and went out to work as a singer, and I made my first performance with other people when I was 13. (interview, July 5, 2010)

Kim Đức's account of studying from a young age and then helping to sustain her family through her art would have been common for many *ca trù* artists before the closure of the singing houses. However, she was among the last generation of singers for whom continuing the *ca trù* tradition was a necessity and a way of making a living. Thanks to her work as a *chèo* opera artist, Kim Đức was able to keep her family's music alive, but most *ca trù* families lost their tradition as *ca trù* disappeared from the public eye.

Since the late 1980s, a few families have revived their *ca trù* traditions, but for aspiring *ca trù* musicians who did not have the opportunity to learn from close relatives, finding a teacher is often complicated. Lê Thị Bạch Vân, founder of the *Hanoi Ca trù Club* and one of the pioneers in the *ca trù* revival in Hanoi, spent years trying to convince old singers to teach her *ca trù*:

> In the 1980s I tried to find a *ca trù* teacher. For several years I regularly visited one famous old singer, but she did not want me as a student. She taught me three sentences of a song. That was all. I went on to another singer who bluntly told me that she never had sung *ca trù*, although I knew she had. I think they did not want to teach anyone because of *ca trù*'s bad reputation, they did not want to be called *cô đầu* [a word for the female singer that had taken on derogatory meanings by the mid-20th century]. Not giving up, I went to see yet another famous singer; she taught me one sentence and told me that if you can

sing it well after 3 years I will teach you. Unfortunately we could not get along and I did not go back to her. In the end I got help from the *đàn đáy* player Chu Văn Du, who comes from a long line of *ca trù* singers and musicians. He taught me *ca trù*. (interview, July 1, 2010; summarized by Esbjörn Wettermark)

For an outsider, finding a suitable teacher was still a problem 20 years later, in the early 2000s, when Phạm Thị Huệ, founder of *Ca trù Thăng Long*, wanted to learn *ca trù*. It took her several years of asking and visiting musicians before she was accepted as a student (personal communication, February 24, 2009).

Ca trù's underlying philosophy of high skill, refinement, and devotion to the genre and its institutions was once a strength of the genre, but its new social–cultural contexts have made it hard for musicians to sustain the high standards. The development of education in *ca trù* clubs has improved the prospect for students outside of family traditions to learn *ca trù*, but was initially met with skepticism from older artists (T. B. V. Lê, 2008). Nevertheless, a couple of clubs have actively molded their practices on the old *giáo phường* system, and in many cases there is a certain blurring of boundaries between family tradition and club teaching (Wettermark, 2010).

Learning and Teaching Practices and Approaches

Among the Hanoian *ca trù* clubs, *Ca trù Thăng Long* has positioned itself as focusing strongly on music education. The founder of the club, Phạm Thị Huệ, is a relatively new actor in the *ca trù* community, but she has quickly become one of the central characters in the revival movement. Originally trained as a *tỳ bà* lute player at the Vietnam National Academy of Music in Hanoi, and for many years a teacher at that institution, she has taken a keen interest in traditional music beyond the walls of the academy. In 2005, she began to study *đàn đáy* and singing with singer Nguyễn Thị Chúc (1930–2014) and lutenist Nguyễn Phú Đẹ (b. 1923). Only a year later she started her club, whose focus soon moved toward education and developing a new generation of *ca trù* musicians. In the first years, Huệ was heavily critiqued by others in the *ca trù* community, primarily for her quick transition from student to teacher, but also because she was playing the *đàn đáy*, generally considered an instrument for males (Wettermark, 2010). Although some still consider Huệ a controversial figure, the success of her club has dampened some of the initial criticism.

Although the students in *Ca trù Thăng Long* have private lessons with Huệ, most of the teaching takes place during group rehearsals, during which senior students help out with instructing the beginners. All singing and playing is taught aurally, and the members are keen users of recording technology to facilitate learning.

Education in the group is aimed at involving the students in performance activities, and here they are consciously diverging from the views and practices of past *ca trù* musicians, who might not have approved of student performances. However, developing confidence and musicianship are overarching goals, and Huệ wants to prepare her students for a life as practicing musicians. None of the students have to pay tuition fees; instead, they are required to help out with various tasks in the organization. This is part of the club's ethos of developing together as a musical family and creates a social foundation for the students (Wettermark, 2010).

In contrast to this arrangement, members of the family-based group *Ca trù Thái Hà* have occasional students from outside of their immediate family but mainly teach to family members. However, through recordings and a number of workshops, their style of *ca trù* has had a big impact on many musicians within the revival. They do not perform publicly as regularly as *Ca trù Thăng Long* or the *Hanoi Ca trù Club*, but they remain active within their own network of enthusiasts (Dimick, 2013).

For most if not all musicians who learned *ca trù* after the 1950s, recordings have played an important part in their learning, both as an inspiration and as a means to learn new material. In particular, Trần Văn Khê's 1976 recordings of the famous singer Quách Thị Hồ became—and remain even now—the norm for how *ca trù* should be performed. This is regardless of the fact that there has been a wealth of different singing styles within the *ca trù* idiom (Đặng, 2008). It is, however, difficult to learn the intricacies of *ca trù* singing from recordings, and young students are generally advised to follow a master musician (Phạm Thị Huệ, personal communication, February 24, 2009).

There is no established notation system for *ca trù*, although *đàn đáy* and *phách* are often learned using a set of onomatopoetic words, which may also be written down. Teaching in all clubs is predominantly aural, but several artists have developed their own theoretical and analytical methods to teach and conceptualize the music for their students. For example, Phạm Thị Huệ analyzed her own masters' performances to devise a more structured way of learning compared to how they taught her (Wettermark, 2010). Kim Đức, on the other hand, expressed worries that *ca trù* is changing too rapidly, arguing, "if you have too much freedom, things change and people will not understand, especially as *ca trù* has had a long break" (personal communication, July 5, 2010). To prevent this development, she decided to make the melodic frameworks more explicit by creating a more set structure to teach from, which she then ensured her students knew by heart. Members of *Ca trù Thái Hà* have also developed analytical models to be able to make certain aspects of their teaching more explicit (Dimick, 2013). These examples show how analysis and theorizing around *ca trù* have developed due to a need to create structures and tools for learning and teaching, given that former educational structures have largely disappeared. Arguably, developing analytic methods has become a form of "activism" where individuals can assert their own interpretation of the *ca trù* tradition, as well as build credibility in the eyes of outsiders (cf. Tenzer, 2006, p. 19). Although in some cases these analytical projects are influenced by the work of musicologists, they are initiated by the musicians themselves, displaying a great deal of creativity in the *ca trù* community.

Relationship to Institutionalized Music Education

An important outside influence on traditional music education in Vietnam has been the development of institutionalized education in academies of music. Academies teach traditional instruments largely within the scope of so-called "modern folk music", *nhạc dân tộc hiện đại*, as well a selected repertoire from a few older genres, including *chèo, cải lương* opera, and arranged folk songs (Arana, 1999). This "modern folk music" was developed at the Vietnam National Academy of Music in Hanoi during the 1960s and '70s and consists of new music in a style mixing traditional music with Western harmony and composition methods (Arana, 1999; T. H. Lê, 1997). The styles of music and ensembles taught at the academy today have many similarities with "folk music orchestras" in China (Yingfai, 1998) and the former Soviet Union (Buchanan, 2006). *Ca trù* is not taught in these academies of music, although a small number of students at the Vietnam National Academy are learning *ca trù* in clubs outside of that institution. One of these students, Nguyễn Thu Thủy, contrasted the transmission practices within *Ca trù Thăng Long* with the institutional approach for teaching traditional non–*ca trù* repertoire:

> In [the academy] we learn following the "book and pen" and it is very fixed. When you play, you all have to play the same: 100 students, 100 play the same. But when I learn *đàn đáy* [in *Ca trù Thăng Long*] I feel very comfortable. The basic things I have to learn are the same but I can [improvise], I don't play same thing every time, and we learn everything mouth by mouth [by ear]. But in [the academy] we have to learn by the book. It is different. (interview, July 14, 2010)

The importance of improvisation in traditional Vietnamese music, and the lack of improvisation at educational institutions, is often brought up when talking to musicians and musicologists in Vietnam. Trần Văn Khê—one of Vietnam's most respected musicologists and an expert on Vietnamese traditional music—raised the issue in an early interview for this research:

It's quite interesting: you hear a number of the younger traditional music teachers at the Hanoi conservatory who are saying that, at the conservatory we are learning the technique and we are learning the basic repertoire, but if we want to play music we have to go back to the old masters who are teaching by rote in order to get the depth of the music. (interview with Huib Schippers, January 20, 2007)

According to Trần Văn Khê, many students graduate with a degree in traditional music but are not able to play for any of the contexts in which the music is found. Instead, they can only "play on the paper, from transcriptions; the script." His views were echoed by many musicians during the fieldwork for this research.

Implications for Sustainability

With the disbanding of *ca trù* culture in the mid-20th century, traditional transmission processes largely disappeared, including extensive exposure to and engagement with the music, its creative processes, and its performance culture. Two formats are currently used in the transmission of *ca trù*: one-on-one tuition, largely aural and holistic, by old masters with students often 50 or more years their junior, and group learning in *ca trù* clubs. The groups and individuals who teach *ca trù* have largely developed their own teaching methods, taking inspiration from both the *giáo phường* system and the analytic methods used in institutionalized music education. At the moment, education is wholly dependent on the initiative of a small number of groups and individuals, and, for better or worse, it is not likely that *ca trù* will become part of any music academy curriculum in the foreseeable future.

MUSICIANS AND COMMUNITIES
The Musician–Community Relationship

After *ca trù* musicians lost their professional identity, prestige, and livelihood due to the changing sociopolitical circumstances of the mid-20th century, the position of these musicians in their communities has had to be rebuilt from scratch. Only a handful of *ca trù* artists alive today have personal experiences of performing *ca trù* before the closure of Hanoi's singing houses. Phó Thị Kim Đức still has fond memories of her time as a young singer:

There were theaters that invited me and I came there to sing. The people wanted to listen. At that time it was not only me; there were many singers everywhere who had as their job to sing *ca trù*. . . . When I got an invitation, I went to sing. So, I had a job and my family had jobs, and we could make a living. At the time, I was very comfortable and proud that I didn't have any problems. (interview, July 5, 2010)

Kim Đức's possibly idealized description of her early days as a *ca trù* singer gives an indication of the economic independence enjoyed by at least some *ca trù* performers in the 1940s and 1950s. Nowadays, however, it is very difficult to generate sufficient income from performing *ca trù* alone. Although *ca trù* is no longer connected with questionable morals, there are few connoisseurs of the genre, and typically audiences do not know how to engage with it. This is a problem *ca trù* shares with many other genres of Vietnamese music, but its literary heritage and specialized musical system make it especially dependent on a knowledgeable audience. According to Kim Đức, this is reflected in the changing role of the *trống chầu* drummer:

In the past, the drummer was a poet or someone very well versed in literature. They understood about literature and composed the poems and songs of *ca trù*. When they wanted to hear us sing they came to the house, or they invited us to come, and they drummed for us. They were very knowledgeable and they were drummers. It was not like nowadays. Now they are just "drum workers" [i.e., not educated connoisseurs]. (interview, July 5, 2010)

Although the demise of audience drummers and aficionados became more pronounced after the closure of the singing houses, the loss of skills had begun already in the first decades of the 20th century. A number of publications from this period—including manuals on drumbeating—attempted to improve the knowledge of *ca trù* patrons (Dimick, 2013, pp. 83–84). The importance of the praise drum was underscored by the late influential singer Nguyễn Thị Chúc, who considered drumming skills a key to understanding *ca trù* (interview with Huib Schippers, January 18, 2007). Although there have been attempts to educate audiences through interactive performances and dedicated classes, it has proven hard to get the audience to fully engage with the participatory conventions of *ca trù* (Wettermark, 2010).

Free public performances have been a key method to reach out to a new audience. For the two larger clubs, *Hanoi Ca trù Club* and *Ca trù Thăng Long*, these performances have mostly taken place in different *đình* and temples, whereas the smaller *UNESCO Ca trù Club* regularly performs in an old traditional house on the grounds of the Vietnam Museum of Ethnology. At the time of our research, *Ca trù*

Thái Hà had no regular public performances but performed within their own circle of connoisseurs, or when hired for particular events. In Hanoi, most *ca trù* groups have focused largely on the *hát chơi* repertoire. *Ca trù Thăng Long*, however, has seen its involvement with the *đình* not only as a place to practice and perform but also as part of their effort to revive the spiritual aspects of *ca trù*. They often perform interpretations of *hát cửa đình*, singing and dancing in front of the altar for the guardian deities of the *đình*. For them, the revival of these performance practices strengthens the emotional and spiritual relationship between the present and the past of *ca trù*. This ambition can be compared to earlier scholarly attempts to evade *ca trù's* links with courtesan culture by reconnecting with its spiritual roots (Đặng, Phạm, & Hồ, 2008; Đỗ & Đỗ, 1962).

To get around the potential conflict between the spiritual context and performing purely for entertainment, *Ca trù Thăng Long* has adapted its performances in a way that the group members feel retains solemnity but also exhibits something of interest to an unaccustomed audience. This has meant modifying dances, making new arrangements of songs, and experimenting with other ensemble forms to both satisfy the audience and allow the artists to experience a spiritual connection with their art (Wettermark, 2010). Most *ca trù* clubs occasionally arrange performances with ceremonial *ca trù*, but in Hanoi, *Ca trù Thăng Long* is arguably the group that has focused most on this performance context. Outside of the city, a few rural communities have revived *hát cửa đình* for their community rituals, most successfully in Lỗ Khê (Anisensel, 2009).

Being a Musician

Today, most *ca trù* artists need another job in addition to their music career. Knowing that learning *ca trù* is never likely to be a considerable source of income, there is little motivation for young students to practice and develop their art to a high level. The few *ca trù* students who are still determined to make a living as musicians often find themselves having to focus much energy on other, more popular music genres, which leaves less time to develop as *ca trù* performers. If these circumstances persist, they may present a considerable challenge to the long-term viability of the genre. One (anonymous) interviewee with insight into the present revival put it bluntly: "It is very difficult to keep clubs alive. . . . A student can only study a short time before they have to find a job . . . [and] *ca trù* cannot sustain them. . . . It's a fact; they need money both to live and to continue learning" (interview, June 25, 2010).

In Vietnam's patriarchal society, this is especially an issue for young women, who, more than men, may find it hard to defend time spent on a pursuit so unprofitable for their families and partners. As the female voice is the primary focus in a *ca trù* performance, allowing young women the time needed to develop skills is an important aspect for the sustainability of the genre, but, thus far, one that has rarely been addressed to any depth. Economic support for individual students has primarily come from nongovernmental sources or private donations. The socioeconomic situation for *ca trù* musicians has thus changed considerably from the experiences had by artists of Kim Đức's generation, and *ca trù* is unlikely to become a source of substantial income for students learning today.

The Diaspora

The Vietnamese music traditions kept alive and developed in the diaspora tend to be genres such as *cải lương* and popular music, rather than *ca trù*. This has been the case in the United States (Reyes, 1999), the United Kingdom (Fitchett, 1984), Australia (T. H. Lê, 2011), and France (Q. H. Trần, 2001), which all have large Vietnamese communities. However, individuals in the diaspora have played important roles in Vietnamese music research and the revival of the *ca trù* in Vietnam. In France, Trần Văn Khê—who moved back to Vietnam in 2005—has devoted much research to *ca trù*. His 1970s field recordings of *ca trù* musicians in Hanoi became an inspiration for both musicians and scholars to investigate the genre more closely. In the United States, singer and music writer Phạm Duy and, later, Nguyễn Thuyết Phong have helped raise awareness about Vietnamese traditional music, including *ca trù*, in the English-speaking academic community.

Implications for Sustainability

Government cultural policy today is supportive of *ca trù*, and the main issues facing *ca trù* performers are largely economic. The lack of a strong audience base means that few musicians can afford the investment in time and money to learn to a high level, leaving the genre dependent on a small core of devoted artists. This situation will become increasingly problematic as truly knowledgeable artists pass away, leaving an even smaller group of proficient performers to motivate and teach a new generation in a harsh and competitive economic climate.

CONTEXTS AND CONSTRUCTS

Since the revival of *ca trù* activities in the 1980s and 1990s, the social, cultural, and economic contexts for the genre have developed in ways both similar to and different from its contexts during the first half of the 20th century. Interrelated with this development are complex historical and ideological constructs surrounding *ca trù*, including strong views on contested concepts such as "tradition" and "authenticity." This section examines *ca trù* in relation to the contexts that provide the frame for its existence in present-day Vietnam, and the constructs that assist and hinder the development of *ca trù* activities today.

Cultural and Social Contexts

Historical sources list a great number of *ca trù* styles and contexts, many of which had disappeared already before the breakdown of public *ca trù* performances in the late 1950s (Đặng et al., 2008). It is primarily the *hát chơi* (singing for entertainment) repertoire, and to a lesser extent that of *hát cửa đình* (singing at the door of the *đình*), that survive relatively intact into the present day. Dances associated with *hát cửa đình* and other ceremonial forms have been reconstructed recently based on the recollections of old musicians and dancers (Đặng et al., 2008). Present-day performance contexts mainly include gatherings of *ca trù* clubs and formal concerts for a seated audience, and a few rural communities arrange *ca trù* performances for rituals in their village temples (Văn, 2008). In Hanoi and elsewhere, individual groups have also seen an increasing though still limited demand in hiring them for private celebrations or performances.

Ca trù festivals, as well as other public cultural events, have become reoccurring performance opportunities. Biannual national and regional *ca trù* festivals have been arranged since 2005 and allow artists to perform and listen to other groups. Festivals often include a small cash prize for the best performers, and they give musicians some degree of recognition for their work. More recently, tourist performances have become an important market in Hanoi, and ongoing plans to develop cultural tourism in other areas of Vietnam—especially in Bắc Ninh province—may create further performance opportunities (People's Committee of Bắc Ninh Province, 2013).

Constructs

Ca trù today is very much a revivalist movement and shares many similarities with other music revivals around the world, especially with regard to its focus on history and the past as a source of authenticity and justification of practices in the present (Livingstone, 1999; Ronström, 1996). These issues have led to much tension between stakeholders and made it hard to agree on which measures are needed to revitalize the genre (Norton, 2014).

After independence and the division of the country in the 1950s, cultural cadres of the Democratic Republic of Vietnam (North Vietnam) largely endorsed views on *ca trù* as a lost art, diluted and perverted by colonial decadence, backward look-ing in its poems' praise of old times, and, through its role in religious ritual, not congruent with the new Marxist reality (Anisensel, 2013; Endres, 2002). For many years, these views allowed for the active discouragement of "prerevolutionary" cul-tural expressions, including *ca trù* (T. H. Lê, 1997). However, the easing of cultural control following the 1986 economic reforms policy, *đổi mới*, allowed opposing views of the Vietnamese past to demand a place next to a previously strong, but no longer viable, "official" history (Pelley, 2002; Tai, 2001). For *ca trù* artists who had lived through the breakdown of their artistic community in the aftermaths of revolution and independence, the officially sanctioned accounts of the *ca trù* past were often in conflict with their own memories and experiences (Norton, 2005).

Since the mid-1990s, the notion of a shared national heritage has become a central aspect of creating a modern Vietnamese national identity (Meeker, 2013; Salemink, 2013). The concept of "heritage," in its recent transnational form, has been discussed and theorized by a number of researchers (see, e.g., Kirshenblatt-Gimblett, 1995; Lowenthal, 1998; Ronström, 2005), and "intangible cultural heri-tage" has become an increasingly important concept when trying to understand cultural revivals around the world (Bithell & Hill, 2014; Howard, 2012; UNESCO, 2003). The narratives provided by the memories and experiences held by the *ca trù* community, old "revolutionary" history, and contemporary ideas of a shared national and world heritage make up three different ways of constructing the *ca trù* past, and hence its role in the present.

A useful framework to described these kinds of historical narratives, or produc-tions, is Ronström's (2005, 2014) notion of *mindscape*, a concept akin to Appadurai's (1996) notion of "scapes" and "imagined worlds" in the global flows of cultural economies. The mindscape concept refers not only to the historical imagination but also to that which inhabits and supports it in the present (Ronström, 2005). Each mindscape is organized into *domains*—that is, the organizations, practices, and structures that sustain and disseminate it. Although mindscapes are produc-tions of an imagined past, it is this past that justifies and allows for actions in the present, and they are therefore useful tools when analyzing historically oriented cultural movements.

The mindscapes sustaining the *ca trù* revival can be labeled a "heritage mind-scape," a "revolutionary mindscape," and a "*ca trù* mindscape." These mindscapes all produce visions of the past that allow for distinct forms of production, modes of dissemination, ownership, and, ultimately, purpose of culture in the present. Table 11.1 shows some main characteristics in relation to their impact on *ca trù*.

Within the revolutionary mindscape, there is little place for *ca trù*, other than as a possible inspiration for new compositions, or in performances using lyrics praising

TABLE 11.1

The Three Mindscapes and Their Main Domains, Product, Cultural Ownership, Modes of Dissemination, and Purpose

Mindscape	Revolutionary	Heritage	Ca trù
Domain	The Vietnam National Academy of Music	The Vietnamese Institute for Musicology; the Vietnamese Association of Folklorists	Family
	National orchestras and ensembles	UNESCO and international nongovernmental organizations	Community
	Communist Party organizations	International tourism industry	Relationship
Product	The national for the local	The local for the national/global (Kirshenblatt-Gimblett, 1995)	The private for the local
Cultural ownership	The state and, in extension, "the people"	The nation and the world; "everybody's and therefore nobody's" (Ronström, 2014, p. 53)	Local, private
Modes of dissemination	Teaching/creating	Learning/preserving	Doing/sustaining
Purpose	Political and cultural unity (Arana, 1999)	National identity and intrinsic value	Memory and nostalgia (Norton, 2005)

the revolution or the party (see, e.g., Norton, 2005). Where *ca trù* culture has been incorporated into its musical mind-set, it has been as one aspect of the varied landscape of a unified socialist music culture, for example, in the form of electric bass and mandolins in the shape of the *đàn đáy* for the "modern folk music" orchestras (Arana, 1999).

However, today, these views are rare and the revolutionary mindscape has largely been usurped by the heritage mindscape. Within the heritage mindscape, the uniqueness of *ca trù* makes it important, and its connections to a refined elite culture make it possible to connect to a seemingly timeless range of historical dynasties stretching back hundreds if not thousands of years. Its uniqueness makes it intrinsically valuable and in need of preservation, and as such it can be presented to the nation at large as part of a shared national heritage, or to the tourist as part of a world heritage. These two mindscapes are both "official" in the sense that their shared "domains" include cultural institutions under the auspices of government ministries and, by extension, the Vietnamese state. Hence, both can benefit from the government's propaganda machinery to disseminate their visions of the Vietnamese cultural past and its possible future.

The *ca trù* mindscape lacks the strong institutions of the heritage and revolutionary mindscapes, and is sustained in lived experience, practices, and local narratives among groups of *ca trù* musicians and enthusiasts. Here *ca trù* becomes a way of remembering and thinking about a complex past with strong personal and emotional connotations; for example, there might be, as in the case of Kim Đức, fond memories of a life as a young singer, or, as Bạch Vân recalls, resentment about accusations of immorality, or more forward-looking justifications, as in *Ca trù Thăng Long*'s longing to reconnect with the spiritual sentiments of old ritual performance practices.

These three mindscapes represent different narrative projects within the greater discourse on *ca trù*. However, actors in this discourse are not necessarily tied to one specific mindscape but may well adapt to, and be inspired by, any of these narratives. The *ca trù* past—and its possible future—is created in negotiation and conflict between these narratives. Thus, the authority and perceived authenticity of cultural policies, organizations, and individuals depend on how they are positioned within the larger discourse.

Implications for Sustainability

Changes in official and public views on *ca trù* have been crucial for a revival to take place but have created a situation where the history, present, and future for *ca trù* have become areas of dispute. The mindscapes model provides a framework to better understand the discourse surrounding *ca trù* in modern Vietnam. This model also implies that future safeguarding measures would benefit from taking into account the tensions created by opposing narratives within this discourse, rather than treating the revival as a unified movement.

INFRASTRUCTURE AND REGULATIONS
Infrastructure

Management and safeguarding of intangible cultural heritage in Vietnam is the responsibility of the Ministry of Culture, Sports, and Tourism. Since the early 2000s, the Vietnamese Institute for Musicology has been the main ministry institution involved in promoting and reviving *ca trù*. Additional research and safeguarding strategies have been supported by the Association of Vietnamese Folklorists, the Vietnam Cultural Heritage Association, and the Vietnamese Institute for Hán-Nôm Studies, as well as the ministry's own culture departments at the provincial level.

The establishment of *ca trù* clubs has become an important safeguarding strategy and created a structure for the safeguarding of the genre. In the context of *ca trù*, the amateur music clubs, *câu lạc bộ*, have similar connotations to their English equivalents—that is, groups of people meeting on a voluntary and mostly not-for-profit basis to engage in an activity of choice. However, although *ca trù* clubs may have activities that are open and free of charge, most are reliant on a core group of select performers. In the Hanoi clubs, generally only a handful of those who attend perform, and the audience is often expected to pay the musicians, either by donation or through a set fee.

The first *ca trù* club was established in 1991 by Lê Thị Bạch Vân, who secured support from the Ministry of Culture to set up the *Hanoi Ca trù Club* (T. B. V. Lê, 2008). From a humble beginning with few artists attending, the reputation of her club grew and more elderly musicians decided to take up *ca trù* again. The club soon became an important institution for *ca trù* activities in Hanoi. Around the same time, the family members in *Ca trù Thái Hà* began to formalize their activities into a performance group (Đặng, 2008; V. K. Nguyễn, 2008). From the mid-1990s, a number of workshops in *ca trù* localities around Hanoi took place, which led to the establishment of *ca trù* clubs in Lỗ Khê, Hà Tây, and Cổ Đạm (Văn, 2008). In 2002, the Ford Foundation funded a 2-month *ca trù* workshop in Hanoi for a large number of participants from several Vietnamese provinces, and an additional training course was arranged in 2005 (Dimick, 2013, p. 103; Ford Foundation, 2001, 2005; Norton, 2005). After the 2002 course, many of the participants started new *ca trù* clubs in their home provinces, either on their own initiative or encouraged by local officials (T. B. V. Lê, 2008; Văn, 2008). In 2006, by the time the Vietnamese government was preparing to submit its first nomination file to UNESCO, over 25 clubs had sprung up across Vietnam, most in the northern regions but a few as far south as Ho Chi Minh City (N. Nguyễn, 2008). The exact number of clubs active today is uncertain, as several have since closed down and others opened. Inflated accounts of *ca trù* activities abound (see, e.g., Phan, 2013), and less active clubs tend to reassemble in time for festivals, which may also give an inaccurate view on the levels of *ca trù* activities on a more everyday basis.

Although at times controversial—several of the musicians interviewed were skeptical about the quick growth and the quality of the clubs started after the 2002 workshop—*ca trù* clubs have become an important infrastructure for workshops, for performances, and especially for training young performers.

Laws, Regulations, and Funding

Although Vietnam lacks the long history of supportive legislation for intangible cultural heritage that can be found in, for example, Japan and Korea (Howard, 2012), it has recently become very active in the promotion of its intangible cultural heritage (Salemink, 2013). The Law on Cultural Heritage (National Assembly of the SRV, 2001, 2002) was the first explicit legal framework to articulate the responsibilities of the government, institutions, and individuals in protecting and promoting Vietnam's intangible cultural heritage. A few years later, in 2005, Vietnam ratified the 2003 UNESCO *Convention on the Safeguarding of Intangible Cultural Heritage*. Several Vietnamese music genres have been inscribed onto UNESCO's *Representative List of the Intangible Cultural Heritage of Humanity*. Recent additions include *Quan họ* folk songs (2009), *Hát xoan* ceremonial singing (2012), and *Đờn ca tài tử* chamber music (2013). *Ca trù* was considered at high risk of disappearing and was inscribed on the *List of Intangible Cultural Heritage in Need of Urgent Safeguarding* in 2009.

Government support of intangible cultural heritage in Vietnam since the early 1990s has been closely connected to political ideology and concerns about developing a strong national identity based on traditional culture, a project that in turn is seen as threatened by globalization (Norton, 2014; see also Vietnamese Institute for Musicology, 2004). Concerns about the purpose and effectiveness of the existing legislation have been raised from within and outside of Vietnam (Jähnichen, 2011; Norton, 2014; Salemink, 2013). The head of the Vietnamese Association of Folklorists, Tô Ngọc Thanh, said that although he welcomes the government's efforts to develop and preserve the country's heritage, he feels that its involvement is often rather superficial, the biggest problem being the implementation of government policies at the local level:

> We have a policy of preservation and promotion of heritages. But at the same time we have also the awareness that since the heritages were created in the old society, they are containing many backward things which must be cleaned and improved – I don't agree with the last consideration. The second, the other policy, is that we must modernize all things in our "new and modern" life, to be a developed country. I think it is not clear, if not a mistake ... I would like to preserve tradition like it was, because that is our history. (interview with Huib Schippers, July 31, 2010)

Although the Law on Cultural Heritage gives strong support to the preservation of intangible heritage, a few of its articles suggest that some of these old policies critiqued by Tô are still present. For example, Article 22 states that "positive customs [and] ways of life" should be preserved, whereas "outdated customs that harm the people's cultural life shall be abolished" (National Assembly of the SRV, 2001). In a similar vein, the 2002 amendment explicitly bans restoring "backward customs" in traditional festivals (National Assembly of the SRV, 2002, Article 10:2b). This suggests that the Vietnamese state intends to remain in charge of what forms of cultural expressions are to be revived. Nevertheless, the Law on Cultural Heritage and the state's involvement with UNESCO have helped to raise awareness and gain support for threatened Vietnamese music genres, both within Vietnam and internationally.

Vietnam has an established system of honoring its foremost artists with official state titles and a system of "Living Human Treasures" inspired by similar systems in Japan and Korea (K. D. Nguyễn, 2004; Tô, 2010). The most established award systems are the titles "Artist of Merit," *Nghệ Sĩ Ưu Tú* (NSƯT), and the higher level, "People's Artist," *Nghệ Sĩ Nhân Dân* (NSND). These were inspired by similar awards in the USSR and outlined in a government decree from 1981, stating that NSND status should be awarded to "artists with outstanding talents who had contributed much to Vietnam's revolutionary cause" and NSƯT to "highly talented artists dedicated to serving the people" (Government of the SRV, 1981, Article 2). The awards were handed out for the first time in 1984, and the demand of artists to support the revolutionary cause was still present in a 2010 revision of the decree (Ministry of Culture, Sports, and Tourism of the SRV, 2010, Article 4).

Generally these titles have been awarded to musicians in state ensembles, but notable exceptions include *ca trù* musicians Quách Thị Hồ (NSND) in 1988, *Ca trù Thái Hà's* Nguyễn Văn Khuê (NSƯT) in 2007, and Lê Thị Bạch Vân (NSƯT) in 2012.

Several interviewees in this research stated that the system is primarily political, and although awarded artists are generally very proud of their title, one interviewee bluntly claimed that as a sign of quality "it is meaningless and has no value" (anonymous, interview, June 25, 2010).

In 2002, frustrated by the inflexibility of state titles, the Association of Vietnamese Folklorists created its own award by formalizing the appointment of *nghệ nhân*—roughly, "tradition bearer" or "artisan" (Meeker, 2013)—in a set of rules closely fashioned on UNESCO's guidelines for "Living Human Treasures" (Tô, 2010; UNESCO, 2002). In August 2014, a new government award system came into being, *Nghệ Nhân Nhân Dân* (NNND) and *Nghệ Nhân Ưu Tú* (NNƯT), which largely follows the same structure as the NSND/NSƯT system, including a small cash award (Government of the SRV, 2014). However, even before its launch, the selection criteria of this system came under critique for not taking into account the specific issues and difficulties affecting traditional arts and artists (Phương, 2014). In November 2015, NNƯT was awarded for the first time to 618 traditional artists and craftspeople across the country, and among them were many *ca trù* artists, notably *Ca trù Thăng Long's* Phạm Thị Huệ, *Ca trù Thái hà's* Nguyễn Thúy Hoà, and the influential *đàn đáy* player Nguyễn Phú Đệ. The regulations governing this new award system state that an artist must first have received NNƯT to be considered for the higher grade of *Nghệ Nhân Nhân Dân*; therefore, NNND has not yet been awarded, and it is still too early to say what impact this new two-tier system will have for the *ca trù* community.

Implications for Sustainability

The Law on Cultural Heritage and Vietnam's backing of international agreements such as UNESCO's *Convention on the Safeguarding of Intangible Cultural Heritage* place the responsibility for heritage management formally in the hands of the government. Formal recognition, such as awarding musicians with state titles, does give credit to the work of individuals and may raise their profile in greater society, but its value within the *ca trù* community is limited. Although the efficiency and principles behind government involvement in the revival have been questioned, the support and interest from government institutions have nevertheless been crucial.

MEDIA AND THE MUSIC INDUSTRY
Media Engagement

Today *ca trù* is regularly present in Vietnamese newspapers and cultural magazines. This dates back to the early 2000s and the media coverage surrounding the preparation of its nomination file to UNESCO; this began in 2002 and the file was submitted in full in early 2009. During this period, *ca trù* activities were much reported in local and national television, radio, magazines, and newspapers (Norton, 2005). Although the journalistic standard is generally low—texts are often partially or completely copied from other local media, and accompanying pictures are often of other *ca trù* groups than those profiled—news media play an important role in raising awareness for *ca trù* and have had an impact on how individuals and groups are perceived by the public (Wettermark, 2010). Since the UNESCO recognition, *ca trù* has also been increasingly promoted and presented internationally by tours and international exchanges with *ca trù* musicians resident in Vietnam.

Ca trù Thăng Long and the *Hanoi Ca trù Club* both have websites and are active on social media in Vietnamese and English, with Facebook and YouTube being the most popular platforms. These groups also use the Internet to attract visiting tourists for their performances, especially through TripAdvisor.com, an online travel review and discussion site.

Presence in the Music Industry

Several published *ca trù* recordings exist, although most are in the form of documentary field recordings. After the release of Trần Văn Khê's 1976 field recordings (V. K. Trần, 1991), *Ca trù Thái Hà* was among the first clubs to appear on a commercially available album (Ca trù Thái Hà, 1996). Today there are several albums that both profile individual singers and groups. While some of these are well distributed, the recordings remain targeted to a niche market and are not always readily available, even within Vietnam. Although a handful of *ca trù* musicians have engaged in collaborations with the potentially more lucrative experimental and "world music" scenes (Norton, 2014), commercial *ca trù* albums are likely to remain a very specialized market. Within Vietnam, the Hanoi-based Hồ Gươm Audio-Video, the state Dihavina label, and the Vietnamese Institute for Musicology are the main producers of *ca trù* albums.

Although some copyright regulations existed already in the 1960s, Vietnam's commercial record industry was not governed by international copyright laws until the early 2000s (Olsen, 2008, p. 233). Although there is little economic incentive for *ca trù* musicians to produce commercial CDs or DVDs, access to computers and digital recording equipment has made it easy for performers to make their own audio and video recordings. However, unauthorized copying of CDs is still widespread and the enforcement of copyright legislation is not very efficient. Recordings are nevertheless treasured for their promotional value, and homemade CDs, as well as professionally produced ones, are often sold by artists after performances.

Implications for Sustainability

News media, commercial recordings, and the Internet—especially through YouTube and social networking sites—have played an important role in the *ca trù* revival. Exposure in the press has helped raise the status of *ca trù*, particularly at the local level, and recordings have made it possible for an interested audience to listen to *ca trù* more regularly. However, there are no direct major financial benefits from the engagement of *ca trù* with the music industry, nor is this likely to change significantly in the future.

ISSUES AND INITIATIVES FOR SUSTAINABILITY

The inscription of *ca trù* on a UNESCO Intangible Cultural Heritage List in 2009 has helped to develop pride and interest in *ca trù*, among both the public and the Vietnamese government. Although a lot has been done by the Vietnamese Institute for Musicology to document, support, and revive *ca trù* practices, it is the work of cultural activists such as Lê Thị Bạch Vân in the *Hanoi Ca trù Club*, family groups such as *Ca trù Thái Hà*, and individual musicians from the older generation that has made the revival possible. Since 2006, *Ca trù Thăng Long* has further developed the revival movement through its focus on education and work with ceremonial *ca trù*. International researchers' interest has helped to lend the revival movement credibility and raise awareness of the genre through publications in established international journals. In recent years, *ca trù* performers have regularly been invited to festivals around Asia and further abroad. The increase of performances for paying tourists is developing an international awareness of *ca trù* outside of academia.

Although the present situation is better than it has been for many years, skilled performers are still very few. While much work has been done in educating young musicians, many do not learn enough technique or sufficient repertoire to be able to pass this knowledge on. Learning *ca trù* demands long-term devotion, but life in contemporary Vietnam rarely allows for young people to focus on a low-profit activity for an extended period of time. This suggests that *ca trù* knowledge will remain in the hands of a handful of enthusiasts for the foreseeable future.

Key Issues for Sustainability

Ca trù is an art form that puts high demands on the performer's, as well as the listener's, competence in music and poetry. Therefore, education, preferably from a young age, is crucial for the survival of *ca trù* as a living art form with an appreciative audience. Those who are now learning *ca trù* in various clubs may become not only the performers but also the knowledgeable audience of the future.

To attract a Vietnamese audience without previous knowledge of the conventions of *ca trù* and, even more so, to attract paying foreign tourists, compromises will need to be made. This is a sensitive issue, and there have been concerns that staged *ca trù* performances might reduce the genre to a repertoire of standardized songs performed in identical renditions (Jähnichen, 2011). Most *ca trù* performances today are presented to an audience unaccustomed to the genre by singers who are still developing their skills. Therefore, as choices have to be made for repertoire that suits both the singers and the audience, a standardization of the repertoire in public performances is arguably unavoidable to some degree. However, this does not necessarily mean that repertoire will be lost, as in small-scale private contexts there is often room for a wider repertoire.

The transmission that takes place in *ca trù* clubs largely works as a modern version of traditional learning that is basically oral and that includes both spiritual and social contexts. Education in *ca trù* clubs has the potential to be successful in the long run, but the clubs are still vulnerable and at risk. The main obstacles are financial. The lack of funding leads to situations where even well-organized clubs may not have a permanent venue for their activities; moreover, the education does not result in substantial income for those who pursue it. This challenge is further complicated by traditional gender roles and family expectations. *Ca trù* singers are generally young females, but many families do not consider being a singer an appropriate profession for women, especially since it is rarely a source of financial gain (see also Grant, 2014).

Past Initiatives

Even in the 1960s, a few Vietnamese researchers had begun to revaluate *ca trù* as an important part of Vietnam's cultural heritage (Đỗ & Đỗ, 1962). In the late 1970s, Trần Văn Khê's 1976 aforementioned recordings of singer Quách Thị Hồ— which received international attention and awards—opened the way for a few radio broadcasts of *ca trù* (T. B. V. Lê, 2008; Norton, 2005). In the early 1980s, additional research in the area around Hanoi resulted in a book about the *ca trù* traditions of Lỗ Khê and a TV documentary (Chu Hà, 2003; Đ. M. Nguyễn, 2010; Norton, 2005). These projects led to the organization of a *ca trù* workshop for some of the singers in the Vietnamese radio's orchestra in the late 1980s (T. B. V. Lê, 2008). More workshops were held in Lỗ Khê in the mid-1990s and in Hanoi in 2002. Since 2001, a number of *ca trù* festivals have been arranged in Hanoi and other parts of Vietnam, and these have become opportunities for clubs and individuals to showcase their activities for a wider audience.

Current and Planned Initiatives

Since 2011, *Ca trù Thăng Long* and the *Hanoi Ca trù Club* have successfully targeted the tourist market with performances in Hanoi's old quarters. Although there was one previous short-lived attempt to market *ca trù* for tourists (Wettermark, 2010), this is the first time performances have been fully under the control of the *ca trù* groups themselves. Inspired in part by the *Sustainable Futures for Music Cultures* project (see Chapter 1), Phạm Thị Huệ's group *Ca trù Thăng Long* now performs a regular hour-long program three times a week in Đền Quan Đế, a temple on Hàng Buồm street. They give a mixed performance, with *ca trù* singing in the *hát chơi* style, a few dances from the *hát cửa đình* repertoire, and instrumental ceremonial *bát âm* music. They regularly collaborate with *ca trù* musicians from Lỗ Khê and occasionally invite musicians from other traditional genres to be guest performers. Funds are raised by ticket sales, and participating musicians, as well as a couple of student translators, are paid for their involvement. To retain an "old" feeling there is no amplification in the group's concerts, and cameras are generally not allowed (Phạm Thị Huệ, personal communication, February 19, 2013).

The *Hanoi Ca trù Club* has established itself a couple of hundred meters away in Đình Kim Ngân on Hàng Bạc Street. Lê Thị Bạch Vân is the main singer, while her students perform occasional songs and dances. The audience is informed about the history of the genre and the club's role in the revival. As with *Ca trù Thăng Long*'s performances, the audience is invited to have tea and to try the instruments. The two groups are competing for the same audience and keep a close eye on each other's activities. However, to avoid unnecessary rivalry, they have scheduled their performances on different days of the week. The ticket prices for their performances are the same, USD $10 USD or 210,000 VND (January 2015), considerably more expensive than tickets for other tourist performances of traditional music in Hanoi.

After the UNESCO recognition, increasing concerns have been raised regarding the development of the revival. In separate articles, two external examiners for the UNESCO nomination file on *ca trù* (Ministry of Culture, Sports, and Tourism of the SRV, 2009)—Barley Norton (2014) and Gisa Jähnichen (2011)—have called for caution to prevent, in the name of safeguarding and heritage policies, the future of *ca trù* being turned into a concern for central government and international heritage groups, largely disconnected from the ambitions of the *ca trù* community. Jähnichen argues that the popularization and reconstruction of obsolete *ca trù* practices for the sake of international and domestic tourism may be counter-productive to the goal of safeguarding the genre for posterity (Jähnichen, 2011). Although there is reason to take this critique seriously, it may be problematized by looking at the present revival not as one single process but as a number of processes that in some cases are in opposition to each other, even though they involve the same individuals.

In his account on the recent efforts to revive and safeguard *ca trù*, Norton (2014) writes that as *ca trù* is increasingly being used as a symbol for Vietnamese national culture by the government, it stands a real risk of alienating the *ca trù* community:

> In the new climate of UNESCO-driven and state-led revivalism, there is concern in ca trù circles that deep, sustained appreciation for the ritual, musical and literary aesthetics will be overshadowed by the promotion of ca trù as a cultural symbol for domestic and international tourist consumption. (p. 177)

Although both writers are critical about the role of tourist performances in the sustainability of the genre, it could be argued—also through Norton's comments—that these have a potential to develop into new styles of "lighter" *ca trù*, which do not need to be in direct conflict with other forms. Tourism is not likely to be a final solution for *ca trù*, but if managed by skilled musicians, who are not tied to this context as their only opportunity for performance, it could still provide much-needed income and stability. In their survey of water puppetry and cultural tourism in the Red River delta, Pack, Eblin, and Walther (2012) argue that the development of a standard tourist performance repertoire has not led to an end of other forms of performances, and the fear that tourism will impoverish local culture is exaggerated. However, there are less encouraging examples, especially with regard to the music of Vietnamese minorities (Ó Briain, 2012). Tourism will continue to play a role for *ca trù*, and the two clubs that engage with this market are confident in their ability to handle the issues that may arise (personal communication, Phạm Thị Huệ February 19, 2013; Lê Thị Bạch Vân, February 20, 2013).

Implications for Sustainability

The revival movement is still reliant on a handful of enthusiasts who are working very hard to keep their organizations running in a socially and financially unpredictable climate. However, groups and individuals have shown a great deal of creativity and have taken advantage of changing cultural policies, as well as financial opportunities. Even so, the existing infrastructure needs more stability to provide opportunities for professional development and education. The lack of sustained financial and structured support means that there is a risk that clubs will close down or that key individuals within the *ca trù* community will feel forced to move on and focus their energy on more profitable and less taxing areas of work.

The most successful revival projects have been led by artists who are themselves closely connected to the *ca trù* community. A key to further success will be to support this existing infrastructure, and to do so in such a way that it leaves open the opportunity for continued performer-led developments. The mindscape model suggests that future safeguarding measures would benefit from carefully taking into account the complexity of the revival movement and the impact these measures may have on different stakeholders.

A number of publications offer suggestions on how *ca trù* can be supported and developed for the future. The following list of key issues for sustainability adds to, and emphasizes, issues already raised by Đặng et al. (2008), Grant (2014), Jähnichen (2011), Norton (2014), and several papers presented at the 2006 conference *Ca Trù Singing of the Việt People* (Vietnamese Institute for Musicology, 2008):

- The existence of performer-led *ca trù* organizations and contexts
- The existence of suitable venues for *ca trù* organizations
- The establishment of a suitable government funding policy for *ca trù*
- Awareness raising about the Law of Cultural Heritage and its implementation
- The recruitment of young learners of the art
- Increasing appreciation for the art among *ca trù* audiences
- The development of sustainable models for tourist performances
- Strategies to encourage and support females to stay in the profession

The last 25 years have seen *ca trù* transformed from a largely forgotten and disreputable music genre to a celebrated cultural heritage. This journey has largely been driven by changes in cultural policies and the quest for international recognition of the nation's heritage, but it would have been impossible without the passionate involvement of numerous *ca trù* musicians, students, and aficionados. In the end, it is these individuals who have the potential to create a future for *ca trù* in modern Vietnam.

ACKNOWLEDGMENTS

The authors would like to thank everyone who helped us during our fieldwork in Vietnam. In no particular order, we would especially like to thank Phạm Thị Huệ,

Lệ Thị Bạch Vân, Phó Thị Kim Đức, Nguyễn Thị Chúc, Nguyễn Phú Đẹ, Nguyễn Văn Khuê, and Bùi Trọng Hiền. Thanks also to Huib Schippers for use of interview material and Catherine Grant for help with an earlier draft of this text. In addition to support from *Sustainable Futures for Music Cultures*, we are grateful for receiving essential travel and research funds from the Swedish International Development Cooperation Agency (2009–2010); the Faculty of Fine and Performing Arts, Lund University, Sweden (2009–2010, 2013), and the United Kingdom's Arts and Humanities Research Council (2012–2015).

Interview translations were made by Khương Cường (Phó Thị Kim Đức, Lệ Thị Bạch Vân, Nguyễn Thu Thủy, and "Anonymous") and Phạm Thị Huệ (Nguyễn Thị Chúc); if not stated otherwise, all other translations are by Esbjörn Wettermark.

ACRONYMS

CNNP	*Ca trù Nhìn từ' Nhiều Phía* (Đ. M. Nguyễn, 2003)
PISC-CSVP	*Proceedings International Scientific Conference: Ca trù singing of the Việt people* (Vietnamese Institute for Musicology, 2008)
MVC	*Monograph on Vietnamese Ca trù* (Đặng, Phạm, & Hồ, 2008)
SRV	Socialist Republic of Vietnam
VIM	Vietnamese Institute for Musicology

REFERENCES

Addiss, S. (1992). Text and context in Vietnamese sung poetry; The art of Hát Ả Đào. In A. Catlin, E. Fraenkel, & T. Mahoney (Eds.), *Selected reports in ethnomusicology, Vol. IX: Text, Context, and Performance in Cambodia, Laos, and Vietnam* (pp. 203–224). Los Angeles, CA: Department of Ethnomusicology, University of California.

Anisensel, A. (2009). Chanter le Ca trù au village de Lỗ Khê (Nord du Viêt-Nam): Une fête rituelle au temple communal et à la maison des patrons de métier du Ca trù. *Péninsule*, 59(2), 143–169.

Anisensel, A. (2013). Le Parti et le patrimoine: le cas de la tradition musicale du Ca trù. In S. Courtois & C. Goscha (Eds.), *Communisme: Vietnam—de l'insurrection à la dictature, 1920-2012* (pp. 303–318). Paris, France: Vendémiaire.

Appadurai, A. (1996). *Modernity at large: Cultural dimensions of globalization*. Minneapolis, MN: University of Minnesota Press.

Arana, M. (1999). *Neotraditional music in Vietnam*. Kent, OH: Nhac Viet.

Bithell, C., & Hill, J. (Eds.). (2014). *Oxford handbook of music revivals*. Oxford, UK: Oxford University Press.

Buchanan, D. A. (2006). *Performing democracy: Bulgarian music and musicians in transition*. Chicago, IL: University of Chicago Press.

Bùi, T. H. (2008). Culture—Social cultural functions and manifestation forms of ca trù arts. In *MVC* (pp. 65–119). Hanoi, Vietnam: VIM.

Ca trù Thái Hà. (1996). *Việt Nam—Ca trù Tradition du Nord: Ensemble Ca trù Thái Hà de Hà Nội* [CD]. Paris, France: Inedit.

Chu Hà. (2003 [1980]). Hát cửa đình Lỗ Khê. In *CNNP*. Hanoi, Vietnam: Nhà Xuất Bản Văn Hoá Thông Tin.

Đặng, H. L. (2008). Ca trù: What has been found. In *MVC* (pp. 457–540). Hanoi, Vietnam: VIM.

Đặng, H. L., Phạm, M. H., & Hồ, H. D. (Eds.). (2008). *Monograph on Vietnamese ca trù*. Hanoi, Vietnam: VIM.

Dimick, B. F. (2013). *Vietnam's Ca trù: Courtesans' songs by any other name* (PhD thesis). University of Michigan, Ann Arbor, MI. Retrieved from http://hdl.handle.net/2027.42/102379

Đỗ, B. Đ., & Đỗ, T. H. (1962). *Việt Nam Ca Trù Biên Khảo*. Saigon, Vietnam: Van Khoa.

Đỗ, B. Đ., & Đỗ, T. H. (2003). Lược sử ca trù. In *CNNP* (pp. 164–187). Hanoi, Vietnam: NXB Văn Hóa Thông Tin.

Endres, K. W. (2002). Beautiful customs, worthy traditions: Changing state discourse on the role of Vietnamese culture. *Internationales Asienforum, 33*(3–4), 303–322.

Fitchett, R. (1984). *Vietnamese music and musical instruments in Britain* (Unpublished master's thesis). Goldsmiths, University of London, London, UK.

Ford Foundation. (2001). Ford Foundation annual report 2001. Retrieved from http://www.fordfound.org

Ford Foundation. (2005). Ford Foundation annual report 2005. Retrieved from http://www.fordfound.org

Government of the SRV. (1981). *[Regulations for artistic titles]* (Government council decree no: 252-CP, June 18, 1981. Retrieved from *http://www.thuvienphapluat.vn).*

Government of the SRV. (2014). *[Regulations regarding NNND and NNƯT]. (Decree no: 62/2014/NĐ-CP, June 26, 2014.* Retrieved from *http://www.thuvienphapluat.vn).*

Grant, C. (2014). *Music endangerment: How language maintenance can help.* New York, NY: Oxford University Press.

Howard, K. (Ed.). (2012). *Music as intangible cultural heritage: Policy, ideology, and practice in the preservation of East Asian traditions.* London, UK: Ashgate.

Jähnichen, G. (2011). Uniqueness re-examined: The Vietnamese lute Đàn đáy. *Yearbook for Traditional Music, 43*, 147–179.

Jähnichen, G. (2014). Melodic relativization of speech tones in classical Vietnamese singing: The case of "many voices." *Jahrbuch des Phonogrammarchivs der Österreichischen Akademie der Wissenschaften, 4*, 180–194.

Kirshenblatt-Gimblett, B. (1995). Theorizing heritage. *Ethnomusicology, 39*(3), 367–380.

Lowenthal, D. (1998). *The heritage crusade and the spoils of history.* Cambridge, UK: Cambridge University Press.

Lê, T. B. V. (2008). Ca trù in Hà Nội: Reality and some solutions. In *PISC-CSVP* (pp. 281–301). Hanoi, Vietnam: VIM.

Lê, T. H. (1997). Traditional and modern national music in North Vietnam between 1954 and 1975. *Nhac Viet, 6*, 35–70.

Lê, T. H. (2011). Vietnamese music in Australia. A general survey. Retrieved from http://sonic-gallery.org/2014/01/06/epapyrus-2-vietnamese-music-in-australia-a-general-survey

Livingston, T. E. (1999). Music revivals: Towards a general theory. *Ethnomusicology, 43*(1), 66–85.

Meeker, L. (2013). *Sounding out heritage: Cultural politics and the social practice of Quan Họ folk songs in Northern Vietnam*. Honolulu, HI: University of Hawai'i Press.

Ministry of Culture, Sports, and Tourism of the SRV. (2009). *Nomination for inscription on the Urgent Safeguarding List in 2009 (Reference No. 00309)*. Hanoi, Vietnam: UNESCO.

Ministry of Culture, Sports, and Tourism of the SRV. (2010). *[Regulations regarding awarding of NSND/NSUT]. (Decision no: 06/2010/TT-BVHTTDL, July 16, 2010*. Retrieved from *http://moj.gov.vn)*.

National Assembly of the SRV. (2001). *Law on Cultural Heritage (Law no: 28/2001/QH10)* (Tran Manh Ha, Trans.). Hanoi. Retrieved from http://www.unesco.org/culture/natlaws/media/pdf/vietnam/vn_law_cltal_heritage_engtof.pdf

National Assembly of the SRV. (2002). *On the detailed regulations to implement some articles of the Law on Cultural Heritage (Decree no: 92/2002/ND-CP)*. (Tran Manh Ha, Trans.). Hanoi. Retrieved from http://www.unesco.org/culture/natlaws/media/pdf/vietnam/vn_decree_92_engtof.pdf

Nguyễn, Đ. M. (Ed.). (2003). *Ca trù nhìn từ nhiều phía*. Hanoi, Vietnam: NXB Văn Hóa-Thông Tin.

Nguyễn, Đ. M. (2010). *Ca trù Hà Nội: Trong Lịch Sử và Hiện Tại*. Hanoi, Vietnam: NXB Hà Nội.

Nguyễn, Đ. P. (2003 [1923]). Khảo luận về cuộc hát ả đào. In *CNNP*. Hanoi, Vietnam: NXB Văn Hoá Thông Tin.

Nguyễn, K. D. (2004, December 6–11). *Country report: Vietnam*. Paper presented at the Pacific 2004 Workshop on Inventory-Making for Intangible Cultural Heritage Management, Tokyo, Japan. Retrieved from http://www.accu.or.jp/ich/en/pdf/2004_Tokyo.pdf

Nguyễn, N. (2008). Ca trù in the past and in the present in Sài Gòn: A spring of traditional ca trù. In *PISC-CSVP* (pp. 201–221). Hanoi, Vietnam: VIM.

Nguyễn, V. K. (2008). Ca trù restoration, preservation and maintenance in a family. In *PISC-CSVP* (pp. 147–153). Hanoi, Vietnam: VIM.

Nguyễn, X. D. (2010). *Lịch sử và Nghệ Thuật Ca trù: khảo sát nguồn tư liệu tại Viên Nghiên cứu Hán Nôm*. Hanoi, Vietnam: NXB Thế Giới—Tuvan Books.

Norton, B. (2005). Singing the past: Vietnamese ca tru, memory, and mode. *Asian Music, Summer/Fall*, 27–56.

Norton, B. (2014). Music revival, ca trù ontologies, and intangible cultural heritage in Vietnam. In C. Bithell & J. Hill (Eds.), *The Oxford handbook of music revivals*. New York, NY: Oxford University Press.

Ó Briain, L. (2012). *Hmong music in Northern Vietnam: Identity, tradition and modernity* (Unpublished PhD thesis), Sheffield University, Sheffield, UK.

Olsen, D. A. (2008). *Popular music of Vietnam: The politic of remembering, the economics of forgetting*. New York, NY: Routledge.

Pack, S., Eblin, M., & Walther, C. (2012). Water puppetry in the Red River delta and beyond: Tourism and the commodification of an ancient tradition. *ASIANetwork Exchange, 19*(2), 23–31.

People's Committee of Bắc Ninh Province. (2013). *[Project approval for development of Quan Họ and Ca trù singing 2013-2020] (Decision no: 780/QĐ-UBND Bắc Ninh, July 4, 2013*. Retrieved from *http://thuvienphapluat.vn)*.

Pelley, P. M. (2002). *Postcolonial Vietnam: New histories of the national past*. Durham, NC, and London, UK: Duke University Press.

Phan, D. (2013). Ca trù trong lòng người Hà Nội hôm nay. *Tập Chí Văn Hóa Dân Gian, 1*, 45–49.

Phương, T. (2014). Phong tặng danh hiệu nghệ nhân không thể "xong rồi để đấy." Voice of Vietnam Radio website. Retrieved from http://vov.vn/van-hoa/phong-tang-danh-hieu-nghe-nhan-khong-the-xong-roi-de-day-339098.vov

Reyes, A. (1999). *Songs of the caged, songs of the free: Music and the Vietnamese refugee experience.* Philadelphia, PA: Temple University Press.

Ronström, O. (1996). Revival reconsidered. *World of Music, 38*(2), 5–20.

Ronström, O. (2005). Memories, tradition, heritage. In O. Ronström & U. Palmenflet (Eds.), *Memories and visions.* Tartu, Estonia: University of Tartu. Retrieved from http://owe.ompom.se/

Ronström, O. (2014). Traditional music, heritage music. In C. Bithell & J. Hill (Eds.), *Oxford handbook of music revivals.* Oxford, UK: Oxford University Press.

Salemink, O. (2013). Appropriating culture: The politics of intangible cultural heritage in Vietnam. In H-T. H. Tai & M. Sidel (Eds.), *State, society and the market in contemporary Vietnam: Property, power and values* (pp. 158–180). Oxon, UK, and New York, NY: Routledge.

Tai, H-T. H. (Ed.). (2001). *The country of memory: Remaking the past in late socialist Vietnam.* Berkeley and Los Angeles, CA, and London, UK: University of California Press.

Tenzer, M. (2006). Analysis, categorization, and theory of musics of the world. In M. Tenzer (Ed.), *Analytical studies in world music* (pp. 3–38): Oxford, UK, and New York, NY: Oxford University Press.

Tô, N. T. (2010). *Vietnam's living human treasures rewarded by Association of Vietnamese Folklorists 2007-2010.* Hanoi, Vietnam: NXB đại học quốc gia Hà Nội.

Tran, N. T. (2013). The commodification of village songs and dance in seventeenth- and eighteenth-century Vietnam. In H-T. H. Tai & M. Sidel (Eds.), *State, society and the market in contemporary Vietnam: Property, power and values* (pp. 141–157). New York, NY: Routledge.

Trần, Q. H. (2001). Vietnamese music in exile since 1975 and musical life in Vietnam since Perestroika. *World of Music, 43*(2/3), 103–112.

Trần V. K. (1991 [1978]). *Viet Nam Ca tru & Quan Ho traditional music* [CD]. Paris, France: Auvidis-UNESCO.

UNESCO. (2002). *Guidelines for the establishment of living human treasures systems.* Retrieved from http://en.unesco.org/

UNESCO. (2003). *Convention for the safeguarding of the intangible cultural heritage.* Retrieved from http://unesdoc.unesco.org/images/0013/001325/132540e.pdf

Văn, S. (2008). Ca trù activity in today's life. In *MVC* (pp. 191–210). Hanoi, Vietnam: VIM.

Vietnamese Institute for Musicology. (2004). *Kỷ Yếu Hội Thảo Khoa Học Quốc Tế: Âm Nhạc Dân Tộc Cổ Truyền Trong Bối Cảnh Toàn Cầu Hóa.* Hanoi, Vietnam: VIM.

Vietnamese Institute for Musicology. (2008). *Proceedings International Scientific Conference: Ca trù singing of the Việt people.* [June 20, 2006]. Hanoi, Vietnam: VIM.

Vũ, N. T. (2008). Music of ca trù singing. In *MVC* (pp.120–174), Hanoi, Vietnam: VIM.

Wettermark, E. (2010). Thăng Long Ca Trù Club—New ways for old music. *Finnish Journal of Music Education, 13*(1), 72–87.

Yingfai, T. (1998). The Modern Chinese Folk Orchestra: A brief history. *Musical Performance, 2*(2), 19–32.

12

APPROACHING MUSIC CULTURES AS ECOSYSTEMS

A Dynamic Model for Understanding and Supporting Sustainability

Huib Schippers and Catherine Grant

WHILE THERE SEEMS to be little risk of music disappearing from our planet altogether, those who make and care for music are continually faced with choices that affect the vitality and sustainability of music practices. It is no easy matter to determine what makes strategic sense in this regard, either at the local or the global level. The five domains outlined in Chapter 1 (systems of learning music; musicians and communities; contexts and constructs; infrastructure and regulations; and media and the music industry) can act as a tool to assist in making better sense of the playing field, and the mechanics of music vitality and viability. Considered in the context of the growing body of work on music sustainability, they also aid in the task of identifying the similarities and differences between music practices from very diverse backgrounds, social settings, and degrees of vitality.

At first glance, the most striking impression across the nine case studies in this volume is the stunning diversity in how people organize their music practices. That is by no means a new awareness, but it does remind us of the sheer capacity of humans to create and engage with music in myriad ways. It also gives fair warning that there will be no simple solutions to understanding or influencing the sustainability of specific music practices. Aside from the challenges created by global musical diversity, many forces act on any single practice, often without easily discernible patterns of cause and effect. Along with expected—and some unexpected—contrasts between music genres, surprising similarities surface between the case studies. We invite readers to reflect on these findings from the perspective of the music practices they know. The following pages summarize some of the key issues identified in the case studies across the five domains. These in turn contribute to the development of a graphic representation of a generic "music ecosystem," a dynamic model to improve understanding of how sustainability in music "works" and can be supported. We then outline a way to gauge the vitality of specific practices at any given moment, as well as their change in vitality over time, as a step toward developing appropriate interventions. Finally, we suggest how tools like these may be adapted and applied to serve communities in shaping their musical futures on their own terms, in the ways they wish, and in collaborations and partnerships they choose.

SYSTEMS OF LEARNING MUSIC

In all sustained music practices, some aspects are transmitted from one individual or group to another. Often there is a long, formal enculturation process; sometimes the process of transmission is less explicit. But it is almost impossible to name a music where a generation of musicians has not learned from or emulated an earlier generation, or at least chosen to rebel against established forms. So it is unsurprising that systems of learning music play a key role in every music practice represented in this volume, whether formal or informal, aural or notation based, in-person or online, real time or based on recordings, self-driven, community, or institutionally organized. Disruption of these transmission processes, whether caused by social, religious, economic, technological, physical, or attitudinal change, has direct implications for the sustainability of any practice.

In some cultures and for some genres, such as Balinese gamelan and Ewe percussion, young people are likely to say they never learned music; rather, the sounds, techniques, behaviors, and underlying values and attitudes of the music are absorbed without the process being made explicit, in line with Rice's (1985) concept of music "that is learned but not taught." In contrast, learning in Western opera and Hindustani music is consciously highly structured. The case studies in this volume suggest that there is not necessarily a direct relationship, however, between highly formalized and highly structured learning: While the relationship between guru and disciple in north India is highly formalized, for example, the structure of teaching is much less so, and may even seem haphazard at times. Surprisingly, in terms of structured progression, similarities exist between learning Western opera at a conservatorium and certain community-based nonformal transmission processes, such as those in Central Australian Aboriginal communities. In both cases, learning progresses from one stage to the next only when the learner is deemed ready, although of course the nature of the "exams" differs vastly.

When it comes to sustainability, it seems that formal education is not necessarily always the ideal. Formal learning (including, but not limited to, that which takes place in institutions) has advantages in terms of stability and prestige, and this is one reason musicians and communities may aspire toward it (as, for example, with *ca trù* and mariachi). However, in some cases, formal learning may represent last-resort efforts to maintain some form of transmission for a music genre. This risks ossification, turning a fluid practice—which may include improvisation and creation of new work—into a static, museumized artifact. It could be argued that even the teaching of Western opera and classical music in European-style institutions has made these genres financially and organizationally dependent on political and philanthropic goodwill, and therefore more vulnerable to changing tastes and politics than traditions where learning is firmly rooted in the community, as in the cultures of Eweland, Bali, and north India. This view represents a radical challenge to any assumption that formal music education is *the* answer to issues of sustainability with regard to transmission processes.

MUSICIANS AND COMMUNITIES

Community is notoriously difficult to define in the context of music making (cf. Schippers, 2010, pp. 92–97). If community is defined broadly, community engagement is arguably at the core of music sustainability in all of the case studies in this volume, and those beyond it: from village square gathering (gamelan) to first-night crowd (opera), from stadium concert (Hindustani music) to online collaborative production (as in contemporary popular music in several cultures).

The spectrum of degrees and types of engagement in the music practices of musicians themselves—and between musicians and others in the inner and outer circles of a tradition—is evident from the nine genres represented in this volume. Moreover, the impact on music sustainability of online communities, with their broad reach and ability to support niche interests, is only beginning to be understood. These communities have the potential to link practitioners with researchers, music lovers with industry, and those who live in poverty with those who live in affluence across geographical, sociological, ethnic, cultural, and economic divides.

Both within and across communities, a raft of factors drive community engagement with any given music genre. These factors range from entertainment to necessity, from shared beliefs to prestige. Some genres incorporate important quality control mechanisms (such as senior classical musicians in north India climbing on stage and punishing a young musician who strays from the tradition). Single inspired individuals or small, motivated groups can play a remarkable role in maintaining or reinvigorating a tradition, as is evident from the role of Phạm Thị Huệ and Lê Thị Bạch Vân in the revival of *ca trù* (or Ry Cooder in the miraculous resurrection of the Buena Vista Social Club in 1997 and its ensuing worldwide success). Festivals, whether as part of the historical fabric of the genre or as contemporary interventions, play an important part in several of the case studies in engaging both the community and new audiences (cf. Keegan-Phipps & Winter, 2014, pp. 495–499).

In all of the case studies, without exception, community recognition of the value of the music genre (in monetary terms or otherwise) seems to be a significant factor in sustainability. This may work both for and against music genres: Balinese gamelan is accorded ongoing high value (in several spheres, including the community, religious, and touristic) and is, in likelihood at least partly for this reason, correspondingly strong in the sustainability stakes. On the other hand, as younger generations of Australian Indigenous people shift their attention away from genres like *yawulyu*, the viability of those genres is adversely affected.

CONTEXTS AND CONSTRUCTS

The importance of the relationship between music genres and their physical and conceptual environment has been at the center of ethnomusicological explorations for over 50 years (see, e.g., Merriam, 1964). Contexts of some music genres are relatively stable, but most change over time, and often drastically. Many of the genres represented in this volume demonstrate remarkable adaptability: Opera is moving to online and cinematic contexts; mariachi has spread with Hispanic culture all the way up the West Coast of the United States and beyond; *shima-uta* has found a new niche on radio and in recording studios; Hindustani music has shifted from places of worship via courts to a middle-class cultural elite; and *ca trù* is now beginning to engage with tourism, festivals, and international touring circuits. Recontextualization allows a genre to be repositioned where old performance contexts may no longer exist (as in Hindustani music), or allows part of the genre to flourish in diasporic settings (as in mariachi). Similarly, any modern-day performance of Bach's *St Matthew's Passion* is a major transposition from its origin in the 18th-century Lutheran church. In that sense, the ability to recontextualize is an asset rather than a weakness.

That, in turn, raises the complex issue of what is, or should be, sustained of a music genre. The case studies show that genres, or at least the specific music practices within genres, are often quite fluid. The music may be canonized, as in opera and samulnori, but more often new music enters the repertoire, with creativity variously attributed to the brilliance of individuals, proper learning, ancestors, or the gods.

Constructs, from aesthetic to religious to political, can clearly be significantly conducive or obstructive to the vibrancy of music. For Ewe drumming, for example, the common understanding that a musician's social position is low has repercussions for musicians' ability to make a living from their music making, and this in turn adversely influences the vibrancy of the tradition. On the other hand, the belief that gamelan in Bali is essential for the success of religious ceremonies is a positive force in its sustainability. Similarly, commentators on north Indian music maintain that it will continue to remain strong because of its link to the very core of Indian culture and even the cyclical nature of the universe. Equally confident are many proponents of Western opera: It would be remarkable for the genre *not* to survive while its claim to being the pinnacle of Western performance art continues to be embraced by governments, funding bodies, philanthropists, and corporate sponsors.

The presence or lack of prestige in its various incarnations is evidently a key factor in sustainability, one that resonates across the five domains of music sustainability. Prestige benefits a genre in various ways: It may mobilize musician and community support; boost engagement with transmission and learning; lead to resources, infrastructure, and funding being made available; encourage people to buy tickets or recordings; inspire exposure through media and commercial endeavors; or trigger systems that provide sustenance for musicians, whether in money, food, or tally sticks (as in *ca trù*). For some genres, such as Ewe drumming and Aboriginal *yawulyu*, a shortage of prestige can result in diminished interest in the tradition among younger generations.

REGULATIONS AND INFRASTRUCTURE

Specific legislation relating to music is perhaps most obvious in the areas of intellectual property, copyright, and performing rights (all of which directly affect opera, but also the other case study genres with large audiences and a substantial music industry, like mariachi and Hindustani classical music). Royalties and other financial rights do not typically generate a substantial or reliable income stream for the vast majority of musicians. Nevertheless, they can constitute an important moral recognition of their contribution and feed into the sustainability of certain genres by providing visibility.

Relatively few other rules and regulations issued by public authorities (including governments) directly relate or refer to music, with the obvious exception of targeted grants and subsidies. However, some non-music-specific regulations certainly do inadvertently or indirectly affect music making, sometimes in significant ways. Laws governing sound and public spaces impact the ability of musicians to make music. In the case of gamelan and mariachi, for instance, the consequences of an unfavorable such law could be dire.

Most communities of the music genres explored in the nine case studies have access to some support in terms of infrastructure, media exposure, or funding, though the degree of support ranges along the spectrum from very minimal (*yawulyu*) to very considerable (Western opera). However, the correlation between funding and sustainability does not seem to be strong. Opera is strongly dependent on government support throughout Europe and Asia, but Hindustani classical music, though thriving, is barely supported by the Indian government. Between the two, the latter may be stronger in the sustainability stakes: A change in government funding will affect opera, while Hindustani music has a decentralized basis of support. Also, not unlike the dependence on formal education, dependence on grants is a possible weakness from a sustainability point of view, and several of the case study genres thrived in one form or another for decades, even centuries, without dedicated financial backing.

For several (but not all) genres represented in this volume, the need for dedicated performance spaces is modest, with musicians using spaces with multiple functions, such as village squares, bars, private houses, and open-air venues. While instruments and materials are sometimes expensive or difficult to come by (some kinds of gamelan, the *đàn đáy* in *ca trù*, or the deer horn needed for the bridges of sitars), Western opera is perhaps the only one of our nine case study genres where the needs for infrastructure and physical resources are so extensive that their absence would become a major liability.

Archives are an important aspect of infrastructure relating to music sustainability, though they raise tricky questions about what is being preserved; how it is being preserved; the messages that sends to musicians, communities, and other stakeholders; and how or whether this feeds back into the documented music practices (cf. Seeger & Chaudhuri, 2015).

MEDIA AND THE MUSIC INDUSTRY

Since their first rise to prominence on the back of technological developments some hundred years ago, mass media and the music industry have played a sizable role in building reputations of musicians, building knowledge of music genres among diverse and dispersed audiences, disseminating music, and contributing to the sustainable future of specific genres. Even at the height of the recording industry in the second half of the 20th century, few world music practices generated a substantial income for individual musicians or groups (though there are exceptions, like the real stars of Western opera, or sitarist Ravi Shankar). However, in spite of many and varied concerns about commodification and commercialization, there has always been a close reciprocal relationship between media exposure and prestige—and as discussed earlier, prestige can open avenues to financial sustainability, for example, via increased recording sales, concert attendance, and activities like teaching or merchandising. Among the genres represented in this volume, this potential is perhaps most evident in the cases of mariachi and opera.

Recently, online environments have created massive exposure for certain music genres, with an impressive scope for forging niche markets and communities. The Internet has obviously vastly changed the landscape of how music is disseminated and received, not only in the case of highly visible traditions like opera, mariachi, or north Indian music, but also in smaller ones like ca *trù*, Ewe drumming, *shima-uta*, and samulnori. In decades to come, possibilities opened up by information and communications technologies hold significant potential to benefit genres at "the weak end of power distribution" (as Nettl calls it, 2005, p. 168), not least due to the nimbleness they afford in terms of production costs and marketing and dissemination.

UNDERSTANDING MUSIC CULTURES AS ECOSYSTEMS

These considerations across the five domains of music sustainability prepare the way for the next step in considering issues of music sustainability from an ecological perspective. While each of the five domains can be regarded to some extent as a distinct entity, a clearer overall picture of sustainability emerges when a genre is examined across the domains. Precedent for this approach is found in other fields of study that use ecology to arrive at a deeper understanding of interrelatedness within complicated systems. As Pickett and Cadenasso (2002) ask: "Exactly what components and entities are linked to one another? Which ones are only indirectly connected? What parts of a system are tightly coupled and which only weakly coupled?" (p. 4). Surprising connections may arise from viewing music from this holistic perspective.

One approach to making the ecological perspective more concrete, including in the context of the case studies in this volume, is to conceive of specific music genres as operating within "musical ecosystems" (cf. Schippers, 2015). While the concept of the *ecosystem* developed, like *ecology*, in biology (see Chapter 1), the term is both derived from and applicable to a wider intellectual space. Sixty-five years after Haeckel introduced the term *ecology*, Tansley (1935) borrowed from the sciences when he first described an *ecosystem* as

> the whole system (in the sense of physics), including not only the organism complex, but also the whole complex of physical factors forming what we call the environment of the biome, the habitat factors in the widest sense. Though the organism may claim our primary interest, when we are trying to think fundamentally we cannot separate them from their special environment, with which they form one physical system. (p. 299)

The concept of ecosystems has since been used to describe and examine animal habitats, use of energy, cities, and increasingly other environments that can "include humans and their artefacts," arguably to the point "that it is applicable to any case where organisms and physical processes interact in some spatial area" (Pickett & Cadenasso, 2002, p. 2; see also Grant, 2012, and Schippers, 2015). This could include the musical space, though that space is not always defined in geographical terms. Examining forces of music sustainability through an ecological perspective may help identify and clarify the vibrancy, strengths, and weaknesses of a music genre, and the ways in which the factors in its vitality and viability interrelate. The various forces and their interactions may be broadly represented as a diagram with the music practice at the center, surrounded by clusters of forces impacting it— positively and/or negatively, unidirectionally or multidirectionally (see Figure 12.1).

As the case studies make clear, the role and impact of each of the forces shown in Figure 12.1 will vary substantially from genre to genre and situation to situation. (This variance could be represented in the diagram by adjusting the relative size of the "balloons" for any specific genre.) For some genres, certain forces will be absent altogether, such as the recording industry in *yawulyu*, institutional contexts in Ewe drumming, or the need for grants in mariachi (those balloons can be popped). Almost invariably, there are connections and correlations between

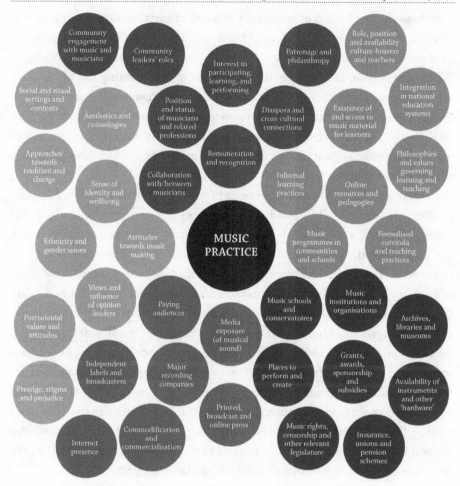

FIGURE 12.1 Ecosystems of music: Major forces working on the sustainability of music practices across five domains (clockwise from the top: musicians and communities; systems of learning music; infrastructure and regulations; media and the music industry; and contexts and constructs).

Adapted from Schippers, H. (2015). Applied ethnomusicology and intangible cultural heritage: Understanding "ecosystems" of music as a tool for sustainability. In S. Pettan & J. T. Titon (Eds.), *The Oxford handbook of applied ethnomusicology*. New York, NY: Oxford University Press, p. 142.

balloons (e.g., between the prestige of a given genre and the amount of patronage and media exposure it receives). The potential impact of compound forces like globalization or social disadvantage (war, disease, poverty) are not represented as single balloons, since in terms of music sustainability they are better understood (and addressed, where possible) at the level of the specific challenges each may present in one or several domains: the destruction of performance spaces, untimely death of musicians, or low esteem for traditional music genres, for example.

Perhaps the key benefit of conceiving of issues of sustainability in terms of ecosystems, and in drawing on the lens of the five domains to do so, is that it provides a consistent framework of analysis. For researchers and organizations working in the applied sphere, for example, it may help avoid "re-inventing the wheel every time we face a community that's trying to preserve its own traditions" (Seeger, in QCRC, 2008). Its deductive approach to understanding music in its social and cultural context, based on five predetermined categories of data, sits in contrast to much ethnomusicological study of the past 50 or 60 years, which has more often worked inductively.

There are certainly risks and limitations to such a deductive approach. Any comparative model may call to mind Lomax's (1976) *Cantometrics* project from the 1960s and 1970s, around which significant scholarly concerns have been raised, not least about the problems of generalizing claims in the face of the complexities of cultural difference and cross-cultural comparison. These are valid concerns, and any application of the ecosystems model (or more specifically the five-domain framework) will benefit from vigilance in this regard. Any model of this nature runs the risk of suggesting "grand narratives" and a "one-size-fits-all" system of understanding music sustainability. That is not our intention. In fact, while we have sought to apply a single framework across genres, each case study remains alert to specific and unique circumstances, including those that are not explicitly captured by the five-domain model. Another key point of difference with *Cantometrics*, and a striking finding of the *Sustainable Futures* project at large, is that the link between musical content and sustainability appears to be very weak: The most influential factors in sustainability lie in realms other than the purely musical.

Beyond these specific concerns about replicating the flaws of *Cantometrics*, others may arise in relation to the use of the ecology and ecosystems metaphors more generally. The metaphor indeed only goes so far, and researchers and cultural stakeholders can and should take account of its limits in developing and implementing initiatives to support music sustainability. The structure and content of the five-domain framework as presented in this volume, then, should not be viewed as either comprehensive or set in stone, but rather used as a guide to explore key issues in sustainability. Similarly, it is important to resist the urge to approach music genres as fixed objects situated in the fluid ecosystem of their music cultures. As the case studies show, genres themselves almost always shift along with the changes in their ecosystems, and this is a crucial consideration in defining, let alone supporting, sustainability.

The approach and use of the model we advocate resonates with the sentiments of Richard Kurin (2007) in relation to the 2003 UNESCO *Convention on Safeguarding Intangible Cultural Heritage*. Kurin believed "the world should try it [the Convention] out, but he doubted if it could really fulfill all the expectations of safeguarding intangible cultural heritage in the world" (in Jacobs, 2014, p. 289). His main reservation was that

> the connection of intangible cultural heritage to the larger matrix of ecological, social, technological, economic and political relationships is too complex, too multi-faceted and nuanced to be reduced to the simple formula proposed by the 2003 treaty. The problem is, we do not have anything better. (Kurin, 2007, p. 18)

Taking an approach informed by these considerations, and with the necessary humility, we offer the five-domain framework and the ecosystems model as tools to enable a more systematic understanding of the threats and opportunities facing specific genres, and music practices more broadly. Understanding music cultures *as* ecosystems not only provides a means to examine issues of sustainability but also can make the discussion and its implications more tangible. Analyzing a genre across the five domains may be a strong foundation not only for developing strategies and resources useful to ethnomusicologists but also in assisting communities to create, perform, and foster the music they value in the way they value it. In addition, it may help gauge improvement or decline in specific aspects of a tradition over time, as we will now show.

MEASURING SUSTAINABILITY

In cases where the sustainable future of a music genre is in jeopardy, and where its community decides that intervention to support the genre is warranted, it is important to have a tool that helps translate the information gathered through the five-domain framework into effective action. One step to this end is a way to gauge the "health" or vitality of a genre. Measuring vitality will enable situations of musics at risk to be identified, and may help determine the urgency of the situation. It may also help to ensure the right focus for sustainability initiatives, since carrying out a "vitality assessment" may help indicate which of the various factors in its sustainability (as identified within the five-domain framework) are playing key roles in its predicament. Having a way to measure the strength of a genre is also important for evaluating sustainability strategies, since two or more measurements of a genre over time will indicate the trajectory of its sustainability (Grant, 2014b).

Several vitality assessment tools have been developed and used by linguists to assess the vitality and viability of endangered languages. One of these, developed on UNESCO's request by an international expert group of linguists in the early 2000s, is the *Language Vitality and Endangerment* framework, which presents nine factors in the level of vitality of any language. Each factor is measured qualitatively (against the best-fitting description) and quantitatively (against a six-grade numeric scale, or in real numbers). Taken together, the nine factors build a picture of the level of vitality of any language (UNESCO, 2003). Since its development almost 15 years ago, the *Language Vitality and Endangerment* framework has been used internationally as the basis for language vitality assessments, including for a large-scale data collection effort coordinated by UNESCO from 2006 to 2009. It has also been the subject of much debate and critique (some of them presented in a document solicited by UNESCO itself as a means to gauge the success of the framework; UNESCO Culture Sector, 2011).

The Music Vitality and Endangerment Framework (MVEF; first presented in Grant, 2014b) is based on this language tool, though it takes into account the sometimes substantial dissimilarities between languages and music genres in relation to their sustainability (the greater role of the mass media and industry for music being one example). The MVEF identifies the following 12 factors that affect the vitality of a music genre, all of which can be relatively easily located in one or several of the five domains:

Factor 1.   Intergenerational transmission
Factor 2.   Change in number of proficient musicians
Factor 3.   Change in number of people engaged with the genre
Factor 4.   Change in the music and music practices
Factor 5.   Change in performance contexts and functions
Factor 6.   Response to mass media and the music industry
Factor 7.   Availability of infrastructure and resources for music practices
Factor 8.   Knowledge and skills for music practices
Factor 9.   Governmental policies affecting music practices
Factor 10. Community members' attitudes toward the genre
Factor 11. Relevant outsiders' attitudes toward the genre
Factor 12. Amount and quality of documentation

Each factor is measured according to a graded scale from 0 (nonvital, inactive) to 5 (vital and vibrant). To assist the choice of a grade, a brief description of each grade is given as a guide. As an example, the graded scale for Factor 10 (community members' attitudes toward the genre) is shown in Table 12.1.

In assisting researchers and communities to identify areas where sustainability may be problematic, and therefore where sustainability initiatives might be of

TABLE 12.1

Grade Descriptions to Assess Factor 10 of the Music Vitality and Endangerment Framework: Community Members' Attitudes Toward the Music Genre

Grade	Community Members' Attitudes Toward the Music Genre
5	Community support for the maintenance of the music genre is very strong.
4	Community support for the maintenance of the music genre is strong.
3	Community support for the maintenance of the music genre is moderate.
2	Community support for the maintenance of the music genre is weak.
1	Community support for the maintenance of the music genre is minimal.
0	No community members support the maintenance of the genre.

Reproduced from Grant, C. (2014). *Music endangerment: How language maintenance can help*. New York, NY: Oxford University Press, p. 123).

most benefit, the MVEF carries forward the intent of the five-domain framework. An assessment of a music genre using the MVEF may be carried out by a community, or by other stakeholders (governments, nongovernment organizations, cultural centers, researchers, etc.) in collaboration with the community. Among other uses, the outcomes of the vitality assessment could form the groundwork for developing appropriate courses of action if required, provide a rigorous basis for funding applications, help inform policies, enable resources to be directed where they will make the most difference, and help steer research and documentation efforts.

As with the five-domain framework, the MVEF carries significant challenges and limitations (some of which are explored in Grant, 2014). In demanding a different way of thinking about music genres, it asks new questions for which data may not be readily available. It may encourage focus on the 12 measures of vitality at the expense of a holistic perspective on the complexity of the ecosystem. Uncarefully applied, it risks confusing causes and characteristics of "vitality" or "endangerment." Depending on who carries out the assessment, and how, it may generate idiosyncratic or politically motivated perspectives on sustainability (e.g., respondents claiming low scores on the 12 factors to make a stronger case for the need for funding support, or conversely, governments claiming high scores to justify a lack of funding). For these reasons (among others), "these twelve factors, and the descriptions and scales for each, are only offered as guidelines, and should be adapted as befits the situation and purpose of the assessment. Under no circumstances should the MVEF be uncritically applied" (Grant, 2014, p. 125).

A research project using the MVEF to measure perspectives on the vitality of over 100 music genres across the world (Grant, 2015) was inspired by the consideration that having a way to systematically gauge the health of specific genres will be an important step in supporting their viable futures. Assessing the vitality of a genre helps improve understanding of its overall vitality, as well as specific factors that may be contributing to its predicament, and enables measurement of trends in music vitality over time—all crucial to developing, implementing, and evaluating initiatives that support music sustainability.

COMMUNITIES AT THE CENTER

We propose that a framework providing insight into the sustainability of music cultures, coupled with an instrument to gauge the relative vitality of a music genre at a given point and over time, can help respond to one of the foremost concerns of—especially applied—ethnomusicology: to strengthen relationships with communities and ensure our work benefits them more directly. As a rule, contemporary ethnomusicologists who go into "the field" no longer consider as their own property the resulting recordings, data, and "new" knowledge. Practical, intellectual, and ethical and moral approaches to ethnography are becoming increasingly sophisticated (Barz & Cooley, 2008), and returning research material to individuals and communities and sharing outcomes in usable formats are common (or at least acknowledged ethical) practices now. But the spectrum of "giving back" is considerable and deserves scrutiny in the context of sustainability.

Many ethnomusicologists working on a single genre over a long period of time have developed approaches and protocols to facilitate meaningful exchange through close and continual consultation and collaboration. Due to its cross-cultural nature and international research teams, the *Sustainable Futures* project has adopted a different approach, even though many of those involved also maintain close long-term relationships with specific communities. From its inception, the project has intended to make its findings on music sustainability useful to communities in two ways.

The first of these is through a free online resource (http://www.soundfutures. org), designed to help communities explore possible approaches to supporting a vibrant future for their music. In some ways, this is a more challenging task than developing genre-specific approaches, since the resource is not targeted at a single group, but at users from cultures around the world. It also inevitably excludes people with no or limited access to the Internet, but as this group is dwindling as a percentage of the world's population at a remarkable rate (web users grew from 394 million people in 2000 to nearly 3 billion in 2014; Statista,

2015), it seems the most realistic and democratic pathway to reach people without being physically present. The project website aims to identify potential strategies and provide examples to communities wishing to take steps to maintain the music they value; it may also assist in planning, executing, and evaluating specific interventions in music ecosystems for the sake of sustainability. Along with summary reports of the *Sustainable Futures* case studies and a short animated introduction to the concepts of music ecosystems and sustainability, the website offers an online "diagnosis" tool that generates impressions, for any given genre, of which aspects of which domain are strong, and which may require attention (see Figure 12.2). The results of assessments using the tool are then linked to examples of how communities elsewhere in the world have dealt with similar challenges to their music.

Caveats like those mentioned earlier in relation to the five-domain framework of music sustainability and the MVEF apply here too: The tool is likely to generate different outcomes based on the knowledge and motivations of the user, and there are risks involved in making claims about appropriate interventions based on the outcomes. Ideally, perhaps, the tool is best used by "insiders"—musicians and other members of the community in question—as a way to better understand challenges and possible pathways forward.

The second way *Sustainable Futures* aims to benefit communities is through opening the way for targeted, genre-specific, community-driven initiatives, and these are continuing to develop in the aftermath of the completed project. For *ca trù*, for example, extensive consultation over several years between members of the research team and one performance group led to the formulation of a project to create a viable performance format and income source for *ca trù* musicians. The project aimed to link the genre to the international cultural tourism to Hanoi:

> Building on its 2009 recognition by UNESCO as Intangible Cultural Heritage in urgent need of safeguarding, *Ca Trù Vietnam* aims to create a context which re-establishes the refined urban expression of this genre in a sustainable environment. Combining the interest of refined Vietnamese and international audiences, this enterprise will open a *ca trù* house in Hanoi (once the home to many such establishments) on a commercially viable basis, using the high-end of cultural tourism to Vietnam as its primary market. This will reconnect the genre to its former basis of support, private patrons, providing a basic but stable income for up to ten *ca trù* musicians, technicians and cultural workers. Linked to this will be performances and lessons for Vietnamese audiences and young people, ensuring the intergenerational

(a)

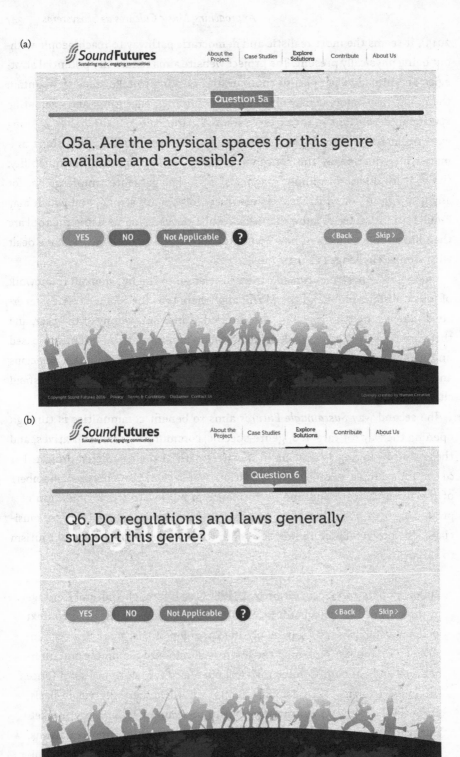

(b)

FIGURE 12.2A–D Stills from the "Explore Solution" section of soundfutures.org, the public website disseminating key findings of *Sustainable Futures*.

(c)

Sound Futures
Sustaining music, engaging communities

About the Project | Case Studies | **Explore Solutions** | Contribute | About Us

Question 9

Q9. Are there currently any specific activities in place that aim to support the sustainability of this genre?

YES   NO   Not Applicable   ?   < Back   Skip >

Copyright Sound Futures 2016   Privacy   Terms & Conditions   Disclaimer   Contact Us   Lovingly created by Human Creative

(d)

Sound Futures
Sustaining music, engaging communities

About the Project | Case Studies | **Explore Solutions** | Contribute | About Us

Question 9a

Q9a. Which area or areas do these sustainability activities currently focus on?

☐ Issues relating to teaching and/or learning the genre

☐ Issues relating to the genre within its community

☐ Issues relating to contexts and constructs (i.e. issues relating to what people think about the music (e.g. positively or negatively), or where the genre is performed, or both)

☐ Issues relating to the infrastructure and/or regulations

☐ Issues relating to media and/or the music industry

< Back   Skip >

Copyright Sound Futures 2016   Privacy   Terms & Conditions   Disclaimer   Contact Us   Lovingly created by Human Creative

FIGURE 12.2A–D Continued

transmission of the genre without continuing dependence on external funding or state support. (Ca Trù Thang Long, 2010)

As Wettermark and Lundström (Chapter 11) mention, the first stage of this project has now been realized. Burns (Chapter 3) reports on how *Sustainable Futures* has enabled commercial recording projects of Ewe dance-drumming. Similar tailored approaches continue to be developed across genres and contexts, drawing on an understanding of the ecosystem to forge new pathways to sustainability—always mindful of Moyle's reminder that "our job as sympathetic and supportive outsiders is properly that of an on-request caretaker and facilitator, but not as an arbiter of what should be preserved and what should not be" (in QCRC, 2008).

We hope the approach outlined in this volume will also prove useful to scholars as a framework to help describe specific music cultures. As the case studies demonstrate, there is no single way to define or ensure sustainability. However, it is possible to identify key forces outside of the musical content and structure that impact on the continuing vibrancy of music practices. Some of these factors can be influenced, others much less so. But the better we understand the challenges and the way they interrelate, the more likely we are to find appropriate strategies to support the sustainable future of these practices.

We hope the work presented in this volume may stimulate and guide discussions among and between stakeholders in music sustainability—musicians, communities, cultural organizations, researchers, government bodies, and others. Across cultures and countries, this might contribute in a small way to fostering a more diverse, vibrant musical future for the planet. Envisaging music cultures as ecosystems is only one way of understanding music sustainability and diversity in all its complexity. It is one, though, that we feel resonates with current ways of thinking about the roles of ethnomusicologists in the 21st century, about the commitment to give more agency to the individuals and communities concerned, and about ways of effectively supporting music sustainability across the world.

REFERENCES

Barz, G. F., & Cooley, T. J. (Eds.). *Shadows in the field: New perspectives for fieldwork in ethnomusicology* (pp. 1–22). New York, NY: Oxford University Press.

Ca Trù Thang Long. (2010). *Ca trù Vietnam Project Plan* (unpublished business manuscript).

Grant, C. (2012). Analogies and links between cultural and biological diversity. *Journal of Cultural Heritage Management and Sustainable Development*, 2(2), 153–163. doi:10.1108/20441261211273644

Grant, C. (2014). *Music endangerment: How language maintenance can help*. New York, NY: Oxford University Press.

Grant, C. (2015). Music vitality and endangerment. Retrieved from http://www.musicendangerment.com

Jacobs, M. (2014). Cultural brokerage. *Volkskunde, 3*, 265–291.

Keegan-Phipps, S., & Winter, T. (2014). Contemporary English folk music and the folk industry. In C. Blithell & J. Hill (Eds.), *The Oxford handbook of music revival* (pp. 489–509). New York, NY: Oxford University Press.

Kurin, R. (2007). Safeguarding intangible cultural heritage: Key factors in implementing the 2003 Convention. *International Journal of Intangible Heritage, 2*, 10–20.

Lomax, A. (1976). *Cantometrics: An approach to the anthropology of music*. Berkeley, CA: University of California Extension Media Center.

Merriam, A. P. (1964). *The anthropology of music*. Chicago, IL: Northwestern University Press.

Nettl, B. (2005). *The study of ethnomusicology: Thirty-one issues and concepts* (2nd ed.). Champaign, IL: University of Illinois Press.

Pickett, S. T. A., & Cadenasso, M. L. (2002). The ecosystem as a multidimensional concept: Meaning, model and metaphor. *Ecosystems, 5*, 1–10.

Queensland Conservatorium Research Centre (QCRC) (2008). *Twelve voices on sustainable futures*. [Unpublished video.] Brisbane: QCRC.

Rice, T. (1985). Music learned but not taught: The Bulgarian case. In D. McAllester (Ed.), *Becoming human through music: The Wesleyan symposium on the perspectives of social anthropology in the teaching and learning of music* (pp. 115–122). Reston, VA: Music Educators' National Conference.

Schippers, H. (2010). *Facing the music: Shaping music education for the 21st century*. New York, NY: Oxford University Press.

Schippers, H. (2015). Applied ethnomusicology and intangible cultural heritage: Understanding "ecosystems" of music as a tool for sustainability. In S. Pettan & J. T. Titon (Eds.), *The Oxford handbook of applied ethnomusicology* (pp. 134–157). New York, NY: Oxford University Press.

Seeger, A., & Chaudhuri, S. (2015). The contribution to sustainable traditions through reconfigured audiovisual archives. *World of Music, 4*(1), 21–34.

Statista. (2015). Number of worldwide internet users from 2000 to 2014 (in millions). Retrieved from http://www.statista.com/statistics/273018/number-of-internet-users-worldwide/

Tansley, A. G. (1935). The use and abuse of vegetational concepts and terms. *Ecology, 16*(3), 284–307.

UNESCO. (2003). *A methodology for assessing language vitality and endangerment*. Retrieved from http://www.unesco.org/new/en/culture/themes/endangered-languages/language-vitality/

UNESCO Culture Sector. (2011). UNESCO's *Language Vitality and Endangerment* methodological guideline: Review of application and feedback since 2003 [background paper]. Retrieved from http://www.unesco.org/new/fileadmin/MULTIMEDIA/HQ/CI/CI/pdf/unesco_language_vitaly_and_endangerment_methodological_guideline.pdf

Index